WESTERN CIVILIZATION

Images and Interpretations

Second Edition

WESTERN CIVILIZATION

Images and Interpretations
Second Edition

&.

Volume II

Edited by

Dennis Sherman

JOHN JAY COLLEGE OF CRIMINAL JUSTICE, CITY UNIVERSITY OF NEW YORK

Alfred A. Knopf New York

COVER ILLUSTRATION: W. H. Egley, *Omnibus Life in London* (1859). Oil on canvas. The Tate Gallery, London.

This painting reveals the wealthy, crowded, controlled style of life of the urban middle class during the mid-nineteenth century.

THIS IS A BORZOI BOOK PUBLISHED BY ALFRED A. KNOPF, INC.

Second Edition

9876

Library of Congress Cataloging in Publication Data

Western civilization, images and interpretations.

    1. Civilizations, Occidental — History — Sources.
2. Civilization, Occidental — History. I. Sherman, Dennis.
CB243.W4835   1987   909'.09821   86–7459
ISBN 0–394–35206–8 (v. 1)
ISBN 0–394–35207–6 (v. 2)

Manufactured in the United States of America

To Pat, Joe, Darryl, Vera, and Raymond

In time choice, change, and obligation merge;
How quietly we listen to ourselves.

PREFACE

This book provides a broad introduction to the sources historians use, the kind of interpretations historians make, and the evolution of Western civilization over the past six thousand years. A large selection of documents, photographs, and maps is presented along with introductions, commentaries, and questions designed to place each selection in a meaningful context and facilitate an understanding of its historical significance. The selections and accompanying notes should also provide insights into how historians work and some of the problems they face.

A brief look at the task facing historians of Western civilization will supply a background to what will be covered in this book. To discover what people thought and did and to organize this into a chronological record of the human past, historians must search for evidence—for the sources of history. Most sources are written materials, ranging from government records to gravestone inscriptions, memoirs, and poetry. Other sources include paintings, photographs, sculpture, buildings, maps, pottery, and oral traditions. In searching for sources, historians usually have something in mind—some tentative goals or conclusions that guide their search. Thus, in the process of working with sources, historians must decide which ones to emphasize. What historians ultimately write is a synthesis of the questions posed, the sources used, and their own ideas.

Historians of Western civilization consider their subject to be what is to-day Europe, along with those offshoots of Europe that have become established in various parts of the world. As they look back into the past, they focus on the origins of today's Western civilization in the Mediterranean basin, a cultural region that includes parts of North Africa and the Near East as well as Europe itself.

STRUCTURE OF THE BOOK

The basic organization of this book is chronological, beginning with the origins of Western civilization in the ancient Near East and gradually moving up to the present. From time to time this chronological approach is modified and certain important developments such as the Renaissance or totalitarianism are pulled out of the chapter covering their period of occurrence and are discussed separately. All the chapters, however, are organized the same way. Each chapter is broken into sections consisting of the following features:

Each chapter opens with a **chapter introduction**, in which the period of history and the general topics to be dealt with in the chapter are described. The introduction provides a brief sketch of some of the most important developments, but no effort is made to cover the period. Instead, the purpose is to introduce the topics, issues, and questions that the sources in the chapter focus on, and to place these sources in the historical context of Western civilization.

The introduction is followed by a **time line**, showing the relevant dates, people, events, and developments of the period, to provide a historical context for the selections in the chapter. In addition, a time line at the beginning of each of the six parts in the book puts the developments covered in each chapter into a broader perspective.

The chapter time line is followed by the **primary sources**. These are documents written by individuals involved in the matter under investigation. Historians consider these documents their main building blocks for learning about and interpreting the past. They are pieces of evidence that show what people thought, how they acted, and what they accomplished. At the same time historians must criticize these sources both externally—to attempt to uncover forgeries and errors—and internally—to find the authors' motives, inconsistencies within the documents, and different meanings of words and phrases.

Each document is preceded by a **headnote.** The headnote provides some information on the nature of the source, places it in a specific historical context, and indicates its particular focus.

The headnotes end with suggestions of points to consider. These points are not simply facts to be searched for in the selection. Rather, they are designed to stimulate analytical thought about the selections and to indicate some of the uses of each source.

The primary sources are followed by visual sources, including maps, and then by **secondary sources.**

Secondary sources are documents written by scholars about the time in question. Usually, they are interpretations of what occurred based on examination of numerous primary documents and other sources. They reflect choices the authors have made and their own particular understandings of what has happened. Often there are important differences of opinion among scholars about how to understand significant historical developments. Secondary sources should therefore be read with these questions in mind: What sort of evidence does the author use? Does the author's argument make sense? What political or ideological preferences are revealed in the author's interpretation? How might one argue against the interpretation presented by the author? At times the distinction between primary and secondary documents becomes blurred, as when the author is a contemporary of the events he or she is interpreting. If a document by that author is read as an interpretation of what occurred, it would be a secondary source. As evidence for the assumptions and attitudes of the author's times, however, the document would be a primary source.

Like the primary documents, all the secondary documents are preceded by headnotes and suggestions for points to consider.

Visual sources are paintings, drawings, sculpture, ceramics, photographs, buildings, monuments, coins, and so forth, that can provide valuable historical insights or information. Although they often include characteristics of secondary documents, they are usually most valuable when used in the same way as primary documents. In this book their purpose is not merely to supplement the documents or provide examples of the great pieces of art throughout history. It is to show how these visual materials can be used as sources of history and to provide insights difficult to gain solely through written documents. To this end, each visual source is accompanied by a relatively extensive interpretive description. Care should be taken in viewing these sources and using these descriptions. By their very nature, visual sources usually have a less clear meaning than written documents. Scholars differ greatly over how sources such as paintings, ceramics, and coins should be interpreted. Therefore, the descriptions accompanying the visual sources are open to debate. They are designed to show how it is possible for historians to use visual materials as sources of history — as unwritten evidence for what people thought and did in the past.

Maps often combine elements of primary documents, secondary documents, and visual sources. However, here they are usually used to help establish relationships, such as the connections between geographical factors and political developments, thereby enabling us to interpret what occurred differently than we could have if we had relied on written sources alone. As is the case with visual sources, each map is accompanied by an interpretive description. These descriptions indicate some of the ways maps might be used by historians.

Each chapter ends with **chapter questions.** These are designed to draw major themes of the chapter together in a challenging way. Answers to these questions require some analytical thought and the use of several of the selections in the chapter.

Since a book of this size can only sample what is available and outline what has occurred, this book is truly an introduction to Western civilization and its sources. Indeed, it is my hope that the materials presented here will reveal the range of sources that can be used to deepen our understanding of Western civilization and serve as a jumping-off point for further exploration into history and the historian's discipline.

Dennis Sherman

CONTENTS

WESTERN CIVILIZATION

Images and Interpretations

Second Edition

Schematic of Evolution of Western Civilization

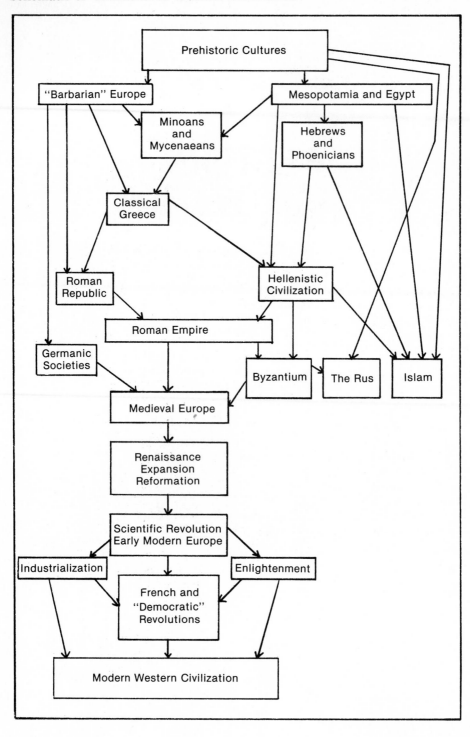

The Evolution of Western Civilization

This chart is a schematic illustration of the development of Western civilization up to modern times. Caution should be exercised when reading such a chart. The connections made are more a matter of judgment than fact. Moreover, what is missing — the how and why of the connections — is of great importance. Nevertheless, such a chart can make it easier to see some of the broadest connections between societies and civilizations, connections that are often lost when a single period or society is examined in detail.

Consider:
Possible reasons for the various connections within the chart; what might be added to this chart to make it more useful.

I

THE
EARLY MODERN
PERIOD

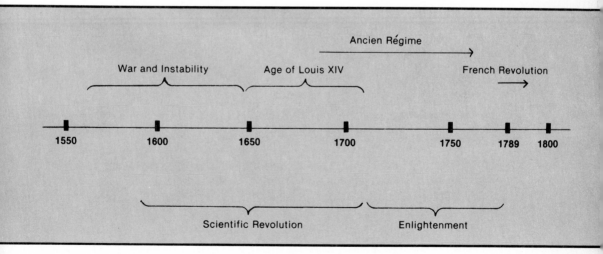

CHAPTER ONE

Aristocracy and Absolutism in the Seventeenth Century

The second half of the seventeenth century was a period of relative political stability in Europe. Although wars still occurred, they lacked the intensity of the preceding period. In the ascendant states, such as France, Prussia, Austria, Russia, and England, central governments were gaining authority. The primary power, and for many states the model of political authority, was France. There, Louis XIV, supported by a strong standing army, a policy of mercantilism, and a growing bureaucracy, wielded absolute power. There were similar situations in Prussia, Austria, and Russia. A different pattern occurred in England, where the central government remained strong while the monarchy itself weakened. There, after the return to power of the Stuart kings between 1660 and 1688, a revolution furthered the authority of Parliament.

During this period, important social, political, and economic changes occurred unevenly and generally benefited those who were already prominent and well to do. Aristocrats lost some of their independence to kings in countries such as France and Prussia, but they continued to staff most of the important government offices, to maintain their elevated prestige, and to influence cultural styles and tastes. For most people, the structure of society, the way of life, and the relevant institutions changed little throughout this period.

This chapter concentrates on two broad topics: the growth of central government and Early Modern society. The selections address a number of questions. For the first topic, what was the nature of monarchical absolutism in France? How did it differ from Prussian monarchical absolutism? How did the pattern of monarchical absolutism compare with the growth of parliamentary power in England? What institutions and policies were developed to facilitate the growth of central governments? For the second topic, what was the nature of the family in Early Modern Europe? What were typical attitudes toward childhood? What were the traditional values and patterns of life for commoners during this period?

This dual focus should provide some broad insights into Europe during the seventeenth century and help establish a background for eighteenth-century developments.

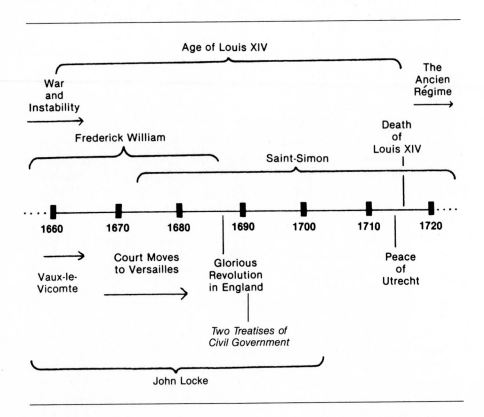

PRIMARY SOURCES

Austria Over All If She Only Will: Mercantilism

Philipp W. von Hornick

Mercantilism, a loose set of economic ideas and corresponding government policies, was a common component of absolutism during the seventeenth century. Typical mercantilist goals were the acquisition of bullion, a positive balance of trade, and economic self-sufficiency. An unusually clear and influential statement of mercantilist policies was published in 1684 by Philipp Wilhelm von Hornick. A lawyer and later a government official, Hornick set down what he considered to be the nine principal rules for a proper economic policy. These are excerpted here.

> **Consider:** *The political and military purposes served by encouraging mercantilist policies; the foreign policy decisions such economic policies would support; the political and economic circumstances that would make it easiest for a country to adhere to and benefit from mercantilist policies.*

NINE PRINCIPAL RULES OF NATIONAL ECONOMY

If the might and eminence of a country consist in its surplus of gold, silver, and all other things necessary or convenient for its *subsistence*, derived, so far as possible, from its own resources, without *dependence* upon other countries, and in the proper fostering, use, and application of these, then it follows that a general national *economy (Landes-Oeconomie)* should consider how such a surplus, fostering, and enjoyment can be brought about, without *dependence* upon others, or where this is not feasible in every respect, with as little *dependence* as possible upon foreign countries, and sparing use of the country's own cash. For this purpose the following nine rules are especially serviceable.

First, to inspect the country's soil with the greatest care, and not to leave the agricultural possibilities or a single corner or clod of earth unconsidered. Every useful form of *plant* under the sun should be experimented with, to see whether it is adapted to the country, for the distance or nearness of the sun is not all that counts. Above all, no trouble or expense should be spared to discover gold and silver.

Second, all commodities found in a country, which cannot be used in their natural state, should be worked up within the country; since the pay-

---

SOURCE: Philipp W. von Hornick, "Austria Over All If She Only Will," in Arthur Eli Monroe, ed., *Early Economic Thought.* Reprinted by permission of Harvard University Press (Cambridge, Mass., 1927), pp. 223–225. Copyright © 1924 by The President and Fellows of Harvard College.

ment for *manufacturing* generally exceeds the value of the raw material by two, three, ten, twenty, and even a hundred fold, and the neglect of this is an abomination to prudent managers.

Third, for carrying out the above two rules, there will be need of people, both for producing and cultivating the raw materials and for working them up. Therefore, attention should be given to the population, that it may be as large as the country can support, this being a well-ordered state's most important concern, but, unfortunately, one that is often neglected. And the people should be turned by all possible means from idleness to remunerative *professions*; instructed and encouraged in all kinds of *inventions*, arts, and trades; and, if necessary, instructors should be brought in from foreign countries for this.

Fourth, gold and silver once in the country, whether from its own mines or obtained by *industry* from foreign countries, are under no circumstances to be taken out for any purpose, so far as possible, or allowed to be buried in chests or coffers, but must always remain in *circulation*; nor should much be permitted in uses where they are at once *destroyed* and cannot be utilized again. For under these conditions, it will be impossible for a country that has once acquired a considerable supply of cash, especially one that possesses gold and silver mines, ever to sink into poverty; indeed, it is impossible that it should not continually increase in wealth and property. Therefore,

Fifth, the inhabitants of the country should make every effort to get along with their domestic products, to confine their luxury to these alone, and to do without foreign products as far as possible (except where great need leaves no alternative, or if not need, wide-spread, unavoidable abuse, of which Indian spices are an example). And so on.

Sixth, in case the said purchases were indispensable because of necessity or *irremediable* abuse, they should be obtained from these foreigners at first hand, so far as possible, and not for gold or silver, but in exchange for other domestic wares.

Seventh, such foreign commodities should in this case be imported in unfinished form, and worked up within the country, thus earning the wages of *manufacture* there.

Eighth, opportunities should be sought night and day for selling the country's superfluous goods to these foreigners in manufactured form, so far as this is necessary, and for gold and silver; and to this end, *consumption*, so to speak, must be sought in the farthest ends of the earth, and developed in every possible way.

Ninth, except for important considerations, no importation should be allowed under any circumstances of commodities of which there is sufficient supply of suitable quality at home; and in this matter neither sympathy nor compassion should be shown foreigners, be they friends, kinsfolk, *allies*, or enemies. For all friendship ceases, when it involves my own weakness and ruin. And this holds good, even if the domestic commodities are of poorer quality, or even higher priced. For it would be better to pay for an article two dollars which remain in the country than only one which goes out, however strange this may seem to the ill-informed.

A Secret Letter: Monarchical Authority in Prussia

Frederick William, The Great Elector

Seventeenth-century monarchs attained unprecedented authority within their realms, often through the skillful use of policies designed to enhance their power. The most dramatic consolidation of power was made by the head of the Hohenzollerns, Frederick William (1640–1688), known as the "great elector" of Brandenburg-Prussia. He instituted new taxes, developed a trained bureaucracy staffed by members of the nobility, modernized his army, and asserted his own authority over competing claims from the nobility and representative institutions. In 1667 he wrote a secret letter of advice to his son, who was in line to inherit the throne. An excerpt of this letter appears here.

> **Consider:** *The greatest threats to monarchical authority according to Frederick William; the policies Frederick William thought were most important for maintaining power; which of Frederick William's recommendations echo the attitudes expressed in mercantilist doctrines.*

It is necessary that you conduct yourself as a good father to your people, that you love your subjects regardless of their religious convictions, and that you try to promote their welfare at all times. Work to stimulate trade everywhere, and keep in mind the population increase of the Mark of Brandenburg. Take advantage of the advice of the clergy and nobility as much as you can; listen to them and be gracious to them all, as befits one of your position; recognize ability where you find it, so that you will increase the love and affection of your subjects toward you. But, it is essential that you always be moderate in your attitudes, in order not to endanger your position and lose respect. With those of your own station in life, be careful never to give way in matters of precedence and in all to which you are entitled; on the contrary, hold fast to the eminence of your superior position. Remember that one can lose one's superior position if one allows too great pomposity and too great a show upon the part of members of the court.

Be keenly interested in the administration of justice throughout your land. See to it that justice is maintained for the poor as well as for the rich

Source: Louis L. Snyder, ed., *Documents of German History.* Reprinted by permission of Rutgers University Press (New Brunswick, N.J., 1958), pp. 94–95. Copyright © 1958 by Rutgers, The State University.

without discrimination of any kind. See to it that lawsuits are carried out without delay, without procrastination, for in doing this, you will solidify your own position. . . .

Seek to maintain friendly relations with the princes and the nobility of the Empire. Correspond with them frequently and maintain your friendship with them. Be certain not to give them cause for ill-will; try not to arouse emotions of jealousy or enmity, but be sure that you are always in a strong position to maintain your weight in disputes that may arise. . . .

It is wise to have alliances, if necessary, but it is better to rely on your own strength. You are in a weak position if you do not have the means and do not possess the confidence of the people. These are the things, God be praised, which have made me powerful since the time I began to have them. I only regret that, in the beginning of my reign, I forsook these policies and followed the advice of others against my will.

Memoires: The Aristocracy Undermined in France

Saint-Simon

Louis XIV of France was the most powerful ruler of his time. He had inherited the throne as a child in 1643. He took personal command by 1661, ruling France until his death in 1715. Contemporary rulers viewed him as a model ruler. One of the ways in which he reinforced his position was by conducting a magnificent court life at his palace of Versailles. There, nobles hoping for favors or appointments competed for his attention and increasingly became dependent upon royal whim. One of those nobles, the Duke of Saint-Simon (1675–1755), felt slighted and grew to resent the king. Saint-Simon chronicled life at Versailles in his Memoires. *In the following excerpt, he shows how Louis XIV used this court life to his own ends.*

> **Consider:** *How the king's activities undermined the position of the nobility; the options available to a noble who wanted to maintain or increase his own power; how the king's activities compare with the Great Elector's recommendations to his son.*

Frequent fetes, private walks at Versailles, and excursions were means which the King seized upon in order to single out or to mortify [individuals] by naming the persons who should be there each time, and in order to keep each person assiduous and attentive to pleasing him. He sensed that he lacked by far enough favors to distribute in order to create a continuous effect. Therefore he substituted imaginary favors for real ones, through jealousy — little preferences which were shown daily, and one might say at each

SOURCE: Orest Ranum and Patricia Ranum, eds. and trans., *The Century of Louis XIV.* Reprinted by permission of Harper & Row (New York, 1972), pp. 81, 83, 87–88.

moment — [and] through his artfulness. The hopes to which these little preferences and these honors gave birth, and the deference which resulted from them — no one was more ingenious than he in unceasingly inventing these sorts of things. Marly, eventually, was of great use to him in this respect; and Trianon, where everyone, as a matter of fact, could go pay court to him, but where ladies had the honor of eating with him and where they were chosen at each meal; the candlestick which he had held for him each evening at bedtime by a courtier whom he wished to honor, and always from among the most worthy of those present, whom he named aloud upon coming out from saying his prayers.

Louis XIV carefully trained himself to be well informed about what was happening everywhere, in public places, in private homes, in public encounters, in the secrecy of families or of [amorous] liaisons. Spies and tell tales were countless. They existed in all forms: some who were unaware that their denunciations went as far as [the King], others who knew it; some who wrote him directly by having their letters delivered by routes which he had established for them, and those letters were seen only by him, and always before all other things; and lastly, some others who sometimes spoke to him secretly in his cabinets, by the back passageways. These secret communications broke the necks of an infinity of persons of all social positions, without their ever having been able to discover the cause, often very unjustly, and the King, once warned, never reconsidered, or so rarely that nothing was more [determined]. . . .

In everything he loved splendor, magnificence, profusion. He turned this taste into a maxim for political reasons, and instilled it into his court on all matters. One could please him by throwing oneself into fine food, clothes, retinue, buildings, gambling. These were occasions which enabled him to talk to people. The essence of it was that by this he attempted and succeeded in exhausting everyone by making luxury a virtue, and for certain persons a necessity, and thus he gradually reduced everyone to depending entirely upon his generosity in order to subsist. In this he also found satisfaction for his pride through a court which was superb in all respects, and through a greater confusion which increasingly destroyed natural distinctions. This is an evil which, once introduced, became the internal cancer which is devouring all individuals — because from the court it promptly spread to Paris and into the provinces and the armies, where persons, whatever their position, are considered important only in proportion to the table they lay and their magnificence ever since this unfortunate innovation — which is devouring all individuals, which forces those who are in a position to steal not to restrain themselves from doing so for the most part, in their need to keep up with their expenditures; [a cancer] which is nourished by the confusion of social positions, pride, and even decency, and which by a mad desire to grow keeps constantly increasing, whose consequences are infinite and lead to nothing less than ruin and general upheaval.

Second Treatise of Civil Government: Legislative Power

John Locke

In England royal absolutism had been under attack throughout the seventeenth century and finally was defeated by the Glorious Revolution of 1688–1689. At that point there was a definitive shift in power to Parliament, which was controlled by the upper classes. John Locke (1632–1704), in his Two Treatises of Civil Government *(1690), justified the revolution and the new political constitution of England and expounded political ideas that became influential during the eighteenth and nineteenth centuries. This work and other writings established Locke as a first-rate empirical philosopher and political theorist. In the following selection from his* Second Treatise of Civil Government, *Locke analyzes legislative power.*

> **Consider:** *The purposes for entering into society; the extent of and limitations on legislative power; how Locke justifies his argument; how these ideas are contrary to monarchical absolutism.*

134. The great end of men's entering into society being the enjoyment of their properties in peace and safety, and the great instrument and means of that being the laws established in that society, the first and fundamental positive law of all commonwealths is the establishing of the legislative power, as the first and fundamental natural law which is to govern even the legislative. Itself is the preservation of the society and (as far as will consist with the public good) of every person in it. This legislative is not only the supreme power of the commonwealth, but sacred and unalterable in the hands where the community have once placed it. Nor can any edict of anybody else, in what form soever conceived, or by what power soever backed, have the force and obligation of a law which has not its sanction from that legislative which the public has chosen and appointed; for without this the law could not have that which is absolutely necessary to its being a law, the consent of the society, over whom nobody can have a power to make laws but by their own consent and by authority received from them; and therefore all the obedience, which by the most solemn ties any one can be obliged to pay, ultimately terminates in this supreme power, and is directed by those laws which it enacts. Nor can any oaths to any foreign power whatsoever, or any domestic subordinate power, discharge any member of the society from his obedience to the legislative, acting pursuant to their trust, nor oblige him to any obedience contrary to the laws so enacted or farther than they do

---

Source: John Locke, *Two Treatises of Civil Government* (London: J. M. Dent, Everyman, 1924), pp. 183–184, 189–190.

allow, it being ridiculous to imagine one can be tied ultimately to obey any power in the society which is not the supreme.

142. These are the bounds which the trust that is put in them by the society and the law of God and Nature have set to the legislative power of every commonwealth, in all forms of government. First: They are to govern by promulgated established laws, not to be varied in particular cases, but to have one rule for rich and poor, for the favourite at Court, and the country-man at plough. Secondly: These laws also ought to be designed for no other end ultimately but the good of the people. Thirdly: They must not raise taxes on the property of the people without the consent of the people given by themselves or their deputies. And this properly concerns only such governments where the legislative is always in being, or at least where the people have not reserved any part of the legislative to deputies, to be from time to time chosen by themselves. Fourthly: Legislative neither must nor can transfer the power of making laws to anybody else, or place it anywhere but where the people have.

VISUAL SOURCES

The Early Modern Château

The picture on page 12 of the château, grounds, and park of Vaux-le-Vicomte in France reveals both the wealth of France and certain trends of the seventeenth century. The château was built between 1657 and 1660 on the orders of France's superintendent of finance, Fouquet, and according to the plans of the architect Le Vau, the painter Lebrun, and the landscape gardener Le Nôtre. With its geometric orderliness and balance, it exemplifies Classical style. In its conquest and manipulation of nature according to the rational plans of humans, it reflects the growing scientific spirit of the age. It also reflects a fundamentally stable society that was still dominated politically, socially, and economically by a small elite. It and buildings like it do not call out for military defense as did medieval castles. It later served as a model for Versailles, which itself became the model of monarchical splendor in seventeenth- and eighteenth-century Europe.

Consider: *Why such buildings and parks might have been built and how Saint-Simon might have viewed such projects.*

Photo 1-1

Alain Perceval

Maternal Care
Pieter de Hooch

This scene of domestic life is painted by the seventeenth-century Dutch artist Pieter de Hooch. Entitled Maternal Care, *it shows a girl kneeling while her mother examines and delouses her head. The scene takes place in Holland, the most urban and commercial European country. The moderate wealth of the rooms, revealed particularly by the paintings and the quality of the drapes, and the emphasis on cleanliness, privacy, and relative austerity indicate that this is a middle-class home.*

Consider: *What the painter intended to communicate to the viewer of this painting.*

Photo 1-2

© Fotocommissie Rijksmuseum, Amsterdam

SECONDARY SOURCES

The Emergence of the Great Powers

John B. Wolf

Although individual kings played an important role in the rise of absolutism, absolutism resulted from more than personal ambition. Economic and political competition with other states and the consequent expansion of the army and the government bureaucracy contributed to the growing sense of the state as a distinct entity. This new sense of the state is analyzed in the following excerpt from The Emergence of the Great Powers. *In it John B. Wolf underscores the movement toward modern politics among European governments during this period.*

> **Consider:** *The evidence of the change in the conception and the reality of the state during this period; how the policies of Louis XIV and the Great Elector relate to Wolf's interpretation of the seventeenth-century state; whether Wolf's claim that "European governments were assuming a characteristically modern shape" is an exaggeration.*

In the Europe of the late seventeenth century the idea that the state encompassed and transcended crown and land, prince and people, was becoming established, reflecting a great revolution in political conceptions. Hailed by Grotius and the coterie of publicists who were developing the concept of international law, this new ideal was written into the public law of Europe by the great treaties from Westphalia (1648) to Nystad (1721). Thenceforth, not princes ruling by divine right, but civil and military bureaucracies provided order and form to society. Driven by the demands of war, kings and statesmen were forced to concentrate their attention upon the political and economic realities and to shape their policies to suit the interests of their states. Machiavelli had insisted upon state interest as the proper basis for politics; in the seventeenth century his ideas, buttressed with doctrines of natural law and natural rights, increasingly became the motive power of political action.

The pace of the revolution that transformed the king into the chief of a bureaucratic machine was accelerated by the very forces that created it. In earlier centuries lay scribes had joined the king's government and, as secretaries, had discharged many administrative and judicial functions. But

SOURCE: John B. Wolf, *The Emergence of the Great Powers, 1685–1715.* Reprinted by permission of Harper & Row (New York, 1951), pp. 3–4. Copyright © 1951 by Harper & Row, Publishers, Inc.

in the course of the seventeenth century these men of the pen had won a sensational victory over the men of the sword even in the domain of political action. At the opening of the century the councils of princes had still been composed of great noblemen and of clergymen who were the sons of noblemen, in short of men whose feudal conceptions were ill suited to the political requirements of the emerging states system. But within the century these aristocrats had been displaced by the rising class of career bureaucrats, whose relatively humble origins made them conscious of the state rather than of estates. These officials, many of them learned jurists with university educations or sons of royal officials with bourgeois backgrounds, together with a sprinkling of great lords who were willing to stake their fortunes on the state, formed the nucleus of the civil and military bureaucracies. Their careers and fortunes depended upon their service to the state and the favor of the prince; their duties almost forced them to see the problems of politics in operational terms. Commerce, finance, fortifications, the delineation of frontiers, the collection of taxes, the administration of revenues, and the organization of armies and navies were their daily tasks. Such problems were becoming the primary concern of governments and therefore became inevitably issues of high politics. Louis XIV may well have dreamed of the Bourbon dynasty's ruling Germany, France, and Spain, but the Rhine frontier, the Dutch commercial monopolies, the growth of English commerce, the strategic importance of fortifications, and the problems of maintaining a navy at sea were the concerns of his principal advisers. In time the exigencies of war and politics forced even Louis to accept the role of chief official, administrator of a civil and military bureaucracy.

The same process was at work elsewhere. As Europe came to be ruled by great military states, those states had to act increasingly in terms of state interest. The great political problems that grew out of the decay of the Holy Roman and Spanish empires seemed to reflect dynastic politics, but in the actual course of events political realities, based upon military, commercial, and financial considerations, became the predominant counters. The rise of great standing armies and their maintenance in the field made strenuous demands upon the treasury and the credit of the kings. In order to assure a continuous flow of revenue from taxation, required to meet the mounting costs, governments had to formulate and implement policies that would increase the riches of their potential taxpayers, and officials primarily interested in maintaining the power of their state inevitably urged policies that coincided with state interest. Thus European governments were assuming a characteristically modern shape and thereby rendering dynastic politics altogether anachronistic.

Politics in France and England

Kingsley Martin

The establishment of monarchical absolutism was not a uniform political trend in the seventeenth century. In England the monarchy lost in its struggle with Parliament for power. Historians have made many attempts to explain why English and French political events differed so greatly. In the following selection Kingsley Martin, British scholar and noted editor of the New Statesman and Nation, *argues that the differences between the royal houses and the aristocracies of England and France help to explain why their political histories were so different.*

> Consider: *The ways in which the royal houses and the aristocracies of England and France differed; other factors that might help to explain the different political patterns in these two countries.*

In the seventeenth century the English and the French monarchies were both engaged in a struggle to secure their sovereignty. In both countries the absolute power of Pope and Emperor had passed to the national King; in France sixteenth-century lawyers had made Henry IV the residuary legatee of the Roman Empire and, in England, Hobbes, with even greater assurance, had justified the irresponsible sovereignty of the Stuarts on a Utilitarian basis. In England Divine Right was effectively countered by the doctrine of fundamental law; behind all human laws, Coke held, there existed a law of nature, a moral law, which no Government was entitled to violate. Its practical expression was to be found not only in Biblical precepts but also in the Common Law of England; English kings had recognized its final authority, embodied in the Coronation Oath and the provisions of Magna Charta. The Puritan House of Commons willingly utilized Coke's theory in its struggle with Charles I, but the revolutionary settlement of 1689 resulted not in the recognition of a fundamental Constitution but in the doctrine of government by consent and the assumption by Parliament of the sovereignty wrested from the Stuarts. "The divine right of the Whig landowner" took the place of the divine right of the monarchy.

In France the seventeenth-century contest ended in the complete triumph of the monarchy. The Bourbons were stronger than the Stuarts for many reasons. The power of the French monarchy, like that of the English, was founded on national opposition to the Papacy and the desire of the trading middle class and populace for the destruction of the lawless power of the feudal aristocracy. But the humiliation of the aristocracy had been of a dif-

---

SOURCE: Kingsley Martin, *The Rise of French Liberal Thought*, J. P. Mayer, ed. Reprinted by permission of New York University Press (New York, 1954), pp. 23–24, 26.

ferent kind in the two countries: in France, as Tocqueville said, the aristocracy had lost their powers and kept their privileges, while in England they had lost their privileges and kept their power. The new English aristocracy, created by the Tudors and employed by them in local and central government, itself led the rebellion against the monarchy which had called it into existence. Religious and economic grievances also united a large section of the middle class against the Stuarts.

The English Revolution, 1688–1689

George Macaulay Trevelyan

In England two blows to monarchical authority proved to be turning points. The first was the Civil War and the execution of Charles I in the 1640s. But although this was a victory for Parliament, the Cromwellian period that followed and the return from exile of Charles II in 1660 cast doubt on the permanence of Parliament's victory. The second was the "Glorious Revolution" of 1688, which removed James II from power without the turmoil of the first revolution. In the following selection, Cambridge historian George Macaulay Trevelyan compares the two revolutions and analyzes the significance of the second one. Following the Whig tradition, Trevelyan views these trends in British history as constructive and progressive. More than most historians, he sees this revolution as an admirable triumph for Parliament.

> **Consider:** *Why the second revolution was a more clear-cut victory for Parliament than the first; factors that contributed to the victory of Parliament; how Kingsley Martin might react to the following analysis.*

The fundamental question at issue in 1688 had been this — Is the law above the King, or is the King above the law? The interest of Parliament was identified with that of the law, because, undoubtedly, Parliament could alter the law. It followed that, if law stood above the King's will, yet remained alterable by Parliament, Parliament would be the supreme power in the State.

James II attempted to make the law alterable wholesale by the King. This, if it had been permitted, must have made the King supreme over Parliament, and, in fact, a despot. The events of the winter of 1688–9 gave the victory to the opposite idea, which Chief Justice Coke and Selden had enunciated early in the century, that the King was the chief servant of the

SOURCE: George Macaulay Trevelyan, *The English Revolution, 1688–1689.* Reprinted by permission of Oxford University Press (Oxford, 1938), pp. 164–166.

law, but not its master; the executant of the law, not its source; the laws should only be alterable by Parliament — Kings, Lords and Commons together. It is this that makes the Revolution the decisive event in the history of the English Constitution. It was decisive because it was never undone, as most of the work of the Cromwellian Revolution had been undone.

It is true that the first Civil War had been fought partly on this same issue: — the Common Law in league with Parliament had, on the field of Naseby, triumphed over the King in the struggle for the supreme place in the Constitution. But the victory of Law and Parliament had, on that occasion, been won only because Puritanism, the strongest religious passion of the hour, had supplied the fighting force. And religious passion very soon confused the Constitutional issue. Puritanism burst the legal bounds and, coupled with militarism, overthrew law and Parliament as well as King. Hence the necessity of the restoration in 1660 of King, law and Parliament together, without any clear definition of their ultimate mutual relations.

Now, in this second crisis of 1688, law and Parliament had on their side not only the Puritan passion, which had greatly declined, but the whole force of Protestant-Anglicanism, which was then at its height, and the rising influence of Latitudinarian scepticism — all arrayed against the weak Roman Catholic interest to which James had attached the political fortunes of the royal cause. The ultimate victor of the seventeenth-century struggle was not Pym or Cromwell, with their Puritan ideals, but Coke and Selden with their secular idea of the supremacy of law. In 1689 the Puritans had to be content with a bare toleration. But law triumphed, and therefore the law-making Parliament triumphed finally over the King.

Centuries of Childhood

Philippe Ariès

Through analysis of paintings such as Maternal Care *by Pieter de Hooch (see p. 13) as well as other kinds of evidence, historians have changed our assumptions about attitudes toward childhood in Early Modern times. The most important of these historians is Philippe Ariès. The following is a selection from his* Centuries of Childhood.

> **Consider:** *How this reading relates to Hooch's painting; the differences between the seventeenth-century family, the medieval family, and the modern family according to Ariès.*

SOURCE: Philippe Ariès, *Centuries of Childhood*, Robert Baldick, trans. Reprinted by permission of Alfred A. Knopf, Inc. (New York, 1962), pp. 403–404. Copyright © 1962 by Alfred A. Knopf, Inc.

Between the end of the Middle Ages and the seventeenth century, the child had won a place beside his parents to which he could not lay claim at a time when it was customary to entrust him to strangers. This return of the children to the home was a great event: it gave the seventeenth-century family its principal characteristic, which distinguished it from the medieval family. The child became an indispensable element of everyday life, and his parents worried about his education, his career, his future. He was not yet the pivot of the whole system, but he had become a much more important character. Yet this seventeenth-century family was not the modern family: it was distinguished from the latter by the enormous mass of sociability which it retained. Where the family existed, that is to say in the big houses, it was a centre of social relations, the capital of a little complex and graduated society under the command of the paterfamilias.

The modern family, on the contrary, cuts itself off from the world and opposes to society the isolated group of parents and children. All the energy of the group is expended on helping the children to rise in the world, individually and without any collective ambition: the children rather than the family.

Parents and Children
in History

David Hunt

Over time the family has remained the most basic institution of social life in Western civilization. In many ways, the family is resistant to change, and thus we can recognize traits of family life in the past as similar to our own. Nevertheless, the family has changed in important ways over time, reflecting the evolving nature of Western societies. In the following selection, David Hunt uses some of the insights of modern psychology and sociology to analyze the family in seventeenth-century France.

Consider: *How the family reflected the broader social system; the importance of the distinction between marriages of love and those of interest; how this reading complements the selection by Ariès and Hooch's painting.*

. . . [I]n the seventeenth century people felt strongly the contrast between the loyalties and duties incumbent upon them as a consequence of their station in society on the one hand, and their natural inclinations on the other. Institutional arrangements always implied a gradation of rank and were thus held to be incompatible with friendship, in which equality between the partners was so important. Far from accepting the fact that personal relations

Source: David Hunt, *Parents and Children in History: The Psychology of Family Life in Early Modern France* (New York: Basic Books, Inc.), pp. 154–155.

were almost always arranged according to hierarchical principles, individuals were made acutely uncomfortable by this situation. In personal letters, writers often distinguished sincere and spontaneous affection from the more perfunctory good will which went with the formal relationship to their correspondent. Thus Madame de Sévigné, in sending good wishes to her daughter, stipulated that, "In this case, maternal love plays less of a part than inclination."

As the quote indicates, the family was caught up in this system. To be a brother, son, or wife was a status, with its special obligations, its place in a grid of rule and submission. Members of the family were supposed to love one another; paternal, maternal, fraternal love were all often cited as models of human fellow feeling. At the same time, even within the family, it was terribly hard to imagine a relationship of mutual affection which was not simultaneously one of ruler and ruled. Like the bond between master and servant, between seigneur and peasant, between king and subject, family ties, while steeped in a folklore of pious harmony, implied as well the power to dominate others, to claim rewards, or, on the contrary, the awareness of a helpless dependence.

This line of argument will help to explain further the distinction which, as we have seen, observers made with such clarity between marriages of love and those of interest. Marriages of love implied spontaneous affection between the two lovers, who were concerned primarily with their own happiness. Marriage of interest involved social and financial considerations to be arranged for the benefit of families. These observers understood very well that in a social system which attempted to subordinate the wishes of marriageable children to the ambitions of their parents, and in which the wife was regarded simply as the means of cementing alliances between families, marriage could not at the same time be expected to provide for the happiness and the emotional satisfaction of the partners.

. . . [G]radations of rank within the household were interpreted simply as a matter of power and of usage, and that people believed this situation discouraged close and mutually satisfying relationships among family members. Ideally, those of lower rank should have accepted the eminence of their superiors and been warmed by the benefits they received from an admittedly unequal partnership. In fact, inequality within the domestic unit filled people not with love and warmth, but with resentment and a feeling of "shame and envy."

The World We Have Lost:
The Early Modern Family

Peter Laslett

The family is a tremendously important institution in any society. Changes in its structure and functions occur very slowly and gradually. With the passage of centuries since Early Modern times, we can see some sharp differences between the family of that period and the family of today. In the following selection Peter Laslett, a social historian from Cambridge who has written extensively on the Early Modern period, points out these differences.

> **Consider:** *The economic and social functions of the family revealed in this selection; what this document adds to the image of the family provided in the painting by Hooch and the accompanying document by Ariès; how the structure of this family differs from a typical twentieth-century family.*

In the year 1619 the bakers of London applied to the authorities for an increase in the price of bread. They sent in support of their claim a complete description of a bakery and an account of its weekly costs. There were thirteen or fourteen people in such an establishment: the baker and his wife, four paid employees who were called journeymen, two apprentices, two maidservants and the three or four children of the master baker himself. . . .

The only word used at that time to describe such a group of people was "family." The man at the head of the group, the entrepreneur, the employer, or the manager, was then known as the master or head of the family. He was father to some of its members and in place of father to the rest. There was no sharp distinction between his domestic and his economic functions. His wife was both his partner and his subordinate, a partner because she ran the family, took charge of the food and managed the womenservants, a subordinate because she was woman and wife, mother and in place of mother to the rest.

The paid servants of both sexes had their specified and familiar position in the family, as much part of it as the children but not quite in the same position. At that time the family was not one society only but three societies fused together: the society of man and wife, of parents and children and of master and servant. But when they were young, and servants were, for the most part, young, unmarried people, they were very close to children in their status and their function. . . .

Apprentices, therefore, were workers who were also children, extra sons or extra daughters (for girls could be apprenticed too), clothed and

SOURCE: Excerpt from *The World We Have Lost* by Peter Laslett. Copyright © 1965 by Peter Laslett. Reprinted by permission of Charles Scribner's Sons.

educated as well as fed, obliged to obedience and forbidden to marry, unpaid and absolutely dependent until the age of twenty-one. If apprentices were workers in the position of sons and daughters, the sons and daughters of the house were workers too. John Locke laid it down in 1697 that the children of the poor must work for some part of the day when they reached the age of three. The sons and daughters of a London baker were not free to go to school for many years of their young lives, or even to play as they wished when they came back home. Soon they would find themselves doing what they could in *bolting*, that is sieving flour, or in helping the maidservant with her panniers of loaves on the way to the market stall, or in playing their small parts in preparing the never-ending succession of meals for the whole household.

We may see at once, therefore, that the world we have lost, as I have chosen to call it, was no paradise or golden age of equality, tolerance or loving kindness. It is so important that I should not be misunderstood on this point that I will say at once that the coming of industry cannot be shown to have brought economic oppression and exploitation along with it. It was there already. The patriarchal arrangements which we have begun to explore were not new in the England of Shakespeare and Elizabeth. They were as old as the Greeks, as old as European history, and not confined to Europe. And it may well be that they abused and enslaved people quite as remorselessly as the economic arrangements which had replaced them in the England of Blake and Victoria. When people could expect to live for only thirty years in all, how must a man have felt when he realized that so much of his adult life, perhaps all, must go in working for his keep and very little more in someone else's family?

Chapter Questions

1. What conditions facilitated the development of monarchical absolutism in the seventeenth century? What policies were used by kings to this end?

2. Why might mercantilist doctrines be particularly appealing to seventeenth-century monarchs?

3. How does family life reflect broader social, economic, and political aspects of the seventeenth century?

CHAPTER TWO

The Scientific Revolution

One of the most important intellectual revolutions of Western civilization occurred in the seventeenth century. Building on some sixteenth-century breakthroughs and a more deeply rooted interest in the workings of the natural world, a small elite of thinkers and scientists—Descartes, Galileo, Newton, Kepler, Bacon, and Boyle—established the foundations for the modern sciences of astronomy, mathematics, physics, and chemistry. Although at first their work was known to only a few, their ideas spread widely during the eighteenth century.

In the process of developing the modern sciences, these thinkers challenged the established conception of the universe as well as previous assumptions about knowledge. This ultimately successful challenge, now known as the scientific revolution, had a number of key elements. First, the view of the universe as being stable, fixed, and finite, with the earth at its center, gave way to a view of the universe as moving and almost infinite, with the earth merely one of millions of bodies, all subject to the laws of nature. Second, earlier methods for ascertaining the truth, which primarily involved referring to traditional authorities such as Aristotle, Ptolemy, and the Church, were replaced by methods that emphasized skepticism, rationalism, and rigorous reasoning based on observed facts and mathematical laws. Third, although these thinkers remained concerned with their own deeply held religious beliefs, the general scientific orientation shifted from theological questions to secular questions that focused on how things worked.

The primary documents in this chapter emphasize two broad questions that faced these seventeenth-century scientists. First, how can one ascertain the truth? The answers of Descartes, Galileo, and Newton are examined. Second, what is the proper line between science and scriptural authority? Galileo, who came most directly into conflict with Church authorities, and Newton, who like most other scientific thinkers of the period remained religious, provide us with clues.

The secondary documents concentrate on the nature and causes of the scientific revolution. In what ways was seventeenth-century science different from the science of earlier centuries? What explains these differences? What were the specific psychological, social, and cultural motives of seventeenth-century scientists?

Most of these intellectual developments were known to only a few throughout Europe. In the eighteenth century these scientific ideas and methods became popularized as part of the intellectual ferment of the Enlightenment.

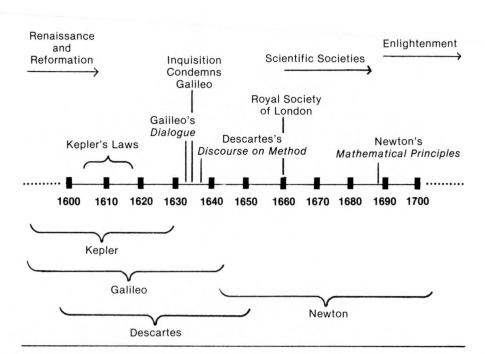

Scientific Revolution

PRIMARY SOURCES

The Discourse on Method
René Descartes

Seventeenth-century science needed new philosophical and methodological stand-ards for truth to replace those traditionally used to support scientific assumptions. These were forcefully provided by René Descartes (1596–1650) in his Discourse on Method *(1637). Born and educated in France, but spending his most productive years in Holland, Descartes gained fame as a mathematician, physicist, and meta-physical philosopher. The following excerpt from his* Discourse *contains the best-known statement of his approach to discovering truth.*

> **Consider:** *The ways in which Descartes' approach constitutes a break with traditional ways of ascertaining the truth; the weaknesses of this approach and how a modern scientist might criticize this method; how this approach reflects Descartes' background as a mathematician.*

In place of the multitude of precepts of which logic is composed, I believed I should find the four following rules quite sufficient, provided I should firmly and steadfastly resolve not to fail of observing them in a single instance.

The first rule was never to receive anything as a truth which I did not clearly know to be such; that is, to avoid haste and prejudice, and not to comprehend anything more in my judgments than that which should pre-sent itself so clearly and so distinctly to my mind that I should have no occa-sion to entertain a doubt of it.

The second rule was to divide every difficulty which I should examine into as many parts as possible, or as might be required for resolving it.

The third rule was to conduct my thoughts in an orderly manner, beginning with objects the most simple and the easiest to understand, in order to ascend as it were by steps to the knowledge of the most composite, assuming some order to exist even in things which did not appear to be naturally connected.

The last rule was to make enumerations so complete, and reviews so com-prehensive, that I should be certain of omitting nothing.

Those long chains of reasoning, quite simple and easy, which geometers are wont to employ in the accomplishment of their most difficult demonstra-tions, led me to think that everything which might fall under the cognizance of the human mind might be connected together in a similar manner, and that, provided only one should take care not to receive anything as true

SOURCE: René Descartes, *The Discourse on Method*, in *The Philosophy of Descartes*, Henry A. P. Torrey, ed. and trans. (New York: Henry Holt, 1892), pp. 46–48.

which was not so, and if one were always careful to preserve the order necessary for deducing one truth from another, there would be none so remote
at which he might not at last arrive, nor so concealed which he might not
discover. And I had no great difficulty in finding those with which to make a
beginning, for I knew already that these must be the simplest and easiest to
apprehend; and considering that, among all those who had up to this time
made discoveries in the sciences, it was the mathematicians alone who had
been able to arrive at demonstrations—that is to say, at proofs certain and
evident—I did not doubt that I should begin with the same truths which
they investigated.

Letter to Christina of Tuscany: Science and Scripture

Galileo Galilei

*The most renowned scientist at the beginning of the seventeenth century was the
Italian astronomer, mathematician, and physicist Galileo Galilei (1564–1642). His
discoveries about gravity, velocity, and the movement of astronomical bodies were
grounded in a scientific method that ran contrary to the accepted standards for
truth and authority. In the following excerpt from a letter to the Grand Duchess
Christina of Tuscany (1615), Galileo defends his ideas and delineates his view of
the correct line between science and scriptural authority.*

> **Consider:** *According to Galileo's view, the kinds of topics or questions that are
> appropriately scientific and those that are appropriately theological; how
> Galileo's views compare with those of Descartes; why Galileo's views are so
> crucial to the scientific revolution.*

I think that in discussions of physical problems we ought to begin not from
the authority of scriptural passages, but from sense-experiences and
necessary demonstrations; for the holy Bible and the phenomena of nature
proceed alike from the divine Word, the former as the dictate of the Holy
Ghost and the latter as the observant executrix of God's commands. It is necessary for the Bible, in order to be accommodated to the understanding of
every man, to speak many things which appear to differ from the absolute
truth so far as the bare meaning of the words is concerned. But Nature, on
the other hand, is inexorable and immutable; she never transgresses the laws
imposed upon her, or cares a whit whether her abstruse reasons and methods

SOURCE: From Galileo Galilei, *Discoveries and Opinions of Galileo*, Stillman Drake, ed. and
trans. Reprinted by permission of Doubleday & Company, Inc. (New York, 1957), pp. 182–183.
Copyright © 1957 by Stillman Drake.

of operation are understandable to men. For that reason it appears that nothing physical which sense-experience sets before our eyes, or which necessary demonstrations prove to us, ought to be called in question (much less condemned) upon the testimony of biblical passages which may have some different meaning beneath their words. For the Bible is not chained in every expression to conditions as strict as those which govern all physical effects; nor is God any less excellently revealed in Nature's actions than in the sacred statements of the Bible. . . .

From this I do not mean to infer that we need not have an extraordinary esteem for the passages of holy Scripture. On the contrary, having arrived at any certainties in physics, we ought to utilize these as the most appropriate aids in the true exposition of the Bible and in the investigation of those meanings which are necessarily contained therein, for these must be concordant with demonstrated truths. I should judge that the authority of the Bible was designed to persuade men of those articles and propositions which, surpassing all human reasoning, could not be made credible by science, or by any other means than through the very mouth of the Holy Spirit.

Yet even in those propositions which are not matters of faith, this authority ought to be preferred over that of all human writings which are supported only by bare assertions or probable arguments, and not set forth in a demonstrative way. This I hold to be necessary and proper to the same extent that divine wisdom surpasses all human judgment and conjecture.

But I do not feel obliged to believe that that same God who has endowed us with senses, reason, and intellect has intended to forgo their use and by some other means to give us knowledge which we can attain by them.

The Papal Inquisition of 1633: Galileo Condemned

Not surprisingly, Galileo found his views under attack from a variety of corners, including important groups within the Church. Ultimately his defense of Copernicanism, which held that the earth was not the center of the universe, was formally condemned by the Church. When he argumentatively summarized these ideas again in his Dialogue Concerning the Two Chief World Systems *(1632), he was brought before the Papal Inquisition, forced to recant his views, and confined to a villa on the outskirts of Florence. The following are some of the main charges against Galileo during his trial for heresy before the Inquisition in 1633.*

> **Consider:** *Why Galileo's views were so threatening to the Church; some of the long-range consequences of such a stance by the Church toward these views.*

SOURCE: Georgio de Santillana, *The Crime of Galileo.* Reprinted by permission of The University of Chicago Press (Chicago, 1955), p. 310. Copyright © 1955.

We say, pronounce, sentence, and declare that you, the said Galileo, by reason of the matters adduced in trial, and by you confessed as above, have rendered yourself in the judgment of this Holy Office vehemently suspected of heresy, namely, of having believed and held the doctrine — which is false and contrary to the sacred and divine Scriptures — that the Sun is the center of the world and does not move from east to west and that the Earth moves and is not the center of the world; and that an opinion may be held and defended as probable after it has been declared and defined to be contrary to the Holy Scripture; and that consequently you have incurred all the censures and penalties imposed and promulgated in the sacred canons and other constitutions, general and particular, against such delinquents. From which we are content that you be absolved, provided that, first, with a sincere heart and unfeigned faith, you abjure, curse, and detest before us the aforesaid errors and heresies and every other error and heresy contrary to the Catholic and Apostolic Roman Church in the form to be prescribed by us for you.

Mathematical Principles of Natural Philosophy

Sir Isaac Newton

The greatest scientific synthesis of the seventeenth century was made by Isaac Newton (1642–1727), who was born in England and attained a post as professor of mathematics at Cambridge University. Newton made his most important discoveries early in life. By the beginning of the eighteenth century he was the most admired scientific figure in Europe. He made fundamental discoveries concerning gravity, light, and differential calculus. Most important, he synthesized various scientific findings and methods into a description of the universe as working according to measurable, predictable, mechanical laws. Newton's most famous work, Mathematical Principles of Natural Philosophy *(1687), contains his theory of universal gravitation. In the following selection from that work, Newton describes his four rules for arriving at knowledge.*

> **Consider:** *Why Newton's rules might be particularly useful for the experimental sciences; ways these rules differ from those of Descartes.*

RULE I

We are to admit no more causes of natural things than such as are both true and sufficient to explain their appearances.

Source: Sir Isaac Newton, *Mathematical Principles of Natural Philosophy*, Andrew Motte, trans., revised by Florian Cajori (Berkeley, Calif.: University of California Press, 1947), pp. 398, 400. Reprinted by permission of the University of California Press.

To this purpose the philosophers say that Nature does nothing in vain, and more is in vain when less will serve; for Nature is pleased with simplicity, and affects not the pomp of superfluous causes.

RULE II

Therefore to the same natural effects we must, as far as possible, assign the same causes.

As to respiration in a man and in a beast; the descent of stones in *Europe* and in *America;* the light of our culinary fire and of the sun; the reflection of light in the earth, and in the planets.

RULE III

The qualities of bodies, which admit neither intensification nor remission of degrees, and which are found to belong to all bodies within the reach of our experiments, are to be esteemed the universal qualities of all bodies whatsoever.

For since the qualities of bodies are only known to us by experiments, we are to hold for universal all such as universally agree with experiments; and such as are not liable to diminution can never be quite taken away.

RULE IV

In experimental philosophy we are to look upon propositions inferred by general induction from phenomena as accurately or very nearly true, notwithstanding any contrary hypotheses that may be imagined, till such time as other phenomena occur, by which they may either be made more accurate, or liable to exceptions.

This rule we must follow, that the argument of induction may not be evaded by hypotheses.

Opticks: God in a Scientific Universe

Sir Isaac Newton

Like Galileo and Descartes, Newton was well aware that his ideas had implications for theology and might be considered contrary to religious doctrine. Yet he was a very religious man and took pains to distinguish the appropriate realms of science and religion. In the following selection from Opticks *(1704), an analysis of light,*

SOURCE: Sir Isaac Newton, *Opticks*, 4th ed. (London: 1730), pp. 400–402.

Newton deals with this issue and emphasizes that behind his ideas and systems there is room for God in the universe.

> **Consider:** *Newton's view of the role played by God in the universe; how Newton's ideas compare with those of Galileo; whether a twentieth-century scientist might have any problems with these ideas.*

All these things being consider'd, it seems probable to me, that God in the Beginning form'd Matter in solid, massy, hard, impenetrable moveable Particles, of such Sizes and Figures, and with such other Properties, and in such Proportion to Space, as most conduced to the End for which he form'd them; and that these primitive Particles being Solids, are incomparably harder than any porous Bodies compounded of them; even so very hard, as never to wear or break in pieces; no ordinary Power being able to divide what God himself made one in the first Creation. . . .

It seems to me farther, that these Particles have not only a *Vis inertiae*, accompanied with such passive Laws of Motion as naturally result from that Force, but also that they are moved by certain active Principles, such as is that of Gravity, and that which causes Fermentation, and the Cohesion of Bodies. These Principles I consider, not as occult Qualities, supposed to result from the specifick Forms of Things, but as general Laws of Nature, by which the Things themselves are form'd; their Truth appearing to us by Phaenomena, though their Causes be not yet discover'd. . . .

Now by the help of these Principles, all material Things seem to have been composed of the hard and solid Particles above-mention'd, variously associated in the first Creation by the Counsel of an intelligent Agent. For it became him who created them to set them in order. And if he did so, it's unphilosophical to seek for any other Origin of the World, or to pretend that it might arise out of a Chaos by the mere Laws of Nature; though being once form'd, it may continue by those Laws for many Ages.

VISUAL SOURCES

A Vision of the New Science

One of the most important figures of the scientific revolution was the astronomer and mathematician Johannes Kepler (1571–1630). On this page from the front of one of his works, first printed in Nuremberg in 1627, the "edifice" of astronomy is presented allegorically. The older but still respectable pillars of astronomy of Hipparchus and Ptolemy give way to the new, sturdy pillars of Kepler's immediate predecessors, Copernicus and Tyco Brahe. In the lower left panel Kepler is

Photo 2-1

pictured in his study; in the center panel is a map of the island where Brahe's observatory was located; in the right-hand panel is a picture of two people working on a printing press. Throughout are various instruments used in astronomy.

The picture reveals much about the scientific revolution. The instruments emphasize how important measurement and observation were to the new science. The depiction of the old and new pillars suggests that the new scientists were replacing if not necessarily challenging the old, accepted scientific authorities by building on the work of their immediate predecessors—here Brahe on Copernicus, and Kepler on Brahe and Copernicus. The importance of communication among scientists is indicated by tribute to the printing press.

> **Consider:** *How this picture illustrates the ways in which seventeenth-century scientists were breaking with earlier scientific assumptions.*

SECONDARY SOURCES

Why Was Science Backward in the Middle Ages?

Michael Postan

The scientific advances of the seventeenth century are commonly considered revolutionary because of their contrast with the previous state of science. One way to gain insight into the origins of the seventeenth-century developments is to look at earlier periods to see whether something was missing then that explains this contrast. In the following selection Michael Postan takes this approach, focusing specifically on the lack of scientific incentives in the Middle Ages.

> **Consider:** *Why scientific incentives were lacking in the Middle Ages; the typically medieval traits that discouraged the men of the Middle Ages from scientific exploration; how the concerns and problems faced by Galileo relate to this argument.*

It is generally agreed that the Middle Ages preserved for the use of later times the science of the ancients. Therein lies both the scientific achievement and the scientific failure of the medieval civilization. . . . What the

Source: Michael Postan, "Why Was Science Backward in the Middle Ages?" in *A Short History of Science: Origins and Results of the Scientific Revolution* (London: Routledge and Kegan Paul), pp. 10–17. Reprinted by permission of Routledge and Kegan Paul, Ltd.

Middle Ages took over they did not very much enrich. Indeed so small was their own contribution that historians of science are apt to regard the Middle Ages as something of a pause. . . .

Thus some advance on planes both purely intellectual and technical there was; yet taken together and placed against the vast panorama of medieval life, or indeed against the achievements of Greek and Hellenistic science in the fourth century B.C., or with the scientific activity of the seventeenth century, all these achievements are bound to appear very poor. Why then this poverty?

To this question many answers can be and have been given. But what most of them boil down to is the absence in medieval life of what I should be inclined to call scientific incentives. Students of science sometimes differ about the true inspiration of scientific progress. Some seek and find it in man's intellectual curiosity, in his desire to understand the workings of nature. Others believe that scientific knowledge grew and still grows out of man's attempts to improve his tools and his methods of production; that, in short, scientific truth is a by-product of technical progress. I do not want here to take sides in this particular controversy; what I want to suggest is that the Middle Ages were doubly unfortunate in that both the inspirations, the intellectual as well as the practical, failed more or less.

The easiest to account for is the intellectual. The Middle Ages were the age of faith, and to that extent they were unfavourable to scientific speculation. It is not that scientists as such were proscribed. For on the whole the persecution of men for their scientific ideas was very rare: rare because men with dangerous ideas, or indeed with any scientific ideas at all, were themselves very rare; and it is indeed surprising that there were any at all. This does not mean that there were no intellectual giants. All it means is that in an age which was one of faith, men of intellect and spirit found the calls of faith itself — its elucidation, its controversies, and its conquests — a task sufficient to absorb them. To put it simply, they had no time for occupations like science.

In fact they had neither the time nor the inclination. For even if there had been enough men to engage in activities as mundane as science, there would still be very little reason for them to do so. In times when medieval religious dogma stood whole and unshaken the intellectual objects and the methods of science were, to say the least, superfluous. The purpose of scientific enquiry is to build up piecemeal a unified theory of the universe, of its origin and of its working. But in the Middle Ages was that process really necessary? Did not medieval man already possess in God, in the story of Creation and in the doctrine of Omnipotent Will, a complete explanation of how the world came about and of how, by what means and to what purpose, it was being conducted? Why build up in laborious and painstaking mosaic a design, which was already there from the outset, clear and visible to all?

So much for intellectual incentive. The practical incentive was almost equally feeble. Greater understanding of nature could not come from technical improvements, chiefly because technical improvements were so few.

Medieval occupations continued for centuries without appreciable change of method. After the great period of initial development, i.e., after the late eleventh century, the routine of medieval farming in the greater part of Europe became as fixed as the landscape itself. In the history of the smithies, the weaving shops, or the potteries, there were occasional periods of innovation, but taking the Middle Ages as a whole technical improvement was very rare and very slow. For this medieval economic policy was largely to blame. In the course of centuries economic activities got surrounded with a vast structure of bye-laws and regulations. . . . For bye-laws were as a rule based on the technical methods in existence when they were framed; and once framed they were to stand in the way of all subsequent change.

What is more, so deeply ingrained was the spirit of protection that in every local trade the technical methods were treated as a secret. . . . The men of the Middle Ages were unable to do more than they did because they were lacking in scientific incentive. What they achieved in advancing the practical arts of humanity or in preserving and transmitting ancient learning, they did in so far and as long as they were not typically medieval.

Early Modern Europe: Motives for the Scientific Revolution

Sir George Clark

By the seventeenth century, certain broad historical developments had set the stage for individuals to make the discoveries we associate with the scientific revolution. In addition, these individuals were motivated in ways that medieval people were not and used the new and growing body of techniques, materials, and knowledge to make their discoveries. In the following selection, British historian Sir George Clark, a recognized authority on the seventeenth century, examines some of the motives that led people to engage in scientific work.

> **Consider:** *The distinctions Clark makes among different people engaged in scientific work; why, more than thirteenth- or fourteenth-century people, these seventeenth-century people had a "disinterested desire to know."*

There were an infinite number of motives which led men to engage in scientific work and to clear the scientific point of view from encumbrances; but we may group together some of the most important under general headings,

SOURCE: Sir George Clark, *Early Modern Europe*. Reprinted by permission of The Oxford University Press (Oxford, 1957), pp. 164–165.

always remembering that in actual life each of them was compounded with the others. There were economic motives. The Portuguese explorers wanted their new instrument for navigation; the German mine-owners asked questions about metallurgy and about machines for lifting and carrying heavy loads; Italian engineers improved their canals and locks and harbours by applying the principles of hydrostatics; English trading companies employed experts who used new methods of drawing charts. Not far removed from the economic motives were those of the physicians and surgeons, who revolutionized anatomy and physiology, and did much more good than harm with their new medicines and new operations, though some of them now seem absurd. Like the doctors, the soldiers called science to their aid in designing and aiming artillery or in planning fortifications. But there were other motives far removed from the economic sphere. Jewellers learnt much about precious and semi-precious stones, but so did magicians. Musicians learnt the mathematics of harmony; painters and architects studied light and colour, substances and proportions, not only as craftsmen but as artists. For a number of reasons religion impelled men to scientific study. The most definite and old-established was the desire to reach absolute correctness in calculating the dates for the annual fixed and movable festivals of the Church: it was a pope who presided over the astronomical researches by which the calendar was reformed in the sixteenth century. Deeper and stronger was the desire to study the wonders of science, and the order which it unravelled in the universe, as manifestations of the Creator's will. This was closer than any of the other motives to the central impulse which actuated them all, the disinterested desire to know.

The Scientific Intellectual: A Psychological Interpretation of the Scientific Revolution

Lewis Feuer

The traditional approach to the scientific revolution has been to view it from a technological perspective, tracing the discovery and use of scientific techniques before and during the seventeenth century. Postan and Clark in the preceding selections deal with the motives that did or did not impel people to engage in scientific work. In both cases a "common sense" view of humans was assumed. In recent years scholars have become more sophisticated in applying the social sciences

SOURCE: Lewis S. Feuer, *The Scientific Intellectual: The Psychological and Sociological Origins of Modern Science*. Reprinted by permission of Basic Books, Inc., Publishers (New York, 1963), pp. 6–8, 17–19. Copyright © 1963 by Basic Books, Inc.

*to the scientific revolution. In the following selection Lewis Feuer uses insights
from modern psychology and social psychology to explain what turned seventeenth-
century men to science.*

> **Consider:** *The spirit common to the scientific revolution and how this spirit
> was manifested in what the scientists were doing; why Postan or Clark might
> be unwilling to accept Feuer's interpretation.*

That the scientific revolution was the outcome of a liberation of curiosity all
would agree. The question, however, remains unsettled: What was the emotional revolution in seventeenth-century thinkers which turned them into men
of science? What was the psychological revolution upon which the scientific
revolution was founded? Modern science, writes Lynn White, Jr., as it first
appeared in the later Middle Ages, "was one result of a deep-seated mutation
in the general attitude toward nature." The new science, he continues, was
an aspect "of an unprecedented yearning for immediate experience of concrete facts which appears to have been characteristic of the waxing third
estate." What, then, was the character of this deep-seated emotional mutation? What changes in attitude and feeling toward human thought, sensation,
and knowledge made possible the emergence of scientific intellectuals? . . .

The scientific intellectual was born from the hedonist-libertarian spirit
which, spreading through Europe in the sixteenth and seventeenth centuries, directly nurtured the liberation of human curiosity. Not asceticism, but
satisfaction; not guilt, but joy in the human status; not self-abnegation, but
self-affirmation; not original sin, but original merit and worth; not gloom,
but merriment; not contempt for one's body and one's senses, but the hymn
of pleasure—this was the emotional basis of the scientific movement of the
seventeenth century. Herbert Butterfield has spoken of "a certain dynamic
quality" which entered into Europe's "secularization of thought" in the
seventeenth century. . . .

The hedonist-libertarian ethic provided the momentum for the scientific
revolution, and was in fact the creed of the emerging movements of scientific
intellectuals everywhere. . . .

The scientists of the seventeenth century swept away the miserable universe of death, famine, and the torture of human beings in the name of
God. They took a world that had been peopled with demons and devils, and
that superstition had thronged with unseen terror at every side. They
cleansed it with clear words and plain experiment. They found an ethic that
advised people to renounce their desires, and to cultivate in a hostile
universe the humility which befitted their impotence, and they taught men
instead to take pride in their human status, and to dare to change the world
into one which would answer more fully to their desires. . . .

The scientific movement in the seventeenth century was not the by-
product of an increase of repression or asceticism. It was the outcome of a

liberation of energies; it derived from a lightening of the burden of guilt. With the growing awareness that happiness and joy are his aims, man could take frank pleasure in the world around him. Libidinal interest in external objects could develop unthwarted; the world was found interesting to live in — an unending stage for fresh experience. Energies were no longer consumed in inner conflicts. With an awakened respect for his own biological nature, self-hatred was cast off. Empiricism was the expression of a confidence in one's senses; the eyes and ears were no longer evidences of human corruption but trusted avenues to a knowledge of nature. The body was not the tainted seat of ignorance, but the source of pleasures and the means for knowledge. Human energies, hitherto turned against themselves, could reach out beyond concern for exclusive self.

The Scientific Role: A Sociocultural Interpretation of the Scientific Revolution

Joseph Ben-David

During the seventeenth century, new institutions such as the Royal Society were formed that helped create a sense of community and permanence among scientists. The achievements of scientists were increasingly recognized, and scientists gained both respect and acceptance into high social circles. These sociological aspects of the scientific revolution are stressed in the following selection by Israeli sociologist Joseph Ben-David. Ben-David argues that step by step scientists gained legitimacy and permanence to the point where science became a "self-perpetuating domain of culture."

> **Consider:** *How science was facilitated by nonscientific segments of society; how Ben-David might have used the ideas of Feuer to support his argument; how Ben-David's argument could be used to explain the previous lack of scientific achievement.*

Traditionally, natural science was subordinated to theology and philosophy. A first step towards the modern efflorescence occurred when it began to become more differentiated from theology and philosophy with respect to its subject-matter and procedures. Even when this point was reached, science continued to be a peripheral and secondary interest, but once its continuity

SOURCE: Joseph Ben-David, "The Scientific Role: The Conditions of Its Establishment in Europe," *Minerva*, Vol. IV, No. 1 (Autumn 1965), pp. 16–17. Reprinted by permission of Edward Shils.

was assured by its patent singularity and the steadiness of the concern which it attracted, it ceased to be subject to intermittent deterioration and there was even a probability of some slow but regular accumulation of scientific knowledge. The next step occurred when this peripheral subject, which had had a low status, relative to other intellectual fields, came to be regarded by groups, with class, religious and political interests opposed to the established order, as intellectually more meaningful to them than the existing theological, philosophical and literary culture. For these groups, the sciences became a central part of their culture. Under these circumstances, men interested in science were impelled to redefine their roles as philosophers in such a way that science became increasingly central instead of peripheral to their conception of what they were doing. With the enhancement of the wealth, power and status of the classes which adopted an outlook sympathetic to science and in opposition to the inherited outlook, the status of the new type of philosopher was elevated. With the advancement of the status of scientific activity, the numbers of intellectuals of the highest quality moving into the field increased. The final steps occurred in the seventeeth century when the political success of the classes adopting the scientistic outlook, combined with the intellectual success of the new philosophers, led to a more elaborate organisation of science and the establishment of scientific journals. In the course of these developments, men who did scientific work came to regard themselves and to be regarded by others as different from philosophers. They came to regard themselves as carrying on a significantly distinctive category of activity, disjunctively separated from the intellectual activity of philosophers and theologians. Increasing in numbers and having more occasion to meet and discuss with each other, they developed their own culture, their own norms and traditions in which their scientific work was embedded. The motivation and curiosity sustained by the stabilised stimulus inherent in such intensified and persistent scientific activity made for a greater continuity in scientific development. With a larger number of persons convinced of the value of science and devoting themselves actively and fully to its cultivation, science became, in a sense, a self-perpetuating domain of culture, and more independent than before of the variations in its environment.

A further contributory factor was the relative openness and decentralisation of the social system of European intellectual life. The Continent, including England, constituted a cultural whole, as a result of the unity of the church and its adoption of Roman traditions; persons and writings travelled across political borders with relative ease. Ideas evolved in one place would be readily appreciated in another. At the same time the various political units were sufficiently different from each other to permit beginnings, which were constricted in their places of origin (because they clashed with important vested interests), to be developed elsewhere, where the same vested interests were for some reason weaker.

Chapter Questions

1. What were the main ways in which the science of the seventeenth century constituted a break from the past? What were some of the main problems facing seventeenth-century scientists in making this break? How did they handle these problems?

2. How would you explain the occurrence of the scientific revolution in the seventeenth century rather than in the sixteenth or eighteenth century?

CHAPTER THREE

Politics and Society in the Ancien Régime

๕.

By the time of the death of Louis XIV in 1715, France no longer threatened to overwhelm the rest of Europe. Indeed, during most of the eighteenth century a rough balance of power developed amid the shifting diplomatic alliances and wars. There were two major sets of rivalries among states between 1715 and 1789. In Central Europe, the older Hapsburg Empire was pitted against the newer, assertive Prussia. Although Prussia acquired the status of a major power as a result of this competition, the Hapsburg Empire managed to hold on to most of its lands and to expand at the cost of weaker states such as Poland and the Ottoman Empire. Outside of Europe, England and France struggled for supremacy over colonial territories in the Great War for Empire.

During this period preceding the French Revolution, referred to as the "Ancien Régime," most of the same political and social trends that had characterized the second half of the seventeenth century continued, namely, aristocratic dominance, strong monarchies, expanding central governments, and traditional ways of life. Important changes that were initiated—such as agricultural, commercial, and industrial developments that strengthened the middle classes and led to urban growth—were limited in scope and area.

The sources in this chapter center on three aspects of the Ancien Régime between 1715 and 1789. First, the nature and position of the still-dominant aristocracy is examined. What was its life style? What were its responsibilities? What was the position of women within the aristocracy? Is it true that the aristocracy was frivolous? How did the aristocracy react to pressures from the monarchy on the one side and the middle classes on the other? Second, the development of the eighteenth-century state, with particular focus on Prussia, is analyzed. What role did Prussia's monarchs play in making her a major power? What institutional developments helped Prussia gain this position? How did wars contribute to and reflect the growing importance of the state? Third, the importance of commerce and the middle class in England is explored. What were the connections between commerce, the middle classes, and the English aristocracy? What was the relationship between the development of commerce and industry and England's colonial concerns and growing nationalism? What were some of the effects of the commerce in slaves engaged in by the English and others?

The sources in this chapter stress the relative political stability that characterized much of the period between 1715 and 1789. Stability was not the rule in intellectual matters, as will be seen in the next chapter.

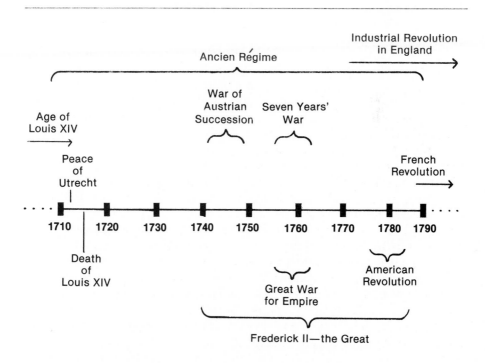

PRIMARY SOURCES

Political Testament

Frederick the Great

From a distance it may seem that eighteenth-century monarchs were much like those of the seventeenth century, similar in powers, position, and prestige. On closer examination, however, some differences are evident. Frederick II (the Great) of Prussia (1712–1786) was one of the most admired eighteenth-century monarchs. He ascended the throne in 1740 and ruled actively until his death in 1786. Frederick II continued the Prussian tradition of relying on a strong army to maintain and increase his holdings and prestige. At the same time he reorganized the army and the bureaucracy and introduced new ideas into both the theory and the practice of government. In the following excerpts from his Political Testament *(1752), he sets out his conception of politics and the proper role of the sovereign.*

> **Consider:** *How this conception of the monarch differs from that expressed by seventeenth-century monarchs; why Frederick emphasized the need to protect and support the nobility; who the crown's greatest potential rivals for power were; the advantages and disadvantages to the monarch of religious toleration.*

Politics is the science of always using the most convenient means in accord with one's own interests. In order to act in conformity with one's interests one must know what these interests are, and in order to gain this knowledge one must study their history and application. . . . One must attempt, above all, to know the special genius of the people which one wants to govern in order to know if one must treat them leniently or severely, if they are inclined to revolt . . . to intrigue. . . .

[The Prussian nobility] has sacrificed its life and goods for the service of the state, its loyalty and merit have earned it the protection of all its rulers, and it is one of the duties [of the ruler] to aid those [noble] families which have become impoverished in order to keep them in possession of their lands: for they are to be regarded as the pedestals and the pillars of the state. In such a state no factions or rebellions need be feared . . . it is one goal of the policy of this state to preserve the nobility.

A well conducted government must have an underlying concept so well integrated that it could be likened to a system of philosophy. All actions taken must be well reasoned, and all financial, political and military matters must flow towards one goal: which is the strengthening of the state and

SOURCE: Frederick II, *Political Testament*, in George L. Mosse, et al., eds., *Europe in Review* (Chicago: Rand McNally, 1957), pp. 110–112. Reprinted by permission of George L. Mosse.

the furthering of its power. However, such a system can flow but from a single brain, and this must be that of the sovereign. Laziness, hedonism and imbecility, these are the causes which restrain princes in working at the noble task of bringing happiness to their subjects . . . a sovereign is not elevated to his high position, supreme power has not been confined to him in order that he may live in lazy luxury, enriching himself by the labor of the people, being happy while everyone else suffers. The sovereign is the first servant of the state. He is well paid in order that he may sustain the dignity of his office, but one demands that he work efficiently for the good of the state, and that he, at the very least, pay personal attention to the most important problems. . . .

You can see, without doubt, how important it is that the King of Prussia govern personally. Just as it would have been impossible for Newton to arrive at his system of attractions if he had worked in harness with Leibnitz and Descartes, so a system of politics cannot be arrived at and continued if it has not sprung from a single brain. . . . All parts of the government are inexorably linked with each other. Finance, politics and military affairs are inseparable; it does not suffice that one will be well administered; they must all be . . . a Prince who governs personally, who has formed his [own] political system, will not be handicapped when occasions arise where he has to act swiftly: for he can guide all matters towards the end which he has set for himself. . . .

Catholics, Lutherans, Reformed, Jews and other Christian sects live in this state, and live together in peace: if the sovereign, actuated by a mistaken zeal, declares himself for one religion or another, parties will spring up, heated disputes ensue, little by little persecutions will commence and, in the end, the religion persecuted will leave the fatherland and millions of subjects will enrich our neighbors by their skill and industry.

It is of no concern in politics whether the ruler has a religion or whether he has none. All religions, if one examines them, are founded on superstitious systems, more or less absurd. It is impossible for a man of good sense, who dissects their contents, not to see their error; but these prejudices, these errors and mysteries were made for men, and one must know enough to respect the public and not to outrage its faith, whatever religion be involved.

The Complete English Tradesman

Daniel Defoe

During the eighteenth century, England was growing in strength and prosperity, particularly in the areas of commerce and manufacturing. A primary beneficiary of these economic developments was the rising commercial middle class. This class was becoming more assertive as the English were becoming more nationalistic. Daniel Defoe (1659?–1731) speaks about these trends in the following selection from The Complete English Tradesman *(1726). Although best known for* Robinson Crusoe, *Defoe wrote many works and followed a commercial career for some time.*

> **Consider:** *The support Defoe offers for his view that commerce rightly dominates the country economically; how the economic policies that Defoe would recommend compare with policies typical of mercantilism; the connections between commerce and social class in England; the apparent advantages of having colonies and the colonial policies that Defoe's views imply.*

I . . . advance these three points in honour of our country — 1. That we are the greatest trading country in the world, because we have the greatest exportation of the growth and product of our land, and of the manufacture and labour of our people; and the greatest importation and consumption of the growth, product, and manufactures of other countries from abroad, of any nation in the world.

2. That our climate is the best and most agreeable to live in, because a man can be more out of doors in England than in other countries.

3. That our men are the stoutest and best, because, strip them naked from the waist upwards, and give them no weapons at all but their hands and heels, and turn them into a room or stage, and lock them in with the like number of other men of any nation, man for man, and they shall beat the best men you shall find in the world.

And so many of our noble and wealthy families, as we have shown, are raised by and derived from trade, so it is true, and indeed it cannot well be otherwise, that many of the younger branches of our gentry, and even of the nobility itself, have descended again into the spring from whence they flowed, and have become tradesmen; and thence it is that, as I said above, our tradesmen in England are not, as it generally is in other countries, always of the meanest of our people. Nor is trade itself in England, as it generally is in other countries, the meanest thing that men can turn their hand to; but, on the contrary, trade is the readiest way for men to raise their

SOURCE: Daniel Defoe, *The Complete English Tradesman*, Vols. 17–18 of *The Novels and Miscellaneous Works of Daniel Defoe* (London: Thomas Tegg, 1840–1841), Chap. 25.

fortunes and families; and therefore it is a field for men of figure and of good families to enter upon. . . .

As to the wealth of the nation, that undoubtedly lies chiefly among the trading part of the people; and though there are a great many families raised within few years, in the late war, by great employments and by great actions abroad, to the honour of the English gentry, yet how many more families among the tradesmen have been raised to immense estates, even during the same time, by the attending circumstances of the war; such as the clothing, the paying, the victualling and furnishing, &c., both army and navy. And by whom have the prodigious taxes been paid, the loans supplied, and money advanced upon all occasions? By whom are the banks and companies carried on, and on whom are the customs and excises levied? Have not the trade and tradesmen borne the burden of the war? And do they not still pay four millions a year interest for the public debts? On whom are the funds levied, and by whom the public credit supported? Is not trade the inexhausted fund of all funds, and upon which all the rest depend?

Again; in how superior a port or figure (as we now call it) do our tradesmen live, to what the middling gentry either do or can support! An ordinary tradesman now, not in the city only, but in the country, shall spend more money by the year, than a gentleman of four or five hundred pounds a year can do, and shall increase and lay up every year too; whereas the gentleman shall at the best stand stock still just where he began, nay, perhaps, decline: and as for the lower gentry, from a hundred pounds a year to three hundred, or thereabouts, though they are often as proud and high in their appearance as the other; as to them, I say, a shoemaker in London shall keep a better house, spend more money, clothe his family better, and yet grow rich too. It is evident where the difference lies; an estate's a pond, but trade's a spring: the first, if it keeps full, and the water wholesome, by the ordinary supplies and drains from the neighbouring grounds, it is well, and it is all that is expected; but the other is an inexhausted current, which not only fills the pond, and keeps it full, but is continually running over, and fills all the lower ponds and places about it.

This being the case in England, and our trade being so vastly great, it is no wonder that the tradesmen in England fill the lists of our nobility and gentry; no wonder that the gentlemen of the best families marry tradesmen's daughters, and put their younger sons apprentices to tradesmen; and how often do these younger sons come to buy the elder sons' estates, and restore the family, when the elder and head of the house, proving rakish and extravagant, has wasted his patrimony, and is obliged to make out the blessing of Israel's family, where the younger son bought the birthright, and the elder was doomed to serve him!

Trade is so far here from being inconsistent with a gentleman, that, in short, trade in England makes gentlemen, and has peopled this nation with gentlemen; for, after a generation or two, the tradesman's children, or at

least their grandchildren, come to be as good gentlemen, statesmen, par-
liamentmen, privy-counsellors, judges, bishops, and noblemen, as those of
the highest birth and the most ancient families; as we have shown. . . .

All this confirms what I have said before, viz., that trade in England
neither is or ought to be levelled with what it is in other countries; or the
tradesmen depreciated as they are abroad, and as some of our gentry would
pretend to do in England; but that as many of our best families rose from
trade, so many branches of the best families in England, under the nobility,
have stooped so low as to be put apprentices to tradesmen in London, and to
set up and follow those trades when they have come out of their times, and
have thought it no dishonour to their blood. . . .

The greatness of the British nation is not owing to war and conquests, to
enlarging its dominions by the sword, or subjecting the people of other
countries to our power; but it is all owing to trade, to the increase of our
commerce at home, and the extending it abroad.

It is owing to trade, that new discoveries have been made in lands
unknown, and new settlements and plantations made, new colonies
planted, and new governments formed, in the uninhabited islands, and the
uncultivated continent of America; and those plantings and settlements
have again enlarged and increased the trade, and thereby the wealth and
power of the nation by whom they were discovered and planted; we have
not increased our power, or the number of our subjects, by subduing the nations which possess those countries, and incorporating them into our own;
but have entirely planted our colonies, and peopled the countries with our
own subjects, natives of this island; and, excepting the negroes, which we
transport from Africa to America, as slaves to work in the sugar and tobacco
plantations, all our colonies, as well in the islands, as on the continent of
America, are entirely peopled from Great Britain and Ireland, and chiefly
the former; the natives having either removed further up into the country,
or, by their own folly and treachery raising war against us, been destroyed
and cut off. . . .

The Slave Trade

Anonymous

*Part of the commercial prosperity enjoyed by several Western nations was built on
the slave trade, which flourished in the seventeenth and eighteenth centuries.
Slaves were generally shipped in British vessels, but the French and others engaged
in this trade as well. Most slaves were taken across the Atlantic to Europe's colonial holdings, which in turn shipped goods such as sugar, metals, and wood prod-*

SOURCE: Leon Apt and Robert E. Herzstein, eds., *The Evolution of Western Society*, Vol. II
(Hinsdale, Ill.: The Dryden Press, 1978), pp. 279–280.

*ucts to the home country. Although there was little widespread opposition to
slavery in Europe during the seventeenth and early eighteenth centuries, by the
middle of the eighteenth century antislavery sentiments were growing. The following is an account of what was involved in the slave trade, written in 1771 by an
anonymous Frenchman who argued for its abolition.*

> **Consider:** *The attitudes that permitted and supported the slave trade; the effects
> of this experience on the blacks; the legacy of this trade for the colonies.*

As soon as the ships have lowered their anchors off the coast of Guinea, the
price at which the captains have decided to buy the captives is announced to
the Negroes who buy prisoners from various princes and sell them to the
Europeans. Presents are sent to the sovereign who rules over that particular
part of the coast, and permission to trade is given. Immediately the slaves
are brought by inhuman brokers like so many victims dragged to a sacrifice.
White men who covet that portion of the human race receive them in a little
house they have erected on the shore, where they have entrenched themselves with two pieces of cannon and twenty guards. As soon as the bargain
is concluded, the Negro is put in chains and led aboard the vessel, where he
meets his fellow sufferers. Here sinister reflections come to his mind; everything shocks and frightens him and his uncertain destiny gives rise to the
greatest anxiety. At first he is convinced that he is to serve as a repast to the
white men, and the wine which the sailors drink confirms him in this cruel
thought, for he imagines that this liquid is the blood of his fellows.

The vessel sets sail for the Antilles, and the Negroes are chained in a hold
of the ship, a kind of lugubrious prison where the light of day does not penetrate, but into which air is introduced by means of a pump. Twice a day
some disgusting food is distributed to them. Their consuming sorrow and
the sad state to which they are reduced would make them commit suicide if
they were not deprived of all the means for an attempt upon their lives.
Without any kind of clothing it would be difficult to conceal from the
watchful eyes of the sailors in charge of any instrument apt to alleviate their
despair. The fear of a revolt, such as sometimes happens on the voyage from
Guinea, is the basis of a common concern and produces as many guards as
there are men in the crew. The slightest noise or a secret conversation among
two Negroes is punished with utmost severity. All in all, the voyage is made
in a continuous state of alarm on the part of the white men, who fear a
revolt, and in a cruel state of uncertainty on the part of the Negroes, who do
not know the fate awaiting them.

When the vessel arrives at a port in the Antilles, they are taken to a ware-
house where they are displayed, like any merchandise, to the eyes of buyers.
The plantation owner pays according to the age, strength and health of the
Negro he is buying. He has him taken to his plantation, and there he is
delivered to an overseer who then and there becomes his tormentor. In order
to domesticate him, the Negro is granted a few days of rest in his new place,

but soon he is given a hoe and a sickle and made to join a work gang. Then he ceases to wonder about his fate; he understands that only labor is demanded of him. But he does not know yet how excessive this labor will be. As a matter of fact, his work begins at dawn and does not end before nightfall; it is interrupted for only two hours at dinnertime. The food a full-grown Negro is given each week consists of two pounds of salt beef or cod and two pots of tapioca meal, amounting to about two pints of Paris. A Negro of twelve or thirteen years or under is given only one pot of meal and one pound of beef or cod. In place of food some planters give their Negroes the liberty of working for themselves every Saturday; others are even less generous and grant them this liberty only on Sundays and holidays. Therefore, since the nourishment of the Negroes is insufficient, their tendency to cheat must be attributed to the necessity of finding the food they lack.

The Defects of Police: The Cause of Immorality

Jonas Hanway

By the eighteenth century it was becoming apparent that the nobility was failing in its performance of the social, political, economic, and military duties that had justified its position in the past. One of these duties involved philanthropy to the poor and others in need of social services. Some saw active participation in social services as a way to revive the status of the aristocracy. This belief is reflected in the following selection by Jonas Hanway, an eighteenth-century British businessman who campaigned for the poor, the sick, the homeless, the insane, and the criminal. Note that his paternal and moralistic approach is typical of eighteenth-century attitudes.

> **Consider:** *The ways Hanway appeals to the nobility and the gentry to become involved in social services; how social problems such as poverty were dealt with in the eighteenth century; how Hanway is critical of the trends he sees occurring in the eighteenth century.*

This general remark must be allowed: The nobility and gentry of this kingdom, where the poor law constitutes so considerable a part of our police,[1] have in process of time fallen-off, and compared with the custom of ancient times, totally neglected the poor. The reason of this is obvious; they suppose the indigent are amply provided for by means of the *parochial tax*; but they do not consider that the administration of this kind of justice, and

---

Source: Jonas Hanway, *The Defects of Police: The Cause of Immorality* (London: J. Dodsley Publishers, 1775), pp. 142–144.

[1] The word "police" had a broader meaning in the eighteenth century than it does today, referring more generally to the maintenance of public welfare.

the proper expenditure of such tax, is as essential a duty as the paying of it. In the mean while the increase of wealth has opened the portals of amusement so very wide, both in town and country, every hour may be filled up in a round of dissipation. At length there is some reason to hope they will grow tired of the vanity of such pursuits, carried to such an excess, and vary their object. Many, at least in the country, *begin* to consider what satisfaction they may derive from entering into the concerns of the poor; by endeavouring to make the parochial taxes produce the happy effects for which they were intended. Frequent occasions point out that which dignifies human nature, and expresses the most cordial *patriotism*. Religion co-operates, and the grand object of life, *immortality*, turns the balance, and influences many whose hearts are not estranged from the great truths contained in the New Testament, to act with consistency. Hence we find them forming themselves into societies for the better government of the *indigent*: and whilst these constitute so large a portion of mankind, in all ages, and in all countries, the office must be honourable: in spite of the depravity of the heart, or the tyranny of custom, it must afford a solid satisfaction.

The county houses of industry, so warmly recommended by the ingenious author of the pamphlet which I have quoted, is a proof of what I advance. When this kind of humanity has had its reign, it will be a higher degree of improvement in moral excellency, for men of fortune and sentiment, in conjunction with the *clergy*, to take care of the indigent in the ordinary method of domestic life; that the virtues of filial duty may be more exercised; fraternal love be less a stranger to the hearts of the labouring poor; and maternal tenderness operate as the God of Nature intended it should do. It would be romantic to expect the golden age to be so far restored, that no misery should be found among *infants*, *aged*, *sickly*, *maimed*, or *insane* persons, without seeking succour, by availing ourselves of such asylums, as the houses of industry now in question so amply supply. The happy regulation of them, especially if they extend to vagrants, without refining on their possible evil consequences, deserves the attention of the ablest politician. In whatever we are defective, in these vast cities, which are so much the *fairs of vanity*, we may learn from country gentlemen, without any great mortification to our pride. Indeed we have but few country gentlemen who are not town gentlemen also: but the *field*, which the country affords, is so vastly superior to the town, for *space*, *air*, *occupation* and *health*; if a true principle were adopted, *all paupers* would be removed into the country, where the same work may be carried on within doors as in town; whilst the culture of the earth, the common parent of us all, might by the hands of *paupers*, contribute towards the furnishing of food as well as raiment. He who should produce a bushel of turnips, might deserve as much as he who has two pair of stockings knit by his own hand.

This general argument may suffice to remove those objections which are urged against the *county houses of industry*, and to give them a preference to the *workhouses* of the respective parishes in the county. According to the gradations of moral improvements among the nobility and gentry, this practice of taking care of *paupers*, will bend their thoughts to the indigent in general, till by precept and example, benevolence and charity, they shall establish a more consistent conduct in their respective towns and villages: and thus they will check the growth of that immorality, which at this time wears so formidable an aspect.

Letter to Lady R., 1716: Women and the Aristocracy

Lady Mary Wortley Montagu

During the eighteenth century women continued to remain limited in the economic and political roles they could play, but it was possible for aristocratic women to take up influential social and cultural roles. In particular, many women used letter writing as an art, and from these letters much insight about the position and attitudes of women can be gained. Lady Mary Wortley Montagu (1689–1762) was a well-known British literary figure, writing essays and poetry in addition to her volumes of letters. The following is a selection from a letter written in 1716 to Lady R.

> **Consider:** *The assumptions about marriage among the aristocracy; connections between marriage, love, and economic interests; the position of aristocratic women reflected by this letter.*

No woman dares appear coquette enough to encourage two lovers at a time. And I have not seen any such prudes as to pretend fidelity to their husbands, who are certainly the best natured set of people in the world, and look upon their wives' gallants as favourably as men do upon their deputies, that take the troublesome part of their business off their hands. They have not however the less to do on that account; for they are generally deputies in another place themselves; in one word, 'tis the established custom for every lady to have two husbands, one that bears the name, and another that performs the duties. And these engagements are so well known, that it would be a downright affront, and publicly resented, if you invited a woman of quality to dinner, without, at the same time, inviting her two attendants of lover and husband, between whom she sits in state with great gravity. The submarriages generally last twenty years together, and the lady often commands the poor lover's estate, even to the utter ruin of his family.

SOURCE: Mary Wortley Montagu, *Works*, Vol. II (London: Richard Phillips, 1803), pp. 57–59.

These connections, indeed, are as seldom begun by any real passion as other matches; for a man makes but an ill figure that is not in some commerce of this nature; and a woman looks out for a lover as soon as she's married, as part of her equipage, without which she could not be genteel; and the first article of the treaty is establishing the pension, which remains to the lady, in case the gallant should prove inconstant. This chargeable point of honour I look upon as the real foundation of so many wonderful instances of constancy. I really know some women of the first quality, whose pensions are as well known as their annual rents, and yet nobody esteems them the less; on the contrary, their discretion would be called in question, if they should be suspected to be mistresses for nothing. A great part of their emulation consists in trying who shall get most. . . .

VISUAL SOURCES

Happy Accidents of the Swing

Jean-Honoré Fragonard

The aristocracy remained dominant culturally during the Ancien Régime, commissioning most of the art of the period. It is not surprising, then, that the art reflected aristocratic values and tastes. Happy Accidents of the Swing *by Jean-Honoré Fragonard (see p. 52) exemplifies a type of painting quite popular among France's eighteenth-century aristocracy.*

Fragonard was commissioned by Baron de Saint-Julien in 1767 to paint a picture of his mistress on a swing being pushed by a bishop who did not know that the woman was the baron's mistress, with the baron himself watching from a strategic place of hiding. In the picture the woman on the swing seems well aware of what is happening, flinging off her shoe toward a statue of the god of discretion in such a way as to cause her gown to billow out revealingly.

This painting reflects a certain religious irreverence on the part of the eighteenth-century aristocracy, for the joke is on the unknowing bishop. The significance of this irreverence is magnified by the fact that Saint-Julien had numerous dealings with the clergy, since he was at this time a government official responsible for overseeing clerical wealth.

The lush setting of the painting and the tenor of the scene suggest the love of romantic luxury and concern for sensual indulgence by this most privileged but soon to be declining part of society.

Consider: *The evidence in this picture of the attitudes and life style of the eighteenth-century French aristocracy.*

Photo 3-1

Act of Humanity

Jean Defraine

In Act of Humanity *(circa 1783), painter Jean Defraine shows that the old tradition of aristocratic responsibility for social welfare is still upheld in the eighteenth century. Here, an aristocrat is visiting a family stricken by both illness and poverty. The realistic depiction of poverty is accompanied by the comforting suggestion that its effects can be alleviated through charitable gestures. Such humanitarian acts on the part of the aristocracy were considered one of the few appropriate cures for social problems of the poor.*

Consider: *How this picture compares with the Hanway document.*

Photo 3-2

Bibliothèque Nationale, Paris

The Battle of Fontenoy

C. C. P. Lawson

War, though still common in the eighteenth century, was more controlled and orderly and less vicious than during the first half of the seventeenth century. This is suggested in this painting by C. C. P. Lawson of a typical eighteenth-century land battle, the Battle of Fontenoy. Aristocratic traditions are maintained by the commanders, who calmly salute each other before the battle begins. The troops are uniformed and orderly, apparently under the firm control of officers. The characteristics of eighteenth-century battles depicted here reflect the realities of military tactics and economics. As argued by the modern historian R. J. White in Europe in the Eighteenth Century *(New York: St. Martin's Press, 1965),*

> *"a supposedly wholesome mixture of aristocrats and scum was the principal substance of the armed forces everywhere in the eighteenth century. Warfare was predominantly defensive, dogged by caution and conducted according to*

Photo 3-3

National Army Museum, Department of Records

strict rules of procedure. The almost baroque movements of armed forces in the stately game of siege warfare, the rigid adherence to the rules of the game as laid down in Fighting Instructions *[a standard military manual], which often appear so ludicrous to modern observers, were not invented to charm later generations, but were the offspring of the peculiar necessities of a world of limited material resources and rationally conceived purposes."*

Consider: *How the arrangement of the troops in this picture reflects the social structure of the eighteenth century.*

SECONDARY SOURCES

The Prussian Bureaucracy

Walter Dorn

Although lacking many of the historical and geographical advantages possessed by other powers such as France and England, Prussia had become a major European power. Traditionally, Prussia's kings and military have been credited for this accomplishment. While not completely disagreeing with this view, Walter Dorn argues that it was the bureaucracy that most distinguished Prussia from other states and that accounted for Prussia's position of power in eighteenth-century Europe. The following selection is from Dorn's Competition for Empire: 1740–1763, *an early effort to apply a comparative approach to eighteenth-century history and still a useful analysis of the period.*

> **Consider:** *How the apparent disadvantage of general poverty in Prussia was turned into an advantage; why it made such a difference that the Prussian bureaucracy was staffed by the nobility as well as the middle class; whether Dorn's interpretation is supported by the views of Frederick the Great.*

The unique role of Prussia among the states of Europe lay not so much in its peculiar mixture of despotism and feudalism, but in the fact that it

---

SOURCE: Walter L. Dorn, *Competition for Empire: 1740–1763.* Reprinted by permission of Harper & Row (New York, 1940), pp. 52–53, 62. Copyright © 1940 by Harper & Row, Publishers, Inc.

accomplished the impossible. A small, poor, still half-feudal and notoriously underpopulated country that was neither a geographic nor racial unit, with a retarded middle class that suffered from both lack of enterprise and capital, Prussia was suddenly thrust into the position of a European power. After his Silesian Wars it was no longer possible for Frederick to retreat from this European position. His only alternative to destruction by stronger neighbors was to mobilize the resources necessary to support his ever growing army, without which his European influence was utterly negligible, by means of superior organization and an unprecedented degree of social discipline. Whatever the cost, the experiment proved successful. In 1750 Prussia was the only large continental state which managed not only to balance its budget but to produce a steady surplus of income over expenditures. This was not due to an equitable distribution of financial burdens among the various classes of Prussian society nor to an intelligent system of taxation. In these matters Prussia was not more advanced than other continental states. The Prussian peasant, who paid about forty per cent of his net income to the state and owed often unlimited services to his feudal lord, had no advantage over the Austrian or French peasant. What made the difference between Prussia and other continental states was the moral force that emanated from the greatest of the Hohenzollern and the superb quality of the Prussian bureaucracy, one of the first great modern civil service systems of Europe. . . .

In this Prussia, devoid of wealth and prosperity, the burdens and obligations of the masses stood in inverse proportion to their economic circumstances. Indeed, it was from the very poverty of its inhabitants that the Prussian state drew its greatest strength. The proud junker, living on an estate too diminutive for a decent standard of life, was constrained to seek public employment, notwithstanding the forbidding severity of its discipline. The ambitious bourgeois intellectual discovered in the Prussian civil service his best, indeed his only, opportunity for advancement. It was not wealth but connection with the army and civil service that guaranteed social position. It was the general poverty that produced the unprecedented concentration of resources, the furor, as Mirabeau was later to call it, of regulating and regimenting every aspect of public and private life, the one-sided emphasis on Spartan virtues and social discipline, in a word, what we generally call Prussianism. It is unthinkable that this Prussianism could ever have sprung from the soil of free, wealthy, parliamentary England. In England the island, as it were, replaced the state; in Prussia the state of the old regime attained its maximum expansion. While England was becoming constantly more individualistic, Prussia remained a collectivist state in which the individual was expected to sacrifice himself for the whole. The only freedom for the eighteenth-century Prussian was the *libertas oboedientiae* — the freedom to obey.

The Resurgent Aristocracy

Leonard Krieger

Historians have at times exaggerated the importance of the rise of the middle class and the decline of the aristocracy in the eighteenth century. Recently, historians have begun to emphasize the middle of the eighteenth century as a period during which the aristocracy was actually resurgent, making efforts to regain its position and increase its influence — often with considerable success. This view is illustrated in the following selection by Leonard Krieger of the University of Chicago.

> **Consider:** *The evidence Krieger offers for a resurgence of the aristocracy; the ways in which the aristocracy adapted to eighteenth-century political needs; how Dorn's analysis of Prussia relates to Krieger's argument.*

In the eighteenth century, surprisingly, aristocracies — or at least important parts of them — were resurgent. Appreciating the principle of what would later become a proverbial prescription for men to join what they could not beat, nobles in the several countries of Europe picked themselves up and began to appropriate commanding positions in the governmental structures of the new states and even in the network of commercial relations. The Whig oligarchy that ruled Britain without serious challenge between the accession of the Hanoverian dynasty in 1714 and George III's assertion of royal influence after 1760 represented a landowning aristocracy that was sponsoring a capitalized and scientific agriculture in response to demands of the market and that had economic ties with merchants and bankers of the City. The French peers, refueled by Louis XIV's calculated infusion of subsidies, made a serious bid to refashion the monarchy in their own image after the death of the Sun King in 1715, and when this attempt failed, a more economically progressive and modern-minded judicial and administrative aristocracy (*noblesse de robe* and *noblesse d'office*) rose to continue the counteroffensive on behalf of the privileged. In Russia various sections of the military and landed nobility dictated the succession to the throne — in general they preferred tsarinas in the expectation that they would behave consistently as members of the "weaker sex" — and dominated the social policy of the government from the death of Peter the Great in 1725 through the accession of Catherine the Great in 1762. The long period from 1718 to 1772 that the Swedes euphemistically called their "era of liberty" was actually an age of aristocratic sovereignty, exercised constitutionally in a

SOURCE: Reprinted from *Kings and Philosophers, 1689–1789*, by Leonard Krieger, with the permission of W. W. Norton & Company, Inc. Copyright © 1970 by W. W. Norton & Company, Inc.

nominal monarchy through the nobles' oligarchic control over both the *Riksdag*, or parliament, and the bureaucracy. The Dutch gave the same high-flown label to the period from 1702 to 1747, when the small but influential class of Regents, an oligarchy comprised of urban patricians, resumed its sway after the death of William III and kept the office of *stadholder* vacant. The seven provinces that made up the Dutch "Republic" were, in this respect, expanded versions of the independent city-states in Europe. Concentrated mainly in Switzerland and Germany, they too were stabilized during the first half of the eighteenth century under the rule of exclusive patrician oligarchies. . . .

The aristocracies' new lease on life for the eighteenth century was thus predicated upon the modernization of their premises, and they thereby shifted the arena of social conflict from outside to inside the structure of the state. Where they had formerly defended their privileged rights to landownership, manorial lordship, judicial immunities, and tax exemptions by denying the jurisdiction of the central governments, they now defended these privileges by occupying and controlling the governmental agencies which exercised the jurisdiction. This aristocratic penetration of the state ran counter to the standards of general law, equal citizenship, and uniform administration which had served and continued to serve bureaucrats as guides in extending the scope of central government. But the hierarchical tendency was no mere atavism. Despite the obvious and reciprocal hostility between it and the leveling tendency with which it shared the state, the coexistence of the two tendencies, however mismatched in logic, was a faithful response to a fundamental social demand of the age. European society required, for the military security of its inhabitants, for the direction and subsidization of its economy, and for the prevention of religious turbulence and popular disorder, the imposition of unified control over a larger area and more people than the contemporary instruments of government could manage. Hence the employment of the traditional social and corporate hierarchies by the government as extensions of the governing arm into the mass of inhabitants. All people were subject, but some were more subject than others.

The Cosmopolitan Aristocracy

J. H. Plumb

The cosmopolitan character of the eighteenth-century aristocracy distinguished it from other classes as well as from the aristocracy of the seventeenth century. Whereas the seventeenth-century aristocracy was educated at home, the

SOURCE: J. H. Plumb, *Men and Centuries* (Boston: Houghton Mifflin, 1963), pp. 54–57. Reprinted by permission of J. H. Plumb. Copyright © 1963 by J. H. Plumb.

eighteenth-century aristocracy was largely educated abroad. In the following selection, J. H. Plumb of Cambridge University describes the significance of the Grand Tour for the aristocracy.

> **Consider:** *The ways in which the Grand Tour made this class more homogeneous; why this change in education might have helped the aristocracy to reassert itself as Krieger argues; how this image of the aristocracy differs from that presented by Dorn.*

Before the end of the seventeenth century, education in England, as elsewhere in Europe, was confined to a narrow compass. At a very tender age gentlemen's sons were boarded out with a country parson to learn their letters, their numbers and the rudiments of Latin grammar — like Robert Walpole, the future Prime Minister of England, who was sent away from home at the age of four. Holidays were sparse — a few days at Christmas and a month at harvest time. At nine or ten the children left the vicarage for the grammar school in the neighbouring county town where they boarded with the master. There they rubbed shoulders with local tradesmen's sons. They dressed alike and spoke the same dialect; in those days a difference in social rank did not inhibit close social intercourse. At adolescence their ways tended to part: the shopkeeper's son went to his apprenticeship, the gentleman's son left for the university or the Inns of Court to acquire that extra knowledge of religion and law that his station required. After two or three years at Oxford and Cambridge (and if his home were distant, there he stayed without a holiday), he returned to help his father with his estate. Apart from a rare visit to London and a more frequent one to the local metropolis — York, Bristol, Norwich, Exeter — his travelling days were over. He lived and died in his neighbourhood. And this, with few variations, was the pattern of education throughout North-Western Europe; it differed only for a few aristocrats attached to courts. . . .

By 1700 all this had changed. The grammar schools and universities were no longer crowded with gentlemen's sons; indeed they were emptying fast (Christ's College, Cambridge, had only three freshmen in 1733, and many of its rooms were deserted). Shopkeepers preferred the new education provided by private enterprise, the schools and academies which taught bookkeeping, languages, geography, navigation — the arts necessary for commercial life; gentlemen sent their sons abroad on a Grand Tour. By 1720, no Englishman or German pretending to a place in society could expect to be regarded as anything but a country bumpkin unless he had spent two or three years in France or Italy. The aristocracy of Scandinavia and Russia quickly followed suit. The effect was to give a remarkable homogeneity of manners and taste to the nobility of eighteenth-century Europe. . . .

To learn manners, to learn the only trades open to an aristocrat — war and diplomacy — to learn the culture of his class made a Grand Tour a necessity for the young English or German peer. Fortunately the new wealth that was seeping into Europe enabled him to afford what was the most expensive form of education ever devised by European society. The young nobleman resided abroad usually for three, but often for four, and at times even five years. More often than not he was accompanied by two tutors: one for bookish study, the other for riding, fencing, the arts of war.

Chapter Questions

1. In what ways did competing groups and historical conditions put pressure on aristocrats who wanted to maintain their position and influence?

2. What were the assets and liabilities of the eighteenth-century aristocracy in the face of pressures to diminish its position and influence?

CHAPTER FOUR

The Enlightenment

As a period of intellectual history in Western civilization, the eighteenth century is known quite appropriately as the Enlightenment. At that time a group of thinkers, called the *philosophes*, developed and popularized related sets of ideas that formed a basis for modern thought. Their methods emphasized skepticism, empirical reasoning, and satire. They spread their ideas through works ranging from pamphlets to the great *Encyclopedia* and numerous meetings in aristocratic "salons." Although centered in France, this intellectual movement took place throughout Europe.

Most of the philosophes believed that Western civilization was on the verge of enlightenment, that reasoning and education could quickly dispel the darkness of the past that had kept people in a state of immaturity. The main objects of their criticism were institutions, such as governments and the Church, and irrational customs that perpetuated old ways of thinking and thus hindered progress. While critical and combative, the philosophes were not political or social revolutionaries. Their ideas were revolutionary in many ways, but in practice these thinkers hoped for rather painless change—often through reform from above by enlightened monarchs. Enlightenment thinkers usually admired England, where liberal ideas and practices were most developed.

The sources in this chapter concern three issues. First, what was the nature of Enlightenment thought? What was the professed spirit of the Enlightenment? What patterns of morality were embodied in Enlightenment ideas? In what ways was authority rejected and nature elevated to great importance? Second, how should we characterize the philosophes? Who were they? What were their common psychological traits, their religious beliefs, and their interactions? Finally, how did Enlightenment thought affect eighteenth-century politics before the French Revolution? Was there such a phenomenon as "enlightened despotism," and if so, what did it mean?

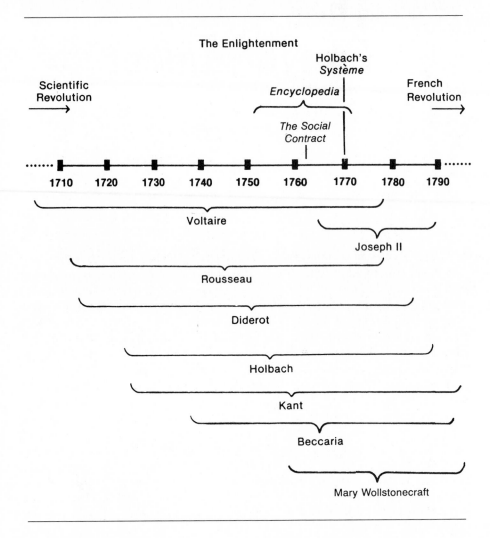

Together, the sources should reveal an intellectual movement still tied to the traditional society of the Ancien Régime but with strikingly modern characteristics. Toward the end of the eighteenth century, many of the ideas of the Enlightenment played an important role in the French Revolution—the subject of the next chapter.

PRIMARY SOURCES

What Is Enlightenment?

Immanuel Kant

One of the most pervasive themes among Enlightenment thinkers was a self-conscious sense of a spirit of enlightenment. This is illustrated in the following excerpt from a short essay by Immanuel Kant (1724–1804) of Königsberg in East Prussia. Kant, one of the world's most profound philosophers, is particularly known for his analysis of the human mind and how it relates to nature, as set forth in his Critique of Pure Reason *(1781). In the following essay, written in 1784, Kant defines the spirit of the Enlightenment and describes some of its implications.*

> **Consider:** *What Kant means by "freedom" and why he feels freedom is so central to the Enlightenment; how people can become enlightened and the appropriate environment to facilitate this enlightenment; what Kant would consider "mature"; how Kant relates enlightenment and politics.*

Enlightenment is man's leaving his self-caused immaturity. Immaturity is the incapacity to use one's intelligence without the guidance of another. Such immaturity is self-caused if it is not caused by lack of intelligence, but by lack of determination and courage to use one's intelligence without being guided by another. *Sapere Aude!* Have the courage to use your own intelligence! is therefore the motto of the enlightenment.

Through laziness and cowardice a large part of mankind, even after nature has freed them from alien guidance, gladly remain immature. It is because of laziness and cowardice that it is so easy for others to usurp the role of guardians. It is so comfortable to be a minor! If I have a book which provides meaning for me, a pastor who has conscience for me, a doctor who will judge

SOURCE: Immanuel Kant, "What Is Enlightenment?" in *The Philosophy of Kant*, Carl J. Friedrich, ed. Reprinted by permission of Random House, Inc. (New York, 1949), pp. 132–134, 138–139. Copyright © 1949 by Random House, Inc.

my diet for me and so on, then I do not need to exert myself. I do not have any need to think; if I can pay, others will take over the tedious job for me. The guardians who have kindly undertaken the supervision will see to it that by far the largest part of mankind, including the entire "beautiful sex," should consider the step into maturity, not only as difficult but as very dangerous. . . .

But it is more nearly possible for a public to enlighten itself: this is even inescapable if only the public is given its freedom. . . .

All that is required for this enlightenment is *freedom*; and particularly the least harmful of all that may be called freedom, namely, the freedom for man to make *public use* of his reason in all matters. . . .

The question may now be put: Do we live at present in an enlightened age? The answer is: No, but in an age of enlightenment. Much still prevents men from being placed in a position or even being placed into position to use their own minds securely and well in matters of religion. But we do have very definite indications that this field of endeavor is being opened up for men to work freely and reduce gradually the hindrances preventing a general enlightenment and an escape from self-caused immaturity. In this sense, this age is the age of enlightenment and the age of Frederick (The Great). . . .

I have emphasized the main point of enlightenment, that is of man's release from his self-caused immaturity, primarily *in matters of religion*. I have done this because our rulers have no interest in playing the guardian of their subjects in matters of arts and sciences. Furthermore immaturity in matters of religion is not only most noxious but also most dishonorable. But the point of view of a head of state who favors freedom in the arts and sciences goes even farther; for he understands that there is no danger in legislation permitting his subjects to make *public* use of their own reason and to submit *publicly* their thoughts regarding a better framing of such laws together with a frank criticism of existing *legislation*. We have a shining example of this; no prince excels him whom we admire. Only he who is himself enlightened does not fear spectres when he at the same time has a well-disciplined army at his disposal as a guarantee of public peace. Only he can say what (the ruler of a) free state dare not say: *Argue as much as you want and about whatever you want but obey!*

The System of Nature

Baron d'Holbach

Most Enlightenment thinkers rejected traditional sources of authority such as the Church or custom. Instead, they argued that people should rely on reason, experience, and nature as their guides. Baron d'Holbach (1723–1789) exemplifies this in his varied writings. A German aristocrat and scientist who assumed French citizenship, d'Holbach is best known for his attacks on organized religion and his contributions to Diderot's Encyclopedia. *In the following selection from his* System of Nature *(1770), Holbach focuses on the meaning of enlightenment and what should be done to obtain this enlightenment.*

> **Consider:** *Why enlightenment is so important; whether "nature" has a meaning similar to* God *for Holbach; the views about the nature of enlightenment that Kant and Holbach share.*

The source of man's unhappiness is his ignorance of Nature. The pertinacity with which he clings to blind opinions imbibed in his infancy, which interweave themselves with his existence, the consequent prejudice that warps his mind, that prevents its expansion, that renders him the slave of fiction, appears to doom him to continual errour. He resembles a child destitute of experience, full of idle notions: a dangerous leaven mixes itself with all his knowledge: it is of necessity obscure, it is vacillating and false: — He takes the tone of his ideas on the authority of others, who are themselves in errour, or else have an interest in deceiving him. To remove this Cimmerian darkness, these barriers to the improvement of his condition; to disentangle him from the clouds of errour that envelop him, that obscure the path he ought to tread; to guide him out of this Cretan labyrinth, requires the clue of Ariadne, with all the love she could bestow on Theseus. It exacts more than common exertion; it needs a most determined, a most undaunted courage — it is never effected but by a persevering resolution to act, to think for himself; to examine with rigour and impartiality the opinions he has adopted. . . .

The most important of our duties, then, is to seek means by which we may destroy delusions that can never do more than mislead us. The remedies for these evils must be sought for in Nature herself; it is only in the abundance of her resources, that we can rationally expect to find antidotes to the mischiefs brought upon us by an ill-directed, by an overpowering enthusiasm. It is time these remedies were sought; it is time to look the evil boldly in the face, to examine its foundations, to scrutinize its superstructure: reason, with its faithful guide experience, must attack in their entrenchments those prejudices to which the human race has but too long been

SOURCE: Baron d'Holbach, *The System of Nature,* H. D. Robinson, trans. (Boston: J. P. Mendum, 1853), pp. viii–ix, 12–13, 15.

the victim. For this purpose reason must be restored to its proper rank, — it must be rescued from the evil company with which it is associated. . . .

Truth speaks not to these perverse beings: — her voice can only be heard by generous minds accustomed to reflection, whose sensibilities make them lament the numberless calamities showered on the earth by political and religious tyranny — whose enlightened minds contemplate with horrour the immensity, the ponderosity of that series of misfortunes with which errour has in all ages overwhelmed mankind.

The *civilized man*, is he whom experience and social life have enabled to draw from nature the means of his own happiness; because he has learned to oppose resistance to those impulses he receives from exterior beings, when experience has taught him they would be injurious to his welfare.

The *enlightened man*, is man in his maturity, in his perfection; who is capable of pursuing his own happiness; because he has learned to examine, to think for himself, and not to take that for truth upon the authority of others, which experience has taught him examination will frequently prove erroneous. . . .

It necessarily results, that man in his researches ought always to fall back on experience, and natural philosophy: These are what he should consult in his religion — in his morals — in his legislation — in his political government — in the arts — in the sciences — in his pleasures — in his misfortunes. Experience teaches that Nature acts by simple, uniform, and invariable laws. It is by his senses man is bound to this universal Nature; it is by his senses he must penetrate her secrets; it is from his senses he must draw experience of her laws. Whenever, therefore, he either fails to acquire experience or quits its path, he stumbles into an abyss, his imagination leads him astray.

Prospectus for the Encyclopedia of Arts and Sciences

Denis Diderot

More than any other work, the Encyclopedia of Arts and Sciences, *edited by Denis Diderot (1713–1784) and Jean-le-Rond d'Alembert (1717–1783), epitomizes the Enlightenment. Written between 1745 and 1780, it presented to the public the sum of knowledge considered important by Enlightenment thinkers. The critical Enlightenment spirit underlying the* Encyclopedia *led traditional authorities to condemn it and to suppress it more than once. The following is an excerpt from*

SOURCE: Denis Diderot, *Prospectus à l' Encyclopédie*, in Diderot, *Oeuvres complètes*, Eds. Jules Assézat and Maurice Tourneux, 20 vols. (Paris, 1875–1877), Vol. XIII, pp. 129–131, in Richard W. Lyman and Lewis W. Spitz, eds., *Major Crises in Western Civilization*, Vol. II, Nina B. Gunzenhauser, trans. (New York: Harcourt, Brace & World, 1965), pp. 11–12. Reprinted by permission of Harcourt Brace Jovanovich, Inc.

the Prospectus *that appeared in 1750, announcing the forthcoming* Encyclopedia. *The* Prospectus *was written by Diderot, a philosopher, novelist, and playwright who had already been in trouble with the authorities for his writings. The* Prospectus *apparently aroused widespread expectations; even before the first volume of the* Encyclopedia *appeared, more than a thousand orders for it had been received.*

> **Consider:** *What a reader could hope to gain by purchasing the* Encyclopedia *and how these hopes themselves reflect the spirit of the Enlightenment; how this selection from the* Prospectus *reflects the same ideas expressed by Kant and Holbach; how the Enlightenment as described here related to the scientific revolution of the seventeenth century.*

It cannot be denied that, since the revival of letters among us, we owe partly to dictionaries the general enlightenment that has spread in society and the germ of science that is gradually preparing men's minds for more profound knowledge. How valuable would it not be, then, to have a book of this kind that one could consult on all subjects and that would serve as much to guide those who have the courage to work at the instruction of others as to enlighten those who only instruct themselves!

This is one advantage we thought of, but it is not the only one. In condensing to dictionary form all that concerns the arts and sciences, it remained necessary to make people aware of the assistance they lend each other; to make use of this assistance to render principles more certain and their consequences clearer; to indicate the distant and close relationships of the beings that make up nature, which have occupied men; to show, by showing the interlacing both of roots and of branches, the impossibility of understanding thoroughly some parts of the whole without exploring many others; to produce a general picture of the efforts of the human spirit in all areas and in all centuries; to present these matters with clarity; to give to each the proper scope, and to prove, if possible, our epigraph by our success: . . . .

The majority of these works appeared during the last century and were not completely scorned. It was found that if they did not show much talent, they at least bore the marks of labor and of knowledge. But what would these encyclopedias mean to us? What progress have we not made since then in the arts and sciences? How many truths discovered today, which were not foreseen then? True philosophy was in its cradle; the geometry of infinity did not yet exist; experimental physics was just appearing; there was no dialectic at all; the laws of sound criticism were entirely unknown. Descartes, Boyle, Huyghens, Newton, Leibnitz, the Bernoullis, Locke, Bayle, Pascal, Corneille, Racine, Bourdaloue, Bossuet, etc., either had not yet been born or had not yet written. The spirit of research and competition did not motivate the scholars: another spirit, less fecund perhaps, but rarer, that of precision and method, had not yet conquered the various divisions of literature; and the academies, whose efforts have advanced the arts and sciences to such an extent, were not yet established. . . . At the end of this project you will find the tree of human knowledge, indicating the connection of ideas, which has directed us in this vast operation.

The Philosophe

Enlightenment thinkers often referred to themselves as "philosophes," which is technically the French word for philosophers. The term had a special meaning bound up with the spirit of the Enlightenment. This is dealt with directly in the following selection, "The Philosopher," from the Encyclopedia. *It has traditionally been assumed that Diderot is the author of "The Philosopher," but it may have been written by another person, perhaps Dumarsis. In any case, it is an authoritative treatment of the topic according to Enlightenment precepts.*

> **Consider:** *The characteristics of the philosopher; how this compares to Kant's definition of enlightenment and Holbach's definition of a civilized or enlightened man; how a twentieth-century philosopher might differ with this definition of a philosopher.*

Other men make up their minds to act without thinking, nor are they conscious of the causes which move them, not even knowing that such exist. The philosopher, on the contrary, distinguishes the causes to what extent he may, often anticipates them, and knowingly surrenders himself to them. In this manner he avoids objects that may cause him sensations that are not conducive to his well being or his rational existence, and seeks those which may excite in him affections agreeable with the state in which he finds himself. Reason is in the estimation of the philosopher what grace is to the Christian. Grace determines the Christian's action; reason the philosopher's.

Other men are carried away by their passions, so that the acts which they produce do not proceed from reflection. These are the men who move in darkness; while the philosopher, even in his passions, moves only after reflection. He marches at night, but a torch goes on ahead.

The philosopher forms his principles upon an infinity of individual observations. The people adopt the principle without a thought of the observations which have produced it, believing that the maxim exists, so to speak, of itself; but the philosopher takes the maxim at its source, he examines its origin, he knows its real value, and only makes use of it, if it seems to him satisfactory.

Truth is not for the philosopher a mistress who vitiates his imagination, and whom he believes to find everywhere. He contents himself with being able to discover it wherever he may chance to find it. He does not confound

---

Source: Merrick Whitcomb, ed., "French Philosophers of the Eighteenth Century," in *Translations and Reprints from the Original Sources of European History*, Vol. VI, No. 1, Department of History of the University of Pennsylvania, ed. (Philadelphia: University of Pennsylvania Press, 1898), pp. 21–23.

it with its semblance; but takes for true that which is true, for false that which is false, for doubtful that which is doubtful, and for probable that which is only probable. He does more—and this is the great perfection of philosophy; that when he has no real grounds for passing judgment, he knows how to remain undetermined.

The world is full of persons of understanding, even of much understanding, who always pass judgment. They are guessing always, because it is guessing to pass judgment without knowing when one has proper grounds for judgment. They misjudge of the capacity of the human mind; they believe it is possible to know everything, and so they are ashamed not to be prepared to pass judgment, and they imagine that understanding consists in passing judgment. The philosopher believes that it consists in judging well: he is better pleased with himself when he has suspended the faculty of determining, than if he had determined before having acquired proper grounds for his decision.

The philosophic spirit is then a spirit of observation and of exactness, which refers everything to its true principles; but it is not the understanding alone which the philosopher cultivates; he carries further his attention and his labors.

Man is not a monster, made to live only at the bottom of the sea or in the depths of the forest; the very necessities of his life render intercourse with others necessary; and in whatsoever state we find him, his needs and his well-being lead him to live in society. To that reason demands of him that he should know, that he should study and that he should labor to acquire social qualities.

Our philosopher does not believe himself an exile in the world; he does not believe himself in the enemy's country; he wishes to enjoy, like a wise economist, the goods that nature offers him; he wishes to find his pleasure with others; and in order to find it, it is necessary to assist in producing it; so he seeks to harmonize with those with whom chance or his choice has determined he shall live; and he finds at the same time that which suits him: he is an honest man who wishes to please and render himself useful.

The philosopher is then an honest man, actuated in everything by reason, one who joins to the spirit of reflection and of accuracy the manners and qualities of society.

Philosophical Dictionary:
The English Model

Voltaire

François Marie Arouet, who later adopted the name Voltaire (1694–1778), was certainly the most famous of the philosophes. Writing almost every type of literature, from drama and satire to history and essays, he exhibited most of the main elements of the Enlightenment. One of these was the philosophes' admiration for and idealization of England's political system. Voltaire gained familiarity with England during a three-year visit, from 1726 to 1729, and played an important role in popularizing the ideas of English scientists and the principles of the English political system. The following is an excerpt from his Philosophical Dictionary, *first published in 1764.*

> **Consider:** *What Voltaire admires about the English constitution; the implied criticism of the French political system; whether Voltaire idealizes the English system.*

The English constitution has, in fact, arrived at that point of excellence, in consequence of which all men are restored to those natural rights, which, in nearly all monarchies, they are deprived of. These rights are, entire liberty of person and property; freedom of the press; the right of being tried in all criminal cases by a jury of independent men — the right of being tried only according to the strict letter of the law; and the right of every man to profess, unmolested, what religion he chooses, while he renounces offices, which the members of the Anglican or established church alone can hold. These are denominated privileges. And, in truth, invaluable privileges they are in comparison with the usages of most other nations of the world! To be secure on lying down that you shall rise in possession of the same property with which you retired to rest; that you shall not be torn from the arms of your wife, and from your children, in the dead of night, to be thrown into a dungeon, or buried in exile in a desert; that, when rising from the bed of sleep, you will have the power of publishing all your thoughts; and that, if you are accused of having either acted, spoken, or written wrongly, you can be tried only according to law. These privileges attach to every one who sets his foot on English ground. A foreigner enjoys perfect liberty to dispose of his property and person; and, if accused of any offence, he can demand that half the jury shall be composed of foreigners.

I will venture to assert, that, were the human race solemnly assembled for the purpose of making laws, such are the laws they would make for their security.

Source: Voltaire, Philosophical Dictionary, in Voltaire, *Works*, trans. W. F. Fleming (New York: E. R. Dumont, 1901), Vol. 5, pp. 293–294.

A Vindication of the Rights of Woman

Mary Wollstonecraft

While the Enlightenment was dominated by men, there were possibilities for active involvement by women. Several women played particularly important roles as patrons and intellectual contributors to the gatherings of philosophes and members of the upper-middle-class and aristocratic elite held in the salons of Paris and elsewhere. It was, however, far more difficult for a woman to publish serious essays in the Enlightenment tradition. Indeed, Enlightenment thinkers did little to change basic attitudes about the inferiority of women. One person who managed to do both was Mary Wollstonecraft (1759–1797), a British author who in 1792 published A Vindication of the Rights of Woman. *The book was a sharply reasoned attack against the oppression of women and an argument for educational change. In the following excerpt, Wollstonecraft addresses the author of a proposed new constitution for France that, in her opinion, does not adequately deal with the rights of women.*

> **Consider:** *Why education is so central to her argument; the ways in which this argument reflects the methods and ideals of the Enlightenment.*

Contending for the rights of woman, my main argument is built on this simple principle, that if she be not prepared by education to become the companion of man, she will stop the progress of knowledge and virtue; for truth must be common to all, or it will be inefficacious with respect to its influence on general practice. And how can woman be expected to co-operate unless she knows why she ought to be virtuous? unless freedom strengthens her reason till she comprehends her duty, and see in what manner it is connected with her real good. If children are to be educated to understand the true principle of patriotism, their mother must be a patriot; and the love of mankind, from which an orderly train of virtues spring, can only be produced by considering the moral and civil interest of mankind; but the education and situation of woman at present shuts her out from such investigations.

In this work I have produced many arguments, which to me were conclusive, to prove that the prevailing notion respecting a sexual character was subversive of morality, and I have contended, that to render the human body and mind more perfect, chastity must more universally prevail, and that chastity will never be respected in the male world till the person of a woman is not, as it were, idolised, when little virtue or sense embellish it with the grand traces of mental beauty, or the interesting simplicity of affection.

Consider, sir, dispassionately these observations, for a glimpse of this truth seemed to open before you when you observed, "that to see one-half of

SOURCE: Mary Wollstonecraft, *The Rights of Woman* (London: J. M. Dent and Sons, Ltd., 1929), pp. 10–11.

the human race excluded by the other from all participation of government was a political phenomenon, that, according to abstract principles, it was impossible to explain." If so, on what does your constitution rest? If the abstract rights of man will bear discussion and explanation, those of woman, by a parity of reasoning, will not shrink from the same test; though a different opinion prevails in this country, built on the very arguments which you use to justify the oppression of woman — prescription.

Consider — I address you as a legislator — whether, when men contend for their freedom, and to be allowed to judge for themselves respecting their own happiness, it be not inconsistent and unjust to subjugate women, even though you firmly believe that you are acting in the manner best calculated to promote their happiness? Who made man the exclusive judge, if woman partake with him of the gift of reason?

The Age of Reason: Deism

Thomas Paine

Many Enlightenment thinkers were strongly opposed to traditional religious institutions and ideas. Yet only a few went so far as to profess atheism. More typical was some form of deism, a belief in a God who created a rational universe with natural laws but who no longer intervened in the course of events. A good example of this belief is found in the following excerpt from Thomas Paine's Age of Reason *(1794). Paine (1737–1809) was an unusually international person. Born in England, he became an American patriot and later a member of the French Convention (1792–1793). His most famous works are* Common Sense *and* The Rights of Man, *in both of which he justifies revolution. In* The Age of Reason *Paine places himself within the tradition of Enlightenment thought and summarizes his religious views.*

Consider: *Why Paine is so opposed to traditional religious institutions; how this opposition is consistent with other Enlightenment thought; how a sincere, sophisticated member of the Catholic Church might have responded to this.*

As several of my colleagues, and others of my fellow-citizens of France, have given me the example of making their voluntary and individual profession of faith, I also will make mine; and I do this with all that sincerity and frankness with which the mind of man communicates with itself.

I believe in one God, and no more; and I hope for happiness beyond this life.

I believe the equality of man, and I believe that religious duties consist in doing justice, loving mercy, and endeavouring to make our fellow-creatures happy.

SOURCE: Moncure Daniel Conway, ed., *The Writings of Thomas Paine*, Vol. IV (New York: G. P. Putnam's Sons, 1896), pp. 21–23.

But, lest it should be supposed that I believe many other things in addition to these, I shall, in the progress of this work, declare the things I do not believe, and my reasons for not believing them.

I do not believe in the creed professed by the Jewish church, by the Roman church, by the Greek church, by the Turkish church, by the Protestant church, nor by any church that I know of. My own mind is my own church.

All national institutions of churches, whether Jewish, Christian, or Turkish, appear to me no other than human inventions set up to terrify and enslave mankind, and monopolize power and profit.

I do not mean by this declaration to condemn those who believe otherwise; they have the same right to their belief as I have to mine. But it is necessary to the happiness of man, that he be mentally faithful to himself. Infidelity does not consist in believing, or in disbelieving; it consists in professing to believe what he does not believe.

It is impossible to calculate the moral mischief, if I may so express it, that mental lying has produced in society. When a man has so far corrupted and prostituted the chastity of his mind, as to subscribe his professional belief to things he does not believe, he has prepared himself for the commission of every other crime. He takes up the trade of a priest for the sake of gain, and, in order to qualify himself for that trade, he begins with a perjury. Can we conceive anything more destructive to morality than this?

Soon after I had published the pamphlet *Common Sense*, in America, I saw the exceeding probability that a revolution in the system of government would be followed by a revolution in the system of religion. The adulterous connection of church and state, wherever it had taken place, whether Jewish, Christian, or Turkish, had so effectually prohibited, by pains and penalties, every discussion upon established creeds, and upon first principles of religion, that until the system of government should be changed, those subjects could not be brought fairly and openly before the world; but that whenever this should be done, a revolution in the system of religion would follow. Human inventions and priest-craft would be detected; and man would return to the pure, unmixed, and unadulterated belief of one God, and no more.

On Crimes and Punishments

Cesare Beccaria

The philosophy of the Enlightenment was manifested in analyses of social and political institutions. One of the most influential calls for enlightened reform came from Cesare Beccaria (1735–1794), an Italian aristocrat and government official. In On Crimes and Punishments *(1764), he severely criticized the criminology and penology of the Ancien Régime and suggested reforms. This authoritative work influenced many reforms during the late eighteenth and early nineteenth centuries.*

> **Consider:** *The principles underlying Beccaria's ideas about crime and punishment; how his ideas and suggestions relate to the spirit of the Enlightenment; what makes his views particularly modern.*

We have seen what the true measure of crimes is — namely, the *harm done to society.* This is one of those palpable truths which, though requiring neither quadrants nor telescopes for their discovery, and lying well within the capacity of any ordinary intellect, are, nevertheless, because of a marvelous combination of circumstances, known with clarity and precision only by some few thinking men in every nation and in every age. . . .

They were in error who believed that the true measure of crimes is to be found in the intention of the person who commits them. Intention depends on the impression objects actually make and on the precedent disposition of the mind; these vary in all men and in each man, according to the swift succession of ideas, of passions, and of circumstances. . . .

Others measure crimes rather by the dignity of the injured person than by the importance [of the offense] with respect to the public good. If this were the true measure of crimes, an irreverence toward the Being of beings ought to be more severely punished than the assassination of a monarch, the superiority of nature constituting infinite compensation for the difference in the injury.

Finally, some have thought that the gravity of sinfulness ought to enter into the measure of crimes. The fallacy of this opinion will at once appear to the eye of an impartial examiner of the true relations between men and men, and between men and God. . . .

It is better to prevent crimes than to punish them. This is the ultimate end of every good legislation, which, to use the general terms for assessing the good and evils of life, is the art of leading men to the greatest possible happiness or to the least possible unhappiness. . . .

Do you want to prevent crimes? See to it that the laws are clear and simple and that the entire force of a nation is united in their defense, and that

SOURCE: Cesare Beccaria, *On Crimes and Punishments,* Henry Paolucci, trans. Reprinted by permission of the Bobbs–Merrill Co., Inc., 1963, pp. 64–65, 93–99.

no part of it is employed to destroy them. See to it that the laws favor not so much classes of men as men themselves. See to it that men fear the laws and fear nothing else. . . .

Another way of preventing crimes is to reward virtue. Upon this subject I notice a general silence in the laws of all the nations of our day. If the prizes offered by the academies to discoverers of useful truths have increased our knowledge and have multiplied good books, why should not prizes distributed by the beneficent hand of the soveriegn serve in a similar way to multiply virtuous actions? The coin of honor is always inexhaustible and fruitful in the hands of the wise distributor.

Finally, the surest but most difficult way to prevent crimes is by perfecting education. . . .

From what has thus far been demonstrated, one may deduce a general theorem of considerable utility, though hardly conformable with custom, the usual legislator of nations; it is this: *In order for punishment not to be, in every instance, an act of violence of one or of many against a private citizen, it must be essentially public, prompt, necessary, the least possible in the given circumstances, proportionate to the crimes, dictated by the laws.*

The Social Contract

Jean Jacques Rousseau

More than anyone else, Jean Jacques Rousseau (1712–1778) tested the outer limits of Enlightenment thought and went on to criticize its very foundations. Born in Geneva, he spent much of his life in France (mainly in Paris), where he became one of the philosophes who contributed to the Encyclopedia. *Yet he also undermined Enlightenment thought by holding that social institutions had corrupted people and that human beings in the state of nature were more pure, free, and happy than in modern civilization. This line of thought provided a foundation for the growth of Romanticism in the late eighteenth and early nineteenth centuries. Rousseau's most important political work was* The Social Contract *(1762), in which he argued for popular sovereignty. In the following selection from that work, Rousseau focuses on what he considers the fundamental argument of the book — the passage from the state of nature to the civil state by means of the social contract.*

> **Consider:** *Rousseau's solution to the main problem of* The Social Contract; *the advantages and disadvantages of the social contract; what characteristics of Enlightenment thought are reflected in this selection.*

SOURCE: Jean Jacques Rousseau, *The Social Contract and Discourses* (London: J. M. Dent, Everyman Library, 1913), pp. 14–15, 18–19.

"The problem is to find a form of association which will defend and protect with the whole common force the person and goods of each associate, and in which each, while uniting himself with all, may still obey himself alone, and remain as free as before." This is the fundamental problem of which *The Social Contract* provides the solution.

The clauses of this contract are so determined by the nature of the act that the slightest modification would make them vain and ineffective; so that, although they have perhaps never been formally set forth, they are everywhere the same and everywhere tacitly admitted and recognised, until, on the violation of the social compact, each regains his original rights and resumes his natural liberty, while losing the conventional liberty in favour of which he renounced it.

These clauses, properly understood, may be reduced to one — the total alienation of each associate, together with all his rights, to the whole community; for, in the first place, as each gives himself absolutely, the conditions are the same for all; and, this being so, no one has any interest in making them burdensome to others.

Moreover, the alienation being without reserve, the union is as perfect as it can be, and no associate has anything more to demand: for, if the individuals retained certain rights, as there would be no common superior to decide between them and the public, each, being on one point his own judge, would ask to be so on all; the state of nature would thus continue, and the association would necessarily become inoperative or tyrannical.

Finally, each man, in giving himself to all, gives himself to nobody; and as there is no associate over whom he does not acquire the same right as he yields others over himself, he gains on equivalent for everything he loses, and an increase of force for the preservation of what he has.

If then we discard from the social compact what is not of its essence, we shall find that it reduces itself to the following terms —

Each of us puts his person and all his power in common under the supreme direction of the general will, and, in our corporate capacity, we receive each member as an indivisible part of the whole.

The passage from the state of nature to the civil state produces a very remarkable change in man, by substituting justice for instinct in his conduct, and giving his actions the morality they had formerly lacked. Then only, when the voice of duty takes the place of physical impulses and right of appetite, does man, who so far had considered only himself, find that he is forced to act on different principles, and to consult his reason before listening to his inclinations. Although, in this state, he deprives himself of some advantages which he got from nature, he gains in return others so great, his faculties are so stimulated and developed, his ideas so extended, his feelings so ennobled, and his whole soul so uplifted, that, did not the abuses of this new condition often degrade him below that which he left, he would be bound to bless continually the happy moment which took him from it for ever, and, instead of a stupid and unimaginative animal, made him an intelligent being and a man.

Let us draw up the whole account in terms easily commensurable. What man loses by the social contract is his natural liberty and an unlimited right to everything he tries to get and succeeds in getting; what he gains is civil liberty and the proprietorship of all he possesses. If we are to avoid mistake in weighing one against the other, we must clearly distinguish natural liberty, which is bounded only by the strength of the individual, from civil liberty, which is limited by the general will; and possession, which is merely the effect of force or the right of the first occupier, from property, which can be founded only on a positive title.

We might, over and above all this, add, to what man acquires in the civil state, moral liberty, which alone makes him truly master of himself; for the mere impulse of appetite is slavery, while obedience to a law which we prescribe to ourselves is liberty. But I have already said too much on this head, and the philosophical meaning of the word liberty does not now concern us.

VISUAL SOURCES

Experiment with an Air Pump
Joseph Wright

Few paintings provide a better image of the Enlightenment than Experiment with an Air Pump *(1768) by the British artist Joseph Wright (see p. 78). The experiment takes place in the center of the picture; its apparent success is evidenced by the dead bird inside a closed glass bowl from which the air has been pumped out. The informally dressed experimenter is carefully observing his work. Around him are members of his family and some well-dressed friends.*

The form and content of this picture symbolize the Enlightenment. A small source of light is sufficient to enlighten humanity and reveal the laws of nature. Science is not just for specialists but something amateurs can understand and practice to obtain practical results. That it is a British painting is particularly significant, for the English led in developing useful machines and were identified as having a more pragmatic approach to science and ideas than other peoples. The painting also reveals customary images of the sexes: the experimenter boldly forging on while to his left a friend or associate calmly explains what is happening to a woman and her daughter, whose sensibilities are as appropriately fragile as the dying bird — the main object of their concern.

Consider: *Any common themes in this painting and the documents by Diderot, Kant, and Holbach.*

Photo 4-1

© The Tate Gallery, London

Propaganda and the Enlightened Monarch

Joseph II of Austria

Emperor Joseph II of Austria (1765–1790) is generally thought to have been one of the most enlightened eighteenth-century kings and indeed considered himself to be an enlightened monarch. Some of what this meant is indicated by this picture Joseph II had painted of himself. It shows him plowing a field with a farmer (to his left) and members of his court (to his right). To make sure he and his office were recognizable to viewers, Joseph remained appropriately dressed, including wearing his powdered wig. This scene also affirms the growing interest in agricultural improvements during the eighteenth century, particularly among aristocratic innovators. Joseph II tells of some of his hopes in a number of letters excerpted here.

> **Consider:** *What there was about this scene and these letters that could be considered enlightened; any inconsistencies with these statements and the reality of being a monarch; how Kant might have viewed Joseph II.*

Photo 4-2

Courtesy, Austrian Press & Information Service

SOURCE: "Letters of Joseph II," in *The Pamphleteer*, Vol. XIX (London, 1882), pp. 282, 288–290.

Mr. Vice-Chancellor — The present system of taxation in my dominions, and the inequality of the taxes which are imposed on the nation, form a subject too important to escape my attention. I have discovered that the principles on which it is founded are unsound, and have become injurious to the industry of the peasant; that there is neither equality, nor equity, between the hereditary provinces with each other, nor between individual proprietors, and therefore it can no longer continue.

With this view I give you the necessary orders to introduce a new system of taxation, by which the contribution, requisite for the wants of the state, may be effected without augmenting the present taxes, and the industry of the peasant, at the same time, be freed from all impediments.

Since my accession to the throne, I have ever been anxious to conquer the prejudices against my station, and have taken pains to gain the confidence of my people; I have several times since given proof, that the welfare of my subjects is my passion; that to satisfy it, I shun neither labor, nor trouble, nor even vexations, and reflect well on the means which are likely to promote my views; and yet in my reforms, I everywhere find opposition from people, of whom I least expect it.

Sir, — Till now the Protestant religion has been opposed in my states; its adherents have been treated like foreigners; civil rights, possession of estates, titles, and appointments, all were refused them.

I determined from the very commencement of my reign to adorn my diadem with the love of my people, to act in the administration of affairs according to just, impartial, and liberal principles; consequently, I granted toleration, and removed the yoke which had oppressed the protestants for centuries.

Fanaticism shall in future be known in my states only by the contempt I have for it; nobody shall any longer be exposed to hardships on account of his creed; no man shall be compelled in future to profess the religion of the state, if it be contrary to his persuasion, and if he have other ideas of the right way of insuring blessedness.

In future my Empire shall not be the scene of abominable intolerance. Fortunately no sacrifices like those of Calas and Sirven have ever disgraced any reign in this country.

If, in former times, the will of the monarch furnished opportunities for injustice, if the limits of executive power were exceeded, and private hatred acted her part, I can only pity those monarchs who were nothing but kings.

Tolerance is an effect of that beneficient increase of knowledge which now enlightens Europe, and which is owing to philosophy and the efforts of great men; it is a convincing proof of the improvement of the human mind, which has boldly reopened a road through the dominions of superstition, which was trodden centuries ago by Zoroaster and Confucius, and which, fortunately for mankind, has now become the highway of monarchs. Adieu!

SECONDARY SOURCES

The Age of Reason
Frank Manuel

The Enlightenment owes its substance to the thought of a relatively small group of eighteenth-century philosophes who came from many countries but were centered in France. Although they often argued among themselves, there was a set of approaches and propositions upon which most of them agreed. In the following selection Frank E. Manuel, a historian of ideas from Brandeis and New York University, analyzes the philosophes' new moral outlook, an outlook that seems particularly modern.

> **Consider:** *How the primary documents support or contradict Manuel's interpretation; the ways in which the moral outlook described here is overly optimistic and naive; the elements of this outlook that make the most sense to you for today's world.*

Despite their sharp cleavages and varying interests, there was a common ground on which all the intellectuals could stand, and from their inconsistent and even incompatible tendencies there emerged a moral outlook distinct from that of the previous age. The eighteenth-century philosophers popularized general precepts of conduct which in time were widely accepted in most civilized societies. They made aggressive war look odious and mocked the ideal of military glory. They preached religious toleration, free speech, a free press. They were in favor of the sanctions of law to protect individual liberties and they were against tyranny which governed by caprice. They wanted equality of all citizens before the law and they were opposed to any recognition of social distinctions when men were brought to justice. They abhorred torture and other barbaric punishments and pleaded for their abolition; they believed that punishment should fit the crime and should be imposed only to restrain potential malefactors. They wanted freedom of movement across state boundaries both for individuals and

---

SOURCE: Frank E. Manuel, *The Age of Reason*. Reprinted by permission of Cornell University Press (New York, 1951), pp. 46–47. Copyright © 1951 by Cornell University.

articles of commerce. Most of them believed that it did not require the threat of eternal torment in hell to make moral ideas generally accepted among mankind. They were convinced that the overwhelming number of men, if their natural goodness were not perverted in childhood, would act in harmony with simple rules and the dictates of rational principles without the necessity for severe restraints and awful punishments.

In summary, though the *philosophes* did not solve the problem of the existence of evil and suffering in the world, they did manage to establish in European society a general consensus about conduct which is evil, a moral attitude which still sustains us. Despite their subservient behavior toward some of the European despots and the social anarchy ultimately inherent in their doctrines of absolute self-interest, the eighteenth-century men of letters did formulate a set of moral principles which to this day remain basic to any discussion of human rights. The deficiencies of their optimistic moral and political outlook are by now visible, but they did venture the first bold examination of reality since the Greeks and they dared to set forth brandnew abstractions about man and the universe. They taught their contemporaries to view the institutions of church and state in the light of reason and to judge them by the simple criterion of human happiness.

The Party of Humanity: The Struggling Philosophes

Peter Gay

There are major disagreements among historians who study the Enlightenment and the philosophes. One group holds that the philosophes were shallow, destructive dilettantes who enjoyed rubbing shoulders with the elite while poking fun at eighteenth-century institutions and practices. Another group holds that the philosophes were sincere, thoughtful intellectuals who braved much to express many of the most important precepts of the modern world. Peter Gay takes into account both of these views in his highly respected interpretations of the French Enlightenment, The Party of Humanity: Essays in the French Enlightenment. *In the following selection, Gay focuses on the psychological underpinnings of much of the philosophes' struggle.*

> **Consider:** *What was so difficult about the philosophes' struggle; any connections between what Gay terms the "struggle of the philosophes" and their "two enemies"; what historical or institutional changes the philosophes would have supported, according to Gay.*

SOURCE: Peter Gay, *The Party of Humanity: Essays in the French Enlightenment.* Reprinted by permission of Alfred A. Knopf, Inc. (New York, 1964), pp. 124–126. Copyright © 1964 by Alfred A. Knopf, Inc.

The *philosophes* had two enemies: the institutions of Christianity and the idea of hierarchy. And they had two problems: God and the masses. Both the enemies and the problems were related and woven into the single task of rethinking their world. The old questions that Christianity had answered so fully for so many men and so many centuries, had to be asked anew: What — as Kant put it — what can I know? What ought I to do? What may I hope?

Science itself did not answer these questions. It only suggested — ever more insistently as the century went on — that the old answers were wrong. Now, the *philosophes* were products of Christian homes and Christian schools. If they became enemies of Christianity, they did so not from indifference or ignorance: they knew their Bible, their catechism, their Church Fathers, their apologetics. And they knew, because it had been drummed into them early, the fate that awaits heretics or atheists in the world to come. Their anticlerical humor therefore has the bitter intimacy of the family joke; to embrace materialism was an act of rejection.

The struggle of the *philosophes* was a struggle for freedom. They did not fully understand it, but to the extent that they did understand it, they knew their situation to be filled with terror and delight. They felt the anxiety and exhilaration of the explorer who stands before the unknown.

To use such existentialist language may seem like a rather portentous way of describing men noted for their sociability and frivolity. It is of course true that the *philosophes* did not suffer alone: they had the comforting company of elegant salons and of respectable philosophical forebears.

Yet even the supple Voltaire, who had been initiated into unbelief by fashionable teachers, was not free from the symptoms of this struggle. Much of his mockery was a weapon in a grim fight, and a device to keep up his own morale. Much of his philosophical rumination on free will reveals the persistence of a troublesome inner conflict. . . .

I am not simply arguing that the *philosophes* were less cheerful than they appeared in their social roles — most of us are. Nor that they suffered personal crises — philosophers, especially young philosophers, often do. I am arguing that the *philosophes'* anguish was related to the crisis in their Christian civilization; that (to use different language) whatever childhood experiences made them psychologically vulnerable in adult life, their obsessions, their self-questionings, their anxieties, were poured into their religious, moral, and political speculation.

The Heavenly City of the Eighteenth-Century Philosophers

Carl Becker

Another point of interpretive division among historians of the Enlightenment centers on how modern and secular the philosophes were. Nineteenth- and early-twentieth-century historians argued that the philosophes were more modern than medieval and indeed drew more from the classical pagan world than from the medieval world. This view still predominates among historians of the period. A famous challenge to this view was made some fifty years ago by Cornell historian Carl Becker. His book, The Heavenly City of the Eighteenth-Century Philosophers *(1932), became the most influential book on the subject, although today it is no longer as popular as it once was. In the following selection from this work, Becker presents the substance of his thesis.*

> **Consider:** *The ways in which the philosophes were more medieval than modern; the support Becker offers for his argument that there was much Christian philosophy in the philosophes' writings; how Gay or Manuel would react to Becker's interpretation.*

We are accustomed to think of the eighteenth century as essentially modern in its temper. Certainly, the *Philosophes* themselves made a great point of having renounced the superstition and hocus-pocus of medieval Christian thought, and we have usually been willing to take them at their word. Surely, we say, the eighteenth century was preëminently the age of reason, surely the *Philosophes* were a skeptical lot, atheists in effect if not by profession, addicted to science and the scientific method, always out to crush the infamous, valiant defenders of liberty, equality, fraternity, freedom of speech, and what you will. All very true. And yet I think the *Philosophes* were nearer the Middle Ages, less emancipated from the preconceptions of medieval Christian thought, than they quite realized or we have commonly supposed. . . .

But, if we examine the foundations of their faith, we find that at every turn the *Philosophes* betray their debt to medieval thought without being aware of it. They denounced Christian philosophy, but rather too much, after the manner of those who are but half emancipated from the "superstitions" they scorn. They had put off the fear of God, but maintained a respectful attitude toward the Deity. They ridiculed the idea that the universe had been created in six days, but still believed it to be a beautifully

SOURCE: Carl L. Becker, *The Heavenly City of the Eighteenth-Century Philosophers.* Reprinted by permission of Yale University Press (New Haven, Conn., 1932), pp. 29–31, 102–103.

articulated machine designed by the Supreme Being according to a rational plan as an abiding place for mankind. The Garden of Eden was for them a myth, no doubt, but they looked enviously back to the golden age of Roman virtue, or across the waters to the unspoiled innocence of an Arcadian civilization that flourished in Pennsylvania. They renounced the authority of church and Bible, but exhibited a naïve faith in the authority of nature and reason. They scorned metaphysics, but were proud to be called philosophers. They dismantled heaven, somewhat prematurely it seems, since they retained their faith in the immortality of the soul. They courageously discussed atheism, but not before the servants. They defended toleration valiantly, but could with difficulty tolerate priests. They denied that miracles ever happened, but believed in the perfectibility of the human race. We feel that these Philosophers were at once too credulous and too skeptical. They were the victims of common sense. In spite of their rationalism and their humane sympathies, in spite of their aversion to hocus-pocus and enthusiasm and dim perspectives, in spite of their eager skepticism, their engaging cynicism, their brave youthful blasphemies and talk of hanging the last king in the entrails of the last priest — in spite of all of it, there is more of the Christian philosophy in the writings of the *Philosophes* than has yet been dreamt of in our histories.

Eighteenth-Century Europe: Enlightened Absolutism

M. S. Anderson

Historians have long debated exactly how much the Enlightenment influenced monarchs of the time. Traditionally there has been considerable acceptance of the view that monarchs such as Joseph II of Austria and Frederick II of Prussia were enlightened. In recent years this view has been seriously narrowed and questioned to the point where many historians feel that enlightened despotism and enlightened absolutism are no longer terms that can usefully be applied to these eighteenth-century monarchs. M. S. Anderson, of the London School of Economics and Political Science, supports this newer critical view. In the following selection he analyzes the limited ways in which eighteenth-century monarchs can be considered enlightened.

> **Consider:** *The characteristics of enlightened despotism; why Joseph II (see the primary documents in this chapter) and Frederick II (see primary documents in the preceding chapter) might be considered enlightened despots; how enlightened despotism differs from seventeenth-century absolutism and the "new monarchs" of the sixteenth century.*

SOURCE: M. S. Anderson, *Eighteenth-Century Europe: 1713–1789.* Reprinted by permission of Oxford University Press (Oxford, 1966), pp. 100–102. Copyright © 1966 by Oxford University Press.

It is generally agreed that in the later eighteenth century, notably in the generation from about 1760 to 1790, many of the monarchies of Europe began to display new characteristics. In one state after another rulers or ministers (Catherine II in Russia, Frederick II in Prussia, Gustavus III in Sweden, Charles III in Spain, Struensee in Denmark, Tanucci in Naples) began to be influenced, or to claim that they were influenced, by the ideas which economists and political philosophers, notably in France, had been proclaiming for several decades. This 'enlightened despotism' is in many ways an unsatisfactory subject of study. Except in a few cases — notably those of the Archduke Leopold in Tuscany (1765-90) and his better-known brother Joseph in the Habsburg dominions — it was always largely super-ficial and contrived. Usually the policies actively pursued by the enlightened despots, however warm the welcome they gave to new theories of govern-ment and administration, ran to some extent in traditional channels.

All of them attempted to improve the administration of their states, especially with regard to taxation, and to unify their territories more effec-tively. Many of them attempted or at least envisaged judicial reforms, notably by the drawing up of elaborate legal codes. The code of civil pro-cedure and the penal code issued by Joseph II in 1781 and 1787, and above all the great Prussian code of 1791, the outcome of many years of labour during the reign of Frederick II, are outstanding examples. With few excep-tions the enlightened despots hoped to achieve their ends by increasing their own authority and the power of the central government in their states. But with the partial exception of the desire for legal reform none of these ambi-tions was new. In differing ways they had been seen in the activities of the 'New Monarchs' of the sixteenth century and in those of Louis XIV and his contemporaries; they were to be seen once more, with greater intensity and effect, in those of Napoleon I. Some elements of novelty can, it is true, be detected in the attitude of several rulers and governments of the later eight-eenth century. In particular the growing humanitarianism, which 'enlightened' thought and writing had done much to foster, was now inspir-ing efforts to abolish judicial torture and greater consideration than in the past for the interests of such groups as orphans and old soldiers. But there were few rulers whose policies in practice represented more than the development of ambitions cherished by their predecessors. Thus Frederick II made little real alteration in the administrative system bequeathed him by his father; and most of his territorial ambitions, notably in Poland, were also inherited. Most of the changes which Catherine II attempted or con-templated in Russia — the secularization of church lands in 1764, the reform of local government in 1775, the codification of the law, attempted par-ticularly by the unsuccessful Legislative Commission of 1767 — had been suggested during the reigns of her predecessors. What distinguished Frederick and Catherine from Frederick William I and Peter the Great was not so much their policies as their explicit justification of them (especially in the case of Catherine) in terms of advanced contemporary thought. It was this appeal to intellectual and moral standards rather than to those of mere expediency that made these rulers appear to be doing something new. And this appeal was essentially spurious. No ruler of any major state could allow his policies to be dictated by theory, however attractive. The history, geographical position, and resources of the state he ruled, the power or weakness of its neighbours, and a host of other factors, set limits to what he might reasonably attempt in either internal or external affairs. Joseph II spent his reign in a continuous series of efforts to improve the administration of his territories and the condition of his subjects. More than any other major ruler of the period he was truly inspired by the theories of government then current in enlightened Europe. Yet his disregard of realities in his relations with the Hungarians, with the inhabitants of his Netherlands provinces, and with the Catholic church, and the failure and near-collapse to which this disregard had led by the end of his reign, were the supreme proof that, as always, there was an 'order of possible progress' in politics and all other aspects of life in the eighteenth century, and that this order could be disregarded only to a very limited extent.

Chapter Questions

1. What core of ideas and attitudes most clearly connects Enlightenment thinkers as revealed in these sources? How do these ideas relate to eighteenth-century society and institutions?

2. What policies would an eighteenth-century ruler have to pursue to fit to the greatest degree the ideas and assumptions of Enlightenment thinkers? What hindrances were faced by monarchs who wanted to be more enlightened?

3. What ideas and attitudes of Enlightenment thinkers do you think remain valid for the problems facing today's world? What Enlightenment ideas and attitudes no longer seem valid or appropriate?

II

THE NINETEENTH CENTURY

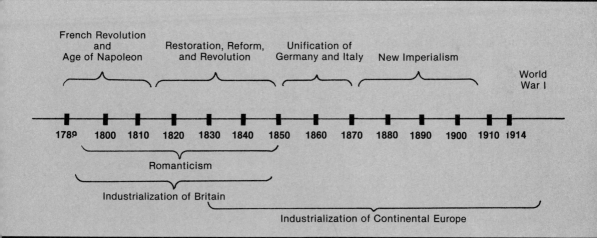

CHAPTER FIVE

The French Revolution

𝕰

In 1789 the French Revolution ended the relative political and social stability of the Ancien Régime. This, and the earlier American Revolution, led to political and social changes that swept through Western civilization in the nineteenth and twentieth centuries.

Although the causes of the French Revolution are deep and controversial, most agree it was precipitated by financial problems that led Louis XVI to call a meeting of an old representative institution, the Estates General, in 1789. A struggle for power soon developed between a resurgent aristocracy and a rising middle class, both demanding support from the king. In an environment where peasants were turning against the aristocracy in the countryside and crowds were resorting to violence in Paris, the king managed to alienate both sides. Revolutionary legislation soon followed. By 1792 France was a constitutional monarchy, feudalism was abolished, liberal principles echoing Enlightenment thought were formally recognized, Church lands were confiscated, and government administration was reorganized. The country was at war internally with counterrevolutionary forces and externally with much of the rest of Europe.

A second revolution in 1792 set France on a more radical course. Louis XVI was executed, and the government was declared a republic. Real power rested in the hands of the small Committee of Public Safety, which attacked internal dissent through the Reign of Terror and external wars through national mobilization. The period ended with a return to a more moderate course in 1794 and 1795, known as Thermidorian Reaction. With power in the hands of the well-to-do middle class, an uneasy balance was maintained between forces clamoring for more radical policies and those wishing to return the monarchy until 1799, when Napoleon Bonaparte rose to power by means of a *coup d'état*.

Historians are fascinated by revolutions, for change is unusually rapid and dramatic. They are particularly interested in the causes of revolutions. In this chapter several primary documents address questions related to the causes of the French Revolution. What were some early signs of revolutionary discontent? What complaints were voiced by the middle class and by the commoners—the Third Estate? How did leaders of this Third Estate see themselves? Related secondary documents explore some of the interpretive debates over the revolution: Was this mainly a social revolution? What was the influence of the Enlightenment on the French Revolution? Should the French Revolution be viewed as part of a broader revolutionary movement throughout Western civilization? Other sources examine the course and effects of the French Revolution. What happened is of particular importance, since the French Revolution was seen as a model for

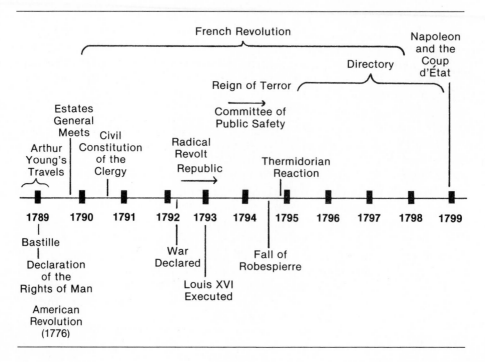

other revolutions and hoped-for revolutions. What were the main changes enacted during the Revolution? How can we explain the most radical phase—the Reign of Terror? What role did women play in revolutionary events? What part did nationalism play in revolutionary developments?

In short, the selections should provide broad insights into the nature and significance of the French Revolution, which more than any other event marks a dividing line between the Early Modern and the Modern eras of Western civilization.

PRIMARY SOURCES

Travels in France: Signs of Revolution

Arthur Young

In one sense, the French Revolution came as a great surprise. One of the last places people might have expected a revolution to occur was in a country so advanced and with such a stable monarchy as France. Yet to some sensitive observers of the time, the signs of revolution were at hand during the late 1780s. One of these observers was Arthur Young (1741–1820), a British farmer and diarist, best known for his writings on agricultural subjects. Between 1787 and 1789 he traveled extensively throughout France, keeping a diary of his experiences. In the following selection from that diary, Young notes deep dissatisfactions among the French.

> **Consider:** *The problems and dissatisfactions that gave the French a sense of impending revolution; the specific problems that seemed most likely to lead to a revolutionary crisis and the steps that might have been taken to avoid such a crisis; how Young felt about these problems and dissatisfactions.*

Paris, October 17, 1787

One opinion pervaded the whole company, that they are on the eve of some great revolution in the government: that every thing points to it: the confusion in the finances great; with a *deficit* impossible to provide for without the states-general of the kingdom, yet no ideas formed of what would be the consequence of their meeting: no minister existing, or to be looked to in or out of power, with such decisive talents as to promise any other remedy than palliative ones: a prince on the throne, with excellent dispositions, but

Source: Arthur Young, *Arthur Young's Travels in France During the Years 1787, 1788, 1789*, Miss Betham-Edwards, ed., 4th ed. (London: Bell, 1892), pp. 97–98, 124, 134.

without the resources of a mind that could govern in such a moment without ministers: a court buried in pleasure and dissipation; and adding to the distress, instead of endeavouring to be placed in a more independent situation: a great ferment amongst all ranks of men, who are eager for some change, without knowing what to look to, or to hope for: and a strong leaven of liberty, increasing every hour since the American revolution; altogether form a combination of circumstances that promise e'er long to ferment into motion, if some master hand, of very superior talents, and inflexible courage, is not found at the helm to guide events, instead of being driven by them. It is very remarkable, that such conversation never occurs, but a bankruptcy is a topic: the curious question on which is, *would a bankruptcy occasion a civil war, and a total overthrow of the government?* These answers that I have received to this question, appear to be just: such a measure, conducted by a man of abilities, vigour, and firmness, would certainly not occasion either one or the other. But the same measure, attempted by a man of a different character, might possibly do both. All agree, that the states of the kingdom cannot assemble without more liberty being the consequence; but I meet with so few men that have any just ideas of freedom, that I question much the species of this new liberty that is to arise. They know not how to value the privileges of THE PEOPLE: as to the nobility and the clergy, if a revolution added any thing to their scale, I think it would do more mischief than good. . . .

RENNES, SEPTEMBER 2, 1788

The discontents of the people have been double, first on account of the high price of bread, and secondly for the banishment of the parliament. The former cause is natural enough, but why the people should love their parliament was what I could not understand, since the members, as well as of the states, are all noble, and the distinction between the *noblesse* and *roturiers* no where stronger, more offensive, or more abominable than in Bretagne. They assured me, however, that the populace have been blown up to violence by every art of deception, and even by money distributed for that purpose. The commotions rose to such a height before the camp was established, that the troops here were utterly unable to keep the peace. . . .

NANTES, SEPTEMBER 22, 1788

Nantes is as *enflammé* in the cause of liberty, as any town in France can be; the conversations I witnessed here, prove how great a change is effected in the minds of the French, nor do I believe it will be possible for the present government to last half a century longer, unless the clearest and most decided talents are at the helm. The American revolution has laid the foundation of another in France, if government does not take care of itself.

The Cahiers: Discontents of the Third Estate

Pressured by discontent and financial problems, Louis XVI called for a meeting of the Estates General in 1789. This representative institution, which had not met for 175 years, reflected the traditional formal divisions in French society: the First Estate, the clergy; the Second Estate, the nobility; and the Third Estate, all the rest from banker and lawyer to peasant. In anticipation of the meeting of the Estates General, the king requested and received cahiers, *lists of grievances drawn up by local groups of each of the three Estates. These* cahiers *have provided historians with an unusually rich source of materials revealing what was bothering people just before the outbreak of the revolution in 1789. The following is an excerpt from a* cahier *from the Third Estate in Carcassonne.*

> **Consider:** *How these grievances of the Third Estate compare to the grievances noted by Young; why these grievances might be revolutionary; the ways in which these grievances are peculiar to the Third Estate and not shared by the First and Second Estates.*

8. Among these rights the following should be especially noted: the nation should hereafter be subject only to such laws and taxes as it shall itself freely ratify.

9. The meetings of the Estates General of the kingdom should be fixed for definite periods, and the subsidies judged necessary for the support of the state and the public service should be noted for no longer a period than to the close of the year in which the next meeting of the Estates General is to occur.

10. In order to assure to the third estate the influence to which it is entitled in view of the number of its members, the amount of its contributions to the public treasury, and the manifold interests which it has to defend or promote in the national assemblies, its votes in the assembly should be taken and counted by head.

11. No order, corporation, or individual citizen may lay claim to any pecuniary exemptions. . . . All taxes should be assessed on the same system throughout the nation.

12. The due exacted from commoners holding fiefs should be abolished, and also the general or particular regulations which exclude members of the third estate from certain positions, offices, and ranks which have hitherto been bestowed on nobles either for life or hereditarily. A law should be passed declaring members of the third estate qualified to fill all such offices for which they are judged to be personally fitted.

SOURCE: "Cahier of the Grievances, Complaints, and Protests of the Electoral District of Carcassone. . . . " From James Harvey Robinson, ed., *Readings in European History*, Vol. II (Boston: Ginn, 1904), pp. 399–400.

13. Since individual liberty is intimately associated with national liberty, his Majesty is hereby petitioned not to permit that it be hereafter interfered with by arbitrary orders for imprisonment. . . .

14. Freedom should be granted also to the press, which should however be subjected, by means of strict regulations, to the principles of religion, morality, and public decency. . . .

What Is the Third Estate?

Emmanuel Joseph Sieyès

Before the Estates General met, issues arose among the Estates, particularly over whether the combined First and Second Estates should be able to hold the preponderance of power when the Estates General met. One of the most wide-ranging attacks on the privileged orders and assertion of Third Estate rights came from Emmanuel Joseph Sieyès (1748–1836). A clergyman strongly influenced by Enlightenment ideas, Sieyès was eventually elected as a representative of the Third Estate and played an active role in events throughout the revolutionary and Napoleonic periods. The following is a selection from his pamphlet, What Is the Third Estate?, *which was published in January 1789 and gained quick popularity.*

> **Consider:** *The basis for the attack by Sieyès on the nobility; why members of the bourgeoisie might find this pamphlet very appealing; how the tone and content of this pamphlet compare with the* cahier.

It suffices here to have made it clear that the pretended utility of a privileged order for the public service is nothing more than a chimera; that with it all that which is burdensome in this service is performed by the Third Estate; that without it the superior places would be infinitely better filled; that they naturally ought to be the lot and the recompense of ability and recognized services, and that if privileged persons have come to usurp all the lucrative and honorable posts, it is a hateful injustice to the rank and file of citizens and at the same time a treason to the public weal.

Who then shall dare to say that the Third Estate has not within itself all that is necessary for the formation of a complete nation? It is the strong and robust man who has one arm still shackled. If the privileged order should be abolished, the nation would be nothing less, but something more. Therefore, what is the Third Estate? Everything; but an everything shackled and oppressed. What would it be without the privileged order? Everything, but an everything free and flourishing. Nothing can succeed without it, everything would be infinitely better without the others. . . .

SOURCE: From Merrick Whitcomb, ed., "French Philosophers of the Eighteenth Century," in *Translations and Reprints from the Original Sources of European History*, Vol. VI, No. 1, Department of History of the University of Pennsylvania, ed. (Philadelphia: University of Pennsylvania Press, 1898), pp. 34–35.

What is a nation? A body of associates, living under a common law, and represented by the same legislature, etc.

It is not evident that the noble order has privileges and expenditures which it dares to call its rights, but which are apart from the rights of the great body of citizens? It departs there from the common order, from the common law. So its civil rights make of it an isolated people in the midst of the great nation. This is truly *imperium in imperio*.

In regard to its political rights, these also it exercises apart. It has its special representatives, which are not charged with securing the interests of the people. The body of its deputies sit apart; and when it is assembled in the same hall with the deputies of simple citizens, it is none the less true that its representation is essentially distinct and separate: it is a stranger to the nation, in the first place, by its origin, since its commission is not derived from the people; then by its object, which consists of defending not the general, but the particular interest.

The Third Estate embraces then all that which belongs to the nation; and all that which is not the Third Estate, cannot be regarded as being of the nation. What is the Third Estate? It is the whole.

Revolutionary Legislation: Abolition of the Feudal System

During the summer of 1789, France was swept with a variety of revolutionary activities. The Third Estate had successfully formed the National Assembly. On July 14 a mob had stormed the Bastille, an act that symbolized a violent tearing down of the Ancien Régime and the beginning of the popular revolution. In the countryside the peasantry rose against the nobility. Faced with these pressures, elements of the nobility in the National Assembly moved on August 4 and 5 to abolish their own feudal rights and privileges. In sum, these laws constituted a formal repudiation of the feudal system and many of the institutions of the Ancien Régime. The following selection comes from that legislation.

> **Consider:** *The extent to which these measures satisfied the grievances of the Third Estate as expressed in the* cahier *and the pamphlet by Sieyès; why members of the nobility proposed and supported these measures themselves; whether these measures should be interpreted as a repudiation of the monarchy as an institution or specifically of Louis XVI as the king.*

ARTICLE I. The National Assembly hereby completely abolishes the feudal system. It decrees that, among the existing rights and dues, . . . all those

SOURCE: From James Harvey Robinson, ed., "The French Revolution, 1789–1791," in *Translations and Reprints from the Original Sources of European History*, Vol. I, No. 5, Department of History of the University of Pennsylvania, ed. (Philadelphia: University of Pennsylvania Press, 1898), pp. 2–5.

originating in or representing real or personal serfdom or personal servitude, shall be abolished without indemnification.

IV. All manorial courts are hereby suppressed without indemnification. . . .

V. Tithes of every description, as well as the dues which have been substituted for them. . . . are abolished, on condition, however, that some other method be devised to provide for the expenses of divine worship, the support of the officiating clergy, for the assistance of the poor, for repairs and rebuilding of churches and parsonages, and for the maintenance of all institutions, seminaries, schools, academies, asylums, and organizations to which the present funds are devoted.

VII. The sale of judicial and municipal offices shall be suppressed forthwith. Justice shall be dispensed *gratis*.

IX. Pecuniary privileges, personal or real, in the payment of taxes are abolished forever. Taxes shall be collected from all the citizens, and from all property, in the same manner and in the same form. . . .

X. . . . All the peculiar privileges, pecuniary or otherwise, of the provinces, principalities, districts, cantons, cities and communes, are once for all abolished and are absorbed into the law common to all Frenchmen.

XI. All citizens, without distinction of birth, are eligible to any office or dignity, whether ecclesiastical, civil or military; and no profession shall imply any derogation.

XVII. The National Assembly solemnly proclaims the King, Louis XVI., the *Restorer of French Liberty*.

XVIII. The National Assembly shall present itself in a body before the King, in order to submit to him the decrees which have just been passed, to tender to him the tokens of its most respectful gratitude. . . .

XIX. The National Assembly shall consider, immediately after the constitution, the drawing up of the laws necessary for the development of the principles which it has laid down in the present decree.

The Declaration of the Rights of Man and Citizen

No document better summarizes the ideals underlying the French Revolution than The Declaration of the Rights of Man and Citizen. *After an extended discussion,*

SOURCE: James Harvey Robinson, ed., "The French Revolution, 1789–1791," in *Translations and Reprints from the Original Sources of European History*, Vol. I, No. 5, Department of History of the University of Pennsylvania, ed. (Philadelphia: University of Pennsylvania Press, 1898), pp. 6–8.

this document was passed by the National Assembly on August 27, 1789; later a revised version of it was incorporated into the Constitution of 1791. Its provisions are a combination of general statements about human rights and specific statements about what the government should and should not do. This document corresponds to the American Declaration of Independence. It is also viewed more broadly as containing the general principles for democratic revolutions in the eighteenth and nineteenth centuries.

> **Consider:** *How this document reflects ideals of the Enlightenment; at which social groups this document was aimed; who would suffer most from or be most infuriated by its provisions; the ways in which this document is inconsistent with monarchical government; how a monarch might retain meaningful powers while still conforming to this document.*

The representatives of the French people, organized as a National Assembly, believing that the ignorance, neglect or contempt of the rights of man are the sole cause of public calamities and of the corruption of governments, have determined to set forth in a solemn declaration the natural, inalienable and sacred rights of man, in order that this declaration, being constantly before all the members of the social body, shall remind them continually of their rights and duties; in order that the acts of the legislative power, as well as those of the executive power, may be compared at any moment with the ends of all political institutions and may thus be more respected; and, lastly, in order that the grievances of the citizens, based hereafter upon simple and incontestable principles, shall tend to the maintenance of the constitution and redound to the happiness of all. Therefore the National Assembly recognizes and proclaims, in the presence and under the auspices of the Supreme Being, the following rights of man and of the citizen: —

ARTICLE 1. Men are born and remain free and equal in rights. Social distinctions may only be founded upon the general good.

2. The aim of all political association is the preservation of the natural and imprescriptible rights of man. These rights are liberty, property, security and resistance to oppression.

3. The principle of all sovereignty resides essentially in the nation. No body nor individual may exercise any authority which does not proceed directly from the nation.

4. Liberty consists in the freedom to do everything which injures no one else; hence the exercise of the natural rights of each man has no limits except those which assure to the other members of the society the enjoyment of the same rights. These limits can only be determined by law.

5. Law can only prohibit such actions as are hurtful to society. Nothing may be prevented which is not forbidden by law, and no one may be forced to do anything not provided for by law.

6. Law is the expression of the general will. Every citizen has a right to participate personally or through his representative in its formation. It must

be the same for all, whether it protects or punishes. All citizens, being equal in the eyes of the law, are equally eligible to all dignities and to all public positions and occupations, according to their abilities, and without distinction except that of their virtues and talents.

7. No person shall be accused, arrested or imprisoned except in the cases and according to the forms prescribed by law. Any one soliciting, transmitting, executing or causing to be executed any arbitrary order shall be punished. But any citizen summoned or arrested in virtue of the law shall submit without delay, as resistance constitutes an offence.

8. The law shall provide for such punishments only as are strictly and obviously necessary, and no one shall suffer punishment except it be legally inflicted in virtue of a law passed and promulgated before the commission of the offence.

9. As all persons are held innocent until they shall have been declared guilty, if arrest shall be deemed indispensable, all harshness not essential to the securing of the prisoner's person shall be severely repressed by law.

10. No one shall be disquieted on account of his opinions, including his religious views, provided their manifestation does not disturb the public order established by law.

11. The free communication of ideas and opinions is one of the most precious of the rights of man. Every citizen may, accordingly, speak, write and print with freedom, but shall be responsible for such abuses of this freedom as shall be defined by law.

12. The security of the rights of man and of the citizen requires public military force. These forces are, therefore, established for the good of all and not for the personal advantage of those to whom they shall be entrusted.

13. A common contribution is essential for the maintenance of the public forces and for the cost of administration. This should be equitably distributed among all the citizens in proportion to their means.

14. All the citizens have a right to decide, either personally or by their representatives, as to the necessity of the public contribution; to grant this freely; to know to what uses it is put; and to fix the proportion, the mode of assessment, and of collection, and the duration of the taxes.

15. Society has the right to require of every public agent an account of his administration.

16. A society in which the observance of the law is not assured, nor the separation of powers defined, has no constitution at all.

17. Since property is an inviolable and sacred right, no one shall be deprived thereof except where public necessity, legally determined, shall clearly demand it, and then only on condition that the owner shall have been previously and equitably indemnified.

The Declaration of Independence

The American Revolution preceded the French Revolution by a few years. Yet its priority in time does not give it priority in historical importance. At that time America was at the fringes of Western civilization while France was at its heart. Nevertheless, the American Revolution influenced the French Revolution in a variety of ways. One similarity between the two is their two great declarations: the American Declaration of Independence *(1776) and the French* Declaration of the Rights of Man and Citizen *(1789). Although it is uncertain whether the French were directly influenced by the American document, both are products of common ideas of the late eighteenth century and show evidence of a strong relationship between these ideas and revolutionary activities in Western civilization. The* Declaration of Independence *was written primarily by Thomas Jefferson. The following selection comes from the beginning of this document.*

> **Consider:** *The usefulness of this standard for evaluating the legitimacy of a revolution; similarities between the French and American declarations; how these two documents differ in purpose and substance.*

When in the Course of human events, it becomes necessary for one people to dissolve the political bands which have connected them with another, and to assume among the powers of the earth, the separate and equal station to which the Laws of Nature and of Nature's God entitle them, a decent respect to the opinions of mankind requires that they should declare the causes which impel them to the separation. — We hold these truths to be self-evident, that all men are created equal, that they are endowed by their Creator with certain unalienable Rights, that among these are Life, Liberty and the pursuit of Happiness. — That to secure these rights, Governments are instituted among Men, deriving their just powers from the consent of the governed, — That whenever any Form of Government becomes destructive of these ends, it is the Right of the People to alter or to abolish it, and to institute new Government, laying its foundation on such principles and organizing its powers in such form, as to them shall seem most likely to effect their Safety and Happiness. Prudence, indeed, will dictate that Governments long established should not be changed for light and transient causes; and accordingly all experience hath shewn, that mankind are more disposed to suffer, while evils are sufferable, than to right themselves by abolishing the forms to which they are accustomed. But when a long train of abuses and usurpations, pursuing invariably the same Object evinces a design to reduce them under absolute Despotism, it is their right, it is their duty, to throw off such Govern-

---

SOURCE: *The Declaration of Independence, 1776* (Washington, D. C.: U. S. Department of State, 1911), pp. 3–8.

ment, and to provide new Guards for their future security. — Such has been the patient sufferance of these Colonies; and such is now the necessity which constrains them to alter their former Systems of Government.

Speech to the National Convention — February 5, 1794: The Terror Justified

Maximilien Robespierre

Between 1793 and 1794, France experienced the most radical phase of the Revolution, known as the Reign of Terror. During this period France was essentially ruled by the twelve-member Committee of Public Safety elected by the National Convention every month. The outstanding member of this committee was Maximilien Robespierre (1758–1794), a provincial lawyer who rose within the Jacobin Club and gained a reputation for incorruptibility and superb oratory. Historians have argued over Robespierre, some singling him out as a bloodthirsty individual with the major responsibility for the executions during the Reign of Terror, others seeing him as a sincere, idealistic, effective revolutionary leader called to the fore by events of the time. In the following speech to the National Convention on February 5, 1794, Robespierre defines the revolution and justifies extreme actions, including terror, in its defense.

> **Consider:** *What Robespierre means when he argues that terror flows from virtue; how the use of terror relates to the essence of the revolution; how this speech might be interpreted as an Enlightenment attack on the Ancien Régime carried to its logical conclusion.*

It is time to mark clearly the aim of the Revolution and the end toward which we wish to move; it is time to take stock of ourselves, of the obstacles which we still face, and of the means which we ought to adopt to attain our objectives. . . .

What is the goal for which we strive? A peaceful enjoyment of liberty and equality, the rule of that eternal justice whose laws are engraved, not upon marble or stone, but in the hearts of all men.

We wish an order of things where all low and cruel passions are enchained by the laws, all beneficent and generous feelings aroused; where ambition is

SOURCE: Raymond P. Stearns, ed., *Pageant of Europe*. Reprinted by permission of Harcourt Brace Jovanovich, Inc. (New York, 1947), pp. 404–405.

the desire to merit glory and to serve one's fatherland; where distinctions are born only of equality itself; where the citizen is subject to the magistrate, the magistrate to the people, the people to justice; where the nation safeguards the welfare of each individual, and each individual proudly enjoys the prosperity and glory of his fatherland; where all spirits are enlarged by the constant exchange of republican sentiments and by the need of earning the respect of a great people; where the arts are the adornment of liberty, which ennobles them; and where commerce is the source of public wealth, not simply of monstrous opulence for a few families.

In our country we wish to substitute morality for egotism, probity for honor, principles for conventions, duties for etiquette, the empire of reason for the tyranny of customs, contempt for vice for contempt for misfortune, pride for insolence, the love of honor for the love of money . . . that is to say, all the virtues and miracles of the Republic for all the vices and snobbishness of the monarchy.

We wish in a word to fulfill the requirements of nature, to accomplish the destiny of mankind, to make good the promises of philosophy . . . that France, hitherto illustrious among slave states, may eclipse the glory of all free peoples that have existed, become the model of all nations. . . . That is our ambition; that is our aim.

What kind of government can realize these marvels? Only a democratic government. . . . But to found and to consolidate among us this democracy, to realize the peaceable rule of constitutional laws, it is necessary to conclude the war of liberty against tyranny and to pass successfully through the storms of revolution. Such is the aim of the revolutionary system which you have set up. . . .

Now what is the fundamental principle of democratic, or popular government—that is to say, the essential mainspring upon which it depends and which makes it function? It is virtue: I mean public virtue . . . that virtue which is nothing else but love of fatherland and its laws. . . .

The splendor of the goal of the French Revolution is simultaneously the source of our strength and of our weakness: our strength, because it gives us an ascendancy of truth over falsehood, and of public rights over private interests; our weakness, because it rallies against us all vicious men, all those who in their hearts seek to despoil the people. . . . It is necessary to stifle the domestic and foreign enemies of the Republic or perish with them. Now in these circumstances, the first maxim of our politics ought to be to lead the people by means of reason and the enemies of the people by terror.

If the basis of popular government in time of peace is virtue, the basis of popular government in time of revolution is both virtue and terror: virtue without which terror is murderous, terror without which virtue is powerless. Terror is nothing else than swift, severe, indomitable justice; it flows, then, from virtue.

A Soldier's Letters to His Mother: Revolutionary Nationalism

François-Xavier Joliclerc

Despite tremendous internal difficulties, including counterrevolutionary movements in a number of provinces, French armies held back foreign forces after war broke out in 1792, but by 1794 the French forces had even made gains beyond the 1789 borders. Part of the reason for this success was the nationalistic enthusiasm that developed along with the revolution. This nationalism is demonstrated by the following letters from François-Xavier Joliclerc, a conscript in the French army, to his mother.

Consider: *The divisions within French society revealed in these letters; why such sentiments among soldiers are so important and how political leaders or military strategists might capitalize on them; whether the nationalism revealed in these letters is inherent in the nature of the French Revolution or in any particular phase of that revolution.*

13 December, 1793

My dear mother,

You continue to point out to me, in all your letters, that we must get out of the army, cost what it may. Here are the difficulties and the obstacles that I can see.

First of all, it is difficult to find replacements despite the enormous sums that are expended for this purpose. Secondly, we have just had a call-up of men eighteen to twenty-five; and the call-up of those from twenty-five to thirty-five is being prepared. As soon as we got home, we would have to get ready to go back, regretting the money we had spent. Thirdly, when *la patrie* calls us to her defense, we ought to fly there as if running to a good meal. Our life, our wealth, and our talents do not belong to us. It is to the nation, *la patrie*, that all that belongs.

I know well that you and all the others in our village do not share these sentiments. They are not aroused by the cries of an outraged fatherland, and all that they do results from being compelled to. But I have been brought up in conscience and thought, and have always been republican in spirit, although obliged to live in a monarchy. These principles of love for *la patrie, la liberté, la république,* are not only engraved in my heart, but are

---

Source: From Ludwig F. Schaefer, Daniel P. Resnick, and George F. Netterville, eds., *The Shaping of Western Civilization*, Vol. II, Daniel P. Resnick, trans. (New York: Holt, Rinehart and Winston, Inc., 1970), p. 216. Reprinted by permission of the editors.

deeply etched and will remain there as long as it will please the Supreme Being to sustain in me the breath of life.

Even if it cost me three quarters of my possessions to have you share these sentiments with me, I would gladly part with them and consider it a very small sacrifice. Oh, if only one day you could know the price of liberty and lose your senseless attachment to material things.

30 May, 1794

What about my lot? I am at my post, where I ought to be, and every good man who knows what's what ought to fly to the aid of his country in danger. If I should perish there, you ought to rejoice. Can one make a finer sacrifice than to die for one's country? Can one die for a more just, glorious, and fairer cause? No! Would you rather see me die on a mattress of straw in my bed at Froidefontaine [his home village] working with wood or stone?

No, dear mother. Think that I am at my post and you will be consoled. If your conscience reproaches you in some way, sell even the last of your petticoats for *la patrie*. She is our only rudder, and it is she who guides us and gives us happiness. . . .

Your son, Joliclerc

VISUAL SOURCES

Allegory of the Revolution
Jeaurat de Bertray

Jeaurat de Bertray's Allegory of the Revolution *(see p. 106) is literally a jumble of historical and revolutionary symbols. At the top is a portrait of Jean Jacques Rousseau, at the time considered by many the spiritual and intellectual father of the French Revolution even though he never advocated revolution and died eleven years before it began. Below him are the new flags of the French Republic, the one on the left with the nationalistic words "love of country." Further to the left is a triangular monument to Equality, below it two maidens representing Goodness and Good Faith, and in the center a bundle of rods and arms topped by a red liberty cap, all symbolizing a fair, forceful republican government. Just below is paper money, the assignats, that helped finance the revolution and pay off debts, and in the center right grows a liberty tree. To the right are two unfinished pillars, the first dedicated to the regeneration of morals and* The Declaration of the Rights of Man and Citizen, *the second to the French Revolution. Just below them and in*

Photo 5-1

Courtesy, Musée Carnavalet/Photographie Bulloz

the background are symbols of forceful determination to uphold and defend the revolution: a guillotine, a cannon, and a soldier. In the right foreground is a peasant wearing a liberty cap and sowing a field. This painting pulls together many symbols and elements of the revolutionary ideology. It was painted in 1794, the time of the most radical phase of the revolution.

Consider: *Connections between this picture,* The Declaration of the Rights of Man and Citizen, *and the Enlightenment; the ways in which the Ancien Régime is rejected symbolically in this picture.*

Internal Disturbances and the Reign of Terror

Understanding of the Reign of Terror has often been distorted by an image of random and purposeless brutality. One way to gain clearer insights into the Terror is through the use of maps and statistics, which reveal where the Terror occurred, how intensive it was, and who its victims were. The two maps presented here compare the amount of civil disturbance facing government officials and the number of executions occurring in the various departments of France during the period of the Terror. The two pie charts compare the estimated percentages of France's population belonging to the various classes in 1789 and during the Terror from March 1793 to August 1794.

Map 5-1   Internal Disturbances

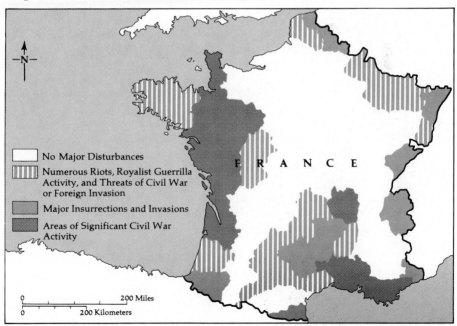

Consider: *How these maps and charts support an argument that the Reign of Terror was not random or purposeless; the hypotheses that might be drawn from these maps and charts about the causes or effects of the Terror.*

Map 5-2   The Incidence of the Terror

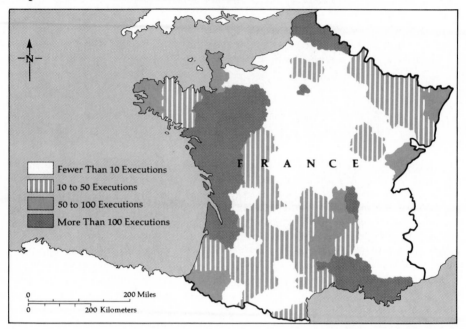

Fewer Than 10 Executions
10 to 50 Executions
50 to 100 Executions
More Than 100 Executions

F R A N C E

0   200 Miles
0   200 Kilometers

Chart 5-1   Classes in France

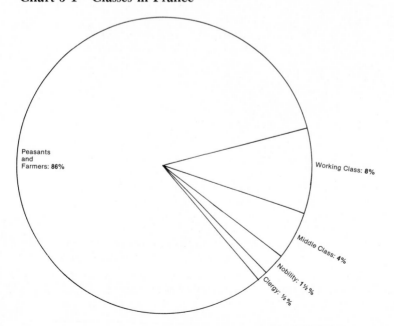

Peasants and Farmers: 86%

Working Class: 8%

Middle Class: 4%

Nobility: 1½%

Clergy: ½%

Chart 5-2   Executions During the Reign of Terror

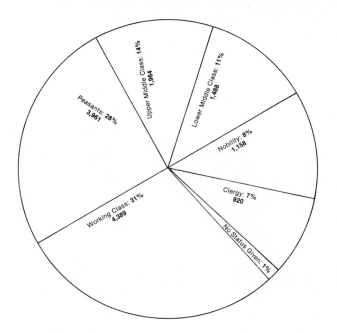

SECONDARY SOURCES

The Coming
of the
French Revolution

Georges Lefebvre

Probably no event in modern history has been interpreted at greater length and with greater passion than the French Revolution. The historiographic tradition related to this event is so extensive that numerous books and articles have been written on this historiography itself. A central controversy involves the cause or causes of the revolution and is dealt with in the following selection from The Coming of the French Revolution *by Georges Lefebvre. Lefebvre held the prestigious*

SOURCE: Georges Lefebvre, *The Coming of the French Revolution*, R. R. Palmer, trans. (Princeton , N.J.: Princeton University Press, 1947), pp. 1–3.

chair of French revolutionary history at the Sorbonne until his death in 1959. His
work on the French Revolution continues to be highly respected and accepted
among historians, many of whom differ greatly among themselves.

> **Consider:** *The most important cause of the French Revolution, according to*
> *Lefebvre; how this interpretation relates the revolution in France to areas out-*
> *side of France; how social, economic, and political factors are linked in this*
> *interpretation of the French Revolution; how this view is supported by the*
> *primary documents.*

The ultimate cause of the French Revolution of 1789 goes deep into the
history of France and of the western world. At the end of the eighteenth
century the social structure of France was aristocratic. It showed the traces
of having originated at a time when land was almost the only form of wealth,
and when the possessors of land were the masters of those who needed it to
work and to live. It is true that in the course of age-old struggles (of which
the Fronde, the last revolt of the aristocracy, was as recent as the seventeenth century) the king had been able gradually to deprive the lords of
their political power and subject nobles and clergy to his authority. But he
had left them the first place in the social hierarchy. Still restless at being
merely his "subjects," they remained privileged persons.

Meanwhile the growth of commerce and industry had created, step by
step, a new form of wealth, mobile or commercial wealth, and a new class,
called in France the bourgeoisie, which since the fourteenth century had
taken its place as the Third Estate in the General Estates of the kingdom.
This class had grown much stronger with the maritime discoveries of the fifteenth and sixteenth centuries and the ensuing exploitation of new worlds,
and also because it proved highly useful to the monarchical state in supply-
ing it with money and competent officials. In the eighteenth century commerce, industry and finance occupied an increasingly important place in the
national economy. It was the bourgeoisie that rescued the royal treasury in
moments of crisis. From its ranks were recruited most members of the
liberal professions and most public employees. It had developed a new
ideology which the "philosophers" and "economists" of the time had simply
put into definite form. The role of the nobility had correspondingly declined;
and the clergy, as the ideal which it proclaimed lost prestige, found its
authority growing weaker. These groups preserved the highest rank in the
legal structure of the country, but in reality economic power, personal
abilities and confidence in the future had passed largely to the bourgeoisie.
Such a discrepancy never lasts forever. The Revolution of 1789 restored the
harmony between fact and law. This transformation spread in the nineteenth century throughout the west and then to the whole globe, and in this
sense the ideas of 1789 toured the world.

The Influence of Eighteenth-Century Ideas on the French Revolution

Henri Peyre

Some historians emphasize economic factors to explain the causes of the French Revolution. Others consider certain ideas, particularly the ideas of the Enlightenment, as the crucial cause of the revolution. This latter reasoning is illustrated in the following selection by Henri Peyre. Born and educated in France, Peyre taught for a long time at Yale. Although his interests ranged widely, most of his work was in the history of French literature.

> **Consider:** *The support Peyre offers for his attack on those stressing economic causes of the French Revolution; how one of these historians might respond; whether documents on the Enlightenment and the primary documents in this chapter support Peyre's interpretation.*

If there is really one almost undisputed conclusion on the origins of the Revolution reached by historical studies coming from radically opposite factions, it is that pure historical materialism does not explain the Revolution. Certainly riots due to hunger were numerous in the eighteenth century and Mornet draws up the list of them; there was discontent and agitation among the masses. But such had also been the case under Louis XIV, such was the case under Louis-Philippe and deep discontent existed in France in 1920 and 1927 and 1934 without ending in revolution. No great event in history has been due to causes chiefly economic in nature and certainly not the French Revolution. France was not happy in 1788, but she was happier than the other countries of Europe and enjoyed veritable economic prosperity. Her population had increased from 19 to 27 millions since the beginning of the century and was the most numerous in Europe. French roads and bridges were a source of admiration for foreigners. Her industries such as ship-fitting at Bordeaux, the silk-industry at Lyons and the textile-industry at Rouen, Sedan and Amiens were active while Dietrich's blast-furnaces and the Creusot were beginning to develop modern techniques in metallurgy. The peasants were little by little coming to be owners of the land. Foreign trade reached the sum of 1,153 million francs in 1787, a figure not to be attained again until 1825. The traffic in colonial spices and San Domingo sugar was a source of wealth. Banks were being founded and France owned

SOURCE: Henri Peyre, "The Influence of Eighteenth-Century Ideas on the French Revolution," Arthur L. Kurth, trans. Reprinted by permission of the *Journal of the History of Ideas*, from that *Journal*, Vol. X, No. 1 (January 1949), pp. 72–73. Copyright © JHI, Inc.

half the specie existing in Europe. So misery in France was no more than relative. But truly wretched peoples such as the Egyptian fellah, the pariah of India or even the Balkan or Polish peasant or Bolivian miners for example rarely bring about revolutions. In order to revolt against one's lot, one must be aware of his wretched condition, which presupposes a certain intellectual and cultural level; one must have a clear conception of certain reforms that one would like to adopt; in short, one must be convinced (and it was on this point that the books of the eighteenth century produced their effect) that things are not going well, that they might be better and that they will be better if the measures proposed by the reformist thinkers are put into practice.

Eighteenth-century philosophy taught the Frenchman to find his condition wretched, or in any case, unjust and illogical and made him disinclined to the patient resignation to his troubles that had long characterized his ancestors. It had never called for a revolution nor desired a change of regime; it had never been republican and Camille Desmouslins was not wrong in stating: "In all France there were not ten of us who were republicans before 1789." Furthermore he himself was not one of those ten. But only an over-simplified conception of influence would indulge in the notion that political upheaval completely embodies in reality the theoretical design drawn up by some thinker. Even the Russian revolution imbued as it was with Marxian dialectic did not make a coherent application of Marxism or quickly found it inapplicable when tried. The reforms of limited scope advocated by *L'Esprit des Lois*, *L'Homme aux quarante écus*, *L'Encyclopédie* and the more moderate writings of Rousseau struck none the less deeply at the foundations of the ancien régime, for they accustomed the Frenchman of the Third Estate to declaring privileges unjust, to finding the crying differences between the provinces illogical and finding famines outrageous. The propaganda of the "Philosophes" perhaps more than any other factor accounted for the fulfillment of the preliminary conditon of the French revolution, namely, discontent with the existing state of things.

The Age of Democratic Revolution

R. R. Palmer

For a long time the French Revolution was studied in relative isolation from other political and social developments of the time. In the years after World War II, some historians viewed the French Revolution in a broader context. The most forceful exponent of this broader view is R. R. Palmer. He places the French

SOURCE: R. R. Palmer, *The Challenge*, Vol. I of *The Age of the Democratic Revolution*. Reprinted by permission of Princeton University Press (Princeton, N.J., 1959), pp. 4–5.

Revolution within the context of the Atlantic civilization and argues that the French Revolution was one aspect of a much broader Age of Democratic Revolution. The following is an excerpt from the first volume of his two-volume work on this age. In it he tells the reader what he will argue.

Consider: *The role the Enlightenment would play in this interpretation; any inconsistencies between this interpretation and the implications of Lefebvre's argument; how this view might elevate the significance of the American Revolution and* The Declaration of Independence.

Let us pass from the concrete image to the broadest of historical generalizations. The present work attempts to deal with Western Civilization as a whole, at a critical moment in its history, or with what has sometimes recently been called the *Atlantic Civilization*, a term probably closer to reality in the eighteenth century than in the twentieth. It is argued that this whole civilization was swept in the last four decades of the eighteenth century by a single revolutionary movement, which manifested itself in different ways and with varying success in different countries, yet in all of them showed similar objectives and principles. It is held that this forty-year movement was essentially "democratic," and that these years are in fact the Age of the Democratic Revolution. "Democratic" is here to be understood in a general but clear enough sense. It was not primarily the sense of a later day in which universality of the suffrage became a chief criterion of democracy, nor yet that other and uncertain sense, also of a later day, in which both Soviet and Western-type states could call themselves democratic. In one way, it signified a new feeling for a kind of equality, or at least a discomfort with older forms of social stratification and formal rank, such as Thomas Shippen felt at Versailles, and which indeed had come to affect a good many of the habitués of Versailles also. Politically, the eighteenth-century movement was against the possession of government, or any public power, by any established, privileged, closed, or self-recruiting groups of men. It denied that any person could exercise coercive authority simply by his own right, or by right of his status, or by right of "history," either in the old-fashioned sense of custom and inheritance, or in any newer dialectical sense, unknown to the eighteenth century, in which "history" might be supposed to give some special elite or revolutionary vanguard a right to rule. The "democratic revolution" emphasized the delegation of authority and the removability of officials, precisely because, as we shall see, neither delegation nor removability were much recognized in actual institutions.

It is a corollary of these ideas that the American and the French Revolutions, the two chief actual revolutions of the period, with all due allowance for the great differences between them, nevertheless shared a good deal in common, and that what they shared was shared also at the same time by various people and movements in other countries, notably in England, Ireland, Holland, Belgium, Switzerland, and Italy, but also in Germany, Hungary, and Poland, and by scattered individuals in places like Spain and Russia.

Loaves and Liberty: Women in the French Revolution

Ruth Graham

Historians have long recognized that women played an important role in certain aspects of the French Revolution. But only in the last twenty years have extensive examinations been made of the significance of the French Revolution for women's history. The following selection by Ruth Graham is a good example of this recent work.

> **Consider:** *Any connections between sex and class lines in the French Revolution; the ways in which women became a "revolutionary force unprecedented in history" during the revolution; what Graham means by women's victories and defeats.*

It would be wrong to assume that because women had come into the Revolution in 1789 asking for bread and liberty and had come out in 1795 with starvation and restriction of their movements, they had gained nothing. They won laws protecting their rights in marriage, property, and education. True, women were denied political rights in the French Revolution (as were the majority of men when the Convention scrapped the democratic constitution of 1793) but nowhere else at the time did women share political rights with men.

Although women were a cohesive group during the Revolution, they responded mainly to the needs of their class and were never an autonomous force. The ideology of the revolutionary authorities who distrusted women's political movements derived seemingly from Rousseau, but actually from the facts of their lives: France's small-scale, home-based economy needed middle- and working-class women to contribute their special skills and labor to their families. Women were not yet a large, independent group in the working class.

In the early days of the French Revolution, women from the middle classes (as can be seen from cahiers written by them) welcomed the restoration of their natural rights as wives and mothers to participate in society as men's "natural companions." Women of the urban poor — wage earners, artisans of women's crafts, owners of small enterprises, such as the market women — agitated for bread rather than for women's rights. There is, however, evidence that "respectable" middle-class women joined them. Although these movements crossed class lines, which were perhaps not rigidly fixed,

---

SOURCE: Ruth Graham, "Loaves and Liberty: Women in the French Revolution," in Renate Bridenthal and Claudia Koonz, eds., *Becoming Visible: Women in European History* (Boston: Houghton Mifflin, 1977), pp. 251–253.

they did not cross sex lines. When men participated, as they did in the October Days of 1789, they came as armed escorts or separate detachments.

As the Revolution entered its more radical phase, as economic crisis
followed war and civil strife, the polarization between the rich and the poor
sharpened the older struggle between aristocrat and patriot. During the last
days of the National Convention, the women who surged into the hall crying "Bread and the Constitution of 1793!" truly represented the poor, whom
the upper classes and their women now feared. The bread riots belonged to
the women of the poor, who incited their men to insurrection, but the insurrection belonged to both of them, the sans-culottes and their women.

Yet, the Revolution had called upon women to make great sacrifices and
they did; in consequence, women became a revolutionary force unprecedented in history. The men in power feared women who challenged the
Revolution's failure to guarantee bread for the poor. So feared were the
women of the French Revolution that they became legendary — they
became Mme. Defarge later to those who feared revolution itself.

A new elite of the upper middle class, men of wealth and talent, rose to
power in the four years of the Directory following the dissolution in 1795 of
the National Convention. Their women had no political rights but emerged
as influential ladies of the salon, such as the brilliant writer Mme. de Staël,
and Mme. Tallien, former wife of an aristocrat and now derisively called
"Our Lady of Thermidor," as a symbol of the reaction. One of these ladies,
Josephine de Beauharnais, the widow of a general, became the mistress of
one of the Directors before she married the young Napoleon Bonaparte,
who soon afterward became general of the armies in Italy.

Outside of Paris, away from the glamour of these women, middle-class
morality prevailed. Napoleon subscribed to this morality. When he became
emperor in 1804, he wrote laws into his code to strengthen the authority of
the husband and father of the family as a safeguard for private property.
Women lost whatever rights they had gained in the Revolution, for now
they had to obey their husbands unconditionally. Napoleon left women the
right to divorce (for Napoleon to use against Josephine when she failed to
provide him an heir), but this right was taken from them after 1815 by the
restoration of the Bourbon monarchy.

What could not be taken from women was their memory of victories during the French Revolution: their march to Versailles in the October Days,
their petitions to the legislature, their club meetings, their processions, their
insurrections. Their defeats served as lessons for next time. "We are simple
women," a women was reported to have said at a club meeting in the days
of the uprising of the Paris Commune in May 1871, nearly a century later,
"but not made of weaker stuff than our grandmothers of '93. Let us not
cause their shades to blush for us, but be up and doing, as they would be
were they living now."

An Evaluation of the French Revolution

John Hall Stewart

Although most would say that rapid and vast changes occurred during the French Revolution, it is difficult to evaluate the extent to which these changes were more apparent than real. Many historians have concluded that while the revolution stood for much, most of the promises made by the Third Estate and contained in The Declaration of the Rights of Man and Citizen *were not carried out. In the following selection John Hall Stewart, compiler of an extensive documentary survey of the revolution, attempts to strike a balance between what was and was not accomplished between 1789 and 1799.*

> **Consider:** *Examples of what Hall calls "disestablishment," "innovation," and "compromise" during the French Revolution between 1789 and 1799; how Hall's argument might be used by those opposing revolutions in general.*

It might safely be said that never in human history, or at least never prior to 1799, had so much been achieved by one people in such a short span of time! Yet, lest the uninformed naïvely assume that between 1789 and 1799 some divine force had transformed France from a purgatory into a paradise, the foregoing impressive list of apparent achievements must be balanced against the *actual* accomplishments. In other words, how much of what was done progressed beyond the "paper" state, how much failed in the effort? And, it must be admitted, here the opponents of the Revolution find much of their material for criticism. A few significant examples will suffice as evidence.

Politically, constitutionalism had been accepted, but the constitution of 1799 was a farce; declarations of rights had been made three times, but each time they had been more form than substance, and in 1799 they were omitted entirely; democracy had never been really tried — 1799 inaugurated a dictatorship; the liberties of the subject had been flagrantly violated during the Terror; in 1799 it appeared that equality and security were preferable to liberty; and protection of property had been of little help to the clergy or the *émigrés*.

Economically, "free" land was a reality only for those who possessed the wherewithal to purchase it; agricultural reforms were still in the future; workers lacked the right to organize and to strike; and the fiscal and financial situation left by the Directory was worse than that facing the Estates General — stability was still lacking.

SOURCE: John Hall Stewart, *A Documentary Survey of the French Revolution*. Reprinted by permission of Macmillan (New York, 1951), pp. 789–790. Copyright © 1951 by Macmillan Publishing Co., Inc., renewed 1979 by John Hall Stewart.

Socially, the bourgeoisie had supplanted the clergy and nobles, but the common man still awaited his due; class consciousness persisted, and privilege was still sought; many of the social reforms proposed never passed outside the legislative halls; and socialism was a dead issue.

Religiously, France was still Catholic, and neither the Revolution nor its attempt at a synthetic faith had altered the situation; anti-Protestantism and anti-Semitism were by no means obliterated; and the revolutionary legislation affecting the Church had produced a schism which remained for Napoleon to heal.

Finally, despite a brief taste of the several freedoms, France was entering upon a period in which censorshop was to keep news of Trafalgar from the columns of the *Moniteur*, and education was to become little more than Bonapartist propaganda; in fact, the educational projects of the Revolution remained, for the most part, decently interred in statute books.

Yet this situation was by no means abnormal. It should neither encourage the counter-revolutionary nor discourage the revolutionary. As fundamental change, the Revolution inevitably worked through a three-fold process: *disestablishment* (of outmoded old institutions); *innovation* (through badly needed new institutions); and *compromise* (by adaptation of existing institutions to the necessities of the moment). The original objectives — which, for convenience, may perhaps best be summed up as *liberty, equality,* and *order* — could be achieved in no other way. What appears to be failure is nothing more than proof that in such movements the forces of reaction are strong, and the ambitions of men usually far exceed the ability of those same men to put their plans to practical use.

Chapter Questions

1. What seems to have motivated many of the revolutionaries, as revealed by the demands made prior to the French Revolution and the actions taken during the revolution?

2. What factors help explain why this revolution occurred in France, one of the most prosperous and powerful nations of Europe? What does this explanation add to the significance of the revolution?

3. With the advantage of hindsight, what might the monarchy have done to retain control and minimize revolutionary changes?

4. In what ways should the French Revolution be considered a middle-class revolution?

CHAPTER SIX

The Age of Napoleon

In 1799 members of the ruling Directory conspired with the well-known military leader Napoleon Bonaparte (1769–1821) to take over the French government by means of a *coup d'état*. It was successful, and Napoleon quickly asserted his own dominance over others. By 1802 he had full power, and by 1804 he was the self-proclaimed Emperor Napoleon I.

The period from 1799 to 1815 is generally known as the Age of Napoleon. Rising with opportunities presented by the French Revolution, Napoleon gained power not only in France, but directly and indirectly throughout much of continental Europe. Within France he crushed threats from both radicals and royalists who wanted to extend or reverse the French Revolution. Through administrative reforms, codification of laws, and settlement with the Church, he institutionalized some of the changes brought about by the revolution and took the heart out of others. Backed by the ideological force of the revolution and strong nationalism, his armies extended French rule, institutions, and influence throughout Europe. In 1814 Napoleon's forces, weakened by overextension and a disastrous Russian campaign, were defeated by a coalition of European powers. After Napoleon's defeat, the major powers, meeting at Vienna, attempted to establish a new stability that would minimize the revolutionary and Napoleonic experiences.

The sources in this chapter focus on the principal interpretive debate connected with Napoleon: How should Napoleon and his policies be understood? Is Napoleon best viewed as a moderate defender of the French Revolution, as an enlightened despot in the eighteenth-century tradition, or as the first of the modern dictators? To provide insight into these issues, the selections will examine Napoleon's rise to power and his ideas, external policies, and internal institutions.

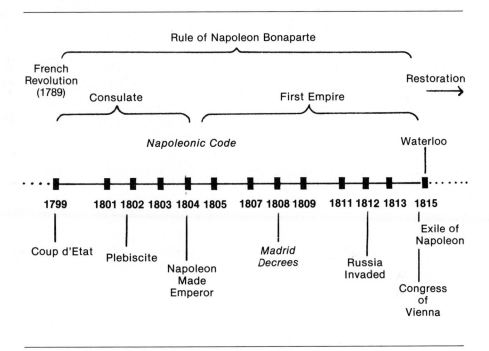

PRIMARY SOURCES

Memoirs: Napoleon's Appeal

Madame de Remusat

Napoleon was neither the candidate of those longing to turn France to a more revolutionary course nor of those who wanted to return France to the legitimacy of the Ancien Régime. He came to power promising to uphold both revolutionary principles and order. Scholars have analyzed the question of why he was able to rise to power. Some see him as a military and political genius; others argue that he was an opportunist who took advantage of circumstances as they arose. One of the earliest analyses of Napoleon's rise to power was written by Madame de Remusat (1780–1821). As a lady in waiting to Empress Josephine and wife of a Napoleonic official, she observed Napoleon firsthand and described him in her Memoirs.

Consider: *Why, according to Remusat, Napoleon was so appealing to the French; the means Napoleon used to secure his power.*

I can understand how it was that men worn out by the turmoil of the Revolution, and afraid of that liberty which had long been associated with death, looked for repose under the dominion of an able ruler on whom fortune was seemingly resolved to smile. I can conceive that they regarded his elevation as a decree of destiny and fondly believed that in the irrevocable they should find peace. I may confidently assert that those persons believed quite sincerely that Bonaparte, whether as consul or emperor, would exert his authority to oppose the intrigue of faction and would save us from the perils of anarchy.

None dared to utter the word "republic," so deeply had the Terror stained that name; and the government of the Directory had perished in the contempt with which its chiefs were regarded. The return of the Bourbons could only be brought about by the aid of a revolution; and the slightest disturbance terrified the French people, in whom enthusiasm of every kind seemed dead. Besides, the men in whom they had trusted had one after the other deceived them; and as, this time, they were yielding to force, they were at least certain that they were not deceiving themselves.

The belief, or rather the error, that only despotism could at that epoch maintain order in France was very widespread. It became the mainstay of Bonaparte; and it is due to him to say that he also believed it. The factions played into his hands by imprudent attempts which he turned to his own advantage. He had some grounds for his belief that he was necessary;

SOURCE: From James Harvey Robinson, ed., *Readings in European History*, Vol. II (Boston: Ginn, 1904), pp. 491–492.

France believed it, too; and he even succeeded in persuading foreign sovereigns that he constituted a barrier against republican influences, which, but for him, might spread widely. At the moment when Bonaparte placed the imperial crown upon his head there was not a king in Europe who did not believe that he wore his own crown more securely because of that event. Had the new emperor granted a liberal constitution, the peace of nations and of kings might really have been forever secured.

Memoirs: Napoleon's Secret Police

Joseph Fouché

Although historians have found various aspects of Napoleonic rule admirable, most condemn Napoleon's use of the secret police. Joseph Fouché, Duke of Otranto (1763–1820), headed this institution for most of the period between 1802 and 1810. Fouché combined the attributes of a powerful politician, a police officer, and an opportunist. In the following selection from his Memoirs, *Fouché boasts of his accomplishments.*

Consider: *The credibility of this document; whether it was reasonable of Napoleon to have Fouché carry out these activities.*

With regard to the interior, an important spring was wanted, that of the general police, which might have rallied the past round the present, and guaranteed the security of the empire. Napoleon himself perceived the void, and, by an imperial decree of the 10th July, re-established me at the head of the police; at the same time investing me with stronger functions that those which I had possessed, before the absurd fusion of the police with the department of justice. . . .

It will not be doubted that I had salaried spies in all ranks and orders; I had some of both sexes, hired at the rate of a thousand or two thousand francs per month, according to their importance and their services. I received their reports directly in writing, having a conventional mark. Every three months, I communicated my list to the emperor, in order that there might be no double employment; and also in order that the nature of the service, occasionally permanent, often temporary, might be rewarded either by places or remunerations.

As to the government's police abroad, it had two essential objects, namely, to watch friendly powers, and counteract hostile governments. In both cases, it was composed of individuals purchased or pensioned, and commissioned to reside near each government, or in each principal town, independ-

SOURCE: Joseph Fouché, *Memoirs* (London: Gibbings and Co., 1894), pp. 188–191.

ent of numerous secret agents sent into all countries, either by the minister of foreign affairs, or by the emperor himself.

I also had my foreign spies. It was in my cabinet, also, that the foreign gazettes, prohibited to the perusal of the French people, were collected, abstracts of which were made for my own use. By that means, I held in my hands the most important strings of foreign politics; and I discharged, in conjunction with the chief of the government, a task capable of controlling or balancing that of the minister charged with foreign relations.

I was thus far from limiting my duties to *espionnage*. All the state prisons were under my control, as well as the *gendarmerie*. The delivery of the *visa* of passports belonged to me. To me was assigned the duty of watching amnestied individuals and foreigners. I established general commissariats in the principal towns of the kingdom, which extended the net-work of the police over the whole of France, and especially our frontiers.

My police acquired so high a renown, that the world went so far as to pretend that I had, among my secret agents, three nobles of the *ancien régime*, distinguished by princely titles, and who daily communicated to me the result of their observations.

I confess that such an establishment was expensive; it swallowed up several millions, the funds of which were secretly provided from taxes laid upon gambling and prostitution, and from the granting of passports. Notwithstanding all that has been said against gambling, reflecting and firm minds must allow, that in the actual state of society, the legal converting of vice into profit is a necessary evil. . . .

It became necessary to organize the gambling-houses upon a much larger scale, for the produce of them was not solely destined to reward my moving phalanxes of spies. I nominated as superintendent-general of the gambling-houses in France, Perrein the elder, who already farmed them, and who, after the coronation, extended his privilege over all of the chief towns of the empire, upon condition of paying fourteen millions yearly, independent of three thousand francs daily to the minister of the police, which, however, did not remain entirely in his hands.

Napoleon's Imperial Decree at Madrid—December 4, 1808

When Napoleon succeeded militarily outside of French soil, more was required of the conquered people than subservience to French rule. Typically some of the reforms and institutions of the French Revolution were applied to the conquered

SOURCE: From James Harvey Robinson, ed., *Readings in European History*, Vol. II (Boston: Ginn, 1904), p. 512.

areas. This is shown in the following decree issued from Napoleon's imperial camp at Madrid on December 4, 1808.

> **Consider:** *The benefits Napoleon might have been hoping for by issuing this decree; to whom this decree would be most threatening; the ways in which these measures were consistent with the acts or spirit of the French Revolution.*

To date from the publication of the present decree, feudal rights are abolished in Spain.

All personal obligations, all exclusive fishing rights and other rights of similar nature on the coast or on rivers and streams, all feudal monopolies (*banalités*) of ovens, mills, and inns are suppressed. It shall be free to every one who shall conform to the laws to develop his industry without restraint.

The tribunal of the Inquisition is abolished, as inconsistent with the civil sovereignty and authority.

The property of the Inquisition shall be sequestered and fall to the Spanish state, to serve as security for the bonded debt.

Considering that the members of the various monastic orders have increased to an undue degree and that, although a certain number of them are useful in assisting the ministers of the altar in the administration of the sacraments, the existence of too great a number interferes with the prosperity of the state, we have decreed and do decree as follows:

The number of convents now in existence in Spain shall be reduced to a third of their present number. This reduction shall be accomplished by uniting the members of several convents of the same order into one.

From the publication of the present decree, no one shall be admitted to the novitiate or permitted to take the monastic vow until the number of the religious of both sexes has been reduced to one third of that now in existence. . . .

All regular ecclesiastics who desire to renounce the monastic life and live as secular ecclesiastics are at liberty to leave their monasteries. . . .

In view of the fact that the institution which stands most in the way of the internal prosperity of Spain is that of the customs lines separating the provinces, we have decreed and do decree what follows:

To date from January 1 next, the barriers existing between the provinces shall be suppressed. The custom houses shall be removed to the frontiers and there established.

Napoleon's Diary

Napoleon's accomplishments and place in history are explained in part by the type of individual he was. The principal sources of information on his personality are his diaries, memoirs, and letters, particularly the portions in which he reflects on himself. The following selection comes from diary entries made between 1798 and 1817.

Consider: *Napoleon's opinions about what made him successful; Napoleon's analysis of his power and his personality; how Napoleon wants to be remembered.*

Paris, January 1, 1798

Paris has a short memory. If I remain longer doing nothing, I am lost. In this great Babylon one reputation quickly succeeds another. After I have been seen three times at the theatre, I shall not be looked at again; I shall therefore not go very frequently.

Paris, January 29, 1798

I will not remain here; there is nothing to be done. They will listen to nothing. I realize that if I stay my reputation will soon be gone. All things fade here, and my reputation is almost forgotten; this little Europe affords too slight a scope; I must go to the Orient; all great reputations have been won there. If the success of an expedition to England should prove doubtful, as I fear, the army of England will become the army of the East, and I shall go to Egypt.

The Orient awaits a man!

Milan, June 17, 1800

I have just reached Milan, somewhat fatigued.

Some Hungarian grenadiers and German prisoners passing by, who had already been prisoners in the campaigns of 1796 and 1797, recognized the First Consul. Many began to shout, with apparent enthusiasm: "Vive Bonaparte!"

What a thing is imagination! Here are men who don't know me, who have never seen me, but who only knew of me, and they are moved by my presence, they would do anything for me! And this same incident arises in all centuries and in all countries! Such is fanaticism! Yes, imagination rules the world. The defect of our modern institutions is that they do not speak to the imagination. By that alone can man be governed; without it he is but a brute.

SOURCE: R. M. Johnston, ed., The Corsican: *A Diary of Napoleon's Life in His Own Words* (Boston: Houghton Mifflin Co., 1910), pp. 74, 140, 166, 492, 496.

December 30, 1802

My power proceeds from my reputation, and my reputation from the victories I have won. My power would fall if I were not to support it with more glory and more victories. Conquest has made me what I am; only conquest can maintain me.

Friendship is only a word; I love nobody; no, not even my brothers. Perhaps Joseph a little; even then it's a matter of habit, it's because he is my elder. — Duroc? Ah, yes, I love him; but why? His character attracts me: he is cool, dry, severe; and Duroc never sheds tears. As for me, you don't suppose I care; I know perfectly well I have no real friends. As long as I remain what I am, I shall have as many as I need so far as the appearance goes. Let the women whimper, that's their business, but for me, give me no sentiment. A man must be firm, have a stout heart, or else leave on one side war and government.

Saint Helena, March 3, 1817

In spite of all the libels, I have no fear whatever about my fame. Posterity will do me justice. The truth will be known; and the good I have done will be compared with the faults I have committed. I am not uneasy as to the result. Had I succeeded, I would have died with the reputation of the greatest man that ever existed. As it is, although I have failed, I shall be considered as an extraordinary man: my elevation was unparalleled, because unaccompanied by crime. I have fought fifty pitched battles, almost all of which I have won. I have framed and carried into effect a code of laws that will bear my name to the most distant posterity. I raised myself from nothing to be the most powerful monarch in the world. Europe was at my feet. I have always been of opinion that the sovereignty lay in the people. In fact, the imperial government was a kind of republic. Called to the head of it by the voice of the nation, my maxim was, *la carrière est ouverte aux talens* without distinction of birth or fortune, and this system of equality is the reason that your oligarchy hates me so much.

Saint Helena, August 28, 1817

Jesus was hanged, like so many fanatics who posed as a prophet, a messiah; there were several every year. What is certain is that at that epoch opinion was setting towards a single God, and those who first preached the doctrine were well received: circumstances made for it. It is just like in my case, sprung from the lower ranks of society I became an emperor, because circumstances, opinion, were with me.

VISUAL SOURCES

Napoleon Crossing the Alps

Jacques Louis David

Jacques Louis David was a leading painter of the late eighteenth and early nineteenth centuries and one of the first great painters to consciously devote his talents to the art of propaganda. A republican during the French Revolution, he painted a

Photo 6-1

Musée Versailles/Giraudon

number of pictures supportive of the revolution and what it stood for. David argued that "the arts should . . . contribute forcefully to the education of the public" and that art "should have grandeur and a moral"; if a painting is properly presented, the "marks of heroism and civic virtue offered the eyes of the people will electrify its soul, and plant the seeds of glory and devotion to the fatherland."

When Napoleon rose to power, David became a Bonapartist. In 1800 he was asked by Napoleon to paint a picture of him leading his army across the Alps. The result, Napoleon Crossing the Alps, shows Napoleon in a heroic pose on a white charger following the glorious footsteps of Hannibal and Charlemagne (whose names are carved in the rocks below) across the Alps. Napoleon is pointing upward, probably both to heaven and to the top of the mountains, while a wind blows at his back—a traditional symbol of victory. Under the horse's belly are troops and cannon moving up the trail. In reality Napoleon wisely rode a sure-footed mule. He also posed only briefly for David, informing him that "it is the character and what animates the physiognomy that needs to be painted. No one inquires if the portraits of great men are likenesses. It is enough that their genius lives in them."

Consider: *The way this painting and the circumstances surrounding its execution by David illustrate connections between politics and art of the period.*

SECONDARY SOURCES

Europe and the French Imperium: Napoleon as Enlightened Despot

Geoffrey Bruun

As with most charismatic figures, it has been difficult to evaluate Napoleon objectively from a historical perspective. Even before his death, a number of myths were developing about him. Since then much of the debate among scholars has dealt with whether Napoleon should be considered a defender or a destroyer of the revolution, whether his rise to power reversed the revolutionary tide or consolidated it. In the following selection Geoffrey Bruun argues that Napoleon should be viewed more as an eighteenth-century enlightened despot than as anything else.

SOURCE: Geoffrey Bruun, *Europe and the French Imperium, 1799–1814*. Reprinted by permission of Harper & Row (New York, 1938), pp. 1–2. Copyright © 1938 by Harper & Row, Publishers, Inc.

Consider: *Bruun's support for his contention that Napoleon was to a considerable degree a "son of the philosophes"; the ways in which Napoleon differed from eighteenth-century monarchs; whether Bruun's view is supported by Napoleon's decree issued from Madrid.*

The major misconception which has distorted the epic of Napoleon is the impression that his advent to power was essentially a dramatic reversal, which turned back the tide of democracy and diverted the predestined course of the revolutionary torrent. That this Corsican liberticide could destroy a republic and substitute an empire, seemingly at will, has been seized upon by posterity as the outstanding proof of his arrogant genius. To reduce his career to logical dimensions, to appreciate how largely it was a fulfillment rather than a miscarriage of the reform program, it is necessary to forget the eighteenth century as the seedtime of political democracy and remember it as the golden era of the princely despots, to recall how persistently the thinkers of that age concerned themselves with the idea of enlightened autocracy and how conscientiously they laid down the intellectual foundations of Caesarism. Napoleon was, to a degree perhaps undreamed of in their philosophy, the son of the *philosophes*, and it is difficult to read far in the political writings of the time without feeling how clearly the century prefigured him, how ineluctably in Vandal's phrase *l'idée a précédé l'homme*.

All the reforming despots of the eighteenth century pursued, behind a façade of humanitarian pretexts, the same basic program of administrative consolidation. The success achieved by Frederick the Great in raising the military prestige and stimulating the economic development of Prussia provided the most notable illustration of this policy, but the same ideals inspired the precipitate decrees of Joseph II in Austria, the cautious innovations of Charles III of Spain, the paper projects of Catherine the Great of Russia and the complex program pursued by Gustavus III in Sweden. Military preparedness and economic self-sufficiency were the cardinal principles guiding the royal reformers, but they also shared a common desire to substitute a unified system of law for the juristic chaos inherited from earlier centuries, to eliminate the resistance and confusion offered by guilds, corporations, provincial estates and relics of feudatory institutions, and to transform their inchoate possessions into centralized states dominated by despotic governments of unparalleled efficiency and vigor. In crowning the work of the Revolution by organizing a government of this type in France, Napoleon obeyed the most powerful political tradition of the age, a mandate more general, more widely endorsed, and more pressing than the demand for social equality or democratic institutions. Read in this light, the significance of his career is seen to lie, not in the ten years of revolutionary turmoil from which he sprang, but in the whole century which produced him. If Europe in the revolutionary age may be thought of as dominated by one nearly universal mood, that mood was an intense aspiration for order. The privileged and the unprivileged classes, philosophers, peasants, democrats, and despots all paid homage to this ideal. Napoleon lent his name to an epoch because he symbolized reason enthroned, because he was the philosopher-prince who gave to the dominant aspiration of the age its most typical, most resolute, and most triumphant expression.

Dictatorship — Its History and Theory: Napoleon as Dictator

Alfred Cobban

There is a tradition of historians much more critical of Napoleon than Bruun or Remusat. They see in Napoleon's rise to power and in the means he used to retain it elements of a modern dictatorship. This view was particularly strong during the 1930s and 1940s, perhaps a reaction to events of those times. The following selection by Alfred Cobban, a scholar from the University of London and a recognized authority on French history, is a good example of this interpretation. Here Cobban analyzes how Napoleon gained power.

> **Consider:** *Cobban's definition of the term "dictator"; how the document by Fouché might be used to support Cobban's view; how Bruun might react to this interpretation.*

Bonaparte came to power because his name provided a new source of authority, but at the same time the principle of the sovereignty of the people had established too firm a hold over men's minds to be abandoned. Some means of reconciling this principle with the rule of one man had to be found. Emotionally this was easy: the sovereignty of the people had become fused with nationalism, and Napoleon through his victories had come to be a living symbol of the national greatness. But to add the appearance of free choice he adopted the method used by the Jacobins in presenting their Constitution of 1793 to the country — the plebiscite. Sieyès and the men of Brumaire had themselves presented this device to Bonaparte, when they incorporated in the Constitution of the year VIII the name of the First Consul, Citizen Bonaparte; so that when it was submitted to the popular vote, it was as much a plebiscite on Bonaparte as a vote for a constitution. The votes on the life consulate in 1802 and on the establishment of the Empire in 1804 are mere sequels. By these popular votes democracy, or at least the principle

SOURCE: Alfred Cobban, *Dictatorship: Its History and Theory* (New York: Charles Scribner's Sons, 1939), pp. 85–86.

that all authority is derived from the people, was to be triumphantly vindicated by the election of Napoleon to the post of supreme power in the state. In this way arose, in the modern world, the idea that one man might himself represent the will of the people, and be invested with all the authority of the most despotic ruler in the name of democracy. The idea of sovereignty, freed from all restraints, and transferred to the people, had at last given birth to the first modern dictatorship. . . .

Napoleon came to power as a dictator from the right — not, of course, as a leader of the old reactionary party, but as a dictator supported by the propertied classes, the financiers and commercial men, the upper bourgeoisie, and speculators, who had made large fortunes out of the revolution and had bought up church or crown lands or the property of *émigrés* with worthless *assignats*.

Napoleon as Preserver of the Revolution

George Rudé

In recent years historians have become more reluctant to categorize Napoleon under any one label. Instead, they tend to interpret more judiciously his words and deeds, taking care to note that both were inconsistent and even contradictory at various times. This tendency among historians is exemplified in the following selection by the well-known British social historian George Rudé. Rudé, who has emphasized looking at history from the bottom up, sees Napoleon as sympathetic to and supportive of the revolution.

Consider: *How Bruun and Cobban might reply to Rudé's interpretation; the ways in which this interpretation is supported or contradicted by the primary documents.*

Napoleon himself believed that his work was a kind of crowning of the Revolution, and he was remarkably honest about his friendship with Robespierre's brother. He defended Robespierre from the charge of being bloodthirsty; he respected him as a man of probity. Napoleon would never have imagined that his own career could have flourished as it did without the surgery performed on French society by the Revolution. He was born in Corsica of poor, proud, petty-noble parents, and before the Revolution he could not possibly have risen above the rank of captain in the French army. Also, he had read Rousseau and sympathized with much of the Jacobin philosophy.

SOURCE: Norman F. Cantor, *Perspectives on the European Past*, Vol. II. Reprinted by permission of Macmillan (New York, 1971), pp. 59–60. Copyright © 1971 by Macmillan Publishing Co., Inc.

Napoleon had two different aspects. He believed in the overthrow of the old aristocracy of privilege; on the other hand, he believed in strong government — and he learned both of these beliefs from the Revolution. He was both an authoritarian and an egalitarian. Yet, admittedly little of this seems to fit the man who created a new aristocracy, who prided himself on being the son-in-law of Francis of Austria, referred to his late "brother" Louis XVI, and aspired to found a new imperial dynasty.

However, if we judge Napoleon on what he actually did and not only on those things that are usually remembered (despotism and foreign conquest), we must concede that his armies "liberalized" the constitutions of many European countries. They overthrew the aristocratic system in Italy and Germany, and even, to some extent, in Poland and Spain. A great many European liberals rallied to Napoleon's banners, particularly where French administration was at its best (as under Napoleon's brother Jerome in Westphalia). Napoleon's armies did bring many of the ideals of the Revolution to Europe: the basic ideas of the overthrow of aristocratic privilege, of a constitution, of the *Code Napoléon* (which was a codification of the laws of the French Revolution). In this sense Napoleon was a revolutionary. He turned his back on revolution to the extent that he was authoritarian and contemptuous of "the little man," but certain important accomplishments of the Revolution — peasant ownership of land free from feudal obligations, expropriation of the possessions of the Church and of the émigré nobility — were retained and even extended beyond France's borders. Napoleon was indeed a military despot, but he did not destroy the work of the Revolution; in a sense, in a wider European context, he rounded off its work.

Chapter Questions

1. Considering the materials in this chapter, how would you explain Napoleon's rise to power and his effective exercise of it?

2. In what ways did Napoleon preserve and support the principles of the French Revolution? In what ways did he undermine these principles?

CHAPTER SEVEN

Reaction, Reform, Revolution, and Romanticism: 1815–1848

The European powers met at the Congress of Vienna (1814–1815) to decide how to proceed now that Napoleon had been defeated. Conservative sentiments, exemplified by the views of Prince Metternich of Austria, predominated at this congress. Although the final settlement was not punitive or humiliating to France, it did represent an effort by conservative leaders to reject changes instituted during the revolutionary and Napoleonic periods, to restore traditional groups and governments to power, and to resist liberalism and nationalism. As a result of this and other developments, the aristocracy regained some of its prominence, monarchs such as Louis XVIII (brother of Louis XVI) returned to power, and armies intervened (as in Spain and Italy) to crush threats to the status quo.

Nevertheless, movements for national liberation and liberal reform surfaced during the 1820s, 1830s, and 1840s. In the 1820s and 1830s, Greece and Belgium gained independence and less successful nationalistic movements arose in Italy and Poland. Liberalism, encompassing demands for greater freedom, constitutional government, and political rights, was particularly strong in Western Europe. In England a series of legislative acts in the

1830s and 1840s clearly recognized liberal demands. In France a revolution in 1830 brought to power groups more open to liberal ideas.

A climax came in 1848, when revolutions erupted across Europe. Although each revolution was different, in general the middle and working classes demanded changes in the name of nationalism or liberalism. At first, established governments weakened or fell, but the revolutionaries found it difficult to remain unified once power was in their hands. Soon groups standing for authoritarian rule took advantage of this disunity and regained power.

The conservatism and liberalism that characterized so many of the political developments of this period were reflected in certain artistic and literary styles. Romanticism was the most important of these, reflecting, in different ways both conservatism and liberalism. From its beginning in the late eighteenth century, it spread until it became the dominant cultural movement of the first half of the nineteenth century. Romanticism rejected the formalism of the previously dominant Classical style, refused to be limited by Enlightenment rationalism or the stark realism of everyday life, and emphasized emotion and freedom.

The documents in this chapter focus on (1) conservatism (What were some of the main characteristics of conservatism? What did it stand against? What policies fit with conservative attitudes? In what ways did the Congress of Vienna reflect the conservatism of the period?), (2) liberalism and movements for reform (What did liberalism mean in the first half of the nineteenth century? What reforms did liberals demand? What was the

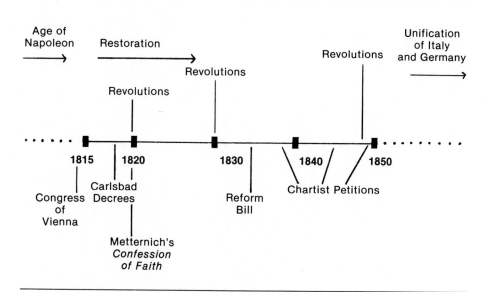

nature of reform movements, as exemplified by Chartism in England?), (3) the revolutions of 1848 (In what ways did the revolutions of 1848 bring to a head some of the main trends of the period? Who might be considered the "winners" and "losers" in these revolutions? Why did a revolution not occur in England at the same time?), and (4) the nature of Romanticism, particularly as it is revealed in literature and art (What were some of the ties between Romanticism and conservatism? How was Romanticism related to liberal and even revolutionary ideals?).

What emerges from these selections is a picture of Europeans trying to deal politically and culturally with the legacy of the French Revolution and the Enlightenment. The economic and social developments of the period will be covered in the next chapter.

PRIMARY SOURCES

Secret Memorandum to Tsar Alexander I, 1820: Conservative Principles

Prince Klemens von Metternich

The outstanding leader of the conservative tide that rose with the fall of Napoleon was Prince Klemens von Metternich (1773–1859). From his post as Austrian Minister of Foreign Affairs, Metternich hosted the Congress of Vienna and played a dominating role within Austria and among the conservative states of Europe between 1815 and 1848. Both in principle and in practice, he represented a conservatism that rejected the changes wrought by the French Revolution and stood against liberalism and nationalism. The following is an excerpt from a secret memorandum that Metternich sent to Tsar Alexander I of Russia in 1820, explaining his political principles. While not a sophisticated statement of political theory, it does reflect key elements of conservative attitudes and ideas.

Consider: *What threats Metternich perceives; how Metternich connects "presumption" with the middle class; how this document reflects the experience of the revolutionary and Napoleonic periods; the kinds of policies that would logically flow from these attitudes.*

SOURCE: Prince Richard Metternich, ed., *Memoirs of Prince Metternich, 1815–1829*, Vol. III, Mrs. Alexander Napier, trans. (New York: Charles Scribner's Sons, 1881), pp. 454–455, 458–460, 468–469.

'*L'Europe*,' a celebrated writer has recently said, '*fait aujourd'hui pitié à l'homme d'esprit et horreur à l'homme vertueux.*'[1]

It would be difficult to comprise in a few words a more exact picture of the situation at the time we are writing these lines!

Kings have to calculate the chances of their very existence in the immediate future; passions are let loose, and league together to overthrow everything which society respects as the basis of its existence; religion, public morality, laws, customs, rights, and duties, all are attacked, confounded, overthrown, or called in question. The great mass of the people are tranquil spectators of these attacks and revolutions, and of the absolute want of all means of defense. A few are carried off by the torrent, but the wishes of the immense majority are to maintain a repose which exists no longer, and of which even the first elements seem to be lost. . . .

Having now thrown a rapid glance over the first causes of the present state of society, it is necessary to point out in a more particular manner the evil which threatens to deprive it, at one blow, of the real blessings, the fruits of genuine civilisation, and to disturb it in the midst of its enjoyments. This evil may be described in one word — presumption; the natural effect of the rapid progression of the human mind towards the perfecting of so many things. This it is which at the present day leads so many individuals astray, for it has become an almost universal sentiment.

Religion, morality, legislation, economy, politics, administration, all have become common and accessible to everyone. Knowledge seems to come by inspiration; experience has no value for the presumptuous man; faith is nothing to him; he substitutes for it a pretended individual conviction, and to arrive at this conviction dispenses with all inquiry and with all study; for these means appear too trivial to a mind which believes itself strong enough to embrace at one glance all questions and all facts. Laws have no value for him, because he has not contributed to make them, and it would be beneath a man of his parts to recognise the limits traced by rude and ignorant generations. Power resides in himself; why should he submit himself to that which was only useful for the man deprived of light and knowledge? That which, according to him, was required in an age of weakness cannot be suitable in an age of reason and vigour amounting to universal perfection, which the German innovators designate by the idea, absurd in itself, of the Emancipation of the People! Morality itself he does not attack openly, for without it he could not be sure for a single instant of his own existence; but he interprets its essence after his own fashion, and allows every other person to do so likewise, provided that other person neither kills nor robs him.

In thus tracing the character of the presumptuous man, we believe we have traced that of the society of the day, composed of like elements, if the denomination of society is applicable to an order of things which only tends

---

[1]Europe . . . is pitied by men of spirit and abhorred by men of virtue.

in principle towards individualising all the elements of which society is composed. Presumption makes every man the guide of his own belief, the arbiter of laws according to which he is pleased to govern himself, or to allow some one else to govern him and his neighbours; it makes him, in short, the sole judge of his own faith, his own actions, and the principles according to which he guides them. . . .

The Governments, having lost their balance, are frightened, intimidated, and thrown into confusion by the cries of the intermediary class of society, which, placed between the Kings and their subjects, breaks the sceptre of the monarch, and usurps the cry of the people — the class so often disowned by the people, and nevertheless too much listened to, caressed and feared by those who could with one word reduce it again to nothingness.

We see this intermediary class abandon itself with a blind fury and animosity which proves much more its own fears than any confidence in the success of its enterprises, to all the means which seem proper to assuage its thirst for power, applying itself to the task of persuading Kings that their rights are confined to sitting upon a throne, while those of the people are to govern, and to attack all that centuries have bequeathed as holy and worthy of man's respect — denying, in fact, the value of the past, and declaring themselves the masters of the future. We see this class take all sorts of disguises, uniting and subdividing as occasion offers, helping each other in the hour of danger, and the next day depriving each other of all their conquests. It takes possession of the press, and employs it to promote impiety, disobedience to the laws of religion and the State, and goes so far as to preach murder as a duty for those who desire what is good.

The Carlsbad Decrees, 1819:
Conservative Repression

One way political leaders tried to assert conservatism against any perceived threats such as liberalism or nationalism was through international cooperation and action, a policy known as the Concert of Europe. Another way was through taking internal measures against the same threats, such as occurred in Germany in 1819 with the issuance of the Carlsbad Decrees. These decrees were pushed through the Diet of the German Confederation by Austria and Prussia, but particularly by Prince Metternich, in reaction to nationalist student movements against the principles of the Congress of Vienna. The following excerpts from those decrees concern the universities, the press, and all "revolutionary plots."

SOURCE: From James Harvey Robinson, ed., "The Reaction after 1815 and European Policy of Metternich," in *Translations and Reprints from the Original Sources of European History*, Vol. I, No. 3, Department of History of the University of Pennsylvania, ed. (Philadelphia: University of Pennsylvania Press, 1898), pp. 16–20.

Consider: *The purposes of these decrees and the means used to effect these purposes; whether these decrees are consistent with attitudes expressed by Metternich in the "confession of faith" he makes in his secret memorandum to Tsar Alexander I; the consequences of the effective enforcement of these decrees.*

PROVISIONAL DECREE RELATING TO THE UNIVERSITIES,
UNANIMOUSLY ADOPTED SEPTEMBER 20, 1819

§ 2. The confederated governments mutually pledge themselves to remove from the universities or other public educational institutions all teachers who, by obvious deviation from their duty or by exceeding the limits of their functions, or by the abuse of their legitimate influence over the youthful minds, or by propagating harmful doctrines hostile to public order or subversive of existing governmental institutions, shall have unmistakably proved their unfitness for the important office intrusted to them. . . .

§ 3. Those laws which have for a long period been directed against secret and unauthorized societies in the universities, shall be strictly enforced. These laws apply especially to that association established some years since under the name Universal Students' Union (*Allegmeine Burschenschaft*), since the very conception of the society implies the utterly unallowable plan of permanent fellowship and constant communication between the various universities. The duty of especial watchfulness in this matter should be impressed upon the special agents of the government.

PRESS LAWS FOR FIVE YEARS

§ 1. So long as this decree shall remain in force no publication which appears in the form of daily issues or as a serial not exceeding twenty sheets of printed matter shall go to press in any state of the Union without the previous knowledge and approval of the state officials.

§ 6. . . . The Diet shall have the right, moreover, to suppress on its own authority, without being petitioned, such writings included in Section 1, in whatever German state they may appear, as in the opinion of a commission appointed by it, are inimical to the honor of the Union, the safety of individual states or the maintenance of peace and quiet in Germany. There shall be no appeal from such decisions and the governments involved are bound to see that they are put into execution.

ESTABLISHMENT OF AN INVESTIGATING COMMITTEE AT MAINZ

ARTICLE 1. Within a fortnight, reckoned from the passage of this decree, there shall convene, under the auspices of the Confederation, in the city and federal fortress of Mainz, an Extraordinary Commission of Investigation to consist of seven members including the chairman.

ARTICLE II. The object of the Commission shall be a joint investigation, as thorough and extensive as possible, of the facts relating to the origin and manifold ramifications of the revolutionary plots and demagogical associations directed against the existing Constitutional and internal peace both of the Union and of the individual states: of the existence of which plots more or less clear evidence is to be had already, or may be produced in the course of the investigation.

English Liberalism

Jeremy Bentham

The roots of liberalism are deep and varied, stretching back to the writings of John Locke in the seventeenth century and further. By the time liberalism started to flourish during the nineteenth century, it had a particularly strong English tradition. Perhaps the most influential of the early-nineteenth-century English liberals was Jeremy Bentham (1748–1832). He is most well-known as the author of the theory of utilitarianism and for advocating reform of many English institutions. The ideas and efforts of Bentham and his followers, who included James Mill and John Stuart Mill, formed one of the mainstreams of English liberalism and liberal reform in the nineteenth century. The first of the following two selections comes from Bentham's An Introduction to the Principles of Morals and Legislation *(1789) and focuses on the principle of utility. The second is from his* A Manual of Political Economy *(1798) and indicates his views toward governmental economic policy.*

> **Consider:** *What exactly Bentham means by the principle of utility; what, according to the principle of utility, the proper role of government in general is; his explanation for the proper role of the government in economic affairs.*

I. Nature has placed mankind under the governance of two sovereign masters, *pain* and *pleasure*. It is for them alone to point out what we ought to do, as well as to determine what we shall do. On the one hand the standard of right and wrong, on the other chains of causes and effects, are fastened to their throne. They govern us in all we do, in all we say, in all we think: every effort we can make to throw off our subjection, will serve to demonstrate and confirm it. In words a man may pretend to abjure their empire: but in reality he will remain subject to it all the while. The *principle of utility* recognizes this subjection, and assumes it for the foundation of that system,

SOURCE: Jeremy Bentham, *An Introduction to the Principles of Morals and Legislation* (Oxford: Claredon Press, 1876), pp. 1–3; John Bowring, ed., *Bentham's Works*, Vol. III (Edinburgh: William Tait, 1843), pp. 33–35.

the object of which is to rear the fabric of felicity by the hands of reason and of law. Systems which attempt to question it, deal in sounds instead of sense, in caprice instead of reason, in darkness instead of light.

But enough of metaphor and declamation: it is not by such means that moral science is to be improved.

II. The principle of utility is the foundation of the present work: it will be proper therefore at the outset to give an explicit and determinate account of what is meant by it. By the principle of utility is meant that principle which approves or disapproves of every action whatsoever, according to the tendency which it appears to have to augment or diminish the happiness of the party whose interest is in question: or, what is the same thing in other words, to promote or to oppose that happiness. I say of every action whatsoever; and therefore not only of every action of a private individual, but of every measure of government.

III. By utility is meant that property in any object, whereby it tends to produce benefit, advantage, pleasure, good, or happiness (all this in the present case comes to the same thing) or (what comes again to the same thing) to prevent the happening of mischief, pain, evil, or unhappiness to the party whose interest is considered: if that party be the community in general, then the happiness of the community: if a particular individual, then the happiness of that individual.

IV. The interest of the community is one of the most general expressions that can occur in the phraseology of morals: no wonder that the meaning of it is often lost. When it has a meaning, it is this. The community is a fictitious *body*, composed of the individual persons who are considered as constituting as it were its *members*. The interest of the community then is, what? — the sum of the interests of the several members who compose it.

V. It is in vain to talk of the interest of the community, without understanding what is the interest of the individual. A thing is said to promote the interest, or to be *for* the interest, of an individual, when it tends to add to the sum total of his pleasures: or, what comes to the same thing, to diminish the sum total of his pains.

VI. An action then may be said to be conformable to the principle of utility, or, for shortness sake, to utility (meaning with respect to the community at large) when the tendency it has to augment the happiness of the community is greater than any it has to diminish it.

VII. A measure of government (which is but a particular kind of action, performed by a particular person or persons) may be said to be conformable to or dictated by the principle of utility, when in like manner the tendency which it has to augment the happiness of the community is greater than any which it has to diminish it. . . .

The practical questions, therefore, are how far the end in view is best promoted by individuals acting for themselves? and in what cases these ends
may be promoted by the hands of government?

With the view of causing an increase to take place in the mass of national
wealth, or with a view to increase of the means either of subsistence or enjoyment, without some special reason, the general rule is, that nothing
ought to be done or attempted by government. The motto, or watchword of
government, on these occasions, ought to be — *Be quiet*.

For this quietism there are two main reasons:

1.   Generally speaking, any interference for this purpose on the part of
      government is needless. The wealth of the whole community is com-
      posed of the wealth of the several individuals belonging to it taken
      together. But to increase his particular portion is, generally speaking,
      among the constant objects of each individual's exertions and care.
      Generally speaking, there is no one who knows what is for your inter-
      est so well as yourself — no one who is disposed with so much ardour
      and constancy to pursue it.

2.   Generally speaking, it is moreover likely to be pernicious, viz. by be-
      ing unconducive, or even obstructive, with reference to the attain-
      ment of the end in view. Each individual bestowing more time and
      attention upon the means of preserving and increasing his portion of
      wealth, than is or can be bestowed by government, is likely to take a
      more effectual course than what, in his instance and on his behalf,
      would be taken by government.

It is, moreover, universally and constantly pernicious in another way, by
the restraint or constraint imposed on the free agency of the individual. . . .

. . . With few exceptions, and those not very considerable ones, the attainment of the maximum of enjoyment will be most effectually secured by
leaving each individual to pursue his own maximum of enjoyment, in proportion as he is in possession of the means. Inclination in this respect will not
be wanting on the part of any one. Power, the species of power applicable to
this case — viz. wealth, pecuniary power — could not be given by the hand of
government to one, without being taken from another; so that by such interference there would not be any gain of power upon the whole.

The gain to be produced in this article by the interposition of government, respects principally the head of knowledge. There are cases in which,
for the benefit of the public at large, it may be in the power of government
to cause this or that portion of knowledge to be produced and diffused,
which, without the demand for it produced by government, would either
not have been produced, or would not have been diffused.

We have seen above the grounds on which the general rule in this behalf —
Be quiet — rests. Whatever measures, therefore, cannot be justified as excep-

tions to that rule, may be considered as *non agenda* on the part of government. The art, therefore, is reduced within a small compass: *security* and *freedom* are all that industry requires. The request which agriculture, manufactures and commerce present to governments, is modest and reasonable as that which Diogenes made to Alexander: "*Stand out of my sunshine.*" We have no need of favour — we require only a secure and open path.

Essay on Liberty and State Power: French Liberalism

Pierre-Claude-François Daunou

Liberalism on the Continent differed from English liberalism in a variety of ways, reflecting the differing historical realities of each nation. In France during the Restoration (1815–1830), which followed the fall of Napoleon, the demands of liberals were milder than those of their counterparts in England, but nevertheless these demands can be recognized as part of the same tradition. This is illustrated in the following selection from an essay on state power and liberty written during the early years of the Restoration by Pierre-Claude-François Daunou (1761–1840), a French historian and politician who was active in the governments of the French Revolutionary and Napoleonic Eras. Here he lists what he considers the proper limitations on, or safeguards against, state power.

> **Consider:** *What is not included on this list; how this compares to* The Declaration of the Rights of Man and Citizen; *what a conservative might object to.*

That none may be arrested or detained without being tried according to ordinary rules of justice with the least possible delay;

That legally held property be inviolable and not subject to arbitrary extortion;

That industry, even if not freed from all impediments, should at least not have to fear a return of those that have already been abolished;

That insult, slander, and sedition be treated as offenses or crimes; and that all other opinions expressed orally or in writing or in the press be free from all censorship, whether prior or subsequent, and from all administrative directives;

That the religion privileged by the state [that is, the Roman Catholic], financially supported by all citizens including those who do not profess it, should in no way or respect restrict the freedom of any other religious belief;

SOURCE: Walter Simon, ed., *French Liberalism, 1789–1848* (New York: John Wiley and Sons, Inc., 1972), pp. 50–51.

These are the only points to be guaranteed, and the only institutions strictly necessary to accomplish this are the following:

That all judges . . . be permanent, not subject to transfer or displacement against their will, and irremovable except by reason of duly pronounced dereliction of duty;

That all matters to be punished as crimes or other offenses be verified and declared as such previously by juries whose selection does not rest with the supreme authority or its agents and may not be influenced by the presidents of courts or tribunals;

Finally, that an assembly of representatives regularly and freely elected . . . without ministerial influence shall in entire independence express its assent to all taxes, loans, and new laws.

The First Chartist
Petition: Demands for
Change in England

Movements for reform occurred throughout Europe between 1815 and 1848 despite the efforts of conservatives to quash them. Eventually almost all countries in Europe experienced the revolutions conservatives feared so much. One exception was England, but even there political movements threatened to turn into violent revolts against the failure of the government to change. The most important of these was the Chartist movement, made up primarily of members of the working class who wanted reforms for themselves. The following is an excerpt from the first charter presented to the House of Commons in 1838. Subsequent charters were presented in 1842 and 1848. In each case the potential existed for a mass movement to turn into a violent revolt, and in each case Parliament rejected the Chartist demands. Only later in the century were most of these demands met.

Consider: *The nature of the Chartists' demands; by what means the Chartists hoped to achieve their ends; how Metternich might analyze these demands.*

Required, as we are universally, to support and obey the laws, nature and reason entitle us to demand that in the making of the laws the universal voice shall be implicitly listened to. We perform the duties of freemen; we must have the privileges of freemen. Therefore, we demand universal suffrage. The suffrage, to be exempt from the corruption of the wealthy and the violence of the powerful, must be secret. The assertion of our right necessarily involves the power of our uncontrolled exercise. We ask for the reality of a good, not for its semblance, therefore we demand the ballot.

SOURCE: From R. G. Gammage, *History of the Chartist Movement*, 2nd ed. (Newcastle-on-Tyne, England: Browne and Browne, 1894), pp. 88–90.

The connection between the representatives and the people, to be beneficial, must be intimate. The legislative and constituent powers, for correction and for instruction, ought to be brought into frequent contact. Errors which are comparatively light, when susceptible of a speedy popular remedy, may produce the most disastrous effects when permitted to grow inveterate through years of compulsory endurance. To public safety, as well as public confidence, frequent elections are essential. Therefore, we demand annual parliaments. With power to choose, and freedom in choosing, the range of our choice must be unrestricted. We are compelled, by the existing laws, to take for our representatives men who are incapable of appreciating our difficulties, or have little sympathy with them; merchants who have retired from trade and no longer feel its harrassings; proprietors of land who are alike ignorant of its evils and its cure; lawyers by whom the notoriety of the senate is courted only as a means of obtaining notice in the courts. The labours of a representative who is sedulous in the discharge of his duty are numerous and burdensome. It is neither just, nor reasonable, nor safe, that they should continue to be gratuitously rendered. We demand that in the future election of members of your honourable house, the approbation of the constituency shall be the sole qualification, and that to every representative so chosen, shall be assigned out of the public taxes, a fair and adequate remuneration for the time which he is called upon to devote to the public service. The management of his mighty kingdom has hitherto been a subject for contending factions to try their selfish experiments upon. We have felt the consequences in our sorrowful experience. Short glimmerings of uncertain enjoyment, swallowed up by long and dark seasons of suffering. If the self-government of the people should not remove their distresses, it will, at least, remove their repinings. Universal suffrage will, and it alone can, bring true and lasting peace to the nation; we firmly believe that it will also bring prosperity. May it therefore please your honourable house, to take this our petition into your most serious consideration, and to use your utmost endeavours, by all constitutional means, to have a law passed, granting to every male of lawful age, sane mind, and unconvicted of crime, the right of voting for members of parliament, and directing all future elections of members of parliament to be in the way of secret ballot, and ordaining that the duration of parliament, so chosen, shall in no case exceed one year, and abolishing all property qualifications in the members, and providing for their due remuneration while in attendance on their parliamentary duties.

"And your petitioners shall ever pray."

An Eyewitness Account of the Revolutions of 1848 in Germany

Annual Register, 1848

In 1848 revolutions broke out throughout Europe. The February Revolution in France seemed to act as a spark for revolutions elsewhere, particularly in the German states. Indeed, within a few days of the outbreak in France, the established governments of the German states were faced with demands for change, demonstrations, and revolutions. The following is an account by an eyewitness of some of the events in Germany during March 1848, as reported in the London Annual Register.

> **Consider:** *Whether this indicates any pattern to the revolutionary activities; the nature of the demands for change; how the established governments reacted.*

In order to give a clear and distinct narrative of the complicated events which have taken place during the present year in Germany, we have had to consider carefully the question of arrangement; for, independently of the revolutionary movements in the separate kingdoms, there has been a long-sustained attempt to construct a new German nationality on the basis of a Confederation of all the states, with one great Parliament or Diet, and a Central Executive at Frankfort. . . .

It was in the southwestern states of Germany that the effects of the French Revolution began first to manifest themselves. On the 29th of February the Grand Duke of Baden received a deputation from his subjects who demanded liberty of the press, the establishment of a national guard, and trial by jury. They succeeded in their object, and M. Welcker, who had distinguished himself as a Liberal leader, was appointed one of the ministers.

On the 3d of March, the Rhenish provinces, headed by Cologne, followed the same example. On the 4th similar demonstrations took place at Wiesbaden and Frankfort, and on the 5th at Düsseldorf. At Cologne, on the 3d of March, the populace assembled in crowds before the Stadthaus, or town hall, where the town council were sitting, and demanded the concession of certain rights, which were inscribed on slips of paper and handed about amongst the mob. They were as follows: (1) Universal suffrage; all legislation and government to proceed from the people. (2) Liberty of the press and freedom of speech. (3) Abolition of the standing army and the armament of the people, who are to elect their own officers. (4) Full rights of

---

SOURCE: Louis L. Snyder, ed., *Documents of German History* (New Brunswick, N.J.: Rutgers University Press, 1958), pp. 174–175.

public meeting. (5) Protection to labor, and a guarantee for the supply of all necessaries. (6) State education for all children.

The military were, however, called out, and the streets were cleared without much difficulty.

At Wiesbaden, in Nassau, a large concourse of people met opposite the palace on the 4th, and demanded a general arming of the people under their own elective leaders; entire liberty of the press; a German Parliament; right of public meeting; public and oral trial by jury; the control of the duchy domain; convocation of the second chamber to frame a new electoral law on the basis of population, and to remove all restrictions on religious liberty. The Duke was absent at Berlin, but the Duchess, from the balcony of the palace, assured the people that their demands would be fully conceded by the Duke, her stepson. Subsequently appeared a proclamation in which the Duchess *guaranteed* the concession of these demands; and on the same day, in the afternoon, the Duke returned, and, immediately addressing the people, he ratified all the concessions made by the Duchess and his ministers.

The Genius of Christianity

René de Chateaubriand

The Romantic movement of the late eighteenth century and first half of the nineteenth century was in part a rebellion against new trends such as rationalism, urbanization, and secularism. Many historians have noted specific connections between Romanticism and conservatism, particularly in the longing for a less complex life, the respect for traditional religion, and the sense of unity between rural life and human institutions. This is illustrated in the following selection from The Genius of Christianity *by René de Chateaubriand (1768–1848), a conservative French politician and writer. Published in 1802, it gained considerable popularity and helped Chateaubriand achieve a leading position among French conservatives. Here Chateaubriand describes the Gothic churches of the Middle Ages.*

Consider: *Why this description might appeal to members of the aristocracy and the Catholic Church; by implication, the aspects of Chateaubriand's own times that he was attacking.*

You could not enter a Gothic church without feeling a kind of awe and a vague sentiment of the Divinity. You were all at once carried back to those times when a fraternity of cenobites, after having meditated in the woods of their monasteries, met to prostrate themselves before the altar and to chant the praises of the Lord, amid the tranquillity and the silence of night. An-

---

SOURCE: Viscount de Chateaubriand, *The Genius of Christianity*, Charles I. White, trans. (Baltimore, Md.: John Murphy, 1856), pp. 385–387.

cient France seemed to revive altogether; you beheld all those singular costumes, all that nation so different from what it is at present; you were reminded of its revolutions, its productions, and its arts. The more remote were these times the more magical they appeared, the more they inspired ideas which always end with a reflection on the nothingness of man and the rapidity of life. . . .

The forests of Gaul were, in their turn, introduced into the temples of our ancestors, and those celebrated woods of oaks thus maintained their sacred character. Those ceilings sculptured into foliage of different kinds, those buttresses which prop the walls and terminate abruptly like the broken trunks of trees, the coolness of the vaults, the darkness of the sanctuary, the dim twilight of the aisles, the secret passages, the low doorways, — in a word, every thing in a Gothic church reminds you of the labyrinths of a wood; every thing excites a feeling of religious awe, of mystery, and of the Divinity.

The two lofty towers erected at the entrance of the edifice overtop the elms and yew-trees of the churchyard, and produce the most picturesque effect on the azure of heaven. Sometimes their twin heads are illumined by the first rays of dawn; at others they appear crowned with a capital of clouds or magnified in a foggy atmosphere. The birds themselves seem to make a mistake in regard to them, and to take them for the trees of the forest; they hover over their summits, and perch upon their pinnacles. But, lo! confused noises suddenly issue from the top of these towers and scare away the affrighted birds. The Christian architect, not content with building forests, has been desirous to retain their murmurs; and, by means of the organ and of bells, he has attached to the Gothic temple the very winds and thunders that roar in the recesses of the woods. Past ages, conjured up by these religious sounds, raise their venerable voices from the bosom of the stones, and are heard in every corner of the ancient Sibyl; loud-tongued bells swing over your head, while the vaults of death under your feet are profoundly silent.

The Tables Turned: The Glories of Nature

William Wordsworth

Romantic themes were reflected in poetry as much as in other cultural forms. The British poet William Wordsworth (1770–1850) focused early on romantic themes in his work. He emphasized the connection between the individual and the glories of nature. Wordsworth gained much recognition in his own lifetime and was eventually appointed Poet Laureate of England. The following poem, "The Tables Turned," was first published in 1798.

> **Consider:** *How this poem might be viewed as a rejection of the Enlightenment; the ways in which this poem relates to themes stressed by Chateaubriand.*

Up! up! my Friend, and quit your books;
Or surely you'll grow double:
Up! up! my Friend, and clear your looks;
Why all this toil and trouble?

The sun, above the mountain's head,
A freshening lustre mellow
Through all the long green fields has spread,
His first sweet evening yellow.

Books! 'tis a dull and endless strife:
Come, hear the woodland linnet,
How sweet his music! on my life,
There's more of wisdom in it.

And hark! how blithe the throstle sings!
He, too, is no mean preacher:
Come forth into the light of things,
Let Nature be your Teacher.

She has a world of ready wealth,
Our minds and hearts to bless—
Spontaneous wisdom breathed by health,
Truth breathed by cheerfulness.

SOURCE: Edward Dowden, ed., *The Poetical Works of William Wordsworth*, Vol. IV (London: George Bell and Sons, 1893), pp. 198–199.

One impulse from a vernal wood
May teach you more of man,
Of moral evil and of good,
Than all the sages can.

Sweet is the lore which Nature brings;
Our meddling intellect
Mis-shapes the beauteous forms of things: —
We murder to dissect.

Enough of Science and of Art;
Close up those barren leaves;
Come forth, and bring with you a heart
That watches and receives.

VISUAL SOURCES

Abbey Graveyard in the Snow

Caspar David Friedrich

Abbey Graveyard in the Snow *(1819) was painted by the well-known North German artist Caspar David Friedrich. In the center are the ruins of a Gothic choir of
a monastic church surrounded by a snow-covered graveyard and leafless winter
forest. To the left a procession of monks follows a coffin into the ruins.*

*This painting exemplifies many elements typical of Romanticism, particularly
German Romanticism. The scene, while visually accurate, goes beyond realism:
The light is too perfectly placed, the church remains are too majestic, the
surrounding forest is too symmetrical a frame, and the funeral procession is out of
place (funerals did not take place in ruins). By implication, this painting rejects
the limits of Enlightenment rationalism and the reality of nineteenth-century urban
life. Instead, a Romantic version of the Middle Ages, the spirituality of nature, and
the glories of Christianity are evoked. The Romantic longing to be overwhelmed
by eternal nature is suggested particularly by the rendering of small human figures
in a large landscape. Romanticism typically exalted the emotional over the rational, even if it was a melancholy sensitivity that was being displayed.*

Consider: *The ways in which the Romanticism of this painting is consistent with that of Wordsworth's poetry and Chateaubriand's description of a Gothic cathedral.*

Photo 7-1

Bildarchiv Preussischer Kulturbesitz

Liberty Leading the People: Romanticism and Liberalism

Eugène Delacroix

A number of historical themes of the first half of the nineteenth century are combined in Liberty Leading the People *(1830) by the French painter Eugène Delacroix. The painting shows an important event of the revolution of 1830 in Paris—revolutionaries fighting off government troops at a bridge in the center of the city. The revolutionaries are led by a feminine figure symbolizing liberty and carrying a Republican flag in one hand, a gun in the other. She is followed by people of all classes and ages.*

In both style and content this painting reveals some of the connections between liberalism and Romanticism. The scene represents the high moral purposes of the

Photo 7-2

Musée du Louvre/Photographie Giraudon

revolution: the people struggling for the ideals of liberalism and nationalism. Despite the turmoil of the event, the people's faces convey a calm, firm, assurance of the rightness and the outcome of their liberal cause. At the same time, the style of the painting is in the Romantic tradition, above all in its emphasis on heroism and the attainment of ideal goals — here liberal goals — beyond the normal expectations of life.

Consider: *The ways in which this painting represents what Metternich and the Congress of Vienna struggled against.*

SECONDARY SOURCES

The Congress of Vienna
Hajo Holborn

Hindsight allows historians to evaluate diplomatic events with a sharply critical eye. Often great settlements between nations have been criticized for not taking into account the historical forces that would soon undo the stability that the peace treaties were supposed to establish. Although this critical view applies to the Congress of Vienna, there are historians who see it as relatively successful, particularly in comparison with the settlement after World War I. One of these historians is Hajo Holborn of Yale University. In the following selection Holborn evaluates the Congress of Vienna from the point of view of what was realistic for the parties at that time.

Consider: *Why Holborn feels that the Congress of Vienna was a constructive peace treaty; how other historians might criticize this view.*

The Vienna settlement created a European political system whose foundations lasted for a full century. For a hundred years there occurred no wars of world-wide scope like those of the twenty-odd years after 1792. Europe experienced frightful wars, particularly between 1854 and 1878, but none of them was a war in which all the European states or even all the great European powers participated. The European wars of the nineteenth century produced shifts of power, but they were shifts within the European political system and did not upset that system as such.

SOURCE: Hajo Holborn, *The Political Collapse of Europe*. Reprinted by permission of Alfred A. Knopf, Inc. (New York, 1965), pp. 27–28. Copyright © 1965 by Alfred A. Knopf, Inc.

The peace settlement of Vienna has more often been condemned than praised. The accusation most frequently levelled against the Congress of Vienna has been that it lacked foresight in appraising the forces of modern nationalism and liberalism. Foresight is, indeed, one of the main qualities that distinguishes the statesman from the mere political professional. But even a statesman can only build with the bricks at hand and cannot hope to construct the second floor before he had modelled the first by which to shelter his own generation. His foresight of future developments can often express itself only by cautious attempts at keeping the way open for an evolution of the new forces.

It is questionable how successful the Congress of Vienna was in this respect. None of the Congress representatives was a statesman or political thinker of the first historic rank. All of them were strong partisans of conservatism or outright reaction, and they found the rectitude of their convictions confirmed by the victory of the old powers over the revolutionary usurper. Still, they did not make a reactionary peace. They recognized that France could not live without a constitutional charter, and they knew, too, that the Holy Roman Empire was beyond resurrection. The new German Confederation represented a great improvement of the political conditions of Germany if one remembers that in Germany as well as in Italy the national movements were not strong enough to serve as pillars of a new order. In eastern Europe, furthermore, the modern ideas of nationality had hardly found more than a small academic and literary audience. A peace treaty cannot create new historical forces; it can only place the existing ones in a relationship most conducive to the maintenance of mutual confidence and least likely to lead to future conflict. The rest must be left to the ever continuing and never finished daily work of the statesmen.

In this light the Vienna settlement was a constructive peace treaty.

Liberalism Defined

David Thomson

Although liberalism varied throughout Europe in accordance with the circumstances facing each country, there were broad similarities among the various liberal ideas and demands during the first half of the nineteenth century. In the following selection David Thomson, a Cambridge University historian who has written extensively on France and Great Britain, summarizes the common elements of liberal doctrine and attitudes in continental Europe.

SOURCE: David Thomson, *Europe Since Napoleon*. Reprinted by permission of Alfred A. Knopf, Inc. (New York: 1958), pp. 103–104. Copyright © 1958 by Alfred A. Knopf, Inc.

Consider: *How these doctrines and attitudes differ from conservatism; why liberalism would be more appealing to the middle class than to the aristocracy or the working class; the significance of the French Revolution for the development of liberal doctrines and attitudes.*

Liberalism, in its continental European sense more clearly than in its English or American sense, was like nationalism in that it rested on the belief that there should be a more organic and complete relationship between government and the community, between state and society, than existed under the dynastic regimes of the eighteenth century. Instead of government and administration existing above and in many respects apart from society — the exclusive affair of kings and their ministers and officials — they should rest on the organized consent of at least the most important sections of the community, and they ought to concern themselves with the interests of the whole community. The ideas that Americans had asserted in 1776 had still not been accepted by European governments: ideas that "governments are instituted among men" to secure individual rights, and derive "their just powers from the consent of the governed." European liberals stood, fundamentally, for these American ideals. The biggest obstacles to a broader basis of government were the powers and privileges of the aristocracy and the Church, and the lack of privileges of the merchant, business, and manufacturing classes. Thus the spearhead of the liberal attack against feudal rights and clericalist power was, in each European country, the underprivileged middle and professional classes. It was these classes, backed in the course of events by the peasants and by the Paris mob, that had been the central driving force of the French Revolution, and the chief gainers from it.

In doctrine, therefore, continental liberalism derived from the rationalist movement of the eighteenth century which had made so corrosive an attack upon inequality and arbitrary power. Its most characteristic method was parliamentary government; it sought in constitutional arrangements and in the rule of law a means of expressing middle-class interests and opinion, a vehicle of social reform, and a safeguard against absolutist government. It was distinct from democracy, or radicalism, in that it favored ideas of the sovereignty of the people; it wanted an extension of the franchise to include all men of property but to exclude men without property; it valued liberty more highly than equality; and it appealed to broadly the same classes as the growing sense of nationalism. To liberals, the French Revolution had condemned itself by its excesses: the Reign of Terror and mob democracy had bred the era of reaction and led to military dictatorship. The most desirable regime was either a constitutional monarchy, guaranteeing certain rights equally to all citizens, or a parliamentary republic, resting on a restricted franchise but upholding the equality of all before the law. Their objections to the settlement of 1815 were less that it violated nationality than that it restored absolutism and threatened to restore aristocratic and clerical privileges.

The Triumph of the Middle Classes: 1848

Charles Morazé

The revolutions of 1848 have been at the center of historical debate for a long time. To some, 1848 represents the end of the system set up by the Congress of Vienna; to others it represents the great battle between the forces of liberalism and conservatism; and to still others, it represents the point at which liberalism, nationalism, socialism, and Romanticism met. Perhaps the most persistent historiographical tradition views 1848 as a point at which history made a "wrong" turn. Some aspects of this historical debate are reflected in the following interpretation of 1848 by the French historian Charles Morazé. Here Morazé views the revolutions from a socioeconomic perspective, emphasizing the revolutions of 1848 as a great victory for middle-class capitalism.

> **Consider:** *According to Morazé, the economic factors that helped cause and end the revolutions of 1848; how Morazé supports his conclusion that this was a victory for middle-class capitalism; in what ways the aristocracy and working classes "lost."*

Thus the revolts of 1848 were an explosion of liberal nationalism which failed, although their effect was to shake the feudal structure so thoroughly that it gave place to a capitalist and bourgeois law, supporting individual ownership, based on a code like that of France. The year 1848 saw the last ineffectual flicker of Romanticism and the first great victory for capitalism.

Eastern Europe then became middle class and shed its tenacious traditions, its feudalism, castes, trade guilds and time-honoured ways of life. It entered the age of codified law, which was kept well up to date by great elected assemblies, and guaranteed the owner his land and the industrialist his credit. In Frankfurt, Rome or Paris there had been little mention of railways, but it was they which had broken up the rigid framework of credit based on personal estate; and by their demands a new monetary and financial world was created, enabling the railways to expand into new areas. The agricultural crisis activated a revolution in the urban industrial economy. Order was re-established in Europe as in England, for gold from the New World no longer enriched either an antiquated feudalism or a radical socialism, but rather strengthened the financial economy imposed by the railways, which gave its shape to capitalism.

The 1848 revolution saw the definitive failure of socialism. French theorists who had severely criticized the middle-class indifference to poverty as being barely concealed under an affectation of charitable virtue, could

SOURCE: Charles Morazé, *The Triumph of the Middle Classes* (Cleveland: World Publishing Co., 1966), p. 208.

not seize power in spite of the vehement eloquence of Proudhon, who dominated the debates in the republican assemblies; they could not even prevent the disastrous failure of the national workshops which were a caricature of the dreams of the first socialist age. Outside France, English chartism collapsed in ridicule, for the worker across the Channel was definitely no revolutionary. In Germany, Marx and his friends had tried to take advantage of the revolutionary movement to win support for their own brand of socialism. After having launched their celebrated manifesto in Paris, they had gone back to Cologne to replace the too liberal *Kölnische Zeitung*, on which Marx had been a collaborator some years earlier, by the *Neue Kölnische Zeitung*. But Marx was expelled in 1849. The crisis of 1846–8 deprived English landlords of the precious Corn Laws and the feudal lords of eastern Germany of the gangs of serf labour and Austria of serfdom itself. Middle-class capitalism was the great victor. From 1850 onwards it was to flourish with extraordinary vigour with the new supplies of American and Australian gold.

The Age of Paradox: 1848 – The English Exception

John Dodds

Although threatened by movements such as Chartism, England avoided the revolutions that struck almost every other European nation in 1848. Why? In the following selection from The Age of Paradox, *John Dodds addresses this question.*

> **Consider:** *Whether the content of the Chartist Petition of 1838 supports Dodds' interpretation; how this interpretation differs from that of Morazé; other differences between England and continental European nations at the time.*

What saved England from the whirlpool of revolution that engulfed the Continent in 1848? Here was a country in which six sevenths of the adult male population could not vote and where the representation in the Commons was so unfairly distributed that the great congested center of Manchester, with twice the population of Buckinghamshire, returned only two members as against the latter's eleven. Hunger and possible starvation looked just as ghastly to the Liverpool Irishman or the Glasgow operative as it did to the French workman. "It is quite new," wrote Greville, "to hear any Englishman coolly recommend assassination." How did England escape catastrophe?

Source: John W. Dodds, *The Age of Paradox* (New York: Rinehart, 1952), pp. 331–332.

In the first place, the Chartist leadership was divided within its own house. Such "moral force" men as Lovett would have nothing to do with the seditious threats of those who urged violent opposition to the Government. The leadership of the "physical force" group was itself vacillating: witness Feargus O'Connor's performance on Kennington Common. There was, too, a new and growing class of superior artisans — notably those essential to the great engineering developments in factories and railways — who wooed respectability, trusted in the developing organization of trade unionism to secure their rights, and threw their social weight with the middle classes. And, unlike the French, the English middle classes were one with the aristocracy in defense of the established order; the householders who patrolled the streets on April 10th as special constables were more important as symbols of a national *esprit* than they knew. Moreover, England had an aristocracy of which even the more stiff-necked members had the sense to bow constitutionally before the inevitable, and many of whom exerted themselves actively to temper the winds of distress. The energetic philanthropic and liberal efforts of such men as Lord Ashley, Sir William Molesworth, Lord Morpeth, and Lord Dudley Stuart (friend of Poland and champion of Kossuth) told heavily. The repeal of the Corn Laws, too, had come just in time; and there had never been any question about the freedom of the British press. The result of all this was that even the underprivileged Englishman felt that he was living under a constitutional government, that he could appeal to a sympathetic Queen and her "most honourable ministers" for relief. Hence an almost pathetic faith in monster petitions. Street barricades were simply not an Englishman's way of life. He might march endlessly with angry banners, but under such a friendly monarchy he would never tear up his own trees in Hyde Park to block Constitution Hill.

Chapter Questions

1. In a debate between liberals and conservatives of the early nineteenth century over how the French Revolution should be evaluated, what points would each side make?

2. In what ways might conservatives find Romanticism to their liking? What aspects of Romanticism might appeal to liberals?

3. Analyze nineteenth-century conservatism, liberalism, and Romanticism as alternative ways in which Europeans attempted to deal with the changes in Western civilization that had been occurring since the second half of the eighteenth century.

CHAPTER EIGHT

Industrialization And Social Change

&.

The Industrial Revolution, which transformed economic life in the West, began in England in the eighteenth century. After the Napoleonic period it spread to Western Europe, and by the end of the nineteenth century it had touched most of Western civilization. The Industrial Revolution was characterized by unprecedented economic growth, the factory system of production, and the use of new, artificially powered machines for transportation and mechanical operations. The potential was tremendous; for the first time, human beings had the ability to produce far more than was needed to sustain a large percentage of the population. Whether that potential would be realized, and at what cost, remained to be seen.

In the wake of industrialization came great social changes. The middle and working classes were most affected by industrialization, and both grew in number and social influence as did the urban areas in which they worked and lived. But it was the middle class that benefited most, enjoying a rising standard of living, increased prestige, and growing political influence. Whether the working class benefited from industrialization during these early decades is a matter for debate among historians. Clearly it was this class that bore the burdens of urban social problems: overcrowded slums, poor sanitation, insufficient social services, and a host of related problems. The aristocracy, the peasantry, and the artisans—classes tied to the traditional agricultural economy and older means of production—slowly diminished in numbers and social importance as industrialization spread.

The selections in this chapter deal with the economic and social aspects of industrialization. Much-debated questions of economic history are addressed. Why did industrialization occur first in England? How did England differ from other areas that were relatively advanced economically? What combination of factors caused this economic transformation? Most of the documents concern the human consequences of industrialization, questions of social history. The most popular area of interest, the effect of industrialization on the workers directly involved, is explored. What were the working conditions in the factories? How did industrialization affect the overall life style of these people? Did their standard of living improve or diminish as a result of industrialization? The middle class is also examined, especially middle-class attitudes and values. How did the middle class view industrial-

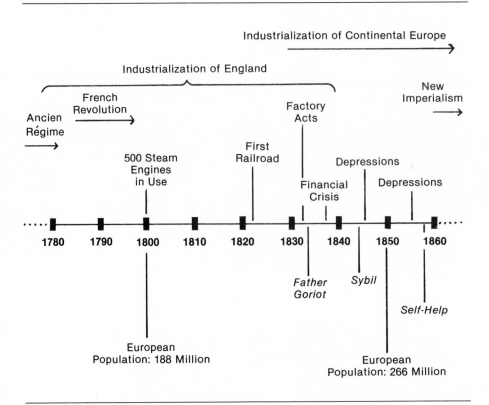

ization? What were its attitudes toward money? How did the attitudes of and toward middle-class women change?

This chapter centers on industrialization in the first half of the nineteenth century. It should be recognized that industrialization spread unevenly, and it was not until the second half of the nineteenth century and even the beginning of the twentieth century that industrialization spread to many areas in Southern and Eastern Europe.

PRIMARY SOURCES

Testimony for the Factory Act of 1833: Working Conditions in England

Industrialization carried with it broad social and economic changes that were quickly felt by those involved. The most striking changes were in the working conditions in the new factories and mines. During the first decades of industrialization, there was little government control over working conditions and few effective labor organizations; laborers were thus at the mercy of factory owners who were pursuing profit in a competitive world. Investigations into conditions in factories and mines conducted by the British Parliament in the 1830s and 1840s led eventually to the enactment of legislation, such as the Factory Act of 1833. These parliamentary investigations provide us with extensive information about working conditions and attitudes toward them. The following selection contains three excerpts from a parliamentary commission's investigations into child labor in factories. The first is a summary by the commission of medical examiners from northeastern England. The second is the testimony of John Wright, a steward in a silk factory. The third is the testimony of William Harter, a silk manufacturer.

> **Consider:** *What these people perceived as the worst abuses of factory labor; the causes of the poor working conditions; how Harter might defend himself against the charges that he was abusing the working class; what biases the witnesses might hold.*

TESTIMONY OF THE COMMISSION OF MEDICAL EXAMINERS

The account of the physical condition of the manufacturing population in the large towns in the North-eastern District of England is less favourable.

SOURCE: Commission for Inquiry into the Employment of Children in Factories, *Second Report, with Minutes of Evidence and Reports by the Medical Commissioners*, Vol. V, Session 29 January–20 August, 1833 (London: His Majesty's Printing Office, 1833), pp. 5, 26–28.

It is of this district that the Commissioners state, "We have found un-doubted instances of children five years old sent to work thirteen hours a day; and frequently of children nine, ten, and eleven consigned to labour for fourteen and fifteen hours." The effects ascertained by the Commis-sioners in many cases are, "deformity," and in still more "stunted growth, relaxed muscles, and slender conformation:" "twisting of the ends of the long bones, relaxation of the ligaments of the knees, ankles, and the like." "The representation that these effects are so common and universal as to enable some persons invariably to distinguish factory children from other children is, I have no hesitation in saying, an exaggerated and unfaithful picture of their general condition; at the same time it must be said, that the individual instances in which some one or other of those effects of severe labour are discernible are rather frequent than rare. . . .

Upon the whole, there remains no doubt upon my mind, that under the system pursued in many of the factories, the children of the labouring classes stand in need of, and ought to have, legislative protection against the conspiracy insensibly formed between their masters and parents, to tax them to a degree of toil beyond their strength."

"In conclusion, I think it has been clearly proved that children have been worked a most unreasonable and cruel length of time daily, and that even adults have been expected to do a certain quantity of labour which scarcely any human being is able to endure. I am of opinion no child under fourteen years of age should work in a factory of any description for more than eight hours a day. From fourteen upwards I would recommend that no individual should, under any circumstances, work more than twelve hours a day; although if practicable, as a physician, I would prefer the limitation of ten hours, for all persons who earn their bread by their industry.

TESTIMONY OF JOHN WRIGHT

How long have you been employed in a silk-mill? — More than thirty years.

Did you enter it as a child? — Yes, betwixt five and six.

How many hours a day did you work then? — The same thirty years ago as now.

What are those hours? — Eleven hours per day and two over-hours: over-hours are working after six in the evening till eight. The regular hours are from six in the morning to six in the evening, and two others are two over-hours: about fifty years ago they began working over-hours.

What are the intervals for meals? — In our factory twenty minutes for breakfast at eight o'clock, one hour for dinner at two, twenty minutes for tea at five o'clock.

Are the meals taken out of the mill, or in? — In the walls of the mill, ex-cept the dinner.

Are the workpeople forbidden to leave the mill for breakfast? — Yes.

Are silk-mills clean in general? — They are; they are swept every day, and white-washed once a year.

What is the temperature of silk-mills? — I don't know exactly the temperature, but it is very agreeable.

Is any artificial heat required? — In the winter it is heated by steam.

To what degree? — I cannot speak positively; but it is not for the work, only to keep the hands warm and comfortable.

Why, then, are those employed in them said to be in such a wretched condition? — In the first place, the great number of hands congregated together, in some rooms forty, in some fifty, in some sixty, and I have known some as many as 100, which must be injurious to both health and growing. In the second place, the privy is in the factory, which frequently emits an unwholesome smell; and it would be worth while to notice in the future erection of mills, that there be betwixt the privy door and the factory wall a kind of a lobby of cage-work. 3dly, The tediousness and the everlasting sameness in the first process preys much on the spirits, and makes the hands spiritless. 4thly, the extravagant number of hours a child is compelled to labour and confinement, which for one week is seventy-six hours, which makes 3,952 hours for one year, we deduct 208 hours for meals within the factory which makes the net labour for one year 3,744; but the labour and confinement together of a child between ten years of age and twenty is 39,520 hours, enough to fritter away the best constitution. 5thly, About six months in the year we are obliged to use either gas, candles, or lamps, for the longest portion of that time, nearly six hours a day, being obliged to work amid the smoke and soot of the same; and also a large portion of oil and grease is used in the mills.

What are the effects of the present system of labour? — From my earliest recollections, I have found the effects to be awfully detrimental to the well-being of the operative; I have observed frequently children carried to factories, unable to walk, and that entirely owing to excessive labour and confinement. The degradation of the workpeople baffles all description: frequently have two of my sisters been obliged to be assisted to the factory and home again, until by-and-by they could go no longer, being totally crippled in their legs. And in the next place, I remember some ten or twelve years ago working in one of the largest firms in Macclesfield, (Messrs. Baker and Pearson,) with about twenty-five men, where they were scarce one half fit for His Majesty's service. Those that are straight in their limbs are stunted in their growth; much inferior to their fathers in point of strength. 3dly, Through excessive labour and confinement there is often a total loss of appetite; a kind of langour steals over the whole frame — enters to the very core — saps the foundation of the best constitution — and lays our strength prostrate in the dust. In the 4th place, by protracted labour there is an alarming increase of cripples in various parts of this town, which has come under my own observation and knowledge. I was fully aware that neither the Commissioners or any other person could form an adequate conception of the wretchedness, except such person canvassed the town in various parts thereof. I entered not into all the streets, but went through eight or nine — some of the cleanliest and prettiest streets in the town; and there I found that which before I had no conception of, although having resided in the town betwixt thirty and forty years.

In Townley Street, the number of cripples	10
George Street	5
Charlotte Street	4
Watercots	15
Bank Top	3
Lord Street	7
Mill Lane	12
Great George Street	2
Workhouse	2
Park Green	1
Pickford Street	2

Are all these cripples made in the silk factories? — Yes, they are, I believe; for when I visited the several families containing the number of cripples afore mentioned, I was particular in my inquiries of the parents, whether their children were crippled entirely through excessive labour and confinement in silk factories; with one consent they all declared they were. I moreover asked whether they considered corporal punishment as any part of the cause; they replied "No;" some declaring they did not think that their children had ever been beaten.

TESTIMONY OF WILLIAM HARTER

What effect would it have on your manufacture to reduce the hours of labour to ten? — It would instantly much reduce the value of my mill and machinery, and consequently of far prejudice my manufacture.

How so? — They are calculated to produce a certain quantity of work in a given time. Every machine is valuable in proportion to the quantity of work which it will turn off in a given time. It is impossible that the machinery could produce as much work in ten hours as in twelve. If the tending of the machines were a laborious occupation, the difference in the quantity of work might not always be in exact proportion to the difference of working time; but in my mill, and silk-mills in general, the work requires the least imaginable labour; therefore it is perfectly impossible that the machines could produce as much work in ten hours as in twelve. The produce would vary in about the same ratio as the working time.

Sybil, or the Two Nations: Mining Towns

Benjamin Disraeli

Nineteenth-century novels contain some of the most effective descriptions of industrial life. In addition to providing such description, Sybil, or the Two Nations (1845), written by Benjamin Disraeli (1804–1881), a novelist and politician who also served as prime minister of England (1867–1868, 1874–1880), illustrates the thinking of a group of reforming Tory aristocrats, sometimes referred to as Young England. They hoped to gain working-class support against their political competitors, the liberal Whigs. In the following selection from this novel, Disraeli describes Marney, a rural mining town.

> **Consider:** *The physical consequences of industrialization for the land and the town; the worst aspects of industrial labor, according to Disraeli; how this description compares with the testimony before the commission on child labor; who, if anyone, Disraeli would blame for all this.*

The last rays of the sun contending with clouds of smoke that drifted across the country, partially illumined a peculiar landscape. Far as the eye could reach, and the region was level, except where a range of limestone hills formed its distant limit, a wilderness of cottages, or tenements that were hardly entitled to a higher name, were scattered for many miles over the land; some detached, some connected in little rows, some clustering in groups, yet rarely forming continuous streets, but interspersed with blazing furnaces, heaps of burning coal, and piles of smouldering ironstone; while forges and engine chimneys roared and puffed in all directions, and indicated the frequent presence of the mouth of the mine, and the bank of the coal-pit. Notwithstanding the whole country might be compared to a vast rabbit warren, it was nevertheless intersected with canals, crossing each other at various levels; and though the subterranean operations were prosecuted with so much avidity that it was not uncommon to observe whole rows of houses awry, from the shifting and hollow nature of the land, still, intermingled with heaps of mineral refuse, or of metallic dross, patches of the surface might here and there be recognised, covered, as if in mockery, with grass and corn, looking very much like those gentlemen's sons that we used to read of in our youth, stolen by the chimneysweeps, and giving some

SOURCE: Benjamin Disraeli, *Sybil, or the Two Nations* (New York: M. Walter Dunne, 1904), pp. 198–200.

intimations of their breeding beneath their grimy livery. But a tree or a shrub, such an existence was unknown in this dingy rather than dreary region.

It was the twilight hour; the hour at which in southern climes the peasant kneels before the sunset image of the blessed Hebrew maiden; when caravans halt in their long course over vast deserts, and the turbaned traveller, bending in the sand, pays his homage to the sacred stone and the sacred city; the hour, not less holy, that announces the cessation of English toil, and sends forth the miner and the collier to breathe the air of earth, and gaze on the light of heaven.

They come forth: the mine delivers its gang and the pit its bondsmen; the forge is silent and the engine is still. The plain is covered with the swarming multitude: bands of stalwart men, broad-chested and muscular, wet with toil, and black as the children of the tropics; troops of youth, alas! of both sexes, though neither their raiment nor their language indicates the difference; all are clad in male attire; and oaths that men might shudder at issue from lips born to breathe words of sweetness. Yet these are to be, some are, the mothers of England! But can we wonder at the hideous coarseness of their language, when we remember the savage rudeness of their lives? Naked to the waist, an iron chain fastened to a belt of leather runs between their legs clad in canvas trousers, while on hands and feet an English girl, for twelve, sometimes for sixteen hours a day, hauls and hurries tubs of coals up subterranean roads, dark, precipitous, and plashy; circumstances that seem to have escaped the notice of the Society for the Abolition of Negro Slavery. Those worthy gentlemen, too, appear to have been singularly unconscious of the sufferings of the little trappers, which was remarkable, as many of them were in their own employ.

See, too, these emerge from the bowels of the earth! Infants of four and five years of age, many of them girls, pretty and still soft and timid; entrusted with the fulfilment of responsible duties, the very nature of which entails on them the necessity of being the earliest to enter the mine and the latest to leave it. Their labour indeed is not severe, for that would be impossible, but it is passed in darkness and in solitude. They endure that punishment which philosophical philanthropy has invented for the direst criminals, and which those criminals deem more terrible than the death for which it is substituted. Hour after hour elapses, and all that reminds the infant trappers of the world they have quitted, and that which they have joined, is the passage of the coal-waggons for which they open the air-doors of the galleries, and on keeping which doors constantly closed, except at this moment of passage, the safety of the mine and the lives of the persons employed in it entirely depend.

Self-Help: Middle-Class Attitudes

Samuel Smiles

Middle-class liberals were not totally unaware of the consequences of industrialization for society. Doctrines were developed that reflected and appealed to their attitudes. Such doctrines served to justify the position of the middle class, to support policies it usually favored, and to rationalize the poor state of the working class. Many of these doctrines appeared in Self-Help, *the popular book by Samuel Smiles, a physician, editor, secretary of two railroads, and author. First published in 1859,* Self-Help *became a best seller in England and was translated into many languages. The following excerpt is a good example of the individualism and moral tone that appear throughout the book.*

> **Consider:** *How Smiles justifies his assertion that self-help is the only answer to problems; how Smiles would analyze the situation of the working class and how he would react to the testimony presented to the parliamentary commission on child labor.*

"Heaven helps those who help themselves" is a well tried maxim, embodying in a small compass the results of vast human experience. The spirit of self-help is the root of all genuine growth in the individual; and, exhibited in the lives of many, it constitutes the true source of national vigor and strength. Help from without is often enfeebling in its effects, but help from within invariably invigorates. Whatever is done *for* men or classes, to a certain extent takes away the stimulus and necessity of doing for themselves; and where men are subjected to over-guidance and over-government, the inevitable tendency is to render them comparatively helpless.

Even the best institutions can give a man no active help. Perhaps the most they can do is, to leave him free to develop himself and improve his individual condition. But in all times men have been prone to believe that their happiness and well-being were to be secured by means of institutions rather than by their own conduct. Hence the value of legislation as an agent in human advancement has usually been much over-estimated. To constitute the millionth part of a Legislature, by voting for one or two men once in three or five years, however conscientiously this duty may be performed, can exercise but little active influence upon any man's life and character. Moreover, it is every day becoming more clearly understood, that the function of Government is negative and restrictive, rather than positive and active; being resolvable principally into protection — protection of life, liberty, and property. Laws, wisely administrated, will secure men in the enjoyment of the fruits of their labor, whether of mind or body, at a com-

SOURCE: Samuel Smiles, *Self-Help* (Chicago: Belford, Clarke, 1881), pp. 21–23, 48–49.

paratively small personal sacrifice; but no laws, however stringent, can make the idle industrious, the shiftless provident, or the drunken sober. Such reforms can only be effected by means of individual action, economy, and self-denial; by better habits, rather than by greater rights. . . .

Indeed, all experience serves to prove that the worth and strength of a State depend far less upon the form of its institutions than upon the character of its men. For the nation is only an aggregate of individual conditions, and civilization itself is but a question of the personal improvement of the men, women, and children of whom society is composed.

National progress is the sum of individual industry, energy, and uprightness, as national decay is of individual idleness, selfishness, and vice. What we are accustomed to decry as great social evils, will for the most part be found to be but the outgrowth of man's own perverted life; and though we may endeavor to cut them down and extirpate them by means of Law, they will only spring up again with fresh luxuriance in some other form, unless the conditions of personal life and character are radically improved. If this view be correct, then it follows that the highest patriotism and philanthropy consist, not so much in altering laws and modifying institutions, as in helping and stimulating men to elevate and improve themselves by their own free and independent individual action.

One of the most strongly marked features of the English people is their spirit of industry, standing out prominent and distinct in their past history, and as strikingly characteristic of them now as at any former period. It is this spirit, displayed by the commons of England, which has laid the foundations and built up the industrial greatness of the empire. This vigorous growth of the nation has been mainly the result of the free energy of individuals, and it has been contingent upon the number of hands and minds from time to time actively employed within it, whether as cultivators of the soil, producers of articles of utility, contrivers of tools and machines, writers of books, or creators of works of art. And while this spirit of active industry has been the vital principle of the nation, it has also been its saving and remedial one, counteracting from time to time the effects of errors in our laws and imperfections in our constitution.

The career of industry which the nation has pursued, has also proved its best education. As steady application to work is the healthiest training for every individual, so is it the best discipline of a state. Honorable industry travels the same road with duty; and Providence has closely linked both with happiness. The gods, says the poet, have placed labor and toil on the way leading to the Elysian fields. Certain it is that no bread eaten by man is so sweet as that earned by his own labor, whether bodily or mental. By labor the earth has been subdued, and man redeemed from barbarism; nor has a single step in civilization been made without it. Labor is not only a necessity and a duty, but a blessing: only the idler feels it to be a curse. The duty of work is written on the thews and muscles of the limbs, the mechanism of the hand, the nerves and lobes of the brain—the sum of whose healthy action is satisfaction and enjoyment. In the school of labor is taught the best practical wisdom; nor is a life of manual employment, as we shall hereafter find, incompatible with high mental culture.

Father Goriot: Money and the Middle Class

Honoré de Balzac

With industrialization the middle class rose in status and wealth. Increasingly, money became a common denominator in society, and the middle class was in a position to benefit from this. But the emphasis on money had its painful side even for the relatively wealthy. Few have focused on this more profoundly and broadly than the French novelist Honoré de Balzac, who himself struggled with financial problems for much of his life. The following is an excerpt from his Father Goriot *(1834), in which Goriot, an old bourgeois, bemoans the way his daughters are treating him now that he is no longer so rich.*

> **Consider:** *How Goriot sees money as both the cause for and the solution to his problems; the connections Balzac makes between money, social structure, and family life; how a worker might react to Goriot's problems.*

"Ah! if I were rich still, if I had kept my money, if I had not given all to them, they would be with me now; they would fawn on me and cover my cheeks with their kisses! I should be living in a great mansion; I should have grand apartments and servants and a fire in my room; and *they* would be about me all in tears, and their husbands and their children. I should have had all that; now—I have nothing. Money brings everything to you; even your daughters. My money. Oh! where is my money? If I had plenty of money to leave behind me, they would nurse me and tend me; I should hear their voices, I should see their faces. Ah, God! who knows? They both of them have hearts of stone. I loved them too much; it was not likely that they should love me. A father ought always to be rich; he ought to keep his children well in hand, like unruly horses. I have gone down on my knees to them. Wretches! this is the crowning act that brings the last ten years to a proper close. If you but knew how much they made of me just after they were married. (Oh! this is cruel torture!) I had just given them each eight hundred thousand francs; they were bound to be civil to me after that, and their husbands too were civil. I used to go to their houses: it was, 'My kind father' here, 'My dear father' there. There was always a place for me at their tables. I used to dine with their husbands now and then, and they were very respectful to me. I was still worth something, they thought. How

SOURCE: Honoré de Balzac, *Father Goriot* (New York: Century Co., 1904), pp. 264–265.

should they know? I had not said anything about my affairs. It is worth while to be civil to a man who has given his daughters eight hundred thousand francs apiece; and they showed me every attention then — but it was all for my money. Grand people are not great. I found that out by experience! I went to the theatre with them in their carriage; I might stay as long as I cared to stay at their evening parties. In fact, they acknowledged me their father; publicly they owned that they were my daughters. But I always was a shrewd one, you see, and nothing was lost upon me. Everything went straight to the mark and pierced my heart. I saw quite well that it was all sham and pretence, but there is no help for such things as these. I felt less at my ease at their dinner-table than I did downstairs here. I had nothing to say for myself. So these grand folks would ask in my son-in-law's ear, 'Who may that gentleman be?' — 'The father-in-law with the dollars; he is very rich.' — 'The devil, he is!' they would say, and look again at me with the respect due to my money.

Woman in Her Social and Domestic Character

Elizabeth Poole Sandford

Industrialization also had its effects on middle-class women. As the wealth and position of these women rose in a changing economic environment, previous models of behavior no longer applied. A variety of books and manuals appeared to counsel middle-class women on their proper role and behavior. The following is an excerpt from one of these, Woman in Her Social and Domestic Character *(1842), written by Mrs. John Sandford.*

> **Consider:** *Woman's ideal function in relation to her husband, according to this document; by implication, the role of the middle-class man in relation to his wife; possible explanations for this view of women.*

The changes wrought by Time are many. It influences the opinions of men as familiarity does their feelings; it has a tendency to do away with superstition, and to reduce every thing to its real worth.

It is thus that the sentiment for woman has undergone a change. The romantic passion which once almost deified her is on the decline; and it is by intrinsic qualities that she must now inspire respect. She is no longer the queen of song and the star of chivalry. But if there is less of enthusiasm entertained for her, the sentiment is more rational, and, perhaps, equally sincere; for it is in relation to happiness that she is chiefly appreciated.

SOURCE: Mrs. John Sandford (Elizabeth Poole Sandford), *Woman in Her Social and Domestic Character* (Boston: Otis, Broaders and Co., 1842), pp. 5–7, 15–16.

And in this respect it is, we must confess, that she is most useful and most important. Domestic life is the chief source of her influence; and the greatest debt society can owe to her is domestic comfort: for happiness is almost an element of virtue; and nothing conduces more to improve the character of men than domestic peace. A woman may make a man's home delightful, and may thus increase his motives for virtuous exertion. She may refine and tranquillize his mind, — may turn away his anger or allay his grief. Her smile may be the happy influence to gladden his heart, and to disperse the cloud that gathers on his brow. And in proportion to her endeavors to make those around her happy, she will be esteemed and loved. She will secure by her excellence that interest and regard which she might formerly claim as the privilege of her sex, and will really merit the deference which was then conceded to her as a matter of course. . . .

Perhaps one of the first secrets of her influence is adaptation to the tastes, and sympathy in the feelings, of those around her. This holds true in lesser as well as in graver points. It is in the former, indeed, that the absence of interest in a companion is frequently most disappointing. Where want of congeniality impairs domestic comfort, the fault is generally chargeable on the female side. It is for woman, not for man, to make the sacrifice, especially in indifferent matters. She must, in a certain degree, be plastic herself if she would mould others. . . .

To be useful, a woman must have feeling. It is this which suggests the thousand nameless amenities which fix her empire in the heart, and render her so agreeable, and almost so necessary, that she imperceptibly rises in the domestic circle, and becomes at once its cement and its charm.

Nothing is so likely to conciliate the affections of the other sex as a feeling that woman looks to them for support and guidance. In proportion as men are themselves superior, they are accessible to this appeal. On the contrary, they never feel interested in one who seems disposed rather to offer than to ask assistance. There is, indeed, something unfeminine in independence. It is contrary to nature, and therefore it offends. We do not like to see a woman affecting tremors, but still less do we like to see her acting the amazon. A really sensible woman feels her dependence. She does what she can; but she is conscious of inferiority, and therefore grateful for support. She knows that she is the weaker vessel, and that as such she should receive honor. In this view, her weakness is an attraction, not a blemish.

In every thing, therefore, that women attempt, they should show their consciousness of dependence. If they are learners, let them evince a teachable spirit; if they give an opinion, let them do it in an unassuming manner. There is something so unpleasant in female self-sufficiency that it not unfrequently deters instead of persuading, and prevents the adoption of advice which the judgment even approves.

VISUAL SOURCES

Gare Saint Lazare

Claude Monet

From a visual standpoint, industrial civilization was strikingly different from its predecessor. This 1877 painting of a railroad station in the heart of nineteenth-century Paris by the French Impressionist Claude Monet epitomizes the new industrial civilization. Steam, powerful engines, rapid transportation, and structures of iron and glass, all in an expanding urban environment, contrast sharply with the typical rural or urban images of previous eras.

Consider: *The associations that a nineteenth-century viewer might have upon viewing this painting.*

Photo 8-1

Courtesy of the Fogg Art Museum, Harvard University.
Bequest, Collection of Maurice Wetheim, Class of 1906.

Illustration from Life and Adventures of Michael Armstrong

This is an illustration from a novel, Life and Adventures of Michael Armstrong *(1840), by the well-known British author, Mrs. Frances Trollope. The illustration*

Photo 8-2

The Bettmann Archive/BBC Hulton

depicts several of the main elements of the Industrial Revolution in England. It shows the inside of a textile factory — a factory in the most advanced of the new industries. Thanks to mechanization and artificial power, a few workers can now do the work of many. The workers — men, women, and children — are obviously poor. In the background stands the stern middle-class owner talking with others of his class while in the foreground a child worker embraces his middle-class counterpart for some kindness he has displayed. The scene is reflective of the typical middle-class view of the poor and poverty — as problems of morals, to be treated with pity and philanthropic concern but not yet requiring substantial social or economic change.

Consider: *The ways in which this illustration reflects aspects of industrialization touched on by other documents in this chapter; the similarities and differences between this illustration and Photo 3-2 in Chapter 3.*

Industrialization and Demographic Change

A comparison of the first two maps (pp. 173–174), which show the population density of England in 1801 and 1851, reveals the relatively rapid increase in population and urbanization in certain areas of England during this period. The third map (p. 159) shows where industry (mainly textiles, metallurgy, and mining) was concentrated in 1851. A comparison of all three maps reveals the connections between shifting population density, urbanization, and industrialization during this period of early, rapid modernization of England's economy.

Consider: *What some of the geopolitical consequences of these connections between demographic and economic changes might be; what some of the social consequences of these same connections might be.*

Map 8-1   Population Density: England, 1801

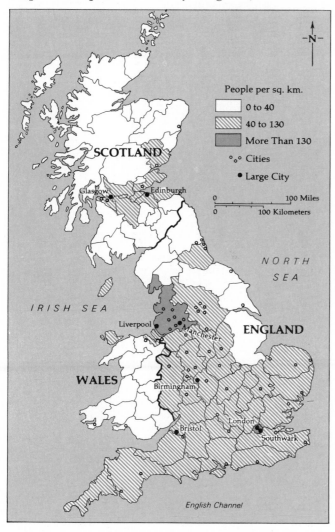

Map 8-2   Population Density: England, 1851

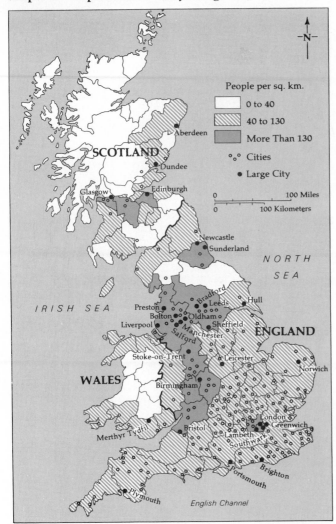

Map 8-3   Concentration of Industry in England, 1851

SECONDARY SOURCES

The Stages of Economic Growth

W. W. Rostow

The entire conception of industrialization has been debated for over a century. For most of that time, scholars have been willing to apply the term "Industrial Revolution," made popular by the elder Arnold Toynbee in the 1880s, to the great economic transformation that occurred in England between the late eighteenth century and the mid-nineteenth century and in other parts of Europe somewhat later. But more recent and more detailed research has led historians to question the usefulness of that term. During the last three decades, economic historians have been turning to such terms as "economic modernization" and "economic growth." Moreover, these historians have been applying new models from the social sciences to these historical processes. One of the most daring and influential works written along these lines is The Stages of Economic Growth *(1960) by W. W. Rostow. A historian and former high official in the Kennedy administration, Rostow argues that industrialization generally takes place in five stages. It is the third stage that constitutes what we usually think of as the Industrial Revolution. In the following selection, Rostow summarizes the first three stages.*

> **Consider:** *What periods each of these three stages would cover; how government action could influence what occurs in each stage.*

It is possible to identify all societies, in their economic dimensions, as lying within one of five categories: the traditional society, the preconditions for take-off, the take-off, the drive to maturity, and the age of high mass-consumption. . . .

First, the traditional society. A traditional society is one whose structure is developed within limited production functions, based on pre-Newtonian science and technology, and on pre-Newtonian attitudes towards the physical world. Newton is here used as a symbol for that watershed in history when men came widely to believe that the external world was subject to a few knowable laws, and was systematically capable of productive manipulation. . . .

The second stage of growth embraces societies in the process of transition; that is, the period when the preconditions for take-off are developed; for it takes time to transform a traditional society in the ways necessary for it to exploit the fruits of modern science, to fend off diminishing returns, and

Source: W. W. Rostow, *The Stages of Economic Growth.* Reprinted by permission of Cambridge University Press (Cambridge, England, 1960), pp. 4, 6–7, 18–19.

thus to enjoy the blessings and choices opened up by the march of compound interest.

The preconditions for take-off were initially developed, in a clearly marked way, in Western Europe of the late seventeenth and early eighteenth centuries as the insights of modern science began to be translated into new production functions in both agriculture and industry, in a setting given dynamism by the lateral expansion of world markets and the international competition for them. But all that lies behind the break-up of the Middle Ages is relevant to the creation of the preconditions for take-off in Western Europe. Among the Western European states, Britain, favoured by geography, natural resources, trading possibilities, social and political structure, was the first to develop fully the preconditions for take-off. . . . We come now to the great watershed in the life of modern societies: the third stage in this sequence, the take-off. The take-off is the interval when the old blocks and resistances to steady growth are finally overcome. The forces making for economic progress, which yielded limited bursts and enclaves of modern activity, expand and come to dominate the society. Growth becomes its normal condition. Compound interest becomes built, as it were, into its habits and institutional structure. . . . The transition we are examining has, evidently, many dimensions. A society predominantly agricultural — with, in fact, usually 75 % or more of its working force in agriculture — must shift to a predominance for industry, communications, trade and services.

A society whose economic, social and political arrangements are built around the life of relatively small — mainly self-sufficient — regions must orient its commerce and its thought to the nation and to a still larger international setting.

The view towards the having of children — initially the residual blessing and affirmation of immortality in a hard life, of relatively fixed horizons — must change in ways which ultimately yield a decline in the birth-rate, as the possibility of progress and the decline in the need for unskilled farm labour create a new calculus.

The income above minimum levels of consumption, largely concentrated in the hands of those who own land, must be shifted into the hands of those who will spend it on roads and railroads, schools and factories rather than on country houses and servants, personal ornaments and temples.

Men must come to be valued in the society not for their connexion with clan or class, or, even, their guild; but for their individual ability to perform certain specific, increasingly specialized functions.

And, above all, the concept must be spread that man need not regard his physical environment as virtually a factor given by nature and providence, but as an ordered world which, if rationally understood, can be manipulated in ways which yield productive change and, in one dimension at least, progress.

All of this — and more — is involved in the passage of a traditional to a modern growing society.

The Making of Economic Society: England, the First to Industrialize

Robert Heilbroner

Although it is clear that industrialization occurred first in England, it is not apparent why this should be so. During the eighteenth century France was prosperous and economically advanced. Other countries such as Belgium and the Netherlands possessed certain economic advantages over England and might have industrialized earlier but did not. In the following selection Robert Heilbroner, an economist and economic historian, addresses the question of why England was first and points out the differences between England and most other European nations in the eighteenth century.

> **Consider:** *Why Heilbroner stresses the role of the "New Men" over the other factors he lists; any disadvantages England had to overcome; whether it was simply the circumstances that gave rise to the "New Men" or whether it was the "New Men" who took advantage of the circumstances when most men in most other nations would not have.*

Why did the Industrial Revolution originally take place in England and not on the continent? To answer the question we must look at the background factors which distinguished England from most other European nations in the eighteenth century.

The first of these factors was simply that England was relatively wealthy. In fact, a century of successful exploration, slave-trading, piracy, war, and commerce had made her the richest nation in the world. Even more important, her riches had accrued not merely to a few nobles, but to a large upper-middle stratum of commercial bourgeoisie. England was thus one of the first nations to develop, albeit on a small scale, a prime requisite of an industrial economy: a "mass" consumer market. As a result, a rising pressure of demand inspired a search for new techniques.

Second, England was the scene of the most successful and thorough-going transformation of feudal society into commercial society. A succession of strong kings had effectively broken the power of the local nobility and had made England into a single unified state. As part of this process, we also find in England the strongest encouragement to the rising mercantile classes. Then too, as we have seen, the enclosure movement, which gained in tempo in the seventeenth and eighteenth centuries, expelled an army of laborers to man her new industrial establishments.

SOURCE: Robert L. Heilbroner, *The Making of Economic Society.* Reprinted by permission of Prentice–Hall, Inc. (Englewood Cliffs, N.J., 1980), pp. 76–77, 80–81.

Third, England was the locus of a unique enthusiasm for science and engineering. The famous Royal Academy, of which Newton was an early president, was founded in 1660 and was the immediate source of much intellectual excitement. Indeed, a popular interest in gadgets, machines, and devices of all sorts soon became a mild national obsession: *Gentlemen's Magazine*, a kind of *New Yorker* of the period, announced in 1729 that it would henceforth keep its readers "abreast of every invention"—a task which the mounting flow of inventions soon rendered quite impossible. No less important was an enthusiasm of the British landed aristocracy for scientific farming: English landlords displayed an interest in matters of crop rotation and fertilizer which their French counterparts would have found quite beneath their dignity.

Then there were a host of other background causes, some as fortuitous as the immense resources of coal and iron ore on which the British sat; others as purposeful as the development of a national patent system which deliberately sought to stimulate and protect the act of invention itself. In many ways, England was "ready" for an Industrial Revolution. But perhaps what finally translated the potentiality into an actuality was the emergence of a group of new men who seized upon the latent opportunities of history as a vehicle for their own rise to fame and fortune. . . .

Pleasant or unpleasant, the personal characteristics fade beside one overriding quality. These were all men interested in expansion, in growth, in investment for investment's sake. All of them were identified with technological progress, and none of them disdained the productive process. An employee of Maudslay's once remarked, "It was a pleasure to see him handle a tool of any kind, but he was *quite splendid* with an 18-inch file." Watt was tireless in experimenting with his machines; Wedgwood stomped about his factory on his wooden leg scrawling, "This won't do for Jos. Wedgwood," wherever he saw evidence of careless work. Richard Arkwright was a bundle of ceaseless energy in promoting his interests, jouncing about England over execrable roads in a post chaise driven by four horses, pursuing his correspondence as he traveled.

"With us," wrote a French visitor to a calico works in 1788, "a man rich enough to set up and run a factory like this would not care to remain in a position which he would deem unworthy of his wealth." This was an attitude entirely foreign to the rising English industrial capitalist. His work was its own dignity and reward; the wealth it brought was quite aside. Boswell, on being shown Watt and Boulton's great engine works at Soho, declared that he never forgot Boulton's expression as the latter declared, "I sell here, sir, what all the world desires to have—Power."

The New Men were first and last *entrepreneurs*—enterprisers. They brought with them a new energy, as restless as it proved to be inexhaustible. In an economic, if not a political, sense, they deserve the epithet "revolutionaries," for the change they ushered in was nothing short of total, sweeping, and irreversible.

Factory Discipline in the Industrial Revolution

Sidney Pollard

One of the most difficult problems in the process of industrialization involved accli-matizing workers to the kind of work and discipline that took place in a factory. From the workers' point of view, this required not only changing how actual tasks were car-ried out, but altering their attitudes, expectations, and behavior patterns. From the employers' point of view, this meant training large numbers of people to work in new ways, to accept new conditions of work, and to develop values appropriate to factory discipline. The following selection by Sidney Pollard, an economic historian from the University of Sheffield, deals with this problem from the employers' point of view during the early period of industrialization in England.

Consider: *The aids the employer had in training his new work force and the problems he faced; the effects on the lives of the workers of these attempts by employers to acclimatize them to factory discipline; the ways in which this perspective on entrepreneurs differs from Heilbroner's.*

First, the acclimatization of new workers to factory discipline is a task dif-ferent in kind, at once more subtle and more violent, from that of maintain-ing discipline among a proletarian population of long standing. Employers in the British Industrial Revolution therefore used not only industrial means but a whole battery of extra-mural powers, including their control over the courts, their powers as landlords, and their own ideology, to impose the control they required.

Secondly, the maintenance of discipline, like the whole field of manage-ment itself, was not considered a fit subject for study, still less a science, but merely a matter of the employer's individual character and ability. No books were written on it before 1830, no teachers lectured on it, there were no en-tries about it in the technical encyclopaedias, no patents were taken out relating to it. As result, employers did not learn from each other, except haphazardly and belatedly, new ideas did not have the cachet of a new technology and did not spread, and the crudest form of deterrents and in-centives remained the rule. Robert Owen was exceptional in ensuring that his methods, at least, were widely known, but they were too closely meshed in with his social doctrines to be acceptable to other employers.

Lastly, the inevitable emphasis on reforming the moral character of the worker into a willing machine-minder led to a logical dilemma that contem-

SOURCE: Sidney Pollard, "Factory Discipline in the Industrial Revolution," *The Economic History Review*, Second Series, Vol. XVI, No. 2 (December 1963), pp. 270–271. Reprinted by permission of the publisher.

poraries did not know how to escape. For if the employer had it in his power to reform the workers if he but tried hard enough, whose fault was it that most of them remained immoral, idle and rebellious? And if the workers could really be taught their employers' virtues, would they not all save and borrow and become entrepreneurs themselves, and who would then man the factories?

The Industrial Revolution happened too rapidly for these dilemmas, which involved the re-orientation of a whole class, to be solved, as it were, *en passant.* The assimilation of the formerly independent worker to the needs of factory routine took at least a further generation, and was accompanied by the help of tradition, by a sharply differentiated educational system, and new ideologies which were themselves the results of clashes of earlier systems of values, besides the forces operating before 1830. The search of a more scientific approach which would collaborate with and use, instead of seeking to destroy, the workers' own values, began later still, and may hardly be said to have advanced very far even to-day.

The First Industrial Revolution

Phyllis Deane

One of the most persistent debates over the early stages of the Industrial Revolution is whether a higher standard of living resulted for factory workers. A number of "optimistic" historians, relying primarily on statistical evidence such as wage rates, prices, and mortality rates, have argued that even during the early period factory workers experienced a rising standard of living. A group of more "pessimistic" historians, emphasizing qualitative data such as descriptions of the psychological, social, and cultural impact of the factory on workers' lives, argues that the standard of living declined for these workers during the first half of the nineteenth century. In the following selection Phyllis Deane, a Cambridge scholar and author of The First Industrial Revolution *(1965), focuses on this debate. Although she is generally associated with the optimistic historians, the conclusion she presents here is a more balanced one that recognizes the validity of points from both sides of the debate.*

Consider: *The aspects of this selection that optimistic historians would emphasize and how pessimistic historians would respond; whether increased wage rates are meaningful without a consideration of the psychological and social costs of that extra money.*

SOURCE: Phyllis Deane, *The First Industrial Revolution.* Reprinted by permission of Cambridge University Press (Cambridge, England, 1965), pp. 268–269.

It seems then that if the working classes earned more and spent more in 1850 than the labouring poor of the pre-industrial times, they paid for it in hard toil. The industrial revolution gave them a chance to better themselves by working harder. It had not yet given them anything for nothing by 1850. If we were to set against the welfare represented by higher money incomes and lower prices for manufactures (though not for food) the disutility of longer, harder working hours, it is doubtful whether the balance would be tipped in their favour. For many of them life on these terms was only acceptable if heavily laced with strong liquor; and drunkenness, together with the degradation and cruelty to which it gives rise, was one of the characteristic features of the English scene in the mid-nineteenth century — as it had been of course a hundred years or so before, in the gin age. Strong drink caused endless trouble to the employers of labour, as the railway builders frequently complained, and it had an important influence on the outcome of parliamentary elections. It drew a firm line between the classes of society, between the respectable and the disreputable, between the two nations of rich and poor, in a way that was not nearly so evident in the eighteenth century.

Compared with what it had been a century before then, the standard of living of the British people in 1850 was higher on the average and a great deal more varied. It was also, for a larger number of people (if a smaller proportion of the population) more vulnerable and more squalid. For many more still, it was achieved at the cost of more labouring effort. The workers in a pre-industrial society have their hours of work dictated by the seasons, by the weather, by the hours of daylight and darkness and by the limited number of opportunities for gainful employment open to the weaker members of the community (the women and children for example). Their leisure is not always of their own choosing, though it is not therefore valueless. In an industrial society work can go on throughout the year and through the night, so long as the output can find a market, and there are many gainful tasks for unskilled and relatively feeble hands.

The Family and Industrialization in Western Europe

Michael Anderson

The tremendous growth of interest in social history over the past twenty years has stimulated scholars from other disciplines to address historical questions. A number of sociologists have applied methods from their own discipline to social aspects of

SOURCE: Michael Anderson, "The Family and Industrialization in Western Europe," *The Forum Series*. Reprinted by permission of Forum Press (St. Louis, Mo., 1978), p. 14. Copyright © 1978 by Forum Press.

nineteenth-century industrialization. In the following selection Michael Anderson, a sociologist from the University of Edinburgh, discusses the effects of industrialization on the working-class family.

> **Consider:** *The specific ways in which the process of industrialization affected working-class families; how Anderson's interpretation might support the "optimists" or the "pessimists" in their debate over the effects of the Industrial Revolution on the working class; how the effects on middle-class families might differ.*

In industrial areas, then, the close interdependence of parents and children which was so important in peasant societies gave way, and this was reflected in changes in family relationships. The early stages of industrialization, however, probably changed relationships between husbands and wives much less, though freedom from such close supervision and a more private domestic situation may have allowed rather more affection to develop between them than had been the case in pre-industrial peasant families. Husband and wife were no longer cooperating in the same productive task, but this had never been universal anyway. There was, however, a continued need and possibility for both husbands and wives to work as producers to keep the family above the subsistence line. In a few areas wives actually left the house to work in the factories. More usually, as women had always done, the wives of factory workers worked at home producing small items of clothing, processing some kind of food or drink, taking in the middle class's washing, or running a small shop or lodging house. The manifold needs of an industrial community were thus met in a way which contributed to working class family solidarity while allowing mothers to supervise and care (perhaps rather better than before) for small children during the lengthening period before they were able to enter the labor force themselves.

Initially, then, it was only in a few areas, especially those specializing in mining, machine-making, metal manufacturing, shipbuilding and sawmilling, that a change occurred in the economic status of women and with it in their family situation. In these areas there were not enough openings for female wage employment and, in consequence, many women were forced into the almost totally new situation of full-time housewife. However, as more and more traditional tasks were taken over by the application of factory production methods to clothing and food preparation, the home increasingly became confined to consumption. Only then did the distinction between male productive work outside the home and female consumption-oriented work inside the home become common among the working class.

Though the evidence is patchy, it seems that, at least in some areas, this had an effect on relationships between husbands and wives. Since the husband became the only income producer, the rest of the family became more dependent on him than he was on them. Whatever the husband did, the wife had little power to resist. While the family as a whole relied materially on the father, he needed them only to the extent that he could obtain from them emotional or other rewards which he could not obtain elsewhere or to the extent to which public opinion in the neighbourhood was effective in controlling his behavior (And with the weakened community control of large industrial cities, neighborhood control was often weak). Thus, in the working class, the idea that a woman's place was in the home and that her role was essentially an inferior domestic one is not of great antiquity. Rather it seems only to have developed as a response to a major shift in the power balance between husbands and wives which reflected the new employment situation of late nineteenth and early twentieth century industrial society.

Chapter Questions

1. Do you feel that industrialization should be considered a great boon, a mixed blessing, or a disaster for nineteenth-century Europeans? Why?

2. In retrospect, what policies might governments have adopted to minimize the pains of industrialization? What factors acted against the adoption of such policies?

3. In a debate over how industrialization should be evaluated, what would be the arguments of middle-class liberals? Of industrial workers?

CHAPTER NINE

The National State, Nationalism, and Imperialism: 1850–1914

Between 1850 and 1914 Europe was characterized politically by the development of the national state, the spread of nationalism, and the rise of the "new imperialism." The development of the national state took place after 1848. Governments, responding to economic and social pressures, increased their involvement in the economic and social life of their countries. This was apparent both in liberal England and in more conservative France under Louis Napoleon. There were similar trends during the national unification movements in Italy and particularly in Germany, where the state took on a wide range of new functions.

Nationalism had deep roots, notably in the experience of and reactions to the French Revolution and the Napoleonic invasions. Nationalism also played a central role in the revolutions of 1848. During the second half of the nineteenth century, nationalism continued to grow and to be capitalized upon by national governments. The most striking manifestations of nationalism came in the successful unification movements in Italy and Germany.

The rise of the new imperialism occurred in the last three decades of the nineteenth century. The European powers engaged in a sudden quest for control over new territories in Asia and Africa. Explorers, missionaries, traders, troops, and government officials quickly followed one another into these lands and established direct political control. In this process the West greatly increased its dominance over much of the rest of the world, bringing Western culture and institutions to the indigenous societies whether they wanted it or not.

The sources in this chapter explore each of these three developments. Some of the documents concentrate on the growth of the national state, particularly in Germany, where the authoritarian government expanded in an effort to adapt to the social and economic pressures of the times, and France, where forces for radical change were still strong. Some of the questions addressed are: How did the government in Germany react to demands for social legislation? What was the role of conservative forces in the German unification process, and how did their dominance affect the subsequent history of Germany? Other documents concern nationalism, particularly its meaning, its appeal, and its connections to liberalism and

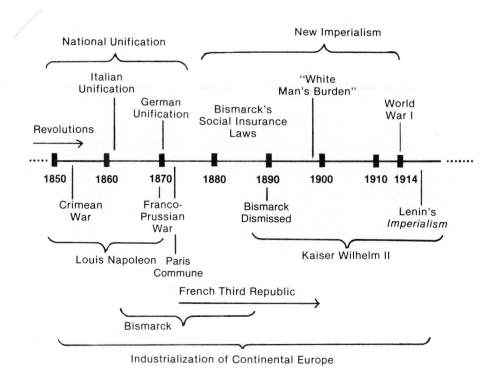

conservatism. How did nationalism change over the nineteenth century? What role did nationalism play in the unification movements in Germany and Italy? How was nationalism tied to the new imperialism of the period? Finally, most of the selections deal with imperialism, for not only was imperialism of far-reaching significance for much of the world, it has been a topic of considerable debate among historians. What were the nationalistic and economic motives for imperialism? What were some of the attitudes toward imperialism, particularly as reflected in materials glorifying it as a Christian and humanitarian movement? How is imperialism understood from a Marxist perspective? What were some of the consequences of imperialism?

Throughout these selections there is evidence for an increasing competitiveness among European states and political strains within those states. As will be seen in Chapter 11, these contributed to the outbreak of World War I and the revolutions that accompanied it.

PRIMARY SOURCES

Speeches on Pragmatism and State Socialism

Otto von Bismarck

The revolutions of 1848 were ultimately a blow to idealistic reform. Thereafter, governments pursued more limited goals. They tended to resort to more authoritarian measures, to avoid doctrinaire policies, and even to adopt certain programs of opposing groups in the hopes of weakening determined opposition to the government. Otto von Bismarck (1815–1898) did this in Germany. Born into a noble Prussian family, Bismarck rose to the position of chief minister under the king in 1862. The first selection below is from an 1862 speech to the Reichstag, in which he argues that the idealism of 1848 must be replaced by a conservative realism.

Bismarck remained in power until 1890. During this time he and his conservative supporters faced opposition from some liberals and from a growing number of socialists representing the working class. In the 1880s Bismarck supported some of the workers' demands for social insurance and pushed through such legislation as the German Workers' Insurance Laws. The remaining excerpts below Bismarck's speeches indicate the rationale behind these policies.

SOURCE: Louis L. Snyder, ed., *Documents of German History* (New Brunswick, N.J.: Rutgers University Press, 1958), p. 202; William H. Dawson, *Bismarck and State Socialism* (London: Swan Sonnenschein and Co., 1890), pp. 29, 34–35, 63–64, 118–119.

Consider: *What Bismarck means when he says the great questions of the day will be decided by iron and blood; how Bismarck justifies his support of "socialist" policies; why Bismarck would support such policies; what conservatives have to gain and who stands to lose by enactment of these policies.*

IRON AND BLOOD

. . . It is true that we can hardly escape complications in Germany, although we do not seek them. Germany does not look to Prussia's liberalism, but to her power. The south German States — Bavaria, Württemberg, and Baden — would like to indulge in liberalism, and because of that no one will assign Prussia's role to them! Prussia must collect her forces and hold them in reserve for an opportune moment, which has already come and gone several times. Since the Treaty of Vienna, our frontiers have not been favorably designed for a healthy body politic. Not by speeches and majorities will the great questions of the day be decided — that was the mistake of 1848 and 1849 — but by iron and blood.

STATE SOCIALISM

Herr Richter has called attention to the responsibility of the State for what it does. But it is my opinion that the State can also be responsible for what it does not do. I do not think that doctrines like those of 'Laissez-faire, laissez-aller,' 'Pure Manchesterdom in politics,' 'He who is not strong enough to stand must be knocked down and trodden to the ground,' 'To him that hath shall be given, and from him that hath not shall be taken away even that which he hath,'—that doctrines like these should be applied in the State, and especially in a monarchically, paternally governed State. On the other hand, I believe that those who profess horror at the intervention of the State for the protection of the weak lay themselves open to the suspicion that they are desirous of using their strength — be it that of capital, that of rhetoric, or whatever it be — for the benefit of a section, for the oppression of the rest, for the introduction of party domination, and that they will be chagrined as soon as this design is disturbed by any action of the Government.

Give the working-man the right to work as long as he is healthy; assure him care when he is sick; assure him maintenance when he is old. If you do that, and do not fear the sacrifice, or cry out at State Socialism directly the words 'provision for old age' are uttered, — if the State will show a little more Christian solicitude for the working-man, then I believe that the gentlemen of the Wyden (Social-Democratic) programme will sound their bird-call in vain, and that the thronging to them will cease as soon as working-men see that the Government and legislative bodies are earnestly concerned for their welfare.

Yes, I acknowledge unconditionally a right to work, and I will stand up for it as long as I am in this place. But here I do not stand upon the ground of Socialism, which is said to have only begun with the Bismarck Ministry, but on that of the Prussian common law.

Many measures which we have adopted to the great blessing of the country are Socialistic, and the State will have to accustom itself to a little more Socialism yet. We must meet our needs in the domain of Socialism by reformatory measures if we would display the wisdom shown in Prussia by the Stein-Hardenberg legislation respecting the emancipation of the peasantry. That was Socialism, to take land from one person and give it to another — a much stronger form of Socialism than a monopoly. But I am glad that this Socialism was adopted, for we have as a consequence secured a free and very well-to-do peasantry, and I hope that we shall in time do something of the sort for the labouring classes. Whether I, however, shall live to see it — with the general opposition which is, as a matter of principle, offered to me on all sides, and which is wearying me — I cannot say. But you will be compelled to put a few drops of social oil into the recipe which you give to the State — how much I do not know. . . . The establishment of the freedom of the peasantry was Socialistic; Socialistic, too, is every expropriation in favour of railways; Socialistic to the utmost extent is the aggregation of estates — the law exists in many provinces — taking from one and giving to another, simply because this other can cultivate the land more conveniently; Socialistic is expropriation under the Water Legislation, on account of irrigation, etc., where a man's land is taken away from him because another can farm it better; Socialistic is our entire poor relief, compulsory school attendance, compulsory construction of roads, so that I am bound to maintain a road upon my lands for travellers. That is all Socialistic, and I could extend the register further; but if you believe that you can frighten any one or call up spectres with the word 'Socialism,' you take a standpoint which I abandoned long ago, and the abandonment of which is absolutely necessary for our entire imperial legislation.

The whole matter centres in the question, Is it the duty of the State, or is it not, to provide for its helpless citizens? I maintain that it is its duty, that it is the duty not only of the 'Christian State,' as I ventured once to call it when speaking of 'practical Christianity,' but of every State. It would be foolish for a corporation to undertake matters which the individual can attend to alone; and similarly the purposes which the parish can fulfil with justice and with advantage are left to the parish. But there are purposes which only the State as a whole can fulfil. To these belong national defence, the general system of communications, and, indeed, everything spoken of in article 4 of the constitution. To these, too, belong the help of the necessitous and the removal of those just complaints which provide Social Democracy with really effective material for agitation. This is a duty of the State, a duty which the State cannot permanently disregard. . . . As soon as the State takes this matter [of insurance] in hand—and I believe it is its duty to take it in hand—it must seek the cheapest form of insurance, and, not aiming at profit for itself, must keep primarily in view the benefit of the poor and needy. Otherwise we might leave the fulfillment of certain State duties—such as poor relief, in the widest sense of the words, is amongst others—like education and national defence with more right to share companies, only asking ourselves, Who will do it most cheaply? who will do it most effectively? If provision for the necessitous in a greater degree than is possible with the present poor relief legislation is a State duty, the State must take the matter in hand; it cannot rest content with the thought that a share company will undertake it.

If an establishment employing twenty thousand or more workpeople were to be ruined . . . we could not allow these men to hunger. We should have to resort to real State Socialism and find work for them, and this is what we do in every case of distress. If the objection were right that we should shun State Socialism as we would an infectious disease, how do we come to organise works in one province and another in case of distress—works which we should not undertake if the labourers had employment and wages? In such cases we build railways whose profitableness is questionable; we carry out improvements which otherwise would be left to private initiative. If that is Communism, I have no objection at all to it; though with such catchwords we really get no further.

The Duties of Man

Giuseppe Mazzini

Nationalism, a growing force since the French Revolution, tended to be associated with liberal and humanitarian ideals during the first half of the nineteenth century. After 1848 it became more pragmatic and conservative, as illustrated by the unification of Germany and Italy. Yet it was still based on some of the earlier ideals. These ideals are illustrated in both the life and writings of the Italian patriot Giuseppe Mazzini (1805–1872). Mazzini was a revolutionary for most of his life and strove continuously for an independent and united Italian Republic. His revolutionary efforts in the 1830s and 1840s failed; unification was ultimately accomplished under the more pragmatic leadership of Cavour in the 1860s. But his ideas represented a strong strain of mid-nineteenth century nationalism both in Italy

SOURCE: Emilie Ashurst Venturi, *Joseph Mazzini: A Memoir* (London: Alexander & Shepheard, 1875), pp. 312–315.

and in other countries. The following is an excerpt from Mazzini's most famous essay, The Duties of Man, *addressed to Italian workingmen.*

Consider: *The bases for Mazzini's nationalism; why these ideas might be appealing to the Italian working class; why Bismarck might approve of these ideas and whether there is anything he might reject.*

Your first duties — first as regards importance — are, as I have already told you, towards Humanity. You are *men* before you are either citizens or fathers. If you do not embrace the whole human family in your affection, if you do not bear witness to your belief in the Unity of that family, consequent upon the Unity of God, and in that fraternity among the peoples which is destined to reduce that unity to action; if, wheresoever a fellow-creature suffers, or the dignity of human nature is violated by falsehood or tyranny — you are not ready, if able, to aid the unhappy, and do not feel called upon to combat, if able, for the redemption of the betrayed or oppressed — you violate your law of life, you comprehend not that Religion which will be the guide and blessing of the future.

But what can each of you, singly, *do* for the moral improvement and progress of Humanity? You can from time to time give sterile utterance to your belief; you may, on some rare occasions, perform some act of *charity* towards a brother man not belonging to your own land; — no more. But charity is not the watchword of the Faith of the Future. The watchword of the faith of the future is *Association*, and fraternal co-operation of all towards a common aim; and this is as far superior to all charity, as the edifice which all of you should unite to raise would be superior to the humble hut each one of you might build alone, or with the mere assistance of lending and borrowing stone, mortar, and tools.

But, you tell me, you cannot attempt united action, distinct and divided as you are in language, customs, tendencies, and capacity. The individual is too insignificant, and Humanity too vast. The mariner of Brittany prays to God as he puts to sea: *Help me, my God! my boat is so small and thy ocean so wide!* And this prayer is the true expression of the condition of each one of you, until you find the means of infinitely multiplying your forces and powers of action.

This means was provided for you by God when he gave you a country; when, even as a wise overseer of labour distributes the various branches of employment according to the different capacities of the workmen, he divided Humanity into distinct groups or nuclei upon the face of the earth, thus creating the germ of Nationalities. Evil governments have disfigured the divine design. Nevertheless you may still trace it, distinctly marked out — at least as far as Europe is concerned — by the course of the great rivers, the direction of the higher mountains, and other geographical conditions. They have disfigured it by their conquests, their greed, and their jealousy even of the righteous power of others; disfigured it so far that if we except England and France — there is not perhaps a single country whose present boundaries correspond to that design.

These governments did not, and do not, recognise any country save their own families or dynasty, the egotism of caste. But the Divine design will infallibly be realized. Natural divisions, and the spontaneous, innate tendencies of the peoples, will take the place of the arbitrary divisions sanctioned by evil governments. The map of Europe will be re-drawn. The countries of the Peoples, defined by the vote of free men, will arise upon the ruins of the countries of kings and privileged castes, and between these countries harmony and fraternity will exist. And the common work of Humanity, of general amelioration and the gradual discovery and application of its Law of life, being distributed according to local and general capacities, will be wrought out in peaceful and progressive development and advance. Then may each one of you, fortified by the power and the affection of many millions, all speaking the same language, gifted with the same tendencies, and educated by the same historical tradition, hope, even by your own single effort, to be able to benefit all Humanity.

O my brothers, love your Country! Our country is our Home, the house that God has given us, placing therein a numerous family that loves us, and whom we love; a family with whom we sympathise more readily, and whom we understand more quickly than we do others; and which, from its being centred round a given spot, and from the homogeneous nature of its elements, is adapted to a special branch of activity. Our country is our common workshop, whence the products of our activity are sent forth for the benefit of the whole world; wherein the tools and implements of labour we can most usefully employ are gathered together: nor may we reject them without disobeying the plan of the Almighty, and diminishing our own strength.

Proclamation of the Paris Commune

While pragmatism and conservatism were strong in the decades after 1848, the forces for radical and even revolutionary reform did not remain dormant for long. This was demonstrated dramatically in 1871 by the establishment of the Paris Commune. The Paris Commune was formed after Paris was brought under siege by the Prussian army during the Franco-Prussian War. After being deserted by most of the wealthier Parisians, the remaining inhabitants refused to accept the authority of the provisional government in Versailles, which was willing to

SOURCE: Stewart Edwards, ed., *The Communards of Paris, 1871* (Ithaca, N.Y.: Cornell University Press), pp. 81–83.

capitulate to the Prussian forces. The self-governing Commune set up by the Parisians was based on a mixture of relatively radical principles, many of which were stated in the following proclamation issued on April 19, 1871.

Consider: *The nature of the demands made by the Commune; how these demands contrast with pragmatism and conservatism; the role of nationalism in this proclamation.*

FRENCH REPUBLIC
LIBERTY EQUALITY FRATERNITY
PARIS COMMUNE
DECLARATION TO THE FRENCH PEOPLE

[In the grievous and terrible conflict which once again exposes Paris to the horrors of siege and bombardment, which causes French blood to flow, our brothers, women and children to perish, flattened by shell and grapeshot, public opinion must not be divided, nor the national consciousness confused.

Paris and the whole nation must be informed of the character, the reason and the aim of the Revolution that is taking place, so that the responsibility for the sorrows, the sufferings and the misfortunes of which we are the victims may be laid on those who, having betrayed France and delivered Paris to the foreigner, are now seeking, with blind and cruel obstinacy, to ruin the capital, in order that the twofold witness of their treachery and their crime may be buried alongside the destruction of the Republic and of Liberty.]

It is the duty of the Commune to confirm and ascertain the aspirations and wishes of the people of Paris. The precise character of the movement of the 18th of March is misunderstood and unknown, and is calumniated by the politicians at Versailles.

[Once more] Paris labours and suffers for the whole of France, for whom she prepares by her battles and intellectual, moral, administrative, and economic regeneration, glory and prosperity.

What does she demand?

The recognition and consolidation of the Republic[, the only form of government compatible with the rights of the People and with the free, regular development of society].

The absolute independence of the Commune extended at all places in France, thus assuring to each the integrity of its rights and to every Frenchman the full exercise of his faculties and aptitudes as a man, a citizen [and a worker].

The independence of the Commune has no other limits [than the right of all the other communes to an equal autonomy] who are adherents of the contract the association of which ought to secure the unity of France.

The inherent rights of the Commune are:

To vote the Communal budget of receipts and expenses; [to fix and assess] taxes; the direction of local services; the organisation of the magistracy, internal policy, and education; the administration of the property belonging to the Commune.

The choice by election or competition, with the responsibility and permanent right of control and revocation, of the Communal magistrates and officials of all classes.

The absolute guarantee of individual liberty, liberty of conscience [and liberty of work].

The permanent intervention of the citizens in Communal affairs by the free manifestation of their ideas and the free defence of their interests; guarantees given for those manifestations by the Commune, which alone is charged with [watching over and ensuring] the free and just exercise of the right of meeting and publicity.

The organisation of urban defence and of the National Guard, which must elect its chiefs and alone watch over the maintenance of order in the city.

Paris wishes nothing more under the head of local guarantees, on the well-understood condition of regaining, in a grand central administration and delegation from the federal communes, the realisation and practice of those same principles.

But [on the strength of] her independence, and profiting by her liberty of action, Paris reserves to herself liberty to bring about as may seem good to her administrative and economic reforms which the people demand, and to create such institutions as may serve to develop and further education, [production,] exchange, and credit; to universalise power and property according to the necessities of the moment, the wishes of those interested, and the data furnished by experience.

Our enemies deceive themselves [and the country] when they accuse Paris of seeking the destruction of French unity, established by the Revolution[, which our fathers acclaimed when they thronged from all corners of old France to the festival of the Federation].

Unity, such has been imposed upon us up to the present by the empire, the monarchy, and parliamentary government, is nothing but centralisation, despotic, unintelligent, arbitrary, and onerous.

Political unity, as desired by Paris, is a voluntary association of all local initiative, the free and spontaneous co-operation of all individual energies with the common object of wellbeing, liberty and security of all.

The Communal Revolution, [begun by popular initiative] on the 18th of March, inaugurated a new era of experimental, positive, and scientific politics.

It [marks the end of the old governmental] and clerical world, of militarism, of bureaucracy, [of exploitation,] of jobbing in monopolies, of privileges, to which the proletariat [owes] its slavery and the country its misfortune and disasters.

[Let this beloved and great country, therefore, deceived by lies and calumnies, be reassured!]

The strife between Paris and Versailles is one of those that cannot be decided by an illusory compromise; the issue should not be doubtful. The victory, fought for with such indomitable energy by the National Guard, will remain [on the side of intelligence (*l'idée*) and of] right.

We appeal to France.

Knowing that Paris in arms possesses as much calmness as courage; [that she maintains] order with as much energy as enthusiasm; [that she] is ready to sacrifice herself with as much reason as heroism; [that she] is only in arms in consequences of her devotion to liberty and to the glory of all [— let France] cause this bloody conflct to cease!

It is for France to disarm Versailles by a solemn manifestation of her irresistible will.

Invited to profit by her conquests, she should declare herself identified with our efforts, she should be our ally in this contest which can only end by the triumph of the Communal idea or the ruin of Paris.

As for ourselves, citizens of Paris, our mission is to accomplish [the] modern Revolution, the greatest and most fruitful of all those which have illuminated history.

It is our duty to fight and conquer.

Speech at Hamburg, 1901: Imperialism

Kaiser Wilhelm II

Imperialism swept through Europe with extraordinary force in the late nineteenth century. For many the step between the increasingly assertive nationalism of the time and the new imperialism was a short one. This view is illustrated in the following speech given at Hamburg in 1901 by Kaiser Wilhelm II (1888–1919) of Germany. Addressing an audience with strong commercial interests, he refers to a recent intervention by European powers in China.

> **Consider:** *How Wilhelm II connects nationalism and imperialism; by what means he hopes to spread German influence throughout the world; the ways in which this speech might appeal to both liberals and conservatives.*

In spite of the fact that we have no such fleet as we should have, we have conquered for ourselves a place in the sun. It will now be my task to see to it that this place in the sun shall remain our undisputed possession, in order that the sun's rays may fall fruitfully upon our activity and trade in foreign parts, that our industry and agriculture may develop within the state and our sailing sports upon the water, for our future lies upon the water. The more Germans go out upon the waters, whether it be in the races of regat-

SOURCE: C. Gauss, *The German Kaiser as Shown in His Public Utterances* (New York: Charles Scribner's Sons, 1915), pp. 181–183.

tas, whether it be in journeys across the ocean, or in the service of the battle-flag, so much the better will it be for us. For when the German has once learned to direct his glance upon what is distant and great, the pettiness which surrounds him in daily life on all sides will disappear. Whoever wishes to have this larger and freer outlook can find no better place than one of the Hanseatic cities.[1] What we have learned out of the previous history of our development amounts really to what I already pointed out when I sent my brother to the East Asiatic station (Dec. 15, 1897). We have merely drawn the logical conclusions from the work which was left us by Emperor William the Great, my memorable grandfather, and the great man whose monument we have recently unveiled. These consequences lie in the fact that we are now making our efforts to do what, in the old time, the Hanseatic cities could not accomplish, because they lacked the vivifying and protecting power of the empire. May it be the function of my Hansa during many years of peace to protect and advance commerce and trade!

In the events which have taken place in China I see the indication that European peace is assured for many years to come; for the achievements of the particular contingents have brought about a mutual respect and feeling of comradeship that can only serve the furtherance of peace. But in this period of peace I hope that our Hanseatic cities will flourish. Our new Hansa will open new paths and create and conquer new markets for them.

As head of the empire I therefore rejoice over every citizen, whether from Hamburg, Bremen, or Lübeck, who goes forth with this large outlook and seeks new points where we can drive in the nail on which to hang our armour. Therefore, I believe that I express the feeling of all your hearts when I recognize gratefully that the director of this company who has placed at our disposal the wonderful ship which bears my daughter's name has gone forth as a courageous servant of the Hansa, in order to make for us friendly conquests whose fruits will be gathered by our descendants.

In the joyful hope that this enterprising Hanseatic spirit may be spread even further, I raise my glass and ask all of those who are my comrades upon the water to join with me in a cheer for sailing and the Hanseatic spirit!

The Rise of Our East African Empire

Lord Lugard

Probably the most apparent motive for the new imperialism was economic. With new conquests made, people expected to develop new commerce and particularly

---

SOURCE: Captain F. D. Lugard, *The Rise of Our East African Empire*, Vol. I (London: William Blackwood and Sons, 1893), pp. 379–382, 473.

[1]The Hanseatic cities formed a league in the Late Middle Ages to facilitate trade.

new markets for manufactured goods. This attitude is reflected by Lord Lugard in his Rise of Our East African Empire *(1893), largely an account of his experiences in colonial service. Lugard, as a British soldier and administrator, helped bring large parts of Africa into the British empire. Here he analyzes the "scramble" for Africa.*

> **Consider:** *How Lugard connects nationalistic and economic motives for imperialism; some of the main arguments presented against imperialism and how Lugard responds to them; Lugard's perceptions of Africans and how such perceptions might facilitate the new imperialism.*

The Chambers of Commerce of the United Kingdom have unanimously urged the retention of East Africa on the grounds of commercial advantage. The Presidents of the London and Liverpool chambers attended a deputation to her Majesty's Minister for Foreign Affairs to urge "the absolute necessity, for the prosperity of this country, that new avenues for commerce such as that in East Equatorial Africa should be opened up, in view of the hostile tariffs with which British manufacturers are being everywhere confronted." Manchester followed with a similar declaration; Glasgow, Birmingham, Edinburgh, and other commercial centres gave it as their opinion that "there is practically no middle course for this country, between a reversal of the free-trade policy to which it is pledged, on the one hand, and a prudent but continuous territorial extension for the creation of new markets, on the other hand." Such is the view of the Chambers of Commerce, and I might quote endless paragraphs from their resolutions and reports in the same sense.

This view has been strongly endorsed by some of our leading statesmen. Space forbids me to quote extracts from speeches by our greatest politicians, which I might else adduce as proof that they held the opinions of the Chambers of Commerce, which I have quoted, to be sound and weighty. . . .

The "Scramble for Africa" by the nations of Europe — an incident without parallel in the history of the world — was due to the growing commercial rivalry, which brought home to civilised nations the vital necessity of securing the only remaining fields for industrial enterprise and expansion. It is well, then, to realise that it is for our *advantage* — and not alone at the dictates of duty — that we have undertaken responsibilities in East Africa. It is in order to foster the growth of the trade of this country, and to find an outlet for our manufactures and our surplus energy, that our far-seeing statesmen and our commercial men advocate colonial expansion. . . .

There are some who say we have no *right* in Africa at all, that "it belongs to the natives." I hold that our right is the necessity that is upon us to provide for our ever-growing population — either by opening new fields for emigration, or by providing work and employment which the development of over-sea extension entails — and to stimulate trade by finding new markets, since we know what misery trade depression brings at home.

While thus serving our own interests as a nation, we may, by selecting men of the right stamp for the control of new territories, bring at the same time many advantages to Africa. Nor do we deprive the natives of their birthright of freedom, to place them under a foreign yoke. It has ever been the key-note of British colonial method to rule through and by the natives, and it is this method, in contrast to the arbitrary and uncompromising rule of Germany, France, Portugal, and Spain, which has been the secret of our success as a colonising nation, and has made us welcomed by tribes and peoples in Africa, who ever rose in revolt against the other nations named. In Africa, moreover, there is among the people a natural inclination to submit to a higher authority. That intense detestation of control which animates our Teutonic races does not exist among the tribes of Africa, and if there is any authority that we replace, it is the authority of the Slavers and Arabs, or the intolerable tyranny of the "dominant tribe." . . .

So far, therefore, as my personal experience goes, I have formed the following estimate: (1) No kind of men I have ever met with — including British soldiers, Afghans, Burmese, and many tribes of India — are more amenable to discipline, more ready to fall into the prescribed groove willingly and quickly, more easy to handle, or require so little compulsion as the African. (2) To obtain satisfactory results a great deal of system, division of labour, supervision, etc., is required. (3) On the whole, the African is very quick at learning, and those who prove themselves good at the superior class of work take a pride in the results, and are very amenable to a word of praise, blame, or sarcasm.

The White Man's Burden
Rudyard Kipling

Imperialism was often glorified both by those actively involved in it and by the public at home. Part of this glorification involved perceiving imperialism as a Christian and nationalistic venture. More broadly it involved portraying imperialism as a heroic deed carried out by idealistic leaders of Western civilization in an effort to spread the "benefits" of "true civilization" to "less advanced" peoples of the world. One of the most popular expressions of this is found in the writings of Rudyard Kipling (1865–1936), particularly in his poem "The White Man's Burden," written in 1899 to celebrate the American annexation of the Philippines.

Consider: *What Kipling means by "the White Man's burden"; how Kipling justifies imperialism; why such a justification might be so appealing.*

SOURCE: Rudyard Kipling, "The White Man's Burden," *McClure's Magazine*, Vol. XII, No. 4 (February 1899), pp. 290–291.

Take up the White Man's burden —
    Send forth the best ye breed —
Go, bind your sons to exile
    To serve your captives' need;
To wait, in heavy harness,
    On fluttered folk and wild —

Your new-caught sullen peoples,
    Half devil and half child.

Take up the White Man's burden —
    In patience to abide,
To veil the threat of terror
    And check the show of pride;
By open speech and simple,
    An hundred times made plain,
To seek another's profit
    And work another's gain.

Take up the White Man's burden —
    The savage wars of peace —
Fill full the mouth of Famine,
    And bid the sickness cease;
And when your goal is nearest
    (The end for others sought)
Watch sloth and heathen folly
    Bring all your hope to nought.

Take up the White Man's burden —
    No iron rule of kings,
But toil of serf and sweeper —
    The tale of common things.
The ports ye shall not enter,
    The roads ye shall not tread,
Go, make them with your living
    And mark them with your dead.

Take up the White Man's burden,
    And reap his old reward —
The blame of those ye better
    The hate of those ye guard —
The cry of hosts ye humour
    (Ah, slowly!) toward the light: —
"Why brought ye us from bondage,
    Our loved Egyptian night?"

Take up the White Man's burden—
    Ye dare not stoop to less—
Nor call too loud on Freedom
    To cloke your weariness.
By all ye will or whisper,
    By all ye leave or do,
The silent sullen peoples
    Shall weigh your God and you.

Take up the White Man's burden!
    Have done with childish days—
The lightly-proffered laurel,
    The easy ungrudged praise:
Comes now, to search your manhood
    Through all the thankless years,
Cold, edged with dear-bought wisdom,
    The judgment of your peers.

VISUAL SOURCES

Imperialism Glorified

George Harcourt

This 1900 painting by George Harcourt conveys some of the meaning of imperialism to Europeans. First displayed at the Royal Academy in 1900, it shows British soldiers leaving by train for the Boer War in South Africa. The soldiers are clearly cast in the role of masculine heroes, both in their own eyes as well as in the eyes of civilians, young and old. This is further evidenced by the couple in the center, representing the epitome of sentimentalized British masculinity and femininity. For many, imperialism enabled Europeans to have a sense of adventure and to prove their superiority to themselves and the rest of the world. Avoided in this picture is the reality of the bloodshed and exploitation to be experienced by these same soldiers and the populations of the colonized lands.

    Consider: *How this painting fits with Kipling's description of "the White Man's burden."*

Photo 9-1

The Bettmann Archive/BBC Hulton

Imperialism in Africa

The first of these two maps shows the approximate divisions among indigenous peoples in nineteenth-century Africa. There were also extremely important cultural and political divisions throughout Africa at this time. The second map shows areas of Africa under European control prior to 1880 and the colonial partition of Africa by European nations by 1914.

Together these maps indicate a number of things about imperialism in Africa. First, the manner and speed with which Africa was divided demonstrates the intense competition involved in this late-nineteenth-century imperial expansion. Second, the European partition of Africa did not take account of the already established social, political, cultural, and ethnic divisions among Africans. From this geopolitical perspective alone, one can imagine some of the disruption to native societies and cultures caused by imperialism. Third, these maps help explain problems experienced by Africans after decolonization occurred. The new African nations were generally formed on the basis of the arbitrary political lines established by European colonizers. Thus many African countries had had to deal with persisting divisions and rivalries among their populations, stemming from the nineteenth-century partition of Africa.

Consider: *How these maps help explain the effects of imperialism on Africans.*

Map 9-1   Divisions Among Indigenous Peoples

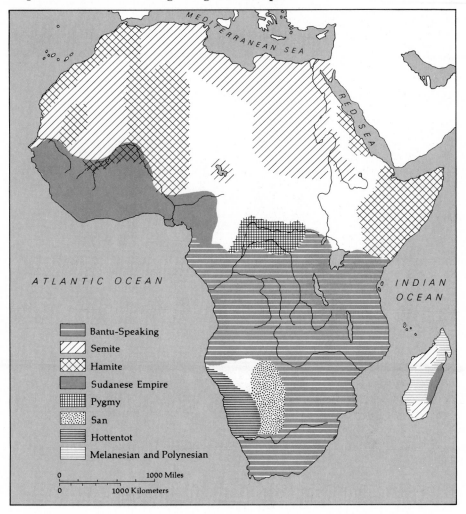

Map 9-2   European Control of Africa

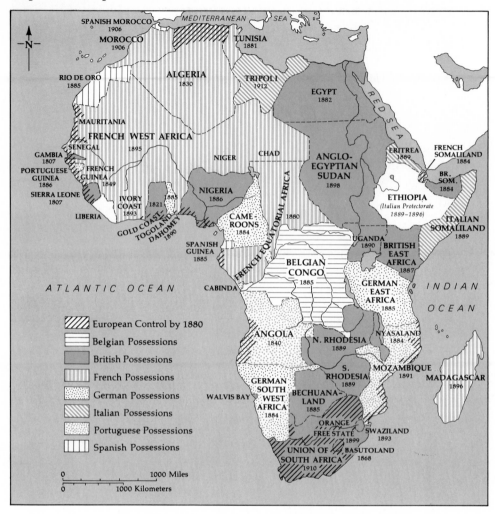

SPANISH MOROCCO
1906
MEDITERRANEAN   SEA
MOROCCO
1906
TUNISIA
1881
-N-
RIO DE ORO
1885
ALGERIA
1830
TRIPOLI
1912
EGYPT
1882
RED SEA
MAURITANIA
FRENCH WEST AFRICA
1895
NIGER
CHAD
ANGLO-
EGYPTIAN
SUDAN
1898
ERITREA
1889
FRENCH
SOMALILAND
1884
GAMBIA
1807
SENEGAL
PORTUGUESE
GUINEA
1886
FRENCH
GUINEA
1849
BR.
SOM.
1884
SIERRA LEONE
1807
NIGERIA
1886
ETHIOPIA
(Italian Protectorate
1889–1896)
IVORY
COAST
1893
1885
CAME-
ROONS
1884
1880
ITALIAN
SOMALILAND
1889
LIBERIA
GOLD COAST
TOGOLAND
DAHOMEY
1890
SPANISH
GUINEA
1885
FRENCH EQUATORIAL AFRICA
UGANDA
1890
BRITISH
EAST
AFRICA
1887
ATLANTIC OCEAN
CABINDA
BELGIAN
CONGO
1885
GERMAN
EAST
AFRICA
1885
INDIAN

OCEAN

European Control by 1880

Belgian Possessions

British Possessions

French Possessions

German Possessions

Italian Possessions

Portuguese Possessions

Spanish Possessions

ANGOLA
1840
N. RHODESIA
1889
NYASALAND
1884
S.
RHODESIA
1889
MOZAMBIQUE
1891
MADAGASCAR
1896
GERMAN
SOUTH
WEST
AFRICA
1884
WALVIS BAY
BECHUANA-
LAND
1885
ORANGE
FREE STATE
1899
SWAZILAND
1893
UNION OF
SOUTH AFRICA
1910
BASUTOLAND
1868

0   1000 Miles

0   1000 Kilometers

SECONDARY SOURCES

Nationalism:
Myth and Reality
Boyd Shafer

Although growing nationalism was a general pattern during the nineteenth century, the forms that nationalism took and its actual meaning differed over time and in various areas. Indeed, "nationalism" is a term that historians have usually used quite loosely, adding to problems of understanding its meaning. In the following selection, Boyd Shafer attempts to define nationalism by listing ten characteristics it embodies.

> **Consider:** *What it would mean to be a German or Italian "nationalist" during the second half of the nineteenth century, according to Shafer's definition of nationalism; what the political implications are of nationalism so defined; the elements of this definition that make nationalism such a historically powerful force.*

1. A certain defined (often vaguely) unit of territory (whether possessed or coveted).
2. Some common cultural characteristics such as language (or widely understood languages), customs, manners, and literature (folk tales and lore are a beginning). If an individual believes he shares these, and wishes to continue sharing them, he is usually said to be a member of the nationality.
3. Some common dominant social (as Christian) and economic (as capitalistic or recently communistic) institutions.
4. A common independent or sovereign government (type does not matter) or the desire for one. The "principle" that each nationality should be separate and independent is involved here.
5. A belief in a common history (it can be invented) and in a common origin (often mistakenly conceived to be racial in nature).
6. A love or esteem for fellow nationals (not necessarily as individuals).
7. A devotion to the entity (however little comprehended) called the nation, which embodies the common territory, culture, social and economic institutions, government, and the fellow nationals, and which is at the same time (whether organism or not) more than their sum.

SOURCE: Boyd C. Shafer, *Nationalism: Myth and Reality*. Reprinted by permission of Harcourt Brace Jovanovich, Inc. (New York, 1955), pp. 7–8.

8. A common pride in the achievements (often the military more than the cultural) of this nation and a common sorrow in its tragedies (particularly its defeats).
9. A disregard for or hostility to other (not necessarily all) like groups, especially if these prevent or seem to threaten the separate national existence.
10. A hope that the nation will have a great and glorious future (usually in territorial expansion) and become supreme in some way (in world power if the nation is already large).

A Sterner Plan for Italian Unity: Nationalism, Liberalism, and Conservatism

Raymond Grew

During the first half of the nineteenth century, nationalism was most often connected to liberalism. After the revolutions of 1848 there were increasing ties between nationalism and conservatism, particularly in the movements for national unification. In the following selection Raymond Grew, an advocate of comparative history from the University of Michigan, analyzes the relationships among nationalism, liberalism, and conservatism in a comparative context.

> **Consider:** *How nationalism could appeal to both liberals and conservatives; why, during the second half of the nineteenth century, liberal ideals were often sacrificed in the name of nationalism; using this and the preceding document, the bases on which nationalism might have been opposed.*

Insofar as politics was the public battle of ideas and interests, then nationalism was a denial of politics. For in stressing the values of unity, loyalty, and duty, nationalism saw political dispute as a source of weakness. It denied that there was conflict in the true interests of classes, groups or regions. The effect of nationalism was therefore inherently conservative in that it provided reason for supporting anyone thought to wield the power of the state effectively in behalf of national unity and strength, Disraeli or Gladstone, Napoleon III or Bismarck. Since order and unity, the cry of the political conservative, are essential to a strong state, and since, to the nationalist, most worthy ends required that strength, the nationalist was always

SOURCE: Raymond Grew, *A Sterner Plan for Italian Unity*. Reprinted by permission of Princeton University Press (Princeton, N.J., 1963), pp. 465–466. Copyright © 1963 by Princeton University Press.

tempted under pressure to move toward the political right, to sacrifice liberty to unity, discussion to authority, ends to means.

Yet the origins of nationalism were usually liberal and reformist; for everywhere it was a demand for change, the doctrine of the modernizers who, while they had too much to lose to want a social revolution, were self-consciously aware that theirs was an "underdeveloped" country. Nationalism could make its denial of politics effective because its ends were so clear, so easily defined in the model of the modern state. For the French that model had been England; for the Italians it was England and France. Italian nationalists were usually liberals, but their liberalism was primarily an admiration for the achievements of the liberal state. Because their model already existed, they looked directly to it, anxious to achieve an efficient bureaucracy, a responsible government, a progressive economic structure, all based on accepted and universally applied laws. Nationalism was a program to obtain these things quickly, not to evolve toward them but, if necessary, to superimpose them. The hurry to achieve these goals where nationalism itself was seriously opposed made a doctrinaire concern for means appear pedantic and unrealistic. Italian nationalists needed nothing so brutal as cynicism to justify "postponement" of controversy or the choice of practical means, though often this meant whittling away at the practices necessary to viable liberalism.

German Unification
Hajo Holborn

As in the case of Italy, nationalism in Germany during the first half of the nineteenth century was closely connected to liberalism. This was particularly so in the early stages of the revolutions of 1848. But with the failure of liberal nationalists to gain the concrete changes they strove for, steps toward unification over the next two decades followed a different path. In the following selection, Hajo Holborn, a noted historian of Germany, analyzes the significance of that path for German history until the outbreak of World War I in 1914.

  Consider: The ways in which liberalism was sacrificed during this period; how the relation between liberalism and nationalism was affected by the position of different social groups in Germany; how Bismarck's social policies support Holborn's interpretation.

The achievement of German unity gave Bismarck the power to force the German liberals to decide whether they were more eager to see unity or liberty achieved in Germany. The majority of them proved willing to com-

SOURCE: Hajo Holborn, *The Political Collapse of Europe*. Reprinted by permission of Alfred A. Knopf, Inc. (New York, 1966), pp. 42–43. Copyright © 1966 Alfred A. Knopf, Inc.

promise with Bismarck. Since centralization went rather far under the new constitution he needed the liberal movement to some extent to counter-balance the particularistic German forces represented chiefly by the German princes. The constitution of the new German empire was, therefore, a bit more centralized and more liberal than Bismarck wished, but he maintained control of the crucial policy-making positions. No decisive power over military and foreign affairs by the constituted popular bodies was allowed in the second German empire. Bismarck made all sorts of concessions in the field of social and economic reform but was absolutely adamant with regard to the powers of the parliament. The direction of foreign and military matters remained a privilege of the Crown.

The pseudo-constitutional character of the new German empire was even more accentuated when in 1878 Bismarck decided to give up free trade and imposed a policy protecting the interests of the Prussian *Junker* agrarians against the importation of cheap Russian and American grain while at the same time introducing tariffs benefiting the growing German iron industries. Just as in 1866 and 1871 the German liberals had had to sacrifice the core of their political faith, so they were forced to jettison the major part of their economic program after 1878. The leading industrial groups of German society readily accepted a protectionist trade policy, and the unity of the liberal *bourgeoisie* crumbled. Thirty years after German liberalism had burst into existence in the Revolution of 1848, it ceased to be an independent political movement. Thereafter the majority of the German *bourgeoisie*, if they did not, like the higher *bourgeoisie*, become absolute supporters of the regime, were driven to further concession and compromise. The appearance of a powerful socialist workers' movement extinguished the last remaining fervor for reform among the liberal *bourgeoisie* and made them take cover under the wings of the established government. The second German empire was founded "by blood and iron" and socially stabilized by "iron and grain." For more than fifty years the German political scene was overshadowed by the alliance of the "barons of the halm" and the "barons of the smokestack," who maintained the army and bureaucracy in power.

Imperialism

V. I. Lenin

Imperialism has been interpreted from a number of perspectives since the early twentieth century. The way that scholars view imperialism often reveals much about their own political and ideological views. Some of the earlier interpretations, such as those by J. H. Hobson and V. I. Lenin, were economic. They criticized im-

SOURCE: V. I. Lenin, *Collected Works*, Vol. XXII (Moscow: Progress Publishers, 1964), pp. 265–267. Reprinted by permission.

perialism as an outgrowth of capitalism, Hobson from the perspective of a liberal socialist, Lenin as a Marxist theorist and political leader. Indeed for Lenin, im-perialism was not only economically determined, it was also a crucial element in a Marxist explanation of how capitalism was evolving historically. This view is illus-trated in the following selection from his Imperialism, *written in 1916 when Lenin was a Bolshevik leader in exile and not yet in power.*

Consider: *Why imperialism is connected to monopoly capitalism; the interest groups that would benefit most from imperialism; in Lenin's view, why England was the greatest imperial nation and why other nations would want to join in the imperial struggle.*

Imperialism emerged as the development and direct continuation of the fundamental characteristics of capitalism in general. But capitalism only became capitalist imperialism at a definite and very high stage of its devel-opment, when certain of its fundamental characteristics began to change in-to their opposites, when the features of the epoch of transition from capital-ism to a higher social and economic system had taken shape and revealed themselves in all spheres. Economically, the main thing in this process is the displacement of capitalist free competition by capitalist monopoly. Free competition is the basic feature of capitalism, and of commodity production generally; monopoly is the exact opposite of free competition, but we have seen the latter being transformed into monopoly before our eyes, creating large-scale industry and forcing out small industry, replacing large-scale by still larger-scale industry, and carrying concentration of production and capital to the point where out of it has grown and is growing monopoly: cartels, syndicates and trusts, and merging with them, the capital of a dozen or so banks, which manipulate thousands of millions. At the same time the monopolies, which have grown out of free competition, do not eliminate the latter, but exist above it and alongside it, and thereby give rise to a number of very acute, intense antagonisms, frictions and conflicts. Monopoly is the transition from capitalism to a higher system. . . .

We must give a definition of imperialism that will include the following five of its basic features:

(1) the concentration of production and capital has developed to such a high stage that it has created monopolies which play a decisive role in economic life; (2) the merging of bank capital with industrial capital, and the creation, on the basis of this "finance capital", of a financial oligarchy; (3) the export of capital as distinguished from the export of commodities ac-quires exceptional importance; (4) the formation of international monopo-list capitalist associations which share the world among themselves, and (5) the territorial division of the whole world among the biggest capitalist powers is completed. Imperialism is capitalism at that stage of development at which the dominance of monopolies and finance capital is established; in

which the export of capital has acquired pronounced importance; in which the division of the world among the international trusts has begun, in which the division of all territories of the globe among the biggest capitalist powers has been completed.

Imperialism as a Nationalistic Phenomenon

Carlton Hayes

Although the economic interpretation of imperialism has not lost its strength, other views have been offered recently as supplements and sometimes as direct alternatives to an economic interpretation. A direct alternative appears in the following selection by Carlton J. H. Hayes. One of the earliest historians to develop a sophisticated understanding of nationalism, Hayes argues that economic motives were at best secondary; on the whole, imperialism was a nationalistic phenomenon.

> **Consider:** *The evidence Hayes uses to reject economic interpretations of nationalism; how Lenin might reply to this interpretation; the ways in which this view fits with the documents on nationalism in this chapter.*

The founding of new colonial empires and the fortifying of old ones antedated the establishment of neo-mercantilism, and that the economic arguments adduced in support of imperialism seem to have been a rationalization *ex post facto*. In the main, it was not Liberal parties, with their super-abundance of industrials and bankers, who sponsored the outward imperialistic thrusts of the '70's and early '80's. Instead, it was Conservative parties, with a preponderantly agricultural clientele notoriously suspicious of moneylenders and big business, and, above all, it was patriotic professors and publicists regardless of political affiliation and unmindful of personal economic interest. These put forth the economic arguments which eventually drew bankers and traders and industrialists into the imperialist camp.

Basically the new imperialism was a nationalistic phenomenon. It followed hard upon the national wars which created an all-powerful Germany and a united Italy, which carried Russia within sight of Constantinople, and which left England fearful and France eclipsed. It expressed a resulting psychological reaction, an ardent desire to maintain or recover national prestige. France sought compensation for European loss in oversea gain. England would offset her European isolation by enlarging and glorifying the British

SOURCE: Carlton J. H. Hayes, *A Generation of Materialism: 1871–1900.* Reprinted by permission of Harper & Row (New York, 1941), pp. 223–224. Copyright © 1941 by Harper & Row, Publishers, Inc., renewed 1969 by Mary Evelyn Hayes.

Empire. Russia, halted in the Balkans, would turn anew to Asia, and before long Germany and Italy would show the world that the prestige they had won by might inside Europe they were entitled to enhance by imperial exploits outside. The lesser powers, with no great prestige at stake, managed to get on without any new imperialism, though Portugal and Holland displayed a revived pride in the empires they already possessed and the latter's was administered with renewed vigor. . . .

Most simply, the sequence of imperialism after 1870 appears to have been, first, pleas for colonies on the ground of national prestige; second, getting them; third, disarming critics by economic argument; and fourth, carrying this into effect and relating the results to the neo-mercantilism of tariff protection and social legislation at home.

The Effects
of Imperialism

David Landes

Earlier in the twentieth century, historians, even those quite critical of imperialism, saw its impact mainly in European terms. In recent decades, the effects of imperialism have been viewed more from the perspective of native populations subject to imperial control. This has led to a more subtle understanding of imperialism and helps explain some of the persisting problems between the West and many "underdeveloped" or "third world" countries. This perspective is illustrated in the following selection by David Landes, an economic historian from Harvard. Here he focuses on Egypt.

> **Consider:** *The nature of the double standard described by Landes; how this double standard affected people's and nations' attitudes; whether this view fits best with the nationalistic or the economic interpretation of imperialism.*

While most Europeans in Egypt lived according to principles, they had two sets of principles: the same rules did not apply in dealing with the in-group of Westerners and the out-group of natives. Some Europeans drew the line between the two societies more sharply than others. There were those for whom the Turk was of his nature treacherous, Moslem justice hopelessly corrupt, the native population mean and despicable. There were others who found the Turk not deliberately false, but lazy and neglectful; who recognized the validity of Moslem law within the framework of Egyptian society, but felt that it offered little protection to foreigners habituated to other codes and that the native tribunals were excessively submissive to govern-

SOURCE: David S. Landes, *Bankers and Pashas.* Reprinted by permission of Harvard University Press (Cambridge, Mass., 1958), pp. 322–323. Copyright © 1958 by David S. Landes.

ment pressure; who had more sympathy than scorn for the Arab, and deplored his inadaptability to the discipline and precision implicit in modern industry and trade. Some saw in every Egyptian a potential enemy whose ill faith required constant vigilance and strong remedies; others looked upon the natives as children whose fumblings and misconduct were best handled by the paternal chastisement of their European friends and protectors. All, however, were agreed that Egyptian society was backward and Egyptian civilization inferior; that the European could not afford to submit to the customs of the country, but that the Egyptian would have to learn the ways and accept the justice of the European; that the standards of behaviour accepted in Europe, the values of honesty, fair play, reasonableness, and so on that shaped — at least in principle — the social and business relations of the West, had to be modified to fit the circumstances of a strange environment. . . .

More than anything, more even than the enormous material costs of imperialism, it was the imposition of inferior social and moral status that shaped the reaction of the Egyptian to the European. Actually, the one implies the other: material exploitation is difficult if not impossible without the sanction of a double set of values and a corresponding double code of behaviour; if they were not there to begin with, the exploiter would have to create them. The fact remains, however, that in the many-sided impact of imperialism, it is the injury to self-respect that hurts most. It is the resentment aroused by spiritual humiliation that gives rise to an irrational response to rational exploitation. The apparently unreasonable, and certainly unprofitable, resistance of many of the world's underdeveloped countries today to Western business enterprise makes sense only in this context.

Chapter Questions

1. What historical links are there between nationalism, the national state, and imperialism during the nineteenth century? How might all three be connected to industrialization, discussed in the previous chapter?

2. How would you explain the rise of imperialism in the late nineteenth century?

3. In what ways have some of our perceptions of imperialism changed since the late nineteenth century?

CHAPTER TEN

Culture, Thought, and Society: 1850–1914

From the mid-nineteenth century to 1914 the urban middle class dominated Europe socially and culturally. It was this class that was benefiting most from the continuing industrialization of the period. As the urban middle class grew in numbers and wealth, it asserted its own values and assumptions. Increasingly this class set the standards of life style, thought, and culture. At the same time, these standards were attacked from all sides, particularly by those sensitive to the problems of the working class. The contrast between the standards being established by the middle class and the challenges to those standards marks this period as one of great social, cultural, and intellectual ferment.

The selections in this chapter exemplify some of the main social, cultural, and intellectual developments of this period. Three broad questions are addressed. First, what were some of the main elements of the middle-class style of life? Some of the materials show how this life style was reflected in the physical setting of the middle class; others concentrate on the role the family played in this style of life. Second, what were some of the dominant intellectual currents favored by the middle class? Here liberalism as it was evolving toward the end of the century and ideas generally referred to as Social Darwinism are examined. Third, what were some of the main challenges to middle-class ideas and institutions? The most pervasive of these were Marxism and related socialist doctrines, but there were also conservative challenges, such as those from the Catholic Church and the challenges of racism.

What emerges from these sources is a picture of a dynamic society with a vast array of cultural and intellectual developments. In the decades following the outbreak of World War I, many would look back to this period as one of unusual progress. Some of the twentieth-century developments that in retrospect make the second half of the nineteenth century seem such a positive time will be examined in the next chapter.

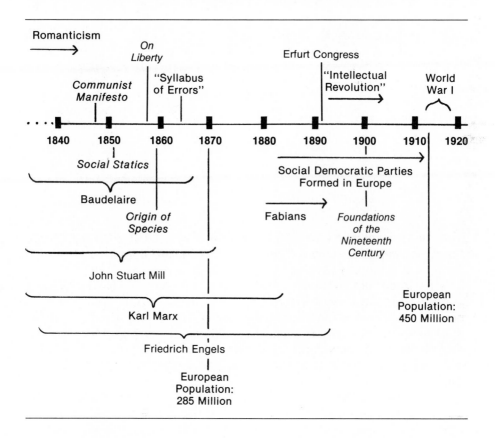

PRIMARY SOURCES

Social Statics: Liberal Philosophy

Herbert Spencer

The works of Herbert Spencer (1820–1903) epitomize the assertive liberal philosophy favored by successful mid-nineteenth-century industrialists. This was a period in which capitalism was relatively unrestrained and social legislation was only in its infancy. It was also the beginning of thinking from a biological and evolutionary perspective, as best evidenced by the publication of Charles Darwin's Origin of Species *in 1859. Spencer reflected all this in his massive writings. He rose from a railroad engineer to become editor of the* London Economist *— which espoused the views of industrial capitalism — and an independent author. Always a supporter of* laissez-faire, *he was best known for his advocacy of social evolution and acceptance of Darwinian ideas applied to society (Social Darwinism). Modern scholars consider him a founder of sociology. The following is an excerpt from* Social Statics, *first published in 1851.*

> **Consider:** *Why Spencer's views would be so appealing to the industrial middle class; on what grounds certain groups might oppose these views; the social policies that would flow from these ideas.*

Pervading all Nature we may see at work a stern discipline which is a little cruel that it may be very kind. That state of universal warfare maintained throughout the lower creation, to the great perplexity of many worthy people, is at bottom the most merciful provision which the circumstances admit of. It is much better that the ruminant animal, when deprived by age of the vigour which made its existence a pleasure, should be killed by some beast of prey, than that it should linger out a life made painful by infirmities, and eventually die of starvation. By the destruction of all such, not only is existence ended before it becomes burdensome, but room is made for a younger generation capable of the fullest enjoyment; and moreover, out of the very act of substitution happiness is derived for a tribe of predatory creatures. Note, further, that their carnivorous enemies not only remove from herbivorous herds individuals past their prime, but also weed out the sickly, the malformed, and the least fleet or powerful. By the aid of which purifying process, as well as by the fighting so universal in the pairing season, all vitiation of the race through the multiplication of its inferior

Source: Herbert Spencer, *Social Statics* (New York: D. Appleton and Co., 1896), pp. 149–151.

samples is prevented; and the maintenance of a constitution completely adapted to surrounding conditions, and therefore most productive of happiness, is ensured.

The development of the higher creation is a progress towards a form of being, capable of a happiness undiminished by these drawbacks. It is in the human race that the consummation is to be accomplished. Civilization is the last stage of its accomplishment. And the ideal man is the man in whom all the conditions to that accomplishment are fulfilled. Meanwhile, the well-being of existing humanity and the unfolding of it into this ultimate perfection, are both secured by that same beneficial though severe discipline, to which the animate creation at large is subject. It seems hard that an unskillfulness which with all his efforts he cannot overcome, should entail hunger upon the artizan. It seems hard that a labourer incapacitated by sickness from competing with his stronger fellows, should have to bear the resulting privations. It seems hard that widows and orphans should be left to struggle for life or death. Nevertheless, when regarded not separately but in connexion with the interests of universal humanity, these harsh fatalities are seen to be full of beneficence — the same beneficence which brings to early graves the children of diseased parents, and singles out the intemperate and the debilitated as the victims of an epidemic.

There are many very amiable people who have not the nerve to look this matter fairly in the face. Disabled as they are by their sympathies with present suffering, from duly regarding ultimate consequences, they pursue a course which is injudicious, and in the end even cruel. We do not consider it true kindness in a mother to gratify her child with sweetmeats that are likely to make it ill. We should think it a very foolish sort of benevolence which led a surgeon to let his patient's disease progress to a fatal issue, rather than inflict pain by an operation. Similarly, we must call those spurious philanthropists who, to prevent present misery, would entail greater misery on future generations. That rigorous necessity which, when allowed to operate, becomes so sharp a spur to the lazy and so strong a bridle to the random, these paupers' friends would repeal, because of the wailings it here and there produces. Blind to the fact that under the natural order of things society is constantly excreting its unhealthy, imbecile, slow, vacillating, faithless members, these unthinking, though well-meaning, men advocate an interference which not only stops the purifying process, but even increases the vitiation — absolutely encourages the multiplication of the reckless and incompetent by offering them an unfailing provision, and *dis*courages the multiplication of the competent and provident by heightening the difficulty of maintaining a family. And thus, in their eagerness to prevent the salutary sufferings that surround us, these sigh-wise and groan-foolish people bequeath to posterity a continually increasing curse.

On Liberty

John Stuart Mill

During the second half of the nineteenth century, liberalism in theory and practice started to change. In general it became less wedded to laissez-faire *policies and less optimistic than it was during the first half of the nineteenth century. This change is reflected in the thought of John Stuart Mill (1806–1873). He was the most influential British thinker of the mid-nineteenth century and probably the leading liberal theorist of the period. When he was young he favored the early liberalism of his father, James Mill, a well-known philosopher, and Jeremy Bentham, the author of utilitarianism. Over time he perceived difficulties with this early liberalism and new dangers. He modified his liberal ideas, a change that would later be reflected in liberal political policies of the late nineteenth and early twentieth centuries. In the following selection from* On Liberty *(1859), his most famous work, Mill analyzes this evolution of liberalism starting with the aims of liberals during the first half of the nineteenth century.*

> **Consider:** *What Mill feels was the essence of early liberalism; what crucial changes occurred to transform liberalism; what Mill means by tyranny of the majority.*

The aim, therefore, of patriots was to set limits to the power which the ruler should be suffered to exercise over the community; and this limitation was what they meant by liberty. It was attempted in two ways. First, by obtaining a recognition of certain immunities, called political liberties or rights, which it was to be regarded as a breach of duty in the ruler to infringe, and which if he did infringe, specific resistance, or general rebellion, was held to be justifiable. A second, and generally a later expedient, was the establishment of constitutional checks, by which the consent of the community, or of a body of some sort, supposed to represent its interests, was made a necessary condition to some of the more important acts of the governing power. To the first of these modes of limitation, the ruling power, in most European countries, was compelled, more or less, to submit. It was not so with the second; and, to attain this, or when already in some degree possessed, to attain it more completely, became everywhere the principal object of the lovers of liberty. And so long as mankind were content to combat one enemy by another, and to be ruled by a master, on condition of being guaranteed more or less efficaciously against his tyranny, they did not carry their aspirations beyond this point.

A time, however, came, in the progress of human affairs, when men ceased to think it a necessity of nature that their governors should be an independent

SOURCE: John Stuart Mill, *Utilitarianism, Liberty, and Representative Government* (London: J. M. Dent and Sons Ltd., Everyman Library, 1910), pp. 66–68.

power, opposed in interest to themselves. It appeared to them much better that the various magistrates of the State should be their tenants or delegates, revocable at their pleasure. In that way alone, it seemed, could they have complete security that the powers of government would never be abused to their disadvantage. By degrees this new demand for elective and temporary rulers became the prominent object of the exertions of the popular party, wherever any such party existed; and superseded, to a considerable extent, the previous efforts to limit the power of rulers. As the struggle proceeded for making the ruling power emanate from the periodical choice of the ruled, some persons began to think that too much importance had been attached to the limitation of the power itself. *That* (it might seem) was a resource against rulers whose interests were habitually opposed to those of the people. What was now wanted was, that the rulers should be identified with the people; that their interest and will should be the interest and will of the nation. The nation did not need to be protected against its own will. There was no fear of its tyrannising over itself. Let the rulers be effectually responsible to it, promptly removable by it, and it could afford to trust them with power of which it could itself dictate the use to be made. Their power was but the nation's own power, concentrated, and in a form convenient for exercise. This mode of thought, or rather perhaps of feeling, was common among the last generation of European liberalism, in the Continental section of which it still apparently predominates. . . .

In time, however, a democratic republic came to occupy a large portion of the earth's surface, and made itself felt as one of the most powerful members of the community of nations; and elective and responsible government became subject to the observations and criticisms which wait upon a great existing fact. It was now perceived that such phrases as "self-government," and "the power of the people over themselves," do not express the true state of the case. The "people" who exercise the power are not always the same people with those over whom it is exercised; and the "self-government" spoken of is not the government of each by himself, but of each by all the rest. The will of the people, moreover, practically means the will of the most numerous or the most active *part* of the people; the majority, or those who succeed in making themselves accepted as the majority; the people, consequently *may* desire to oppress a part of their number; and precautions are as much needed against this as against any other abuse of power. The limitation, therefore, of the power of government over individuals loses none of its importance when the holders of power are regularly accountable to the community, that is, to the strongest party therein. This view of things, recommending itself equally to the intelligence of thinkers and to the inclination of those important classes in European society to whose real or supposed interests democracy is adverse, has had no difficulty in establishing itself; and in political speculations "the tyranny of the majority" is now generally included among the evils against which society requires to be on its guard.

Like other tyrannies, the tyranny of the majority was at first, and is still vulgarly, held in dread, chiefly as operating through the acts of the public authorities. But reflecting persons perceived that when society is itself the tyrant — society collectively over the separate individuals who compose it — its means of tyrannising are not restricted to the acts which it may do by the hands of its political functionaries. Society can and does execute its own mandates: and if it issues wrong mandates instead of right, or any mandates at all in things with which it ought not to meddle, it practises a social tyranny more formidable than many kinds of political oppression, since, though not usually upheld by such extreme penalties, it leaves fewer means of escape, penetrating much more deeply into the details of life, and enslaving the soul itself. Protection, therefore, against the tyranny of the magistrate is not enough: there needs protection also against the tyranny of the prevailing opinion and feeling; against the tendency of society to impose, by other means than civil penalties, its own ideas and practices as rules of conduct on those who dissent from them; to fetter the development, and, if possible, prevent the formation, of any individuality not in harmony with its ways, and compels all characters to fashion themselves upon the model of its own. There is a limit to the legitimate interference of collective opinion with individual independence: and to find that limit, and maintain it against encroachment, is as indispensable to a good condition of human affairs, as protection against political despotism.

The Salon [Art Exhibit] of 1846: Art and the Bourgeoisie

Charles Baudelaire

The rising power of the middle class during the nineteenth century was recognized by observers in all fields. This power was not only economic, social, and political but cultural as well. Even artists, who early developed ambivalent and then hostile feelings toward the bourgeoisie, recognized this cultural power. This is illustrated in the following selection by Charles Baudelaire (1821–1867). Early in his career as an author, Baudelaire gained some popularity as an art critic. The following introduction to his critical account of the Salon of 1846 (art exhibit) held in Paris is addressed to the bourgeoisie.

Consider: *How Baudelaire describes the bourgeoisie; Baudelaire's basis for his appeal to them to support art; how this document reveals the spreading cultural influence of the bourgeoisie.*

SOURCE: Charles Baudelaire, "The Salon of 1846," from *Art in Paris, 1845–1862*, Jonathan Mayne, trans. and ed. Published by Phaidon Press Ltd., Oxford, pp. 41–43. Reprinted by permission of the publisher.

TO THE BOURGEOIS

You are the majority—in number and intelligence; therefore you are the force—which is justice.

Some are scholars, others are owners; a glorious day will come when the scholars shall be owners and the owners scholars. Then your power will be complete, and no man will protest against it.

Until that supreme harmony is achieved, it is just that those who are but owners should aspire to become scholars; for knowledge is no less of an enjoyment than ownership.

The government of the city is in your hands, and that is just, for you are the force. But you must also be capable of feeling beauty; for as not one of you today can do without power, so not one of you has the right to do without poetry.

You can live three days without bread—without poetry, never; and those of you who can say the contrary are mistaken; they are out of their minds.

The aristocrats of thought, the distributors of praise and blame, the monopolists of the things of the mind, have told you that you have no right to feel and to enjoy—they are Pharisees.

For you have in your hands the government of a city whose public is the public of the universe, and it is necessary that you should be worthy of that task.

Enjoyment is a science, and the exercise of the five senses calls for a particular initiation which only comes about through goodwill and need.

Very well, you need art.

Art is an infinitely precious good, a draught both refreshing and cheering which restores the stomach and the mind to the natural equilibrium of the ideal.

You understand its function, you gentlemen of the bourgeoisie—whether law-givers or businessmen—when the seventh or the eighth hour strikes and you bend your tired head towards the embers of your hearth or the cushions of your armchair.

That is the time when a keener desire and a more active reverie would refresh you after your daily labours.

But the monopolists have decided to keep the forbidden fruit of knowledge from you, because knowledge is their counter and their shop, and they are infinitely jealous of it. If they had merely denied you the power to create works of art or to understand the processes by which they are created, they would have asserted a truth at which you could not take offence, because public business and trade take up three quarters of your day. And as for your leisure hours, they should be used for enjoyment and pleasure.

But the monopolists have forbidden you even to enjoy, because you do not understand the technique of the arts, as you do those of the law and of business.

And yet it is just that if two-thirds of your time are devoted to knowledge, then the remaining third should be occupied by feeling—and it is by feeling alone that art is to be understood; and it is in this way that the equilibrium of your soul's forces will be established.

Truth, for all its multiplicity, is not two-faced; and just as in your politics you have increased both rights and benefits, so in the arts you have set up a greater and more abundant communion.

You, the bourgeois — be you king, law-giver, or business-man — have founded collections, museums and galleries. Some of those, which sixteen years ago were only open to the monopolists, have thrown wide their doors to the multitude.

You have combined together, you have formed companies and raised loans in order to realize the idea of the future in all its varied forms — political, industrial and artistic. In no noble enterprise have you ever left the initiative to the protesting and suffering minority, which anyway is the natural enemy of art.

For to allow oneself to be outstripped in art and in politics is to commit suicide; and for a majority to commit suicide is impossible.

And what you have done for France, you have done for other countries too. The Spanish Museum is there to increase the volume of general ideas that you ought to possess about art; for you know perfectly well that just as a national museum is a kind of communion by whose gentle influence men's hearts are softened and their wills unbent, so a foreign museum is an international communion where two peoples, observing and studying one another more at their ease, can penetrate one another's mind and fraternize without discussion.

You are the natural friends of the arts, because you are some of you rich men and the others scholars.

When you have given to society your knowledge, your industry, your labour and your money, you claim back your payment in enjoyments of the body, the reason and the imagination. If you recover the amount of enjoyments which is needed to establish the equilibrium of all parts of your being, then you are happy, satisfied and well-disposed, as society will be satisfied, happy and well-disposed when it has found its own general and absolute equilibrium.

And so it is to you, the bourgeois, that this book is naturally dedicated; for any book which is not addressed to the majority — in number and intelligence — is a stupid book.

1st May 1846

The Communist Manifesto

Karl Marx and Friedrich Engels

Although initially only one of many radical doctrines, Marxism proved to be the most dynamic and influential challenge to industrial capitalism and middle-class civilization in general. Its most succinct and popular statement is contained in the Communist Manifesto, *written by Karl Marx (1818–1883) and Friedrich Engels (1820–1895) and first published in 1848. Karl Marx was born in Germany, studied history and philosophy, and entered a career as a journalist, writer, and revolutionary. For most of his life he lived in exile in London. His collaborator, Friedrich Engels, was also born in Germany and lived in England, but there he helped manage his family's cotton business in Manchester. Their doctrines directly attacked the middle class and industrial capitalism, presenting communism as a philosophically, historically, and scientifically justified alternative that would inevitably replace capitalism. They saw themselves as revolutionary leaders of the growing proletariat (the working class). The following is a selection from the* Communist Manifesto.

> **Consider:** *The appeal of the ideas presented here; the concrete policies advocated by Marx and Engels; the historical and intellectual trends reflected in the* Manifesto.

A specter is haunting Europe—the specter of Communism. All the powers of old Europe have entered into a holy alliance to exorcise this specter; Pope and Czar, Metternich and Guizot, French radicals and German police spies.

Where is the party in opposition that has not been decried as Communistic by its opponents in power? Where the opposition that has not hurled back the branding reproach of Communism, against the more advanced opposition parties, as well as against its reactionary adversaries?

Two things result from this fact.

I. Communism is already acknowledged by all European powers to be in itself a power.

II. It is high time that Communists should openly, in the face of the whole world, publish their views, their aims, their tendencies, and meet this nursery tale of the Specter of Communism with a Manifesto of the party itself.

To this end the Communists of various nationalities have assembled in London, and sketched the following manifesto to be published in the English, French, German, Italian, Flemish and Danish languages.

In what relation do the Communists stand to the proletarians as a whole?

The Communists do not form a separate party opposed to other working class parties.

SOURCE: Karl Marx and Friedrich Engels, *Manifesto of the Communist Party*, 2nd ed. (New York: National Executive Committee of the Socialist Labor Party, 1898), pp. 30–32, 41–43, 60.

They have no interests separate and apart from those of the proletariat as a whole.

They do not set up any sectarian principles of their own by which to shape and mould the proletarian movement.

The Communists are distinguished from the other working class parties by this only: 1. In the national struggles of the proletarians of the different countries, they point out and bring to the front the common interests of the entire proletariat, independently of all nationality. 2. In the various stages of development which the struggle of the working class against the bourgeoisie has to pass through, they always and everywhere represent the interests of the movement as a whole.

The Communists, therefore, are on the one hand, practically, the most advanced and resolute section of the working class parties of every country, that section which pushes forward all others; on the other hand, theoretically, they have over the great mass of the proletariat the advantage of clearly understanding the line of march, the conditions, and the ultimate general results of the proletarian movement.

The immediate aim of the Communists is the same as that of all the other proletarian parties: formation of the proletariat into a class, overthrow of the bourgeois supremacy, conquest of political power by the proletariat.

The theoretical conclusions of the Communists are in no way based on ideas or principles that have been invented, or discovered, by this or that would-be universal reformer.

They merely express, in general terms, actual relations springing from an existing class struggle, from a historical movement going on under our very eyes. The abolition of existing property relations is not at all a distinctive feature of Communism.

All property relations in the past have continually been subject to historical change, consequent upon the change in historical conditions.

The French revolution, for example, abolished feudal property in favor of bourgeois property.

The distinguishing feature of Communism is not the abolition of property generally, but the abolition of bourgeois property. But modern bourgeois private property is the final and most complete expression of the system of producing and appropriating products, that is based on class antagonisms, on the exploitation of the many by the few.

In this sense the theory of the Communists may be summed up in the single sentence: Abolition of private property.

We have seen above that the first step in the revolution by the working class is to raise the proletariat to the position of the ruling class; to win the battle of democracy.

The proletariat will use its political supremacy to wrest, by degrees, all capital from the bourgeoisie; to centralize all instruments of production in the hands of the State, *i. e.*, of the proletariat organized as the ruling class; and to increase the total of productive forces as rapidly as possible.

Of course, in the beginning this cannot be effected except by means of despotic inroads on the rights of property and on the conditions of bourgeois production; by means of measures, therefore, which appear economically insufficient and untenable, but which, in the course of the movement, outstrip themselves, necessitate further inroads upon the old social order and are unavoidable as a means of entirely revolutionizing the mode of production.

These measures will, of course, be different in different countries.

Nevertheless in the most advanced countries the following will be pretty generally applicable:

1. Abolition of property in land and application of all rents of land to public purposes.
2. A heavy progressive or graduated income tax.
3. Abolition of all right of inheritance.
4. Confiscation of the property of all emigrants and rebels.
5. Centralization of credit in the hands of the State, by means of a national bank with State capital and an exclusive monopoly.
6. Centralization of the means of communication and transport in the hands of the State.
7. Extension of factories and instruments of production owned by the State; the bringing into cultivation of waste lands, and the improvement of the soil generally in accordance with a common plan.
8. Equal liability of all to labor. Establishment of industrial armies, especially for agriculture.
9. Combination of agriculture with manufacturing industries: gradual abolition of the distinction between town and country, by a more equable distribution of the population over the country.
10. Free education for all children in public schools. Abolition of children's factory labor in its present form. Combination of education with industrial production, etc., etc.

When, in the course of development, class distinctions have disappeared and all production has been concentrated in the hands of a vast association of the whole nation, the public power will lose its political character. Political power, properly so called, is merely the organized power of one class for oppressing another. If the proletariat during its contest with the bourgeoisie is compelled, by the force of circumstances, to organize itself as a class, if, by means of a revolution, it makes itself the ruling class, and, as such, sweeps away by force the old conditions of production, then it will, along with these conditions, have swept away the conditions for the existence of class antagonisms, and of classes generally, and will thereby have abolished its own supremacy as a class.

In place of the old bourgeois society with its classes and class antagonisms we shall have an association in which the free development of each is the condition for the free development of all.

Programme of the Social Democratic Party of Germany:

The Erfurt Congress, 1891

Initially Marxism attracted few adherents, but within a few decades it had become extremely influential, particularly among left-wing working-class organizations and parties. This was particularly so in Germany, where the Social Democratic Party, founded in 1875, grew to the point at which after 1890 it gained more votes than any other party in Germany and became Europe's strongest socialist party. At the Erfurt Congress of 1891 the party defined its official program. The following excerpt from that program indicates the party's ideological basis.

> **Consider:** *How this relates to the ideas contained in the* Communist Manifesto; *the policies the party would support; what is appealing and what is threatening about this program.*

PROGRAMME OF THE SOCIAL DEMOCRATIC PARTY OF GERMANY

The economic development of bourgeois society leads necessarily to the disappearance of production on a small scale *(Kleinbetrieb)*, the principle of which consists in the worker's owning the means of production. This economic development separates the worker from his means of production, and transforms him into an unpropertied proletarian, while the means of production become the property of a comparatively small number of capitalists and great landlords.

Hand in hand with the monopolising of the means of production, goes the supplanting of scattered small businesses by colossal businesses, the development of the tool into the machine, and a gigantic growth of the productivity of human labour. But all the advantages of this change are monopolised by the capitalists and great landlords. For the proletariat and the sinking intermediate layers — small masters, peasants — it betokens growing increase of the insecurity of their existence, of misery, of oppression, of slavery, of humiliation and of exploration.

Ever greater grows the number of the proletariat, ever more extensive the army of superfluous workers, ever sharper the contrast between exploiters and exploited, and ever bitterer the class-warfare between bourgeoisie and proletariat, which divides modern society into two hostile camps, and is the common characteristic of all industrial countries.

The chasm between propertied and unpropertied is further widened by crises, rooted in the essence of the capitalistic method of production, which

---

SOURCE: Bertrand Russell, *German Social Democracy* (London: Longmans, 1896), pp. 137–139.

grow ever more far-reaching and more ravaging, which make general in-security into the normal condition of society, and furnish the proof that the productive powers of modern society have outgrown its control, that private property in the means of production is irreconcilable with the due applica-tion and full development of those powers.

Private property in the means of production, which was formerly the means of securing to the producer the possession of his own product, has to-day become the means of expropriating peasants, handicraftsmen and small producers, and of putting the non-workers, capitalists and great landlords in possession of the product of the workers. Only the conversion of capitalistic private property in the means of production — land, quarries, and mines, raw material, tools, machines, means of communication — into common property, and the change of the production of goods into a socialistic production, worked for and through society, can bring it about that production on a large scale, and the ever-growing productiveness of human labour, shall develop, for the hitherto exploited classes, from a source of misery and oppression, into a source of the highest well-being and perfect universal harmony.

This social change betokens the emancipation, not only of the proletariat, but of the whole human race, which is suffering under the present condi-tions. But it can only be the work of the working classes, because all other classes, in spite of conflicts of interests among themselves, take their stand on the ground of private property in the means of production, and have, for their common aim, the maintenance of the foundations of existing society.

The struggle of the working class against capitalistic exploitation is of nec-essity a political struggle. The working class cannot carry on its economic con-tests, and cannot develop its economic organisation, without political rights. It cannot bring about the transference of the means of production into the possession of the community, without having obtained political power.

To give to this fight of the working class a conscious and unified form, and to show it its necessary goal — that is the task of the Social Democratic Party.

The interests of the working classes are the same in all countries with a capitalistic mode of production. With the extension of the world's com-merce, and of production for the world-market, the position of the worker in every country grows ever more dependent on the position of the worker in other countries. The liberation of the working class, accordingly, is a work in which the workmen of all civilised countries are equally involved. In rec-ognition of this, the Social Democratic Party of Germany feels and declares itself to be *one* with the class-conscious workmen of all other countries.

The Social Democratic Party of Germany does not fight, accordingly, for new class-privileges and class-rights, but for the abolition of class-rule and of classes themselves, for equal rights and equal duties of all, without distinction of sex or descent. Starting from these views, it combats, within existing society, not only the exploitation and oppression of wage-earners, but every kind of exploitation and oppression, whether directed against a class, a party, a sex, or a race.

Fabian Essays

Sidney Webb

Numerous varieties of socialist thought arose in the nineteenth century. Although Marxism was the most influential of these, its revolutionary nature frightened many. Moreover, it, like other socialist doctrines, was subject to differing interpretations. Some of the best-known revisions of socialism, all of which drew heavily from Marxism but which offered more moderate programs, were those of Jean Jaurès (1859–1914) in France, Eduard Bernstein (1850–1932) in Germany, and the Fabians in England. The following selection is from one of the leading Fabians, Sidney Webb (1859–1947). He and a number of other intellectuals, such as George Bernard Shaw, Beatrice Webb, and H. G. Wells, wrote numerous essays urging socialist reforms through democratic means and within the context of an evolving British heritage. The Fabians ultimately became influential in the British Labour party.

> **Consider:** *The ways in which Fabianism accepts Marxism and yet modifies it; what groups this view would most appeal to and why; the major nineteenth-century trends this document accepts or rejects.*

In the present Socialist movement these two streams are united: advocates of social reconstruction have learnt the lesson of Democracy, and know that it is through the slow and gradual turning of the popular mind to new principles that social reorganization bit by bit comes. All students of society who are abreast of their time, Socialists as well as Individualists, realize that important organic changes can only be (1) democratic, and thus acceptable to a majority of the people, and prepared for in the minds of all; (2) gradual, and thus causing no dislocation, however rapid may be the rate of progress; (3) not regarded as immoral by the mass of the people, and thus not subjectively demoralizing to them; and (4) in this country at any rate, constitutional and peaceful. Socialists may therefore be quite at one with Radicals in their political methods. Radicals, on the other hand, are perforce realizing that mere political levelling is insufficient to save a State from anarchy and despair. Both sections have been driven to recognize that the root of the difficulty is economic; and there is every day a wider census that the inevitable outcome of Democracy is the control by the people themselves, not only of their own political organization, but, through that, also of the main instruments of wealth production; the gradual substitution of organized cooperation for the anarchy of the competitive struggle; and the consequent recovery, in the only possible way, of what John Stuart Mill calls "the enormous share which the possessors of the instruments of industry are able to take from the produce." The economic side of the democratic ideal is, in fact, Socialism itself.

Source: Sidney Webb, "Fabian Essays," from *Fabian Essays in Socialism*, G. Bernard Shaw, ed. (London: Walter Scott, 1889), pp. 34–35.

Syllabus of Errors

Pope Pius IX

Critics of middle-class liberalism were not limited to those demanding more rapid, radical changes such as the Marxists and Fabians. From the time of the French Revolution, the conservative Catholic Church was usually hostile to most of the changes favored by the middle class and by doctrines of liberalism. Indeed, in the decades just after mid-century, when it had become apparent that traditional society was on the wane, the Church became more intransigent than ever. In 1864 Pius IX, who served as pope from 1846 to 1878, issued the famous "Syllabus of Errors," in which most of the major forces of the nineteenth century were formally rejected. The following excerpts from that document should be read with care; they present views the Church specifically rejected as errors, not views accepted by the Church.

> **Consider:** *Why Pius IX took this stand; the dilemma faced by Catholics who were also middle class and liberal; the groups that might favor the Church's view as expressed here.*

15. Every man is free to embrace and profess the religion he shall believe true, guided by the light of reason.

16. Men may in any religion find the way of eternal salvation, and obtain eternal salvation.

39. The commonwealth is the origin and source of all rights, and possesses rights which are not circumscribed by any limits.

45. The entire direction of public schools, in which the youth of Christian states are educated, except (to a certain extent) in the case of episcopal seminaries, may and must appertain to the civil power, and belong to it so far that no other authority whatsoever shall be recognized as having any right to interfere in the discipline of the schools, the arrangement of the studies, the taking of degrees, or the choice and approval of the teachers.

47. The best theory of civil society requires that popular schools open to the children of all classes, and, generally, all public institutes intended for instruction in letters and philosophy, and for conducting the education of the young, should be freed from all ecclesiastical authority, government, and interference, and should be fully subject to the civil and political power, in conformity with the will of rulers and the prevalent opinions of the age.

SOURCE: From William E. Gladstone, *The Vatican Decrees in Their Bearing on Civil Allegiance: A Political Expostulation* (New York: Harper and Brothers, 1875), pp. 109–129.

56. Moral laws do not stand in need of the divine sanction, and there is no necessity that human laws should be conformable to the laws of nature, and receive their sanction from God.

57. Knowledge of philosophical things and morals, and also civil laws, may and must depart from divine and ecclesiastical authority.

78. In the present day, it is no longer expedient that the Catholic religion shall be held as the only religion of the State, to the exclusion of all other modes of worship.

80. The Roman Pontiff can and ought to reconcile himself to, and agree with, progress, liberalism, and civilization as lately introduced.

Foundations of the Nineteenth Century: Racism

Houston Stewart Chamberlain

During the second half of the nineteenth century, elements of nationalism, Darwinism, and Romanticism were combined by various writers to produce racist theories and provide justification for the growth of racist views. One of the most famous of these writers was Houston Stewart Chamberlain (1855–1927), an Englishman who moved to Germany and became a naturalized German. There he wrote The Foundations of the Nineteenth Century *(1900), which soon became a popular success. In it he stressed the importance of racism for the development of civilization. The following selection from that book deals with the "German race."*

Consider: *The characteristics of the "German race"; the ways in which this selection reflects racist thought; how this might relate to German nationalism.*

Let us attempt a glance into the depths of the soul. What are the specific intellectual and moral characteristics of this Germanic race? Certain anthropologists would fain teach us that all races are equally gifted; we point to history and answer: that is a lie! The races of mankind are markedly different in the nature and also in the extent of their gift, and the Germanic races belong to the most highly gifted group, the group usually termed Aryan. Is this human family united and uniform by bonds of blood? Do these stems really all spring from the same root? I do not know and I do not much care; no affinity binds more closely than elective affinity, and in this sense the Indo-European Aryans certainly form a family. . . .

SOURCE: Houston Stewart Chamberlain, *Foundations of the Nineteenth Century* (New York: Howard Fertig, 1968), Vol. I, pp. 542–543.

Physically and mentally the Aryans are pre-eminent among all peoples; for that reason they are by right, as the Stagirite expresses it, the lords of the world. Aristotle puts the matter still more concisely when he says, "Some men are by nature free, others slaves"; this perfectly expresses the moral aspect. For freedom is by no means an abstract thing, to which every human being has fundamentally a claim; a right to freedom must evidently depend upon capacity for it, and this again presupposes physical and intellectual power. One may make the assertion, that even the mere conception of freedom is quite unknown to most men. Do we not see the *homo syriacus* develop just as well and as happily in the position of slave as of master? Do the Chinese not show us another example of the same nature? Do not all historians tell us that the Semites and half-Semites, in spite of their great intelligence, never succeeded in founding a State that lasted, and that because every one always endeavoured to grasp all power for himself, thus showing that their capabilities were limited to despotism and anarchy, the two opposites of freedom?

Judaism in Music:
Anti-Semitism

Richard Wagner

One of the darkest aspects of racist thought during the second half of the nineteenth century was its growing stress on anti-Semitism. Anti-Semitism has a long history, but it welled up with new strength after mid-century, particularly in Germany, where it became an important social and political force. An example of this bitter anti-Semitism comes from the pen of the great German composer, Richard Wagner (1813–1883). The following is an excerpt from "Judaism in Music," an article he published in a German journal in 1850.

> **Consider:** *The elements of Wagner's anti-Semitism; the support he uses for his arguments against the Jew; how this relates to the ideas of Houston Stewart Chamberlain.*

It is necessary for us to explain the *involuntary repugnance* we possess for the nature and personality of the Jews. . . . According to the present constitution of the world, the Jew in truth is already more than emancipate: He rules, and will rule, as long as Money remains the power before which all

SOURCE: Louis L. Snyder, ed., *Documents of German History* (New Brunswick, N.J.: Rutgers University Press, 1958), pp. 192–193.

our doings and our dealings lose their force. . . . The public art taste has been brought between the busy fingers of the Jews, who reside over an art bazaar. . . . The Jew's outward appearance always has something disagreeably foreign about it. . . .

The Jew speaks the language of the nation in whose midst he dwells from generation to generation, but he always speaks it as an alien. Our whole European art and civilization have remained to the Jew a foreign tongue. In this speech, this art, the Jew can only after-speak and after-patch — cannot truly make a poem of his words, an artwork of his doings. In the peculiarities of Semitic pronunciation the first thing that strikes our ear as quite outlandish and unpleasant, in the Jew's production of the voice sounds, is a creaking, squeaking, buzzing snuffle. . . . The Jew who is innately incapable of enouncing himself to us artistically through either his outward appearance or his speech, and least of all through his singing, has, nevertheless, been able in the widest-spread of modern art varieties, to wit, in Music, to reach the rulership of public taste. . . . Control of money through usury has led the Jews to power, for modern culture is accessible to none but the well-to-do. . . .

The Jews have never produced a true poet. [Heinrich Heine] reached the point where he duped himself into a poet, and was rewarded by his versified lies being set to music by our own composers. He was the conscience of Judaism, just as Judaism is the evil conscience of our modern civilization.

VISUAL SOURCES

The Hatch Family: The Upper Middle Class

Eastman Johnson

This 1871 portrait of the Hatch family by the American artist Eastman Johnson shows a number of elements of the condition, style of life, and values of the upper middle class. Both the quality and quantity of the furnishings and the clothes indicate how materially well to do this family is. The clothes and demeanor convey the strong sense of propriety; yet the activities of the children and the position of their toys denote how child-centered this family is. The appropriate sexual roles are suggested: the father at center right in an authoritative pose, with pen in hand sitting at his desk, the grandfather on the left, keeping up on the news by reading a paper, the mother on the right, generally surveying her children, and the grand-

Photo 10-1

The Metropolitan Museum of Art, Gift of Frederick H. Hatch

mother on the left, knitting. The large painting on the left as well as the sculptures on the right show this family to be properly supportive and appreciative of the arts. The large bookcase on the right indicates a respect for literature and learning. Heavy curtains largely block out the outside world; values of domesticity and privacy are evident.

Consider: *How this portrait supports the description of middle-class life by Reader.*

The Lunch Hour: The Working Class

Käthe Kollwitz

Accompanying the rise to prominence of the upper middle class was the growth of the urban working class, the two economically dependent on one another but in strikingly different conditions. This 1909 drawing by the German artist Käthe Kollwitz, entitled Lunch Hour, *gives an impression of the condition and spirit of the German working class. The workers seem to be part of an almost undifferentiated mass, dully and similarly clothed, eating low-quality meals in uncomfortable circumstances, and above all displaying a physical and psychological fatigue and a pervasive sense of discouragement.*

Consider: *How this drawing relates to the views of Marx and Engels.*

Photo 10-2

Private Collection. Photo courtesy Galerie St. Etienne, New York.

SECONDARY SOURCES

Life in Victorian England

W. J. Reader

Being middle class in the nineteenth century meant carrying out a certain style of life. Any short description of this style of life requires making generalizations that in each particular case are violated. Yet there is something useful in even a stereotypical picture of how middle-class families lived. In the following selection W. J. Reader, while quite aware of distinctions between different elements of the middle class, describes the home and some aspects of the life of the Victorian middle-class family. Here he emphasizes changes occurring over the course of the century.

> **Consider:** *The values embodied in this style of life; the principal ways in which this style of life changed by the last decades of the century and why these changes occurred; how this description might differ from a description of working-class or aristocratic life styles.*

Towards the end of the century, one can picture the well-to-do Victorian middle-class family in its solid suburban house, with a semi-circular carriage drive running from the gate past the shrubbery up to the front door and out again on the other side. The carriage drive was likely to symbolize aspiration rather than fact, unless the family was really wealthy, for it needed a great deal of money to run a carriage, and most middle-class families had to wait for the motor car before they could have their own private transport. But at least there would be ample money to staff the house, to take the whole family to the seaside every year (with appropriate servants), or perhaps abroad, to educate the boys and launch them into professional life, and to provide for the girls adequately.

In the family's general way of life, it was likely that there would be little enough of puritan austerity. Drink might still be suspect, but on the other hand there might be an excellent cellar of wines. The head of the family, whose father might have gone to work at nine in the morning and stayed till nine at night, would be likely now to leave at five; work was not quite the all-consuming necessity it once had been. For amusement, it was unlikely that theatres or dancing would be barred. Certainly relations between the sexes would be somewhat easier than thirty or forty years before, partly because new amusements — croquet, lawn tennis, roller-skating, cycling —

SOURCE: W. J. Reader, *Life in Victorian England*. Reprinted by permission of Capricorn Books (New York, 1967), and B. T. Batsford Ltd. (London, 1967), pp. 152–154. Copyright © 1967 by Capricorn Books (U.S. Rights), and B. T. Batsford Ltd. (Canadian Rights).

had brought young men and young women much more informally into each other's presence. . . .

By the seventies, that is to say, the force of the middle-class attack on the privileged position of the upper classes had carried them well within it. They had impressed their own notions on many aspects of upper-class life; in return, they were allowing upper-class notions to modify some of their own. In the process, some of the grimness of middle-class life rubbed off; some of the wilder excesses of aristocratic self-indulgence were tamed. A kind of life emerged which, if it had a good deal of snobbery, purse-pride and smugness about it, was nevertheless a good deal more humane and civilized than either aristocratic or middle-class life in the not very distant past.

The Decline of Political Liberalism

F. H. Hinsley

Despite the apparent failures of 1848, political liberalism was at its zenith during the middle of the nineteenth century. By the last two decades of the century it was clearly on the decline or was at least evolving in striking new ways. This evolution is analyzed in the following selection from The New Cambridge Modern History *by F. H. Hinsley of Cambridge.*

> **Consider:** *The causes of the decline of political liberalism; the intellectual or ideological developments that occurred in the second half of the nineteenth century, as reflected by the decline of political liberalism.*

The politics of the age was distinguished, even in the least authoritarian of states, as much by the growth of authority as by the extension of democracy; and less by the extension of democracy and the democratisation of government than by an advance towards the democratisation of government policies and of the political context in which governments operated. It is these facts which account for the collapse of liberalism — for its exhaustion in more democratic countries as well as for its frustration in less democratic circumstances and its distortion in situations that were in between.

In the advanced countries of western Europe during the 1870's, when liberalism was at its zenith in its European home, liberal governments, abandoning the liberal opposition to the power of the state and seeing the state as the most effective means of securing the liberal conception of

Source: F. H. Hinsley, "Introduction," in *The New Cambridge Modern History,* Vol. XI, F. H. Hinsley, ed. (Cambridge, England: Cambridge University Press, 1962), pp. 32–34. Reprinted by permission of the publisher.

freedom in changed circumstances, accepted the early steps towards the inevitable extension of the functions of government and the use of unprecedented state compulsion on individuals for social ends — embracing the notion of state education, legalising trade unions, justifying public health measures, adopting even insurance and factory legislation. No governments in such countries, whatever their political complexion, could, indeed, have opposed such developments. From the end of the 1870's, however, they were overrun and overturned in those countries by the further progress of those twin forces, the masses and the modern state. Every advance in the role of the state, every new aspect of the social problem, every recognition of the emergence of the masses, every new turn of policy — whether towards protectionism and imperialism or towards social regulation and the extension of the franchise — conflicted with the liberal belief in freedom of contract and of enterprise, in free trade, in individual liberty, in public economy, in the minimum of government interference. Liberalism's great contribution, the constitutional state, and its guiding principles, the freedom of the individual, legal equality and conflict with the Church, were — to the varying extents that they had been already established in these states — taken over by more empirical and conservative politicians. Liberalism became more doctrinaire and more narrowly associated with urban and big business interests — even while industrial organisation itself, with the movement from personal to corporate control, was deserting it. The liberal parties split into moderate (national, social or imperialist) and radical wings on these current issues and lost office. Liberal rule or its equivalent ended in Great Britain in 1885, in Germany in 1878, in Austria and the Netherlands in 1879, in Sweden in 1880, in Belgium in 1884, in France in 1885. In Italy under Depretis and Crispi and in some states beyond western Europe liberal parties remained in power. But, liberal only in name, they embraced protectionism and imperialism, undertook social regulation and retained of the old liberal creed only opposition to the extension of the franchise and to the pretensions of the Church. In these states, as in even more authoritarian countries, authentic liberalism remained a relevant if a weakened basis for opposition to established authority. But even in that role, and even when it was not proscribed by the increased possibilities of repression, it was doomed to frustration by the growth of the need for social regulation and strong government and by the demand for those things by the mass of the population.

The Unfinished Revolution: Marxism Interpreted

Adam B. Ulam

Critical analyses of Marx and Marxism abound and from almost all points of view. From the historian's perspective, one of the most useful ways to approach Marx and Marxism is to place both in their historical context. This is done in the following excerpt from The Unfinished Revolution *by Adam Ulam, a professor of government at Harvard who has written extensively on the history of Marxism and the Soviet Union. Here he attempts to explain aspects of both the content and the appeal of Marxism by pointing to intellectual traditions affecting Marx and social realities conditioning those who accepted it.*

> **Consider:** *Why Marxism is most appealing during the early period of industrialization; how Ulam would explain the apparent failure of Marxism to take hold in twentieth-century nations such as the United States; what Ulam means when he calls Marx a child of rationalistic optimism; how a more pro-Marxist scholar might respond to this interpretation.*

Here, then, is a theory attuned even more closely than other parts of Marxism to the facts and feelings of an early period of industrialization. The class struggle is the salt of Marxism, its most operative revolutionary part. As a historical and psychological concept, it expresses a gross oversimplification, but it is the oversimplification of a genius. The formula of the class struggle seizes the essence of the mood of a great historical moment — a revolution in basic economy — and generalizes it into a historical law. It extracts the grievances of groups of politically conscious workers in Western Europe, then a very small part of the whole proletariat, and sees in it the portent and meaning of the awakening of the whole working class everywhere. The *first* reaction of the worker to industrialization, his feelings of grievance and impotence before the machine, his employer, and the state which stands behind the employer, are assumed by Marx to be typical of the general reactions of the worker to industrialization. What does change in the process of the development of industry is that the worker's feeling of impotence gives way to class consciousness, which in turn leads him to class struggle and socialism. Marx's worker is the historical worker, but he is the historical worker of a specific period of industrial and political development.

Even in interpreting the psychology of the worker of the transitional period, Marx exhibited a rationalistic bias. The worker's opposition to the capitalist order is a total opposition to its laws, its factories, and its govern-

---

SOURCE: Adam B. Ulam, *The Unfinished Revolution* (New York: Random House, Inc., 1960), pp. 42–44. Reprinted by permission of the author.

ment. But this revolutionary consciousness of the worker is to take him next to Marxist socialism, where he will accept the factory system and the state, the *only* difference being the abolition of capitalism. Why shouldn't the revolutionary protest of the worker flow into other channels: into rejection of industrialism as well as capitalism, into rejection of the socialist as well as the capitalist state? It is here that Marx is most definitely the child of his age, the child of rationalistic optimism: the workers will undoubtedly translate their anarchistic protests and grievances into a sophisticated philosophy of history. They will undoubtedly realize that the forces of industrialism and modern life, which strip them of property, status, and economic security, are in themselves benevolent in their ultimate effects and that it is only capitalism and the capitalists which make them into instruments of oppression. The chains felt by the proletariat are the chains of the industrial system. The chains Marx urges them to throw off are those of capitalism. Will the workers understand the difference? And if they do, will they still feel that in destroying capitalism they have a "world to win"?

Consciousness and Society:
The Generation of the 1890s

H. Stuart Hughes

Most historians agree that the most logical historical dividing line between the nineteenth and twentieth centuries is World War I. Yet some historians place the dividing line earlier. This is particularly so for those espousing intellectual history, as illustrated by H. Stuart Hughes in the following selection from Consciousness and Society. *A historian well known for his work on nineteenth- and twentieth-century thought, Hughes argues that a revolution in intellectual history came with the generation of the 1890s.*

   Consider: *The unifying characteristics of this "intellectual revolution"; the ways in which this intellectual change can be related to Freudian thought.*

From the perspective of the post-Second World War era, the work of the generation of the 1890's can be viewed as a "first attempt" at accommodation to a "new concept of reality." It represented a great deal more than a "return of the older idealism" — although the restatement of certain familiar idealist principles, in vastly altered form, was one aspect of this wider revolution in thought. In their most general significance, the three decades

Source: H. Stuart Hughes, *Consciousness and Society: The Reorientation of European Social Thought 1890–1930.* Reprinted by permission of Alfred A. Knopf, Inc., pp. 33, 66, 427–428. Copyright © 1958 by H. Stuart Hughes.

from about 1890 to the early 1920's marked the period in which the more imaginative thinker came to the conclusion that "the former conceptions of a rational reality" were insufficient, and that human thought would have to make "concessions" to a reality that could no longer be conceived as an orderly system. In this process of concession and adaptation, the "activity of human consciousness" for the first time became of paramount importance. For consciousness seemed to offer the only link between man and the world of society and history.

"The nature of reality" itself "no longer afforded a coherent totality": the natural world and with it reality in the broader sense were now seen as approachable only through conventional fictions. "But society, which represented the mediating sphere between man and this general reality and partook of elements of both, was still accessible to man." As Vico had declared two centuries earlier, man was capable of understanding the "civil world" *because he had made it.* By an effort of imaginative *construction*, human thought could mimic the process of creation, and hence of understanding.

There are certain periods in history in which a number of advanced thinkers, usually working independently one of another, have proposed views on human conduct so different from those commonly accepted at the time—and yet so manifestly interrelated—that together they seem to constitute an intellectual revolution. The decade of the 1890's was one of such periods. In this decade and the one immediately succeeding it, the basic assumptions of eighteenth- and nineteenth-century social thought underwent a critical review from which there emerged the new assumptions characteristic of our own time. "A revolution of such magnitude in the prevailing empirical interpretations of human society is hardly to be found occurring within the short space of a generation, unless one goes back to about the sixteenth century. What is to account for it?"

Such, indeed, is the most general characterization we may give to the new intellectual concerns of the 1890's. They had displaced the axis of social thought from the apparent and objectively verifiable to the only partially conscious area of unexplained motivation. In this sense the new doctrines were manifestly subjective. Psychological process had replaced external reality as the most pressing topic for investigation. It was no longer what actually existed that seemed most important: it was what men thought existed. And what they felt on the unconscious level had become rather more interesting than what they had consciously rationalized. Or—to formulate the change in still more radical terms—since it had apparently been proved impossible to arrive at any sure knowledge of human behavior—if one must rely on flashes of subjective intuition or on the creation of convenient fictions—then the mind had indeed been freed from the bonds of positivist method: it was at liberty to speculate, to imagine, to create. At one stroke the realm of human understanding had been drastically reduced and immensely broadened. The possibilities of social thought stretched out to infinity. It was perhaps this that Freud had in mind when in 1896 he spoke of "metapsychology"—the definition of the origin and nature of humanity—as his "ideal and problem child," his most challenging task for the future.

Chapter Questions

1. Give support for the argument that the nineteenth century was above all a middle-class century.
2. What common elements are there among the various criticisms of the middle class, its ideas, and its life style?
3. How would you explain the rise of Marxist and socialist ideas and movements during the second half of the nineteenth century?

III

THE TWENTIETH CENTURY
1914 to the Present

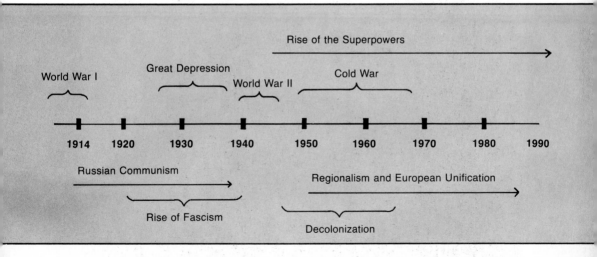

CHAPTER ELEVEN

War and Revolution: 1914–1920

Historians usually mark the end of the nineteenth century not at the turn of the century but with the outbreak of World War I in 1914. Although a number of wars took place after 1815, none covered all of Europe, none were long, and none were very costly. Indeed, many Europeans optimistically believed that the Western nations had become too economically interdependent and culturally mature to become involved in massive wars ever again. At the outbreak of World War I no one expected it to be so widespread or long-lasting. In fact, the fighting continued for four years before the war was finally concluded. The destruction was so unprecedented and the fighting so brutal that one had to question whether Western civilization had progressed at all. The war was such a strain that the most modernized nations, England, France, and Germany, for example, mobilized the total resources of their societies, while less modernized nations such as Russia were unable to support the effort.

Revolutions occurred in a number of areas, most notably in Germany, the Austro-Hungarian Empire, and Russia. The revolutions in Russia were the most significant. In March 1917 the tsarist government was swept from power by relatively moderate, liberal groups. In November of that year the new Provisional government was toppled by the Bolsheviks, who initiated a communist regime that proved surprisingly resilient. Under this government, the Soviet Union was to become a significant force in world politics.

In some ways the Paris Peace Conference in 1919 brought the period to a close, but the problems facing diplomats and heads of state meeting in Versailles were overwhelming. The Soviet Union was not invited to the conference, and the Germans were virtually ignored. Few left the conference satisfied and many harbored resentments that would color domestic and international politics during the 1920s and 1930s.

This chapter focuses on World War I and the Russian Revolution. With World War I, the two major issues for historians are the cause and the settlement. What caused this apparently unwanted war to break out and who, if anyone, was most to blame? Was the Peace of Paris a success or a failure? What role did Wilson play in working out this peace? Some of the selections also explore tactics used to fight the war, people's experiences during the war, and the results of the war. With the Russian Revolution, the question is not only why it occurred but moreover how and why the Bolsheviks—through most of 1917 only a small party—were ultimately able to gain and maintain power against extremely long odds. A number of

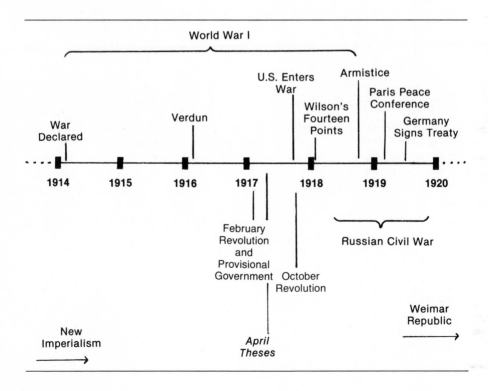

documents illustrate Lenin's strategy and Bolshevik policy as well as the variety of scholarly efforts to answer these questions.

Many feel that the events during this period of war constituted a fundamental break with the past. The significance of World War I and the Russian Revolution are shown in the developments in the two decades that followed. These will be covered in Chapters 12 and 13.

PRIMARY SOURCES

Letter to the Editor of the London Times: War and Political Ideology

V. Bourtzeff

At the beginning of World War I, there was tremendous popular enthusiasm and unity behind governments for the war effort. What is most surprising was that even socialist and other leftist political parties joined in this support. Socialists had long argued that working-class interests transcended national boundaries and that they would not support a nationalistic war entered into by a government dominated by capitalists. The following letter from V. Bourtzeff, a Russian Socialist, appeared in the London Times *about six weeks after the outbreak of the war in 1914.*

> **Consider:** *Why Bourtzeff supported the government's war effort; how Bourtzeff connects his opposition to the government's policies and his support for the government in the war; assuming these to be typical expectations at the beginning of the war, the ways World War I was a psychologically shattering experience for Europeans.*

TO THE EDITOR OF "THE TIMES":

Sir — May I be allowed to say a few words in connection with the excellent letter by my compatriot, Professor Vinogradov, which appeared in your paper today (September 14)? Professor Vinogradov is absolutely right when he says that not only is it desirable that complete unity of feeling should exist in Russian political circles, but that this unity is already an accomplished fact.

SOURCE: From Frank A. Golder, *Documents of Russian History, 1914–1917*, Emanuel Aronsberg, trans. Reprinted by permission of Prentice–Hall, Inc., pp. 38–39. Copyright © 1927 by Prentice–Hall, Inc.

The representatives of all political parties and of all nationalities in Russia are now at one with the Government, and this war with Germany and Austria, both guided by the Kaiser, has already become a national war for Russia.

Even we, the adherents of the parties of the Extreme Left, and hitherto ardent anti-militarists and pacifists, even we believe in the necessity of *this* war. *This* war is a war to protect justice and civilization. It will, we hope, be a decisive factor in our united *war against war*, and we hope that after it, it will at last be possible to consider seriously the question of disarmament and universal peace. There can be no doubt that victory, and decisive victory at that (personally I await this in the immediate future), will be on the side of the Allied nations—England, France, Belgium, Servia, and Russia.

The German peril, the curse which has hung over the whole world for so many decades, will be crushed, and crushed so that it will never again become a danger to the peace of the world. The peoples of the world desire peace.

To Russia this war will bring regeneration.

We are convinced that after this war there will no longer be any room for political reaction, and Russia will be associated with the existing group of cultured and civilized countries.

Professor Vinogradov is right when he says that in Russia not one of the political Left parties has at the present time modified its program in any way in view of the war. The word on all lips in Russia now is "Freedom." All are hungrily awaiting a general amnesty, freedom of the Press and of national life.

All the parties without any exceptions have supported the Government without even waiting for it to make any definite announcement about these crying needs. This is the measure of the belief of the people in the inevitableness of liberal reforms. The Government unfortunately still seems irresolute, and has up till now only done the minimum to justify the popular belief in it, but we are convinced that circumstances will develop in such a way that the Government will not be able to delay for long that which has become for Russia a *historical necessity*. And the sooner this happens the better.

To ensure the complete success of Russia in this war against Germany and Austria, and also for the time when the terms of peace will be discussed, the strongest and most firm national unity is necessary. And this unity of all nationalities and all parties will be possible only when the Russian Government will frankly and resolutely inaugurate a new and free era in the political life of the country.

We are convinced that we have supporting us both the public opinion of England and that of her Allies—France and Belgium.

Yours truly,
V. Bourtzeff

Reports from the Front:
The Battle for Verdun, 1916

The widely anticipated short war typified by heroic offensive thrusts failed to materialize. Instead, it turned into a long, extraordinarily brutal struggle. On the Western front, opposing armies slaughtered each other from their trenches. There are numerous reports of life at the front, such as the following account by a French Army officer of the battle for Verdun in 1916.

> **Consider:** *Why the defense was at such an advantage; why there was a willingness to sacrifice so much for such small advances.*

The Germans attacked in massed formation, by big columns of five or six hundred men, preceded by two waves of sharpshooters. We had only our rifles and our machine guns, because the 75's could not get to work.

Fortunately the flank batteries succeeded in catching the Boches on the right. It is absolutely impossible to convey what losses the Germans must suffer in these attacks. Nothing can give the idea of it. Whole ranks are mowed down, and those that follow them suffer the same fate. Under the storm of machine gun, rifle and 75 fire, the German columns were plowed into furrows of death. Imagine if you can what it would be like to rake water. Those gaps filled up again at once. That is enough to show with what disdain of human life the German attacks are planned and carried out.

In these circumstances German advances are sure. They startle the public, but at the front nobody attaches any importance to them. As a matter of fact, our trenches are so near those of the Germans that once the barbed wire is destroyed the distance between them can be covered in a few minutes. Thus, if one is willing to suffer a loss of life corresponding to the number of men necessary to cover the space between the lines, the other trench can always be reached. By sacrificing thousands of men, after a formidable bombardment, an enemy trench can always be taken.

There are slopes on Hill 304 where the level of the ground is raised several meters by mounds of German corpses. Sometimes it happens that the third German wave uses the dead of the second wave as ramparts and shelters. It was behind ramparts of the dead left by the first five attacks, on May 24th, that we saw the Boches take shelter while they organized their next rush.

We make prisoners among these dead during our counterattacks. They are men who have received no hurt, but have been knocked down by the falling of the human wall of their killed and wounded neighbors. They say very little. They are for the most part dazed with fear and alcohol, and it is several days before they recover.

Source: From *Source Records of the Great War*, Vol. IV, Charles F. Horne, ed. (New York: National Alumni, 1923), pp. 222–223.

Dulce et Decorum Est: Disillusionment

Wilfred Owen

The experience of World War I was profoundly disillusioning to those who believed in nineteenth-century ideals. After World War I, Europe was no longer characterized by the sense of optimism, progress, and glory that had typified Europe for most of the period between the eighteenth century and 1914. This is evidenced in war poems that no longer glorified the struggle but instead conveyed a sense of the horror and futility about it. One of the best of these antiwar poets was Wilfred Owen, born in England in 1893 and killed in action in 1918, one week before the armistice. The following poem has the ironic ending, "It is sweet and proper to die for one's country."

Consider: *The psychological consequences of the war for the soldiers; other ways this same disillusionment might be shown in novels, plays, paintings, or even historical analyses of the time.*

DULCE ET DECORUM EST

Bent double, like old beggars under sacks,
Knock-kneed, coughing like hags, we cursed through sludge,
Till on the haunting flares we turned our backs
And towards our distant rest began to trudge.
Men marched asleep. Many had lost their boots
But limped on, blood-shod. All went lame; all blind;
Drunk with fatigue; deaf even to the hoots
Of tired, outstripped Five-Nines that dropped behind.

Gas! Gas! Quick, boys! — An Ecstasy of fumbling,
Fitting the clumsy helmets just in time;
But someone still was yelling out and stumbling
And flound'ring like a man in fire or lime . . .
Dim, through the misty panes and thick green light,
As under a green sea, I saw him drowning.

In all my dreams, before my helpless sight,
He plunges at me, guttering, choking, drowning.

If in some smothering dreams you too could pace
Behind the wagon that we flung him in,

SOURCE: C. Day Lewis, *Collected Poems of Wilfred Owen.* Reprinted by permission of New Directions and Chatto & Windus, p. 55. Copyright © Chatto & Windus, Ltd., 1946, 1963, and The Owen Estate.

And watch the white eyes writhing in his face,
His hanging face, like a devil's sick of sin;
If you could hear, at every jolt, the blood
Come gargling from the froth-corrupted lungs,
Obscene as cancer, bitter as the cud
Of vile, incurable sores on innocent tongues, —
My friend, you would not tell with such high zest
To children ardent for some desperate glory,
The old Lie: Dulce et decorum est
Pro patria mori.

Minutes of the Tsar's Council of Ministers, 1915: Breakdown in Russia

When the war did not come to an end after the first few months of fighting, the strains of supporting a long-term military struggle began to appear in those countries that were least modernized politically and economically. This was clearest in the case of Russia, which had been struggling to modernize under the leadership of an inefficient autocratic government. As early as 1915 the government found itself increasingly unable to establish control over a country experiencing tremendous needs. Some of this sense of things out of control and the problems caused by the strains of war are revealed in the minutes of a meeting of the Council of Ministers on August 24, 1915.

> **Consider:** *Why the Russian government was experiencing such difficulty in establishing control; how the war fueled already existing problems within Russia.*

AUGUST 24, 1915

Scherbatov: The Council of Ministers knows that there were disturbances in Moscow which ended in bloodshed. . . . There were even more serious disorders at Ivanovo-Voznesensk when it was necessary to fire on the crowd with the result that sixteen were killed and thirty wounded. There was a critical moment when it was uncertain what the garrison would do. . . .

Shakhovskoi: I have information . . . that the workmen are quite aroused. Any kind of spark may start a fire. . . .

Goremykin: . . . I should like to ask the Minister of the Interior what measures he is taking to put an end to the lawlessness . . . going on every-

---

SOURCE: *Documents of Russian History, 1914–1917*, Frank A. Golder, ed., Emanuel Aronsberg, trans. Reprinted by permission of Prentice–Hall, Inc., pp. 184–185. Copyright © 1927 by Prentice–Hall, Inc.

where. His principal function is to protect the State from disorder and danger.

Scherbatov: The Minister of the Interior is taking all the measures which his duty and present circumstances permit. I have more than once called your attention to the abnormal position of the Minister. Half of European Russia is out of his jurisdiction. Elsewhere in the rear the real government is in the hands of lieutenants who have despotic inclinations and little understanding. I have brought to your notice the fact that even in Petrograd, which gives tone to the whole of Russia, the Minister of the Interior is a mere resident. He has only as much power as the war lords will grant him. . . . How can you expect me to fight the growing revolutionary movement when I am refused the support of the troops on the ground that they are unreliable, that one can not be certain that they will fire on the mob? You can not quiet the whole of Russia by the police alone, especially now when the ranks of the police are being thinned out . . . hourly and the population is growing daily more excited by the speeches in the Duma, by newspaper stories, by continuous defeats, and rumors of disorders in the rear. The demonstrations and disorders come about from most unforeseen causes. At Moscow patriotic reasons were responsible. Newspapers gave out that the Dardanelles had been taken and that our troops had recaptured Kovno. One silver-tongued orator was arrested and trouble started. . . . I agree that something ought to be done. But how can you do anything when you have no support, when those in responsible places [ministers] can not get a hearing [Emperor] on questions on which the fate of the State may depend? . . . I have in my portfolio several telegrams from governors. They inform me that the flow of refugees, German-colonists and Jews driven out by the military authorities is ever rising and that the local population is so aroused against the newcomers that they receive them with clubs. . . . The governors ask for instructions and help. What can the Minister of the Interior reply. . . . Among the workmen, as among the population in general, there are terrible reports of graft in connection with war orders. . . .

Program of the Provisional Government in Russia

In the spring of 1917 a revolution finally toppled the disintegrating tsarist government in Russia. A relatively moderate, liberal Provisional Government was formed under the leadership of men such as Prince Lvov and Paul Miliukov. While the provisional government had to share and even compete for power with the more radical workers' political organizations – the soviets – it initially acted with speed

Source: F. A. Golder, ed., E. Aronsberg, tr., *Documents of Russian History, 1914–1917* (New York: Appleton-Century-Crofts, Inc., 1927).

to make important changes. The following is the early program of the Provisional Government, issued on March 16, 1917.

> **Consider:** *The attitudes revealed by this document; the nature of the reforms initiated; what this implies about the problems under the tsarist government and the discontents that supported the revolution.*

Citizens, the Provisional Executive Committee of the members of the Duma, with the aid and support of the garrison of the capital and its inhabitants, has triumphed over the dark forces of the Old Régime to such an extent as to enable it to organize a more stable executive power. . . .

The Cabinet will be guided in its actions by the following principles:

1. An immediate general amnesty for all political and religious offenses, including terrorist acts, military revolts, agrarian offenses, etc.
2. Freedom of speech and press; freedom to form labor unions and to strike. These political liberties should be extended to the army in so far as war conditions permit.
3. The abolition of all social, religious and national restrictions.
4. Immediate preparation for the calling of a Constituent Assembly, elected by universal and secret vote, which shall determine the form of government and draw up the Constitution for the country.
5. In place of the police, to organize a national militia with elective officers, and subject to the local self-governing body.
6. Elections to be carried out on the basis of universal, direct, equal, and secret suffrage.
7. The troops that have taken part in the revolutionary movement shall not be disarmed or removed from Petrograd.
8. On duty and in war service, strict military discipline should be maintained, but when off duty, soldiers should have the same public rights as are enjoyed by other citizens.

The Provisional Government wishes to add that it has no intention of taking advantage of the existence of war conditions to delay the realization of the above-mentioned measures of reform.

April Theses: The Bolshevik Opposition

V. I. Lenin

Faced with a continuing war and deep discontent, the Provisional Government soon came under attack by those such as Vladimir Ilyich Lenin (1870–1924),

SOURCE: From V. I. Lenin, *Collected Works*, Vol. XXIV (Moscow: Progress Publishers, 1964), pp. 21–24. Reprinted by permission of the Copyright Agency of the USSR.

who called for more radical changes. Lenin, who spent much of his life as a revolutionary—often in exile—had risen to the leadership of the Bolshevik faction of the Russian Marxists. He combined the skills of a superb Marxist theoretician and a revolutionary organizer. In April 1917 the Germans aided his return to Russia in an effort to weaken the new government there. On his arrival, Lenin presented his April Theses, at first criticized by Russian Marxists but eventually accepted by the Bolshevik Central Committee.

> **Consider:** *Why Lenin rejects support for the Provisional Government; to whom this program might be appealing and why; the ways in which this program is particularly Marxist.*

1. In our attitude towards the war, which under the new government of Lvov and Co. unquestionably remains on Russia's part a predatory imperialist war owing to the capitalist nature of that government, not the slightest concession to a "revolutionary defencism" is permissible. . . .

2. The specific feature of the present situation in Russia is that the country is *passing* from the first stage of the revolution—which, owing to the insufficient class-consciousness and organisation of the proletariat, placed power in the hands of the bourgeoisie—to its *second* stage, which must place power in the hands of the proletariat and the poorest sections of the peasants. . . .

3. No support for the Provisional Government; . . .

5. Not a parliamentary republic—to return to a parliamentary republic from the Soviets of Workers' Deputies would be a retrograde step—but a republic of Soviets of Workers', Agricultural Labourers' and Peasants' Deputies throughout the country, from top to bottom.
   Abolition of the police, the army and the bureaucracy.
   The salaries of all officials, all of whom are elective and displaceable at any time, not to exceed the average wage of a competent worker.

6. The weight of emphasis in the agrarian programme to be shifted to the Soviets of Agricultural Labourers' Deputies.
   Confiscation of all landed estates.
   Nationalisation of *all* lands in the country, the land to be disposed of by the local Soviets of Agricultural Labourers' and Peasants' Deputies. The organisation of separate Soviets of Deputies of Poor Peasants. The setting up of a model farm on each of the large estates (ranging in size from 100 to 300 dessiatines, according to local and other conditions, and to the decisions of the local bodies) under the control of the Soviets of Agricultural Labourers' Deputies and for the public account.

7. The immediate amalgamation of all banks in the country into a single national bank, and the institution of control over it by the Soviet of Workers' Deputies.

8. It is not our *immediate* task to "introduce" socialism, but only to bring social production and the distribution of products at once under the *control* of the Soviets of Workers' Deputies.

Speech to the Petrograd Soviet — November 8, 1917: The Bolsheviks in Power

V. I. Lenin

The Provisional government fell in a revolution in November 1917. Under the leadership of Lenin and Leon Trotsky (1877–1940), the tightly organized Bolsheviks quickly took control. On November 8, 1917, Lenin made the following speech to a meeting of the Petrograd Soviet.

> **Consider:** *The policies Lenin supported and how they compare with the program in his* April Theses; *the ways in which Lenin was relying on forces outside of Russia to sustain the initial success of this revolution.*

Comrades, the workmen's and peasants' revolution, the need of which the Bolsheviks have emphasized many times, has come to pass.

What is the significance of this revolution? Its significance is, in the first place, that we shall have a soviet government, without the participation of bourgeoisie of any kind. The oppressed masses will of themselves form a government. The old state machinery will be smashed into bits and in its place will be created a new machinery of government by the soviet organizations. From now on there is a new page in the history of Russia, and the present, third Russian revolution shall in its final result lead to the victory of Socialism.

One of our immediate tasks is to put an end to the war at once. But in order to end the war, which is closely bound up with the present capitalistic system, it is necessary to overthrow capitalism itself. In this work we shall have the aid of the world labor movement, which has already begun to develop in Italy, England, and Germany.

A just and immediate offer of peace by us to the international democracy will find everywhere a warm response among the international proletariat masses. In order to secure the confidence of the proletariat, it is necessary to publish at once all secret treaties.

SOURCE: *Documents of Russian History, 1914–1917*, Frank A. Golder, ed., Emanuel Aronsberg, trans. Reprinted by permission of Prentice–Hall, Inc., pp. 618–619. Copyright © 1927 by Prentice–Hall, Inc.

In the interior of Russia a very large part of the peasantry has said: Enough playing with the capitalists; we will go with the workers. We shall secure the confidence of the peasants by one decree, which will wipe out the private property of the landowners. The peasants will understand that their only salvation is in union with the workers.

We will establish a real labor control on production.

We have now learned to work together in a friendly manner, as is evident from this revolution. We have the force of mass organization which has conquered all and which will lead the proletariat to world revolution.

We should now occupy ourselves in Russia in building up a proletarian socialist state.

Long live the world-wide socialistic revolution.

The Fourteen Points

Woodrow Wilson

Each nation entered World War I for its own mixture of pragmatic and idealistic reasons. In considering their war aims and a possible peace settlement, governments did not anticipate the changes that would occur in this unexpectedly long and costly war. By 1918 various governments had fallen and the United States had entered the conflict. On January 8, 1918, in an address to a joint session of the U. S. Congress, President Woodrow Wilson (1856–1924) presented his Fourteen Points, a delineation of American war aims and proposals for a peace settlement. The Fourteen Points served as a basis for debate at the Paris Peace Conference in 1919 and represented the most idealistic statement of what might be gained in a final peace settlement.

> **Consider:** *The ideals that hold these points together; the grievances recognized and unrecognized in these points; the assumptions about what measures would preserve peace in the postwar world.*

We entered this war because violations of right had occurred which touched us to the quick and made the life of our own people impossible unless they were corrected and the world secured once for all against their recurrence. What we demand in this war, therefore, is nothing peculiar to ourselves. It is that the world be made fit and safe to live in; and particularly that it be made safe for every peace-loving nation which, like our own, wishes to live its own life, determine its own institutions, be assured of justice and fair dealing by the other peoples of the world as against force and selfish aggression. All the peoples of the world are in effect partners in this interest, and for our own part we see very clearly that unless justice be done to others it

SOURCE: Woodrow Wilson, "Fourteen Points," *Congressional Record*, Vol. LVI, Part I (1918) Washington, D. C.: U. S. Government Printing Office, pp. 680–681.

will not be done to us. The program of the world's peace, therefore, is our program; and that program, the only possible program, as we see it, is this:

I. Open covenants of peace, openly arrived at, after which there shall be no private international understandings of any kind but diplomacy shall proceed always frankly and in the public view.

II. Absolute freedom of navigation upon the seas, outside territorial waters, alike in peace and in war, except as the seas may be closed in whole or in part by international action. . . .

III. The removal, so far as possible, of all economic barriers and the establishment of an equality of trade conditions among all the nations consenting to the peace and associating themselves for its maintenance.

IV. Adequate guarantees given and taken that national armaments will be reduced to the lowest point consistent with domestic safety.

V. A free, open-minded, and absolutely impartial adjustment of all colonial claims, based upon a strict observance of the principle that in determining all such questions of sovereignty the interests of the populations concerned must have equal weight with the equitable claims of the government whose title is to be determined.

VI. The evacuation of all Russian territory and such a settlement of all questions affecting Russia as will secure the best and freest cooperation of the other nations of the world in obtaining for her an unhampered and unembarrassed opportunity for the independent determination of her own political development and national policy and assure her of a sincere welcome into the society of free nations under institutions of her own choosing; and, more than a welcome, assistance also of every kind that she may need and may herself desire. The treatment accorded Russia by her sister nations in the months to come will be the acid test of their good will, of their comprehension of her needs as distinguished from their own interests, and of their intelligent and unselfish sympathy.

VII. Belgium, the whole world will agree, must be evacuated and restored, without any attempt to limit the sovereignty which she enjoys in common with all other free nations. No other single act will serve as this will serve to restore confidence among the nations in the laws which they have themselves set and determined for the government of their relations with one another. Without this healing act the whole structure and validity of international law is forever impaired.

VIII. All French territory should be freed and the invaded portions restored, and the wrong done to France by Prussia in 1871 in the matter of Alsace-Lorraine, which has unsettled the peace of the world for nearly fifty years, should be righted, in order that peace may once more be made secure in the interest of all.

IX. A readjustment of the frontiers of Italy should be effected along clearly recognizable lines of nationality.

X. The peoples of Austria-Hungary, whose place among the nations we wish to see safeguarded and assured, should be accorded the freest opportunity of autonomous development.

XI. Rumania, Serbia, and Montenegro should be evacuated; occupied territories restored; Serbia accorded free and secure access to the sea; and the relations of the several Balkan states to one another determined by friendly counsel along historically established lines of allegiance and nationality; and international guarantes of the political and economic independence and territorial integrity of the several Balkan states should be entered into.

XII. The Turkish portions of the present Ottoman Empire should be assured a secure sovereignty, but the other nationalities which are now under Turkish rule should be assured an undoubted security of life and an absolutely unmolested opportunity of autonomous development, and the Dardanelles should be permanently opened as a free passage to the ships and commerce of all nations under international guarantes.

XIII. An independent Polish state should be erected which should include the territories inhabited by indisputably Polish populations, which should be assured a free and secure access to the sea, and whose political and economic independence and territorial integrity should be guaranteed by international covenant.

XIV. A general association of nations must be formed under specific covenants for the purpose of affording mutual guarantes of political independence and territorial integrity to great and small states alike.

In regard to these essential rectifications of wrong and assertions of right we feel ourselves to be intimate partners of all the governments and peoples associated together against the Imperialists. We cannot be separated in interest or divided in purpose. We stand together until the end.

For such arrangements and covenants we are willing to fight and to continue to fight until they are achieved; but only because we wish the right to prevail and desire a just and stable peace such as can be secured only by removing the chief provocations to war, which this program does remove. We have no jealousy of German greatness, and there is nothing in this program that impairs it. We grudge her no achievement or distinction of learning or of pacific enterprise such as have made her record very bright and very enviable. We do not wish to injure her or to block in any way her legitimate influence or power. We do not wish to fight her either with arms or with hostile arrangements of trade if she is willing to associate herself with us and the other peace-loving nations of the world in covenants of justice and law and fair dealing. We wish her only to accept a place of equality among the peoples of the world, — the new world in which we now live, — instead of a place of mastery.

Neither do we presume to suggest to her any alteration or modification of her institutions. But it is necessary, we must frankly say, and necessary as a preliminary to any intelligent dealings with her on our part, that we should know whom her spokesmen speak for when they speak to us, whether for the Reichstag majority or for the military party and the men whose creed is imperial domination.

We have spoken now, surely, in terms too concrete to admit of any further doubt or question. An evident principle runs through the whole program I have outlined. It is the principle of justice to all peoples and nationalities, and their right to live on equal terms of liberty and safety with one another, whether they be strong or weak. Unless this principle be made its foundation no part of the structure of international justice can stand. The people of the United States could act upon no other principle; and to the vindication of this principle they are ready to devote their lives, their honor, and everything that they possess. The moral climax of this the culminating and final war for human liberty has come, and they are ready to put their own strength, their own highest purpose, their own integrity and devotion to the test.

VISUAL SOURCES

World War I:
The Front Lines

This photo displays the physical and psychological realities of life on the Western front during World War I. The war is being fought from trenches with soldiers at machine guns guarding land made barren by artillery barrages, throwing hand grenades at the often unseen enemy, and using poison gas (note the gas mask). It is difficult to find in such a scene a sense of a progressive civilization, of the dignity of the individual, or of reasoned interaction among nations — the ideals held by nineteenth-century Western civilization. Considering the use of such weapons, we can easily imagine the carnage and the sense of futility that resulted from the "heroic" offensive charges of the foot soldiers that were so common for most of the war.

Consider: *How this supports the description of life on the front lines during the Verdun battle.*

Photo 11-1

World War I:
The Home Front

This picture of a British war plant gives an idea of how industrialization and technology have helped turn any extended war into a massive strain. Large factories had to be built or converted to the production of war munitions, here heavy artillery shells. A new labor force had to be trained, often involving a change of values: Here women and older men predominate to make up for the drain on manpower caused by the armed services. Finally, this picture suggests the enormous logistical organization and government cooperation with capitalist enterprises necessary to keep a modern war effort going.

> **Consider:** *The ways in which a modern war effort affects a nation's people and economy even though the war is being fought on foreign soil.*

Photo 11-2

Courtesy, The Trustees of the Imperial War Museum

Revolutionary Propaganda

This Russian poster of 1919 illustrates some of the message and appeal of the Communists. It shows capitalist, Church, and monarch in league in a ruthlessly commanding position over exploited workers and peasants: Death trails in their wake.

Consider: *How this poster reflects the ideas contained in the documents by Lenin.*

Photo 11-3

SECONDARY SOURCES

The Struggle for Mastery in Europe

A. J. P. Taylor

Almost before World War I was over, scholars were debating its causes. With the depth of emotional involvement characterizing this war, objective evaluation was difficult. Scholars often had difficulty distinguishing analysis of causes from place-ment of blame. After World War II most historians stressed the "Balance of Power" system of international relations as an important cause of World War I. At the same time, most of these historians reemphasized Germany's responsibility for the war. In the following selection, historian A. J. P. Taylor of Oxford agrees that Germany was most responsible but rejects the typical emphasis on the Balance of Power for causing the war.

> **Consider:** *Taylor's reasons for blaming Germany and Austria-Hungary for the war and the arguments that might be used to refute this interpretation; how the Balance of Power system might have contributed to the outbreak of World War I and why Taylor rejects this as an important factor.*

On 4 August the long Bismarckian peace ended. It had lasted more than a generation. Men had come to regard peace as normal; when it ended, they looked for some profound cause. Yet the immediate cause was a good deal simpler than on other occasions. Where, for instance, lay the precise respon-sibility for the Crimean war, and when did that war become inevitable? In 1914 there could be no doubt. Austria-Hungary had failed to solve her na-tional problems. She blamed Serbia for the South Slav discontent; it would be far truer to say that this discontent involved Serbia, against her will, in Habsburg affairs. In July 1914 the Habsburg statesmen took the easy course of violence against Serbia, ... Berchtold launched war in 1914, ...

Berchtold counted rightly on support from Germany; he would not have persisted in a resolute line if it had not been for the repeated encouragements which came from Berlin. The Germans did not fix on war for August 1914, but they welcomed it when the occasion offered. They could win it now; they were more doubtful later. Hence, they surrendered easily to the dictates of a military time-table. Austria-Hungary was growing weaker; Germany believed herself at the height of her strength. They decided on war from opposite motives; and the two decisions together caused a general European war.

SOURCE: A. J. P. Taylor, *The Struggle for Mastery in Europe: 1848–1918* (Oxford, England: Clarendon Press, 1954), pp. 526–529. Reprinted by permission of Oxford University Press.

The Powers of the Triple Entente all entered the war to defend themselves. The Russians fought to preserve the free passage of the Straits, on
which their economic life depended; France for the sake of the Triple
Entente, which she believed, rightly, alone guaranteed her survival as a
Great Power. The British fought for the independence of sovereign states
and, more remotely, to prevent a German domination of the Continent. It is
sometimes said that the war was caused by the system of alliances or, more
vaguely, by the Balance of Power. This is a generalization without reality.
None of the Powers acted according to the letter of their commitments,
though no doubt they might have done so if they had not anticipated them.
Germany was pledged to go to war if Russia attacked Austria-Hungary. Instead, she declared war before Russia took any action; and Austria-Hungary
only broke with Russia, grudgingly enough, a week afterwards. France was
pledged to attack Germany, if the latter attacked Russia. Instead she was
faced with a German demand for unconditional neutrality and would have
had to accept war even had there been no Franco-Russian alliance, unless
she was prepared to abdicate as a Great Power. Great Britain had a moral
obligation to stand by France and a rather stronger one to defend her Channel coast. But she went to war for the sake of Belgium and would have done
so, even if there had been no Anglo-French entente and no exchange of letters between Grey and Cambon in November 1912. Only then, the British
intervention would have been less effective than it was.

As to the Balance of Power, it would be truer to say that the war was
caused by its breakdown rather than by its existence. There had been a real
European Balance in the first decade of the Franco-Russian alliance; and
peace had followed from it. The Balance broke down when Russia was
awakened by the war with Japan; and Germany got in the habit of trying to
get her way by threats. This ended with the Agadir crisis. Russia began to
recover her strength, France her nerve. Both insisted on being treated as
equals, as they had been in Bismarck's time. The Germans resented this and
resolved to end it by war, if they could end it no other way. They feared that
the Balance was being re-created. Their fears were exaggerated . . . .

In fact, peace must have brought Germany the mastery of Europe within
a few years. This was prevented by the habit of her diplomacy and, still
more, by the mental outlook of her people. They had trained themselves
psychologically for aggression.

The German military plans played a vital part. The other Great Powers
thought in terms of defending themselves. No Frenchman thought seriously
of recovering Alsace and Lorraine; and the struggle of Slav and Teuton in
the Balkans was very great nonsense so far as most Russians were concerned.
The German generals wanted a decisive victory for its own sake.

The Origins of World War I: Militant Patriotism

Roland Stromberg

Many observers were struck by the almost universal enthusiasm with which people greeted the news that war had been declared in August 1914. This has led some scholars to reevaluate traditional interpretations of the causes for World War I and emphasize the underlying social forces that led people to welcome its outbreak. In the following selection, Roland Stromberg, a historian of modern Europe at the University of Wisconsin, examines various attempts to explain the outbreak of war and suggests that the willingness of European peoples to go to war may have been more important than "the system of sovereign states" or any other cause for World War I.

> **Consider:** *The explanations that Stromberg rejects and why he rejects them; the problems with blaming the war on "the system of sovereign states"; how militant patriotism played a role in the outbreak of the war; how this interpretation differs from A. J. P. Taylor's.*

No wonder the sudden outbreak of a major international war at the beginning of August caught everyone by surprise. The sobering lesson was that war could happen without anybody seeming to want it or to will it. All kinds of myths grew up later, as bewildered people attempted to explain the outbreak of war. As usual, conspiracy theories flourished. In particular it was alleged that the Germans plotted war; Wilhelm II, the unhappy German monarch, was depicted in the Allied countries as a monster with tentacles reaching out to ensnare small countries. That "Prussian militarism" was the canker in the olive branch became an article of faith in France and England and later, after she had joined the war, in the United States. For their part, the Germans believed that jealous neighbors plotted to encircle and destroy a country whose only crime was her economic success.

Then, too, the theory arose that the capitalistic economic system, far from being a force for peace, had engineered the war because war was profitable or because there was competition for markets and raw materials. Although they may contain germs of truth, all such simple-minded "devil theories" must be dismissed as inadequate to the serious study of events, more interesting as folklore than as history.

Though it is tempting to look for it, no single all-embracing cause can successfully explain the war or any other major historical event. We can, of course, say that the basic cause was something like the "system of sovereign states"; and this was in fact probably the most widespread diagnosis during

SOURCE: Roland N. Stromberg, *Europe in the Twentieth Century* (Englewood Cliffs: Prentice-Hall, Inc., 1980), pp. 43–44, 74.

the war. This diagnosis led to the many schemes that proliferated from 1914 on for a League of Nations or an association of nations or even a world state. However, people must be politically organized in one way or another; one might almost as well say that the "people system" caused the war. One could cite human nature, or more specifically humanity's relentless pursuit of power, as the cause. Such explanations are too general to take us far; human nature is the necessary condition for *any* human activity, but it does not explain why this particular war happened at this particular time. Were the sovereign states more sovereign, human nature more aggressive, power more sought after in 1914 than in 1890 or 1880? Evidently not.

We may get an idea of the differences of opinion among those who sought to account for the war by noting how contradictory the explanations were. Some blamed it on lack of democratic control over foreign policy, which was said to be the monopoly of a secret elite; but others said that an erratic and frequently bellicose public opinion had taken over the reins of power from the professionals. Some blamed it on military men, who were madly eager to try out their weapons; but others argue that the military was far from eager to go to war. . . .

The states of Europe were like individuals living in a primeval state of nature marked by incessant strife between one and another. They acknowledged no higher authority that might have forced them to keep the peace. What was called "international law" was not in fact binding on them, being backed by no more than a moral or customary sanction. . . .

Of course, they exchanged diplomatic representatives and negotiated treaties and other agreements with each other. The traditions surrounding this activity, reaching back to ancient times and particularly to the fifteenth century, were numerous and complex. But underneath the velvet glove of diplomacy one could see clearly enough the iron fist of national self-interest backed by armed force. Within this tradition, war, the ultimate court of appeal, had its recognized place. It was itself the formalization of violence. . . .

More and more people had acquired a larger stake in defending the state. This was the natural result of democratization and increase in wealth. However imperfectly or inequitably these had come about, the large majority of citizens had some interest in defending the political community of which they were a part. All over Europe, 1914 was to prove that the masses as well as the classes were militantly patriotic when they thought their country was being attacked. . . .

Virtually no one had expected war; it came with dramatic suddenness. When it did come, the typical reaction was not that of Edward Grey. Standing at his office window on the night of August 4 and watching the lamps flicker off as the British ultimatum to Germany to withdraw from Belgium expired, Grey said, "The lights are going out all over Europe, and no one now living will ever see them come back again." The historian must regretfully record that a sense of joy rather than of gloom prevailed. Huge cheering crowds surrounded the kaiser, stood outside Buckingham Palace, saluted departing French troops at the railroad stations, made love publicly in St. Petersburg. A Parisian observer on August 2 described a "human torrent, swelling at ever corner" screaming, shouting singing the "Marseillaise." In Berlin, crowds passed through the streets incessantly for two days singing "Deutschland über alles" and "Wacht am Rhein." A mob attacked the German embassy in St. Petersburg. An "indescribable crowd" blocked the streets around government offices in London a few minutes after midnight August 4–5, and continued to fill the streets for days. It was with exultation, not sorrow, that the peoples of Europe greeted the war, a fact that in the last analysis may go farther to explain its coming than all the details of diplomacy. . . .

The Revolution in War and Diplomacy

Gordon A. Craig

The technology and tactics used in World War I were strikingly different from those used in previous wars. This, combined with the war's length and the waning distinction between civilian and military targets, made it difficult for people to perceive the enemy in terms other than extreme hatred. This was reflected in the demands for retribution made both during and at the end of the war, inevitably affecting the peace settlements that followed. In the following selection Gordon Craig of Princeton and Stanford, a noted military and diplomatic historian who has done extensive work on German history, analyzes these attitudes and their causes while comparing World War I with previous wars.

> **Consider:** *How the primary documents on the experience of World War I relate to this interpretation; why it was difficult for governments of belligerent nations to compromise; whether this description of what happened in World War I is likely to be true for almost any extended twentieth-century war.*

The war of 1914 was the first total war in history, in the sense that very few people living in the belligerent countries were permitted to remain unaffected by it during its course. This had not been true in the past. Even during the great wars against Napoleon many people could go on living as if the world were at peace. . . .

This kind of detachment, which was true also of the wars in Central Europe in the 1860s, was wholly impossible during World War I. This was, for one thing, the first war in which the distinction between soldier and civilian broke down, a development that was partly due to the expansion of warfare made possible by . . . technological innovations. . . . When dirigibles began to drop bombs over London and submarines began to sink merchant ships, war had invaded the civilian sphere and the battle line was everywhere. . . .

Moreover . . . precisely because war became so total and was so prolonged, it also became ideological, taking on a religious cast that had not characterized warfare in the West since the Thirty Years' War. . . .

The civilian . . . could not look the enemy in the face and recognize him as another man; he knew only that it was "the enemy," an impersonal, generalized concept, that was depriving him of the pleasures of peace. As his own discomfort grew, his irritation hardened into a hatred that was often encouraged by government propagandists who believed that this was the best way of maintaining civilian morale. Before long, therefore, the enemy was considered to be capable of any enormity and, since this was true, any idea of compromise with him became intolerable. The foe must be beaten to his knees, no matter what this might cost in effort and blood; he must be made to surrender unconditionally; he must be punished with peace terms that would keep him in permanent subjection.

The result of this was . . . that rational calculation of risk versus gain, of compromise through negotiation . . . became virtually impossible for the belligerent governments.

Wilson the Diplomatist

Arthur S. Link

Historians have traditionally condemned the settlement of World War I worked out at Versailles. They usually argue that it compared poorly with the previous Vienna settlement ending the Napoleonic Wars and that Wilson's efforts were naive and mostly unsuccessful. Yet some historians have challenged this view. In the following selection, American historian Arthur S. Link, who has written extensively on Woodrow Wilson, argues that Wilson was, for the most part, quite successful.

   Consider: *The significance of Wilson's "failures"; whether Wilson deserves credit for these "successes"; how Link's interpretation compares to that of Craig.*

. . . The Versailles Treaty, measured by the standards that Wilson had enunciated from 1916 to 1919, obviously failed to fulfill entirely the liberal

SOURCE: Arthur S. Link, *Wilson the Diplomatist* (Baltimore, Md.: Johns Hopkins Press, 1957), pp. 121–122, 124–125. Reprinted by permission of Arthur S. Link. Copyright © 1957 by Arthur S. Link.

peace program. It was not, as Wilson had demanded in his Peace without Victory speech and implicitly promised in the Fourteen Points, a peace among equals. It was, rather, as the Germans contended then and later, a *diktat* imposed by victors upon a beaten foe. It shouldered Germany with a reparations liability that was both economically difficult to satisfy and politically a source of future international conflict. It satisfied the victors' demands for a division of the enemy's colonies and territories. In several important instances it violated the principle of self-determination. Finally, it was filled with pin pricks, like the provision for the trial of the former German Emperor, that served no purpose except to humiliate the German people. It does not, therefore, require much argument to prove that Wilson failed to win the settlement that he had demanded and that the Allies had promised in the Pre-Armistice Agreement. . . .

In spite of it all Wilson did succeed in winning a settlement that honored more of the Fourteen Points — not to mention the additional thirteen points — than it violated and in large measure vindicated his liberal ideals. There was the restoration of Belgium, the return of Alsace-Lorraine to France, and the creation of an independent Poland with access to the sea. There was the satisfaction of the claims of the Central European and Balkan peoples to self-determination. There was the at least momentary destruction of German military power. Most important, there was the fact that the Paris settlement provided machinery for its own revision through the League of Nations and the hope that the passing of time and American leadership in the League would help to heal the world's wounds and build a future free from fear.

As it turned out, many of Wilson's expectations were fulfilled even though the American people refused to play the part assigned to them. For example, the reparations problem was finally solved in the 1920's in a way not dissimilar from the method that Wilson had proposed. Germany was admitted to the League in 1926, and that organization ceased to be a mere league of victors. Effective naval disarmament was accomplished in 1921 and 1930. Even the great and hitherto elusive goal of land disarmament and the recognition of Germany's right to military equality was being seriously sought by international action in the early 1930's. In brief, the Paris settlement, in spite of its imperfections, did create a new international order that functioned well, relatively speaking. And it failed, not because it was imperfect, but because it was not defended when challenges arose in the 1930's.

The February Revolution in Russia

Michael T. Florinsky

Historians often respond to the challenge of explaining the occurrence of a major revolution by constructing a complex set or theory of causes. For Marxist historians, the February Revolution in Russia, which brought down the tsar in 1917, was of extraordinary importance. These historians and others point to long-term economic and social factors as crucial in causing this revolution. Many historians, however, argue that the causes were more immediate and less complex. Michael T. Florinsky, a highly respected author of several works on Russian history, represents the latter group of historians, focusing on World War I as the key cause for the revolution. In the following excerpt, Florinsky refers to the Rasputin episode, in which the reactionary tsarina — who held considerable power — came under the influence of the corrupt mystic, Grigori Rasputin.

> **Consider:** *The explanations for the revolution that Florinsky rejects; Florinsky's explanation and whether he provides support for his explanation; how a Marxist historian might react to this explanation.*

The Reason Why. The Rasputin episode — for in the context of Russian history it was no more than an episode — did much harm to the prestige of the monarchy with the educated classes, as did the hostility of the government towards any manifestation of liberalism, however modest, including the program of the Progressive Bloc. Nevertheless these developments cannot be regarded as the true or a major cause of the revolution. The empress was unpopular with the masses, not because of Rasputin or of her meddling in the affairs of state, but because she was of German birth (she was, indeed, frequently referred to as "the German") and was suspected of pro-German sympathies, which is contrary to all available evidence. Nor is it reasonable to ascribe the revolution to the skillful propaganda of subversive groups, to say nothing of a carefully-thought-out master plan devised by Lenin or someone else. During the war the organized revolutionary movement was at low ebb. The strikes of July 1914, staged on the occasion of the visit of the French president to St. Petersburg, were followed by massive police retaliation that all but wiped out the revolutionary organizations. Their leaders, who were soon to acquire world-wide fame, were scattered, and many of them behind bars. Lenin was in Switzerland, Trotsky in New York, Stalin in Siberia. The revolution took many of them by surprise. Revolutionary policies had numerous adherents in wartime organizations and in the armed

SOURCE: Michael T. Florinsky, *Russia: A Short History*, 2nd ed. (New York: Macmillan Publishing Company, 1969), pp. 409–410.

forces, but if their preachments proved successful it was because they fell on fertile ground. The true and basic causes of the revolution were military defeats, staggering losses, demoralization of the army, plight of the refugees, economic hardships, lack of understanding of the objects of the war, and general longing for peace at any price.

An unsuccessful war is never popular, and the war of 1914–1917 on the Russian front was unsuccessful. Russian casualties were officially estimated at over 7 million, half of them missing and prisoners-of-war. According to confidential official reports, refusals to fight and mass surrender to the enemy began in 1914 and became widespread during the retreat in 1915. The Russian steamroller, in which the Western allies put their hope in the dark hours of the war, did not come up to expectation. Food shortages, the patent inability of the government to cope with mounting emergencies, frustration, and near chaos bred weariness, disaffection, and disillusionment. It is the sum total of these conditions that spelled the end of the monarchy and made the revolution inevitable.

Red October: The Bolshevik Revolution of 1917

Robert V. Daniels

How one interprets the Russian Revolution has much to do with how one views Marxism in general and the Russian application of Marxism during the twentieth century in particular. As with the French Revolution, a body of highly ideological historiography has grown up that is difficult to separate from the times in which it was written. In the following selection Robert Daniels, professor of Russian history at the University of Vermont, describes different schools of interpretation and emphasizes the difficulty of the task facing the Bolsheviks.

> **Consider:** *The relative strengths and weaknesses of both the official Communist and anti-Communist interpretations; how historians from each side might utilize the primary documents in this chapter to support their own views.*

The official Communist history of the revolution has held rigidly to an orthodox Marxist interpretation of the event: it was an uprising of thousands upon thousands of workers and peasants, the inevitable consequence of the international class struggle of proletariat against bourgeoisie, brought to a head first in Russia because it was "the weakest link in the chain of capitalism." At the same time it is asserted, though the contradiction is pa-

SOURCE: Robert V. Daniels, *Red October: The Bolshevik Revolution of 1917* (New York: Charles Scribner's Sons, 1967), p. 215.

tent, that the revolution could not have succeeded without the ever-present genius leadership of Lenin. This attempt to have it both ways has been ingrained in Communist thinking ever since Lenin himself campaigned in the name of Marx for the "art of insurrection."

Anti-Communist interpretations, however they may deplore the October Revolution, are almost as heavily inclined to view it as the inescapable outcome of overwhelming circumstances or of long and diabolical planning. The impasse of the war was to blame, or Russia's inexperience in democracy, or the feverish laws of revolution. If not these factors, it was Lenin's genius and trickery in propaganda, or the party organization as his trusty and invincible instrument. Of course, all of these considerations played a part, but when they are weighed against the day by day record of the revolution, it is hard to argue that any combination of them made Bolshevik power inevitable or even likely.

The stark truth about the Bolshevik Revolution is that it succeeded against incredible odds in defiance of any rational calculation that could have been made in the fall of 1917. The shrewdest politicians of every political coloration knew that while the Bolsheviks were an undeniable force in Petrograd and Moscow, they had against them the overwhelming majority of the peasants, the army in the field, and the trained personnel without which no government could function. Everyone from the right-wing military to the Zinoviev-Kamenev Bolsheviks judged a military dictatorship to be the most likely alternative if peaceful evolution failed. They all thought — whether they hoped or feared — that a Bolshevik attempt to seize power would only hasten or assure the rightist alternative.

Chapter Questions

1. In what ways was World War I an outgrowth of the major trends of the late nineteenth century? Why is World War I nevertheless often considered a dividing line between the nineteenth and twentieth centuries?

2. What role did World War I play in explaining the Russian Revolution and the Bolsheviks' rise to power?

3. What was there about the causes and process of World War I that made the peace settlement at the end of the war so difficult?

CHAPTER TWELVE

Democracy, Depression, and Instability: The 1920s and 1930s

The two decades following World War I were marked by instability and uncertainty. Except in Russia, where the Bolsheviks had taken power, it appeared that liberal democracy had been established throughout Europe as a result of World War I. But soon a trend toward authoritarianism appeared, with many nations suffering from political fluctuations. The economic problems left from World War I and the immediate postwar period did not disappear despite a brief period of fragile prosperity in the mid-1920s. In 1929 the stock market crash in New York initiated the Great Depression in the United States, which quickly spread to Europe. Huge numbers of people suffered economically, and governments were pressured to effect radical solutions to the problems. Not surprisingly, there were great social strains through all of this. The difficulty of recovering from World War I was exacerbated by this political and economic instability. Swept by uncertainty about the present and the future, society seemed to polarize into opposing classes and around opposing ideologies.

A similar uncertainty characterized intellectual trends. The optimism and faith in rationality typical of the eighteenth and nineteenth centuries gave way to movements such as relativism in the physical and social sciences, Freudianism in psychology, and seeming anarchy in the arts. The West was no longer so confident, and events of the 1920s and 1930s added to that lack of confidence.

The selections in this chapter exemplify these trends. Historians usually focus on Germany during the 1920s in describing the general unrest and the efforts made to respond to it. What was the nature of the political and economic disorder in Germany during the 1920s? In what ways was there a sense that things were out of hand and that the population was comprised of many opposing factions? The Great Depression dealt the worst blow to the industrial economy. How did the Depression make the future of capitalism uncertain? What policies were pursued by governments to deal with the Depression? How was the Depression related to political disorder during the 1930s? What was the long-term significance of the Depression? Finally, a general sense of disillusionment and uncertainty characterized intellectual life. How did Freudian psychoanalysis reflect this? In what ways was there a feeling that nineteenth-century ideals were gone and that twentieth-century people might be worse off than their predecessors? Why have the post–World War I decades been viewed as an age of unreason?

A gloomy picture of life during the 1920s and 1930s emerges from these materials. The growth of totalitarianism during this period, to be examined in the next chapter, will add to this negative image.

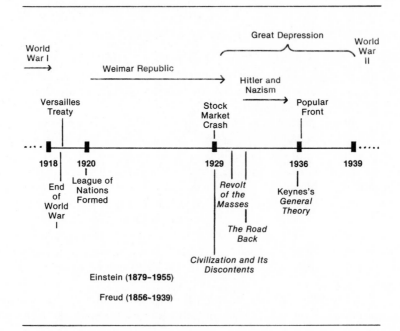

PRIMARY SOURCES

The Road Back
Erich Maria Remarque

and

Restless Days
Lilo Linke

With the establishment of the Weimar Republic at the end of World War I, Germany had a government system much like those of the other Western democracies. But the German government was burdened with tremendous economic problems, continued social turmoil, and inexperienced politicians laboring with the legacy of World War I. This society and its mood are particularly well reflected in the cultural productions of the period, for example, in the following selections from Erich Maria Remarque and Lilo Linke. Remarque, whose All Quiet on the Western Front *(1929) and* The Road Back *(1931), were two of the most popular books of the period, was a German soldier during World War I. The first selection is from* The Road Back, *which focuses on the life in Germany faced by the returning soldier. The second selection is from Linke's autobiography,* Restless Days.

> **Consider:** *Any connections between World War I and subsequent economic problems; the political problems facing the Weimar Republic; how such an environment might prove fertile for the rise of a political figure such as Hitler.*

Demonstrations in the streets have been called for this afternoon. Prices have been soaring everywhere for months past, and the poverty is greater even than it was during the war. Wages are insufficient to buy the bare necessities of life, and even though one may have the money it is often impossible to buy anything with it. But ever more and more gin palaces and dance halls go up, and ever more and more blatant is the profiteering and swindling.

Scattered groups of workers on strike march through the streets. Now and again there is a disturbance. A rumour is going about that troops have been concentrated at the barracks. But there is no sign of it as yet.

Here and there one hears cries and counter-cries. Somebody is haranguing at a street corner. Then suddenly everywhere is silence.

A procession of men in the faded uniforms of the front-line trenches is moving slowly toward us.

It is formed up by sections, marching in fours. Big white placards are carried before: *Where is the Fatherland's gratitude? — The War Cripples are starving.*

The men with one arm are carrying the placards, and they look around continually to see if the procession is still coming along properly behind them, for they are the fastest.

These are followed by men with sheep dogs on short, leather leads. The animals have the red cross of the blind at their collars. . . .

Behind the blind come the men with one eye, the tattered faces of men with head wounds: wry, bulbous mouths, faces without noses and without lower jaws, entire faces one great red scar with a couple of holes where formerly were a mouth and a nose. But above this desolation, quiet, questioning, sad human eyes.

On these follow the long lines of men with legs amputated. Some already have artificial limbs that spring forward obliquely as they walk and strike clanking on the pavement, as if the whole man were artificial, made up of iron and hinges. Others have their trouser legs looped up and made fast with safety pins. These go on crutches or sticks with black rubber pads.

Then come the shakers, the shell-shocked. Their hands, their heads, their clothes, their bodies quake as though they still shudder with horror. They no longer have control of themselves; the will has been extinguished, the muscles and nerves have revolted against the brain, the eyes become void and impotent.

It was no good to go on assuming that a common basis for all the different groups and classes in Germany could be found. The break between them became daily wider and more irreparable. The plebiscite of the Right "against the Young Plan and the war-guilt lie" proved just as unsuccessful as those arranged in former years by the Left, but the poison of the defamatory agitation remained in the body of the community, and we watched its effects with anxiety.

In my own family the political antagonism was growing past endurance. In October Fritz had finished his apprenticeship in an old-established export house, at the precise moment when the firm went bankrupt — a minor incident compared with such events as the breakdown of the Frankfurt General Insurance Company and the Civil Servants' Bank or the enforced reorganization and amalgamation of the Deutsche Bank and the Disconto-Gesellschaft, which all happened in the course of the year and dangerously damaged the whole economic life of Germany. Yet for my brother the bankruptcy of his firm overshadowed all other happenings, since it meant that he lost his job. His three years' training was in vain — there was not a single export firm which was not forced to dismiss as many of its employees as possible. . . .

"Yes, that's just it — millions! If it isn't my fault, whose fault is it? I tell you — your friends, the French, the English, the Americans, all those damnable nations who inflict on us one dishonorable penalty after the other — they are to blame for all this. Before the war the whole world bought German goods. My firm exported to Africa, to the German colonies. Hundreds of thousands we turned over every year. But they have robbed us of our colonies, of all our foreign markets. They have stolen the coal-mines in the Saar and in Upper Silesia, they squeeze millions of marks out of our bleeding country. We'll never rise again unless we free ourselves by another war."

"Don't be foolish, Fritz. Things are bad in the whole world."

"I don't care about the world, I care only about Germany, which you and your pacifists have delivered into the hands of our enemies. I despise you, you are not worthy to call yourself a German."

Program of the Popular Front — January 11, 1936

The Great Depression of the 1930s was a major blow to Western stability. In many areas it led to the fall of established governments and the rise of right-wing groups. In France in 1934, Socialists and Communists, in part fearing the rise of fascism, drew together into the Popular Front. In 1936, under the leadership of Léon Blum (1872–1950), the Popular Front came to power, but only for about two years. The following is an excerpt from the program of the Popular Front, January 11, 1936.

> **Consider:** *The ways in which this document reflects the turmoil of public life during the 1930s; how the Popular Front proposes to deal with the Depression; to what groups such a program would most appeal and why.*

I. *Defence of Freedom.*
 1. A general amnesty.
 2. Measures against the Fascist Leagues:
     (*a*) The effective disarmament and dissolution of all semi-military formations, in accordance with the law.
     (*b*) The enforcement of legal measures in cases of incitement to murder or any attempt against the safety of the State.

SOURCE: From David Thomson, *Democracy in France*. Reprinted by permission of Oxford University Press (Oxford, 5th edition, 1969), pp. 310–314.

3. Measures for the cleansing of public life, especially by forbidding Deputies to combine their parliamentary functions with certain other forms of activity.
4. The Press:
    (a) The repeal of the laws and decrees restricting freedom of opinion.
    (b) Reform of the Press by the following legislative measures:
        (i) Measures effectively repressing libel and blackmail.
        (ii) Measures which will guarantee the normal means of existence to newspapers, and compel publication of their financial resources.
        (iii) Measures ending the private monopoly of commercial advertising and the scandals of financial advertising, and preventing the formation of newspaper trusts.
    (c) Organization by the State of wireless broadcasts with a view to assuring the accuracy of wireless news and the equality of political and social organizations in relation to radio.
5. Trade Union Liberties:
    (a) Application and observance of trade union freedom for all.
    (b) Recognition of women's labour rights.

6. Education and freedom of conscience:
    (a) Measures safeguarding the development of public education, by the necessary grants and by reforms such as the raising of the age for compulsory education to fourteen and, in secondary education, the proper selection of pupils as an essential accompaniment of grants.
    (b) Measures guaranteeing to all concerned, pupils and teachers, perfect freedom of conscience, particularly by ensuring the neutrality of education, its non-religious character, and the civic rights of teachers.
7. Colonies: formation of a Parliamentary committee of inquiry into the political, economic and cultural situation in France's territories overseas, especially French North Africa and Indo-China.

II. *Defence of Peace.*
    1. Appeal to the people, and especially the working classes, for collaboration in the maintenance and organization of peace.
    2. International collaboration within the framework of the League of Nations for collective security, by defining the aggressor and by joint application of sanctions in cases of aggression.
    3. Ceaseless endeavour to pass from armed peace to disarmed peace, first by a convention of limitation, and then by the general, simultaneous and effectively controlled reduction of armaments.
    4. Nationalization of war industries and suppression of private trade in armaments.

5. Repudiation of secret diplomacy; international action and public negotiation to bring back to Geneva the states which have left it, without weakening the essential principles of the League of Nations, which are the principles of collective security and indivisible peace.
6. Greater flexibility in the procedure provided by the League of Nations' Covenant for the peaceful adjustment of treaties which have become dangerous to the peace of the world.
7. Extension of the system of pacts open to all nations, particularly in Eastern Europe, on the lines of the Franco-Soviet Pact.

III. *Economic Demands.*
  1. Restoration of purchasing power destroyed or reduced by the crisis.
    (*a*) Against unemployment and the crisis in industry.
        (i) Establishment of a national unemployment fund.
        (ii) Reduction of the working week without reduction of the weekly wage.
        (iii) Bringing young workers into employment by establishing a system of adequate pensions for aged workers.
        (iv) Rapid execution of a public works programme, both urban and rural, linking local investments with schemes financed by the State and local authorities.
    (*b*) Against the agricultural and commercial crisis.
        (i) Revaluation of agricultural produce, combined with measures against speculation and high prices, in order to reduce the gap between wholesale and retail prices.
        (ii) Establishment of a National Grain Board (*Office du Blé*) to abolish the tribute levied by speculators against both the producer and consumer.
        (iii) Strengthening of agricultural co-operatives, and supply of fertilizers at cost prices by the National Boards for Nitrogen and Potash, control and certification of sales of superphosphates and other fertilizers, extension of agricultural credits, reduction of leasehold rents. . . .
  2. Against the robbery of investors and for the better organization of credit:
    (*a*) Regulation of banking business. Regulation of balance sheets issued by banks and joint-stock companies. Further regulation of the powers of directors of joint-stock companies.
    (*b*) State officials who have retired or are on the reserve-list to be prohibited from joining the board of directors of a joint-stock company.
    (*c*) In order to remove credit and investment from the control of the economic oligarchy, the Bank of France must cease to be a private concern, and 'The Bank of France' must become 'France's Bank.'. . .

IV. *Financial Purification.*
　　1. Control of the trade in armaments, in conjunction with the nationalization of armaments industries. Prevention of waste in the civil and military departments.
　　2. Establishment of a War Pensions Fund.
　　3. Democratic reform of the system of taxation so as to relax the fiscal burden blocking economic recovery, and raising revenue by measures against large fortunes. Rapid steepening of income tax on incomes above 75,000 francs a year; reorganization of death duties; special taxes on monopoly profits, but in such a way as to have no effects on retail prices. Measures against tax evasions, in connexion with transferable ('bearer') securities.
　　4. Control of export of capital, and punishment of evasion by rigorous measures, including confiscation of property concealed abroad or of its equivalent value in France.

The Revolt of the Masses

José Ortega y Gasset

The disillusionment of the 1920s and 1930s, often associated with the effects of World War I, is reflected in many of the more profound attempts to understand Western civilization and the human condition. But this intellectual trend should not be seen only as a reaction to World War I. In The Revolt of the Masses *(1930), one of the most influential works of the period, José Ortega y Gasset (1883–1955) laments the population increase, the rise of the "masses," and the decline of the elite, cultured, liberal civilization of the nineteenth century. Ortega, a strong liberal and antimonarchist, became professor of metaphysics at the University of Madrid in 1910 and Spain's leading intellectual. Anticipating the defeat of the Republicans, he fled Spain in 1936. In the following excerpt from* The Revolt of the Masses, *he introduces the themes he will deal with in the rest of the book.*

　　Consider: *Why the rise to power of the masses is so serious; how Ortega distinguishes the "masses" from the "qualified minorities"; whether he presents a valid criticism of modern democracy.*

There is one fact which, whether for good or ill, is of utmost importance in the public life of Europe at the present moment. This fact is the accession of the masses to complete social power. As the masses, by definition, neither should nor can direct their own personal existence, and still less rule society in general, this fact means that actually Europe is suffering from the great-

---

Source: José Ortega y Gasset, *The Revolt of the Masses.* Reprinted by permission of W. W. Norton & Co., Inc. (New York, 1932), pp. 11, 16, 18.

est crisis that can afflict peoples, nations, and civilisation. Such a crisis has occurred more than once in history. Its characteristics and its consequences are well known. So also is its name. It is called the rebellion of the masses. . . .

There exist, then, in society, operations, activities, and functions of the most diverse order, which are of their very nature special, and which consequently cannot be properly carried out without special gifts. For example: certain pleasures of an artistic and refined character, or again the functions of government and of political judgment in public affairs. Previously these special activities were exercised by qualified minorities, or at least by those who claimed such qualification. The mass asserted no right to intervene in them; they realised that if they wished to intervene they would necessarily have to acquire those special qualities and cease being mere mass. They recognised their place in a healthy dynamic social system. . . .

The characteristic of the hour is that the commonplace mind, knowing itself to be commonplace, has the assurance to proclaim the rights of the commonplace and to impose them wherever it will. As they say in the United States: "to be different is to be indecent." The mass crushes beneath it everything that is different, everything that is excellent, individual, qualified and select. Anybody who is not like everybody, who does not think like everybody, runs the risk of being eliminated. And it is clear, of course, that this "everybody" is not "everybody." "Everybody" was normally the complex unity of the mass and the divergent, specialised minorities. Nowadays, "everybody" is the mass alone. Here we have the formidable fact of our times, described without any concealment of the brutality of its features.

Civilization and Its Discontents

Sigmund Freud

Psychoanalysis became one of the most powerful intellectual influences in the twentieth century. In part, it was based on the older eighteenth- and nineteenth-century optimism about the power of human rationality and scientific investigation: It assumed that human behavior could be even more deeply understood than before through scientific observation and that rational understanding could alleviate pain and problems. In other ways, however, it reflected the late-nineteenth- and early-twentieth-century attack on rationality: It argued that much of human behavior is irrational, unconscious, and instinctual. Finally, it echoed some of the pessimism fostered by the experience of World War I: Civilization was increasingly threat-

Source: Sigmund Freud, *Civilization and Its Discontents*, in *The Standard Edition of the Complete Psychological Works of Sigmund Freud*, James Strachey, trans. and ed. Reprinted by permission of W. W. Norton & Co., Inc. (New York, 1961), pp. 58–59, 92, The Hogarth Press, Ltd., Sigmund Freud Copyrights Ltd., and The Institute of Psycho-Analysis.

ened by deep, antisocial drives such as for sex or aggression. Sigmund Freud (1856–1939), the person most responsible for developing psychoanalysis, was a Viennese neurologist who became increasingly interested in psychoanalysis as a theory of human behavior, as a method of investigation, and as a treatment for certain illnesses. The following is a selection from Civilization and Its Discontents *(1929), written in the aftermath of World War I and toward the end of Freud's life. In it Freud speaks of the fragility of civilization.*

> **Consider:** *How this selection reflects the experience of World War I; the ways in which this document reflects and contributes to the sense of uncertainty common in this period; similarities between Ortega and Freud.*

The element of truth behind all this, which people are so ready to disavow, is that men are not gentle creatures who want to be loved, and who at the most can defend themselves if they are attacked; they are, on the contrary, creatures among whose instinctual endowments is to be reckoned a powerful share of aggressiveness. As a result, their neighbour is for them not only a potential helper or sexual object, but also someone who tempts them to satisfy their aggressiveness on him, to exploit his capacity for work without compensation, to use him sexually without his consent, to seize his possessions, to humiliate him, to cause him pain, to torture and to kill him. *Homo homini lupus.*[1] Who, in the face of all his experience of life and of history, will have the courage to dispute this assertion? As a rule this cruel aggressiveness waits for some provocation or puts itself at the service of some other purpose, whose goal might also have been reached by milder measures. In circumstances that are favourable to it, when the mental counter-forces which ordinarily inhibit it are out of action, it also manifests itself spontaneously and reveals man as a savage beast to whom consideration towards his own kind is something alien. Anyone who calls to mind the atrocities committed during racial migrations or the invasions of the Huns, or by the people known as Mongols under Jenghiz Khan and Tamerlane, or at the capture of Jerusalem by the pious Crusaders, or even, indeed, the horrors of the recent World War — anyone who calls these things to mind will have to bow humbly before the truth of this view.

The existence of this inclination to aggression, which we can detect in ourselves and justly assume to be present in others, is the factor which disturbs our relations with our neighbour and which forces civilization into such a high expenditure [of energy]. In consequence of this primary mutual hostility of human beings, civilized society is perpetually threatened with disintegration. The interest of work in common would not hold it together; instinctual passions are stronger than reasonable interests. Civilization has to use its utmost efforts in order to set limits to man's aggressive instincts and to hold the manifestations of them in check by psychical reaction-formations.

---

[1] ['Man is a wolf to man.' Derived from Plautus, *Asinaria* II, iv, 88.]

Hence, therefore, the use of methods intended to incite people into identifications and aim-inhibited relationships of love, hence the restriction upon sexual life, and hence too the ideal's commandment to love one's neighbour as oneself — a commandment which is really justified by the fact that nothing else runs so strongly counter to the original nature of man. In spite of every effort, these endeavours of civilization have not so far achieved very much. It hopes to prevent the crudest excesses of brutal violence by itself assuming the right to use violence against criminals, but the law is not able to lay hold of the more cautious and refined manifestations of human aggressiveness.

The fateful question for the human species seems to me to be whether and to what extent their cultural development will succeed in mastering the disturbance of their communal life by the human instinct of aggression and self-destruction. It may be that in this respect precisely the present time deserves a special interest. Men have gained control over the forces of nature to such an extent that with their help they would have no difficulty in exterminating one another to the last man. They know this, and hence comes a large part of their current unrest, their unhappiness and their mood of anxiety. And now it is to be expected that the other of the two 'Heavenly Powers,' eternal Eros, will make an effort to assert himself in the struggle with his equally immortal adversary. But who can foresee with what success and with what result?[2]

VISUAL SOURCES

Decadence in the Weimar Republic

George Grosz

This 1921 drawing by the German artist George Grosz shows some of the problems facing Western societies, particularly Germany, shortly after World War I. The wealthy few indulge in leisure activities while guards protect their factories. The rest of the people are crippled veterans, bankrupt businessmen, old women, young children, and the poor. They appear to feel isolated, distrustful, and out of place. The subject matter of this drawing is typical of art and literature that attacked capitalism and militarism between the wars.

Consider: *How this drawing relates to the selection by Linke or the one by Remarque.*

---

[2][The final sentence was added in 1931 — when the menace of Hitler was already becoming apparent.]

Photo 12-1

The Granger Collection

SECONDARY SOURCES

Government and the Governed:
The Interwar Years

R. H. S. Crossman

Many scholars saw the 1920s as a period of failure and missed opportunities. This was particularly true of liberal or left-wing scholars from Western democracies, for they looked for the origins of the disastrous rise of dictatorships and the Great

Source: R. H. S. Crossman, *Government and the Governed*. Reprinted by permission of G. P. Putnam's Sons (New York, 1940), pp. 255–257. Copyright © 1940 by G. P. Putnam's Sons.

Depression in those years. The following selection by R. H. S. Crossman exemplifies
this perspective. Educated at Oxford, Crossman became a leading figure in the
Labour Party's left wing and wrote numerous works on philosophy and politics. Here,
in a work published in 1940, Crossman analyzes the period between 1918 and 1933.

Consider: *Opportunities that were missed in 1918 and 1919; policies that the*
Western democracies might have initiated during this period that could have
changed the course of events.

Seen in retrospect, the period from 1918–1933 is marked by a growing
lethargy in the victor nations. Neither at home nor abroad did democracy
undertake a single great constructive enterprise. Victory seemed to have
deprived France and Britain of their dynamic: their Conservatives ceased to
be ardent imperialists, and their Socialists lost their revolutionary fervour. A
spirit of collective pacifism possessed them, and made the people content
with the lazy approval of high ideals, the verbal condemnation of injustice,
chicanery and oppression. Holding all the power, the Western democracies
disdained to use it, so long as the status quo was in any way tolerable. The
attitude of America was not dissimilar, except that here the League idea was
rejected and the Monroe doctrine was still regarded as America's contribution to world peace.

A myth is only justifiable if it stimulates to action. But "Collective
Pacifism" was a sedative, not a stimulant. It intoxicated the democracies
with a feeling of moral superiority and well-being, while it sapped their
sense of responsibility. Gradually statesmen and peoples alike began to
believe that the League of Nations was a force able to do the work which
previously fell to the various nations. Instead of relying on themselves and
on co-operation with their allies, they began to rely on the League to
preserve peace. Since the League had no coercive power at its disposal, this
trust was wholly unjustified.

No one Party or section of the population can be blamed for this collapse
of democratic morale. The great opportunity had been missed in 1918–19:
and it was difficult for the Western democracies to recover from that failure.
They had encouraged nationalism as the basis of government; they had
retained economic imperialism and permitted international finance to function independently of government policy. In brief, they had as far as possible returned to pre-war conditions. Having done so, they sought to
humanize them. That they failed is an indication that good intentions and
kindness, unbacked by resolution and knowledge, may disguise injustices
but never eradicate them. Kindness and good-will no doubt console the
patient suffering from cancer, but they will not cure the cancer; and the patient whose practitioner only displays these qualities, may, in his intolerable
agonies, turn to a quack and curse the Christian humanity which his practitioner displays.

The Great Depression in Europe

James Laux

*Most scholars agree that the Great Depression was very important, but they dis-
agree over its precise significance. For Marxists, it was the greatest in a series of
periodic economic crises inevitably flowing from the capitalist system and an indication that this system would soon collapse. For liberal economic historians, it was
an indictment of conservative, nationalistic economic policies that would be forced
to give way to modern Keynesian policies characterized by greater government activity and planning. For others, it was a crucial cause of the rise of nazism and
World War II itself. In the following selection James Laux of the University of
Cincinnati analyzes the impact of the Great Depression, emphasizing various
changes in attitude that stemmed from it.*

> **Consider:** *Whether, as some scholars argue, the Great Depression forced govern-
> ments to modify* laissez-faire *just enough to save capitalism as a whole; why
> economic planning appeared more attractive after the experience of the Depression.*

The Depression, perhaps, had the most serious impact in Europe on people's
thinking about economic matters. Looking back on the experience, most
Europeans agreed that the orthodoxy of laissez-faire no longer held. They
would not again accept the view that a government must interfere as little
as possible in the operation of the economic system. Governments must accept wider responsibilities than balancing their own budgets. The value of
the currency in terms of gold must give way to economic expansion if the
two appear to conflict. Laissez-faire already was wheezing and laboring in
the 1920s; after the decade of the 1930s it was nearly prostrate. As so often
happens, a philosophy came along to justify this changed attitude, a new
approach to theoretical economics worked out by the Englishman John
Maynard Keynes. The most influential economist of the twentieth century,
Keynes published his classic work in 1936, *The General Theory of Employment, Interest and Money.* He argued that governments can and should
manipulate capitalist economies, by running surpluses or deficits, by investing heavily in public works, by changing the size of the money and
credit supply, and by altering rates of interest. In his analysis he emphasized
the total economy, the relations among savings, investment, production,
and consumption, what is called macroeconomics, rather than an investigation of a single firm or sector. A critic of socialism, Keynes scorned the signif-

SOURCE: James M. Laux, from "The Great Depression in Europe" (*The Forum Series*).
Reprinted by permission of Forum Press (St. Louis, Mo., 1974), pp. 13–14. Copyright © 1974 by
Forum Press.

icance of government ownership of production facilities, but promoted government intervention in an economy to make capitalism work better.

Bolstering this view were the remarkable production achievements of many European industrial states during the two world wars. In these crises national economies expanded military production enormously under government direction. Many asked why such techniques could not be applied in peacetime also, but to make consumer products rather than tools of destruction.

The upshot was that by 1945 if not 1939 most Europeans abandoned the idea that they lived at the mercy of an impersonal economic system whose rules could not be changed and accepted the proposition that the economy could operate the way people wanted it to. From this it was a short step to the concept of planning the future development of the economy — both the whole and particular segments of it. Economic planning became an acceptable posture for capitalist societies and enjoyed a considerable reputation. Some of those who supported it perhaps under-estimated the possible merits of free markets as guiding production decisions and did seem to assume that planners somehow possess more wisdom than ordinary human beings.

Economic nationalism was a more immediate result of the Depression — the policy that short-run national economic interests have highest priority and that international economic cooperation and trade must give way before narrowly conceived national interests. Economic nationalism showed its sharpest teeth in those European states where political nationalism reached a peak — Germany, Italy, and the Soviet Union. Its strength declined in western Europe after the Second World War as people saw once again that economic prosperity among one's neighbors could bring great benefits to oneself. In an expanding continental or world economy everyone can get richer. But one wonders if economic nationalism may not revive in western Europe, especially if it seems a popular policy in a crisis.

The Great Depression had important political repercussions too. In Germany, the Depression's tragic gloom made the dynamism of the Nazi movement seem more attractive. It is difficult to imagine the Nazis achieving power without the Depression and its pervasive unemployment in the background. In France, the Depression convinced many that the regime of the Third Republic had lost its élan and relevance to twentieth-century problems, but the lack of a widely popular alternative meant that the Republic could limp along until a disastrous military defeat brought it down. In Britain, the Depression was less serious and no fundamental challenge to the political regime developed. The Conservatives held power for most of the interwar period and their failure to work actively to absorb the large unemployment that continued there until late in the 1930s brought widespread rancor and bitterness against them. Doubts as to the Conservatives' ability to manage a peacetime economy led to the first majority Labour government in the 1945 election. More profoundly, the years of heavy unemployment bred a very strong anticapitalist sentiment in much of British labor, a sentiment that led them after the war to demand moves toward socialism, such as nationalization of major industries.

The Depression helped convince Europeans that their governments must try to manage their economies. Most agreed that full employment and expanding output should be the goals. They did not agree on the means to achieve these ends.

Our Age of Unreason

Franz Alexander

Interpreters of the interwar period often see it as a period of irrationality. They cite evidence from political affairs, cultural trends, and general attitudes to support this view. Moreover, the rise and spread of Freudian psychology seemed both to reflect and to prove the strength of irrational trends within our civilization. The following excerpt from Our Age of Unreason *by Franz Alexander illustrates this perception. An early psychoanalyst, Alexander trained in Budapest and taught in Berlin during the 1920s. In the 1930s he moved to the United States, where he became director of the Chicago Institute for Psychoanalysis. This selection, written in 1942, combines autobiographical and interpretive insights into the interwar period.*

> **Consider:** *Why the interwar period seems more irrational than any other period; how Alexander connects political, cultural, and psychological events to support his argument.*

I spent the eleven years following the Versailles and Trianon Peace Treaties in Europe, the next twelve years in the United States. In Europe I saw the world of my youth rapidly disintegrate and standards and ideals which had become second nature to me vanish. Like most European observers of these eventful years I saw that a cultural epoch was in process of dissolution. What would follow was not clear, but much clearer was what was specifically disappearing, the highest values I had known; science and artistic creation for their own sakes, the gradual improvement of human relations by the use of knowledge and reason were giving way to a chaotic sense of insecurity, fear, and distrust among mechanically minded men who had been corrupted by technical accomplishments. Everyone expected the worst, was worried, strained, and was concerned with himself, with his uncertain future, and with the pressing and practical problems of the present. The maxim *Primum vivere deinde philsophare* ("First live; then philosophize") became the ruling principle. . . .

Source: Franz Alexander, *Our Age of Unreason* (New York: J. B. Lippincott Co., 1942), pp. 7, 19. Reprinted by permission of California First Bank as trustee for Anita Alexander.

Current events impress us with their irrationality. We are witnessing on an unprecedented scale the wholesale destruction of life and property. All this happens in an era of the utmost scientific enlightenment and of the greatest technical achievements which, if intelligently used, could render the life of all the inhabitants of the earth easier and more carefree than ever before. There is little doubt that a council of economists and political scientists could work out a peaceful social organization and a rational world order which could satisfy the vital needs of all. That such a rational world order is today, as in Plato's time, a utopia is due to the fact that human relationships are not governed primarily by reason but by essentially irrational emotional forces. The dominance of irrational forces in human nature has perhaps never been as complete as at the present moment. It is no wonder that in the face of current world events many turn for an explanation to the psychiatrist, the specialist in irrational behavior.

The Freudian Model of Human Nature

Erich Fromm

Sigmund Freud had many followers and many critics. The German psychoanalyst Erich Fromm (1900–1980) falls into both categories: He was a neo-Freudian who nevertheless differed with Freud on a number of important points. In the following selection from The Crisis of Psychoanalysis, *Fromm examines the social and historical bases of Freud's thoughts and presents a brief analysis of the Freudian model of human nature.*

Consider: *The ways in which this interpretation is supported by the selections from Freud's* Civilization *and* Its Discontents; *how Freud's views reflect his times.*

To appreciate the social basis of Freud's views, it is useful to recognize from the outset that he was a liberal critic of bourgeois society, in the sense in which liberal reformers in general were critical. He saw that society imposes unnecessary hardships on man, which are conducive to worse results rather than the expected better ones. He saw that this unnecessary harshness, as it operated in the field of sexual morality, led to the formation of neuroses that, in many cases, could have been avoided by a more tolerant attitude. (Political and educational reform are parallel phenomena.) But Freud was never a radical critic of capitalistic society. He never questioned its socio-economic bases, nor did he criticize its ideologies — with the exception of those concerning sexuality.

SOURCE: Erich Fromm, *The Crisis of Psychoanalysis* (New York: Holt, Rinehart and Winston, 1970), pp. 30–31, 34–35.

As for his concept of man, it is important to point out first that Freud, rooted in the philosophy of humanism and enlightenment, starts out with the assumption of the existence of *man* as such — a universal man, not only man as he manifests himself in various cultures, but someone about whose structure generally valid and empirical statements can be made. Freud, like Spinoza before him, constructed a "model of human nature" on the basis of which not only neuroses, but all fundamental aspects, possibilities, and necessities of man, can be explained and understood.

What is this Freudian model?

Freud saw man as a closed system driven by two forces: the self-preservative and the sexual drives. The latter are rooted in chemophysiological processes moving in a phased pattern. The first phase increases tension and unpleasure; the second reduces the built-up tension and in so doing creates that which subjectively is felt as "pleasure." Man is primarily an isolated being, whose primary interest is the optimal satisfaction of both his ego and his libidinous interest. Freud's man is the physiologically driven and motivated *homme machine*. But, secondarily, man is also a social being, because he needs other people for the satisfaction of his libidinous drives as well as those of self-preservation. The child is in need of mother (and here, according to Freud, libidinous desires follow the path of the physiological needs); the adult needs a sexual partner. Feelings like tenderness or love are looked upon as phenomena that accompany, and result from, libidinous interests. Individuals need each other as means for the satisfaction of their physiologically rooted drives. Man is primarily unrelated to others, and is only secondarily forced — or seduced — into relationships with others.

Freud's *homo sexualis* is a variant of the classic *homo economicus*. It is the isolated, self-sufficient man who has to enter into relations with others in order that they may mutually fulfill their needs. *Homo economicus* has simply economic needs that find their mutual satisfaction in the exchange of goods on the commodity market. The needs of *homo sexualis* are physiological and libidinous, and normally are mutually satisfied by the relations between the sexes. In both variants the persons essentially remain strangers to each other, being related only by the common aim of drive satisfaction. This social determination of Freud's theory by the spirit of the market economy does not mean that the theory is wrong, except in its claim of describing the situation of *man as such*; as a description of interpersonal relations in bourgeois society, it is valid for the majority of people.

More important, however, is Freud's new appreciation of the role of human destructiveness. Not that he had omitted aggression in his first theoretical model. He had considered aggression to be an important factor, but it was subordinated to the libidinous drives and those for self-preservation. In the new theory destructiveness becomes the rival of, and eventually the victor over the libido and the ego drives. Man cannot help wanting to destroy, for the destructive tendency is rooted in his biological constitution. Although he can mitigate this tendency to a certain point, he can never deprive it of its strength. His alternatives are to direct his destructiveness either against himself or against the world outside, but he has no chance of liberating himself from this tragic dilemma.

There are good reasons for the hypothesis that Freud's new appreciation of destructiveness has its roots in the experience of the first World War. This war shook the foundations of the liberal optimism that had filled the first period of Freud's life. Until 1914 the members of the middle class had believed that the world was rapidly approaching a state of greater security, harmony and peace. The "darkness" of the middle ages seemed to lift from generation to generation; in a few more steps, so it seemed, the world — or at least Europe — would resemble the streets of a well-lighted, protected capital. In the bourgeois euphoria of the *belle époque* it was easily forgotten that this picture was not true for the majority of the workers and peasants of Europe, and even less so for the populations of Asia and Africa. The war of 1914 destroyed this illusion; not so much the beginning of the war, as its duration and the inhumanity of its practices. Freud, who during the war still believed in the justice and victory of the German cause, was hit at a deeper psychic level than the average, less sensitive person. He probably sensed that the optimistic hopes of enlightenment thought were illusions, and concluded that man, by nature, was destined to be destructive. Precisely because he was a reformer, the war must have hit him all the more forcefully. Since he was no radical critic of society and no revolutionary, it was impossible for him to hope for essential social changes, and he was forced to look for the causes of the tragedy in the nature of man.

Chapter Questions

1. Which developments focused on in this chapter are most closely related to the experience and results of World War I?
2. In what ways do the trends of the 1920s and 1930s support the argument that Western civilization reached its apogee between 1789 and 1914, and that starting with World War I it was clearly on the decline? What factors might be pointed out to mitigate or counter this interpretation?

CHAPTER THIRTEEN

Totalitarianism

𝓈.

The end of World War I and the arrangements made at the Paris Peace Conference in 1919 seemed to represent success for parliamentary democracy. But during the 1920s and 1930s, that success proved to be more apparent than real. The 1917 revolution had already brought a Communist regime to power in Russia. During the following two decades, Communist parties spread throughout Europe and were perceived as a great threat, but they did not come to power outside of the Soviet Union. Authoritarian movements of the right became the most immediate danger to parliamentary democracy. The first of these movements was Mussolini's fascism, which became dominant in Italy in 1922. By the end of the decade regimes in Eastern and Southern Europe were becoming more authoritarian. This trend became stronger during the Depression of the 1930s. There was a retreat toward nationalistic economic policies and greater central control by governments attempting to deal with the despair, destruction, and dislocation accompanying the Depression. In Central, Eastern, and Southern Europe, the Depression fueled already strong tendencies toward dictatorships and fascism. The most extreme of rightist ideology was Hitler's nazism, which became dominant in Germany in 1933. By the end of that decade, Europe was embroiled in a new World War even greater than World War I.

Historians and social scientists looking at this period typically focus on the rise of totalitarianism. This is a controversial term that is hard to evaluate objectively. Generally, it refers to a form of government that shares certain traits. It rejects individualism, a single party is in power, and the state controls almost all aspects of life (economic activities, social organizations, cultural institutions, the military, and politics). It has one official, revolutionary ideology, and terror, propaganda, and mass communications are used as tools of power. Yet there have been important differences among totalitarian states. Communism in Russia under Stalin and its professed opposite, nazism in Germany, sprang from different sources and ideologies. Even though German nazism and Italian fascism resembled each other, some scholars question whether Italian fascism was thorough and effective enough to be considered totalitarian. Other nationalistic authoritarian regimes of the right, from Eastern Europe to Spain and Portugal, shared only certain elements of totalitarian fascism. Nevertheless, the concept of totalitarianism does provide us with a tool to use in interpreting important developments between the two world wars.

This chapter addresses a number of broad questions. What were the main features of the totalitarian regimes? How were they similar to and different from each other? How can their appeal and the power they commanded over people be explained? In what ways were they related to nineteenth- and early-twentieth-century trends?

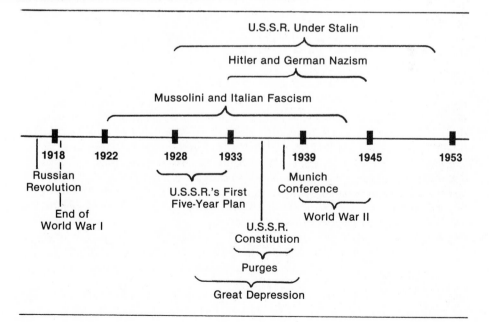

The selections in this chapter survey totalitarianism from a variety of perspectives. The concept itself is questioned. How useful is it? Is it historically bound to a few regimes of the 1920s, 1930s, and 1940s, or is it more broadly applicable? What characteristics do totalitarian regimes share and how do these regimes differ from nontotalitarian systems? The three regimes most commonly identified with totalitarianism—fascism, nazism, and communism—are examined. The selections on Mussolini and Italian fascism focus on the ideology of fascism and its historical place. An effort is made to distinguish German nazism from Italian fascism, to analyze nazism's appeal, to understand the extremes possible under such a system, and to evaluate the role of Hitler in shaping nazism. Three of the most controversial aspects of Stalin and Russian communism are examined: Stalin's justification for the policy against the *kulaks* in 1929, his analysis of democracy as part of his defense of the 1936 Soviet Constitution, and his massive purges of the 1930s.

In addition to offering broad insights into totalitarianism during the 1920s and 1930s, the selections in this chapter provide some of the background of World War II, which will be covered in the next chapter.

PRIMARY SOURCES

The Doctrine of Fascism

Benito Mussolini

Italy was the first European power to turn to fascism. She was one of the victors in World War I, but the war was costly and Italy did not gain much. After the war the country was marked by instability, weak governments, and an apparent threat from the left. Benito Mussolini (1883–1945), a former leader of the Socialist party and a veteran of the war, organized the Italian Fascist Party in 1919. Strongly nationalistic, the party stood against the Versailles Treaty, left-wing radicalism, and the established government. After leading his Blackshirts in a march on Rome in 1922, Mussolini was invited by King Victor Emmanuel III to form a government. Over the next few years Mussolini effectively eliminated any opposition and installed his fascist state system, which would last some twenty years. The following document contains excerpts from "The Political and Social Doctrine of Fas-

Source: Benito Mussolini, "The Political and Social Doctrine of Fascism," *International Conciliation*, No. 306 (January 1935), pp. 7–17. Originally published by the Carnegie Endowment for International Peace, as part of the *International Conciliation Series*.

cism," an article signed by Mussolini and written with the philosopher Giovanni
Gentile that originally appeared in the Enciclopedia Italiana *in 1932. It describes*
the ideological foundations of Italian fascism. These excerpts emphasize the rejec-
tion of traditional democracy, liberalism, and socialism as well as faith in the
authoritarian, fascist state.

> **Consider:** *The greatest sources of appeal in the doctrine according to Mussolini;*
> *the ways in which this doctrine can be considered a rejection of major*
> *historical trends that had been developing over the previous century; the*
> *government policies that would logically flow from such a doctrine.*

Fascism, the more it considers and observes the future and the development of humanity quite apart from political considerations of the moment, believes neither in the possibility nor the utility of perpetual peace. It thus repudiates the doctrine of Pacifism — born of a renunciation of the struggle and an act of cowardice in the face of sacrifice. War alone brings up to its highest tension all human energy and puts the stamp of nobility upon the peoples who have the courage to meet it. . . .

The Fascist accepts life and loves it, knowing nothing of and despising suicide; he rather conceives of life as duty and struggle and conquest, life which should be high and full, lived for oneself, but above all for others — those who are at hand and those who are far distant, contemporaries, and those who will come after. . . .

Such a conception of life makes Fascism the complete opposite of that doctrine, the base of so-called scientific and Marxian Socialism, the materialist conception of history. . . . Fascism, now and always, believes in holiness and in heroism; that is to say, in actions influenced by no economic motive, direct or indirect. . . .

Fascism repudiates the conception of "economic" happiness, to be realized by Socialism and, as it were, at a given moment in economic evolution to assure to everyone the maximum of well-being. Fascism denies the materialist conception of happiness as a possibility, and abandons it to its inventors, the economists of the first half of the nineteenth century. . . .

After Socialism, Fascism combats the whole complex system of democratic ideology, and repudiates it, whether in its theoretical premises or in its practical application. Fascism denies that the majority, by the simple fact that it is a majority, can direct human society; it denies that numbers alone can govern by means of a periodical consultation, and it affirms the immutable, beneficial, and fruitful inequality of mankind, which can never be permanently leveled through the mere operation of a mechanical process such as universal suffrage. . . .

Fascism denies, in democracy, the absurd conventional untruth of political equality dressed out in the garb of collective irresponsibility, and the myth of "happiness" and indefinite progress. But, if democracy may be conceived in diverse forms — that is to say, taking democracy to mean a state of society in which the populace are not reduced to impotence in the State — Fascism may write itself down as "an organized, centralized, and authoritative democracy."

Fascism has taken up an attitude of complete opposition to the doctrines of Liberalism, both in the political field and the field of economics. . . . Fascism uses in its construction whatever elements in the Liberal, Social, or Democratic doctrines still have a living value; it maintains what may be called the certainties which we owe to history, but it rejects all the rest — that is to say, the conception that there can be any doctrine of unquestioned efficacy for all times and all peoples. Given that the nineteenth century was the century of Socialism, of Liberalism, and of Democracy, it does not necessarily follow that the twentieth century must also be a century of Socialism, Liberalism, and Democracy: political doctrines pass, but humanity remains; and it may rather be expected that this will be a century of authority, a century of the Left, a century of Fascism. For if the nineteenth century was a century of individualism (Liberalism always signifying individualism) it may be expected that this will be the century of collectivism, and hence the century of the State. It is a perfectly logical deduction that a new doctrine can utilize all the still vital elements of previous doctrines. . . .

The foundation of Fascism is the conception of the State, its character, its duty, and its aim. Fascism conceives of the State as an absolute, in comparison with which all individuals or groups are relative, only to be conceived of in their relation to the State. The conception of the Liberal State is not that of a directing force, guiding the play and development, both material and spiritual, of a collective body, but merely a force limited to the function of recording results: on the other hand, the Fascist State is itself conscious, and has itself a will and a personality — thus it may be called the "ethic" State. . . .

If every age has its own characteristic doctrine, there are a thousand signs which point to Fascism as the characteristic doctrine of our time. For if a doctrine must be a living thing, this is proved by the fact that Fascism has created a living faith; and that this faith is very powerful in the minds of men, is demonstrated by those who have suffered and died for it.

Fascism has henceforth in the world the universality of all those doctrines which, in realizing themselves, have represented a stage in the history of the human spirit.

Mein Kampf

Adolf Hitler

The most extreme and racist form of fascism arose in Germany under the Nazis, led by Adolf Hitler (1889–1945). After serving in World War I, Hitler joined and soon took control of the small National Socialist German Workers party. In the early 1930s, after years of relative obscurity, the Nazi party gained popularity with a nationalistic program attacking the Versailles Treaty, the Weimar Republic, the Communists, and above all the Jews. In 1933 Hitler was appointed chancellor and Germany was soon transformed into a Nazi state. Hitler's ideology, his mental processes, and some of the ideas behind nazism are illustrated in his rather formless book Mein Kampf *("My Struggle"). It was written in 1924 while he was in jail for his efforts to overthrow the government of Bavaria in southern Germany. With the growing popularity of the Nazi party in the early 1930s, the book became a best seller. In these selections from* Mein Kampf, *Hitler displays his anti-Semitism, argues that a racial analysis is central to an understanding of history, and indicates his vision of German expansion eastward at the expense of Russia.*

> **Consider:** *How Hitler connects the Jews, the Marxists, and German expansion eastward; on what points Mussolini might agree with Hitler here; the ways in which these ideas might be appealing, popular, or acceptable in the historical circumstances of Germany in the early 1930s.*

If we were to divide mankind into three groups, the founders of culture, the bearers of culture, the destroyers of culture, only the Aryan could be considered as the representative of the first group. From him originate the foundations and walls of all human creation, and only the outward form and color are determined by the changing traits of character of the various peoples. He provides the mightiest building stones and plans for all human progress and only the execution corresponds to the nature of the varying men and races. . . .

Blood mixture and the resultant drop in the racial level is the sole cause of the dying out of old cultures; for men do not perish as a result of lost wars, but by the loss of that force of resistance which is contained only in pure blood.

All who are not of good race in this world are chaff. . . .

With satanic joy in his face, the black-haired Jewish youth lurks in wait for the unsuspecting girl whom he defiles with his blood, thus stealing her from her people. With every means he tries to destroy the racial foundations of the people he has set out to subjugate. Just as he himself systematically ruins women and girls, he does not shrink back from pulling down the blood barriers for others, even on a large scale. It was and it is Jews who bring the Negroes into the Rhineland, always with the same secret thought and clear aim of ruining the hated white race by the necessarily resulting bastardization, throwing it down from its cultural and political height, and himself rising to be its master.

For a racially pure people which is conscious of its blood can never be enslaved by the Jew. In this world he will forever be master over bastards and bastards alone.

And so he tries systematically to lower the racial level by a continuous poisoning of individuals.

And in politics he begins to replace the idea of democracy by the dictatorship of the proletariat.

In the organized mass of Marxism he has found the weapon which lets him dispense with democracy and in its stead allows him to subjugate and govern the peoples with a dictatorial and brutal fist.

He works systematically for revolutionization in a twofold sense: economic and political.

Around peoples who offer too violent a resistance to attack from within he weaves a net of enemies, thanks to his international influence, incites them to war, and finally, if necessary, plants the flag of revolution on the very battlefields.

In economics he undermines the states until the social enterprises which have become unprofitable are taken from the state and subjected to his financial control.

In the political field he refuses the state the means for its self-preservation, destroys the foundations of all national self-maintenance and defense, destroys faith in the leadership, scoffs at its history and past, and drags everything that is truly great into the gutter.

Culturally he contaminates art, literature, the theater, makes a mockery of natural feeling, overthrows all concepts of beauty and sublimity, of the noble and the good, and instead drags men down into the sphere of his own base nature.

Religion is ridiculed, ethics and morality represented as outmoded, until the last props of a nation in its struggle for existence in this world have fallen.

Now begins the great last revolution. In gaining political power the Jew casts off the few cloaks that he still wears. The democratic people's Jew becomes the blood-Jew and tyrant over peoples. In a few years he tries to exterminate the national intelligentsia and by robbing the peoples of their natural intellectual leadership makes them ripe for the slave's lot of permanent subjugation.

The most frightful example of this kind is offered by Russia, where he killed or starved about thirty million people with positively fanatical savagery, in part amid inhuman tortures, in order to give a gang of Jewish journalists and stock exchange bandits domination over a great people.

The end is not only the end of the freedom of the peoples oppressed by the Jew, but also the end of this parasite upon the nations. After the death of his victim, the vampire sooner or later dies too. . . .

8.

And so we National Socialists consciously draw a line beneath the foreign policy tendency of our pre-War period. We take up where we broke off six hundred years ago. We stop the endless German movement to the south and west, and turn our gaze toward the land in the east. At long last we break off the colonial and commercial policy of the pre-War period and shift to the soil policy of the future.

If we speak of soil in Europe today, we can primarily have in mind only *Russia* and her vassal border states.

Here Fate itself seems desirous of giving us a sign. By handing Russia to Bolshevism, it robbed the Russian nation of that intelligentsia which previously brought about and guaranteed its existence as a state. For the organization of a Russian state formation was not the result of the political abilities of the Slavs in Russia, but only a wonderful example of the state-forming efficacity of the German element in an inferior race. Numerous mighty empires on earth have been created in this way. Lower nations led by Germanic organizers and overlords have more than once grown to be mighty state formations and have endured as long as the racial nucleus of the creative state race maintained itself. For centuries Russia drew nourishment from this Germanic nucleus of its upper leading strata. Today it can be regarded as almost totally exterminated and extinguished. It has been replaced by the Jew. Impossible as it is for the Russian by himself to shake off the yoke of the Jew by his own resources, it is equally impossible for the Jew to maintain the mighty empire forever. He himself is no element of organization, but a ferment of decomposition. The Persian empire in the east is ripe for collapse. And the end of Jewish rule in Russia will also be the end of Russia as a state. We have been chosen by Fate as witnesses of a catastrophe which will be the mightiest confirmation of the soundness of the folkish theory.

Nazi Propaganda Pamphlet

Joseph Goebbels

Propaganda was strongly emphasized by the Nazis as a method of acquiring and maintaining power. Joseph Goebbels (1897–1945), an early leader in the Nazi party, was made chief of propaganda in 1929, minister for propaganda and national enlightenment in 1933, and a member of Hitler's cabinet council in 1938. The following is an excerpt from a 1930 pamphlet, written by Goebbels, describing why the Nazis are nationalists, "socialists," and against Jews and Marxists.

> **Consider:** *How this document reflects the character of life in Germany during the 1920s; to whom this document was designed to appeal and in what ways it might be a convincing piece of propaganda; in tone, quality, and ideas, how this compares with Mussolini's "Doctrine of Fascism"; how Nazi "socialism" differs from more traditional or Marxist conceptions of socialism.*

WHY ARE WE NATIONALISTS?

We are NATIONALISTS because we see in the NATION the only possibility for the protection and the furtherance of our existence.

The NATION is the organic bond of a people for the protection and defense of their lives. He is nationally minded who understands this IN WORD AND IN DEED.

Today, in GERMANY, NATIONALISM has degenerated into BOURGEOIS PATRIOTISM, and its power exhausts itself in tilting at windmills. It says GERMANY and means MONARCHY. It proclaims FREEDOM and means BLACK-WHITE-RED.

WE ARE NATIONALISTS BECAUSE WE, AS GERMANS, LOVE GERMANY. And because we love Germany, we demand the protection of its national spirit and we battle against its destroyers.

WHY ARE WE SOCIALISTS?

We are SOCIALISTS because we see in SOCIALISM the only possibility for maintaining our racial existence and through it the reconquest of our political freedom and the rebirth of the German state. SOCIALISM has its peculiar form first of all through its comradeship in arms with the forward-driving energy of a newly awakened nationalism. Without nationalism it is nothing, a phantom, a theory, a vision of air, a book. With it, it is everything, THE FUTURE, FREEDOM, FATHERLAND!

It was a sin of the liberal bourgeoisie to overlook THE STATE-BUILDING POWER OF SOCIALISM. It was the sin of MARXISM to degrade SOCIALISM to a system of MONEY AND STOMACH.

SOURCE: From Louis L. Snyder, *The Weimar Republic*. Reprinted by permission of D. Van Nostrand Co. (New York, 1966), pp. 201–203. Copyright © 1966 by Litton Educational Publishing, Inc.

SOCIALISM IS POSSIBLE ONLY IN A STATE WHICH IS FREE IN-SIDE AND OUTSIDE.

DOWN WITH POLITICAL BOURGEOIS SENTIMENT: FOR REAL NATIONALISM!

DOWN WITH MARXISM: FOR TRUE SOCIALISM!

UP WITH THE STAMP OF THE FIRST GERMAN NATIONAL SO-CIALIST STATE!

AT THE FRONT THE NATIONAL SOCIALIST GERMAN WORKERS PARTY!

WHY DO WE OPPOSE THE JEWS?

We are ENEMIES OF THE JEWS, because we are fighters for the freedom of the German people. THE JEW IS THE CAUSE AND THE BENE-FICIARY OF OUR MISERY. He has used the social difficulties of the broad masses of our people to deepen the unholy split between Right and Left among our people. He has made two halves of Germany. He is the real cause for our loss of the Great War.

The Jew has no interest in the solution of Germany's fateful problems. He CANNOT have any. FOR HE LIVES ON THE FACT THAT THERE HAS BEEN NO SOLUTION. If we would make the German people a unified community and give them freedom before the world, then the Jew can have no place among us. He has the best trumps in his hands when a people lives in inner and outer slavery. THE JEW IS RESPONSIBLE FOR OUR MISERY AND HE LIVES ON IT.

That is the reason why we, AS NATIONALISTS and AS SOCIALISTS, oppose the Jew. HE HAS CORRUPTED OUR RACE, FOULED OUR MORALS, UNDERMINED OUR CUSTOMS, AND BROKEN OUR POWER.

THE JEW IS THE PLASTIC DEMON OF THE DECLINE OF MAN-KIND.

WE ARE ENEMIES OF THE JEWS BECAUSE WE BELONG TO THE GERMAN PEOPLE. THE JEW IS OUR GREATEST MISFORTUNE.

It is not true that we eat a Jew every morning at breakfast.

It is true, however, that he SLOWLY BUT SURELY ROBS US OF EVERYTHING WE OWN.

THAT WILL STOP, AS SURELY AS WE ARE GERMANS.

The Theory and Practice of Hell: The Nazi Elite

Eugene Kogon

The SS was Hitler's special corps, serving as his bodyguard and elite police force. Members of the SS usually became extremely dedicated to the ideas and practices of nazism and carried out its precepts with extraordinary ruthlessness. The following is a statement from an SS officer recorded in a 1937 interview conducted by Eugene Kogon, less than one year before Kogon was arrested and taken to the concentration camp at Buchenwald. The officer was being trained as one of the elite of the Nazi state. Here he reveals his assumptions as a committed follower of Hitler and nazism.

> **Consider:** *The role this officer assumes the SS will play in the Nazi state and the ways this role was particularly appropriate to a fascist system; how this document helps account for the appeal of the SS to those deciding to join it; how the ideas revealed here might serve as psychological justification for some of the atrocities committed by the SS.*

"What we trainers of the younger generation of Führers aspire to is a modern governmental structure on the model of the ancient Greek city states. It is to these aristocratically run democracies with their broad economic basis of serfdom that we owe the great cultural achievements of antiquity. From five to ten per cent of the people, their finest flower, shall rule; the rest must work and obey. In this way alone can we attain that peak performance we must demand of ourselves and of the German people.

"The new Führer class is selected by the SS — in a positive sense by means of the National Political Education Institutes (*Napola*) as a preparatory stage, of the *Ordensburgen* as the academies proper of the coming Nazi aristocracy, and of a subsequent active internship in public affairs; in a negative sense by the extermination of all racially and biologically inferior elements and by the radical removal of all incorrigible political opposition that refuses on principle to acknowledge the philosophical basis of the Nazi State and its essential institutions.

"Within ten years at the latest it will be possible for us in this way to dictate the law of Adolf Hitler to Europe, put a halt to the otherwise inevitable decay of the continent, and build up a true community of nations, with Germany as the leading power keeping order."

SOURCE: Eugene Kogon, *The Theory and Practice of Hell*, Heinz Norden, trans. Reprinted by permission of Farrar, Straus and Giroux, Inc. Published by Farrar, Straus and Giroux, Inc. (New York, 1950), pp. 15–16.

The Informed Heart: Nazi Concentration Camps

Bruno Bettelheim

Organized, official racial persecution was a direct consequence of Nazi theories, attitudes, and practices. During the 1920s and early 1930s, however, the extent of the persecution was unanticipated. The most extreme form of this occurred in the late 1930s, with the introduction of forced labor and concentration camps, later to be followed by camps in which a policy of literal extermination was pursued. In the following selection, Bruno Bettelheim, a psychoanalyst in Austria at the time and now a leading psychoanalyst in the United States, describes his experiences in the concentration camps at Dachau and Buchenwald. He focuses on the dehumanizing processes involved and some of the ways prisoners adapted in an effort to survive.

> **Consider:** *The methods used to gain control over the prisoners; the psychological means developed by Bettelheim and other prisoners to cope with and survive this experience; how the existence, nature, and functioning of these camps reflect the theory and practice of Nazi totalitarianism.*

Usually the standard initiation of prisoners took place during transit from the local prison to the camp. If the distance was short, the transport was often slowed down to allow enough time to break the prisoners. During their initial transport to the camp, prisoners were exposed to nearly constant torture. The nature of the abuse depended on the fantasy of the particular SS man in charge of a group of prisoners. Still, they all had a definite pattern. Physical punishment consisted of whipping, frequent kicking (abdomen or groin), slaps in the face, shooting, or wounding with the bayonet. These alternated with attempts to produce extreme exhaustion. For instance, prisoners were forced to stare for hours into glaring lights, to kneel for hours, and so on.

From time to time a prisoner got killed, but no prisoner was allowed to care for his or another's wounds. The guards also forced prisoners to hit one another and to defile what the SS considered the prisoners' most cherished values. They were forced to curse their God, to accuse themselves and one another of vile actions, and their wives of adultery and prostitution. . . .

The purpose of this massive initial abuse was to traumatize the prisoners and break their resistance; to change at least their behavior if not yet their personalities. This could be seen from the fact that tortures became less and less violent to the degree that prisoners stopped resisting and complied immediately with any SS order, even the most outrageous. . . .

SOURCE: Bruno Bettelheim, *The Informed Heart: Autonomy in a Mass Age.* Reprinted by permission of Macmillan Publishing Co., Inc. Copyright © 1960 by The Free Press, a corporation.

It is hard to say just how much the process of personality change was speeded up by what prisoners experienced during the initiation. Most of them were soon totally exhausted; physically from abuse, loss of blood, thirst, etc.; psychologically from the need to control their anger and desperation before it could lead to a suicidal resistance. . . .

If I should try to sum up in one sentence what my main problem was during the whole time I spent in the camps, it would be: to protect my inner self in such a way that if, by any good fortune, I should regain liberty, I would be approximately the same person I was when deprived of liberty. So it seems that a split was soon forced upon me, the split between the inner self that might be able to retain its integrity, and the rest of the personality that would have to submit and adjust for survival. . . .

I have no doubt that I was able to endure the horrors of the transport and all that followed, because right from the beginning I became convinced that these dreadful and degrading experiences were somehow not happening to "me" as a subject, but only "me" as an object. . . .

All thoughts and feelings I had during the transport were extremely detached. It was as if I watched things happening in which I took part only vaguely. . . .

This was taught me by a German political prisoner, a communist worker who by then had been at Dachau for four years. I arrived there in a sorry condition because of experiences on the transport. I think that this man, by then an "old" prisoner, decided that, given my condition, the chances of my surviving without help were slim. So when he noticed that I could not swallow food because of physical pain and psychological revulsion, he spoke to me out of his rich experience: "Listen you, make up your mind: do you want to live or do you want to die? If you don't care, don't eat the stuff. But if you want to live, there's only one way: make up your mind to eat whenever and whatever you can, never mind how disgusting. Whenever you have a chance, defecate, so you'll be sure your body works. And whenever you have a minute, don't blabber, read by yourself, or flop down and sleep."

Problems of Agrarian Policy in the U.S.S.R.: Soviet Collectivization

Joseph Stalin

Joseph Stalin (1879–1953) rose from his working-class origins to become a leading member of the Bolsheviks before the 1917 revolution, the general secretary of the Russian Communist party in 1922, and the unchallenged dictator of the U.S.S.R.

SOURCE: J. V. Stalin, "Problems of Agrarian Policy in the U.S.S.R.," in *Problems of Leninism*, J. V. Stalin, ed. (Moscow: Foreign Languages, 1940), pp. 303–305, 318–321. Reprinted by permission of the Copyright Agency of the U.S.S.R.

by 1929. In 1927 Stalin and the leadership of the Russian Communist party decided on a policy for the planned industrialization of the U.S.S.R. — the First Five-Year Plan. At the same time they decided on a policy favoring the collectivization of agriculture. By 1929 Stalin made that policy more drastic, using massive coercion against the kulaks (relatively rich independent peasants). Kulaks resisted this enforced collectivization and widespread death and destruction resulted. Nevertheless, by 1932 much of Russian agriculture was collectivized. The following is an excerpt from a 1929 speech delivered by Stalin at the Conference of Marxist Students of the Agrarian Question. In it he explains and justifies the policy of collectivization and the need to eliminate the kulaks as a class.

> **Consider:** *The relations of this policy toward the kulaks to the policy for the planned industrialization of the U.S.S.R.; how Stalin justifies this policy as "socialist" as opposed to "capitalist"; the differences between Stalin's attitudes and ideas toward the kulaks and Hitler's toward the Jews.*

Can we advance our socialized industry at an accelerated rate while having to rely on an agricultural base, such as is provided by small peasant farming, which is incapable of expanded reproduction, and which, in addition, is the predominant force in our national economy? No, we cannot. Can the Soviet government and the work of Socialist construction be, for any length of time, based on two *different* foundations; on the foundation of the most large-scale and concentrated Socialist industry and on the foundation of the most scattered and backward, small-commodity peasant farming? No, they cannot. Sooner or later this would be bound to end in the complete collapse of the whole national economy. What, then, is the solution? The solution lies in enlarging the agricultural units, in making agriculture capable of accumulation, of expanded reproduction, and in thus changing the agricultural base of our national economy. But how are the agricultural units to be enlarged? There are two ways of doing this. There is the *capitalist* way, which is to enlarge the agricultural units by introducing capitalism in agriculture — a way which leads to the impoverishment of the peasantry and to the development of capitalist enterprises in agriculture. We reject this way as incompatible with the Soviet economic system. There is a second way: the *Socialist* way, which is to set up collective farms and state farms, the way which leads to the amalgamation of the small peasant farms into large collective farms, technically and scientifically equipped, and to the squeezing out of the capitalist elements from agriculture. We are in favour of this second way.

And so, the question stands as follows: either one way or the other, either *back* — to capitalism or *forward* — to Socialism. There is no third way, nor can there be. The "equilibrium" theory makes an attempt to indicate a third way. And precisely because it is based on a third (non-existent) way, it is Utopian and anti-Marxian. . . .

Now, as you see, we have the material base which enables us to *substitute* for kulak output the output of the collective farms and state farms. That is why our offensive against the kulaks is now meeting with undeniable success. That is how the offensive against the kulaks must be carried on, if we mean a real offensive and not futile declamations against the kulaks.

That is why we have recently passed from the policy of *restricting* the exploiting proclivities of the kulaks to the policy of *eliminating the kulaks as a class.*

Well, what about the policy of expropriating the kulaks? Can we permit the expropriation of kulaks in the regions of solid collectivization? This question is asked in various quarters. A ridiculous question! We could not permit the expropriation of the kulaks as long as we were pursuing the policy of restricting the exploiting proclivities of the kulaks, as long as we were unable to launch a determined offensive against the kulaks, as long as we were unable to substitute for kulak output the output of the collective farms and state farms. At that time the policy of not permitting the expropriation of the kulaks was necessary and correct. But now? Now the situation is different. Now we are able to carry on a determined offensive against the kulaks, to break their resistance, to eliminate them as a class and substitute for their output the output of the collective farms and state farms. Now, the kulaks are being expropriated by the masses of poor and middle peasants themselves, by the masses who are putting solid collectivization into practice. Now, the expropriation of the kulaks in the regions of solid collectivization is no longer just an administrative measure. Now, the expropriation of the kulaks is an integral part of the formation and development of the collective farms. That is why it is ridiculous and fatuous to expatiate today on the expropriation of the kulaks. You do not lament the loss of the hair of one who has been beheaded.

There is another question which seems no less ridiculous: whether the kulak should be permitted to join the collective farms. Of course not, for he is a sworn enemy of the collective-farm movement. Clear, one would think.

Report to the Congress of Soviets, 1936: Soviet Democracy

Joseph Stalin

In 1936 a new constitution for the U.S.S.R. was established. Although in form it was democratic and apparently rather liberal, in fact it did nothing to challenge Stalin's power or the Communist party as the only legitimate political organiza-

SOURCE: James H. Meisel and Edward S. Kozera, eds., *Materials for the Study of the Soviet System* (Ann Arbor, Mich.: The George Wahr Publishing Co., 1950), pp. 236–237. Reprinted by permission of the publisher.

tion. Part of the problem has to do with differing conceptions of the word "democracy." In the following selection from his report to the Extraordinary Eighth Congress of Soviets of the U.S.S.R. in 1936, Stalin defends the constitution, comparing the meanings of "democracy" and "political freedom" in the U.S.S.R. with their significance in other societies.

> **Consider:** *The concerns revealed by this document; why Stalin goes to such pains to justify the new constitution; the legitimacy of the distinction made between democracy in capitalist countries and democracy in the U.S.S.R.*

I must admit that the draft of the new Constitution does preserve the regime of the dictatorship of the working class, just as it also preserves unchanged the present leading position of the Communist Party of the U.S.S.R. [Loud applause.] If the esteemed critics regard this as a flaw in the Draft Constitution, that is only to be regretted. We Bolsheviks regard it as a merit of the draft Constitution. [Loud applause.]

As to freedom for various political parties, we adhere to somewhat different views. A party is a part of a class, its most advanced part. Several parties, and, consequently, freedom for parties, can exist only in a society in which there are antagonistic classes whose interests are mutually hostile and irreconcilable — in which there are, say, capitalists and workers, landlords and peasants, kulaks and poor peasants, etc. But in the U.S.S.R. there are no longer such classes as the capitalists, the landlords, the kulaks, etc. In the U.S.S.R. there are only two classes, workers and peasants, whose interests — far from being mutually hostile — are, on the contrary, friendly. Hence there is no ground in the U.S.S.R. for the existence of several parties, and, consequently, for freedom for these parties. In the U.S.S.R. there is ground only for one party, the Communist Party. In the U.S.S.R. only one party can exist, the Communist Party, which courageously defends the interests of the workers and peasants to the very end. . .

They talk of democracy. But what is democracy? Democracy in capitalist countries, where there are antagonistic classes, is, in the last analysis, democracy for the strong, democracy for the propertied minority. In the U.S.S.R., on the contrary, democracy is democracy for the working people, i.e., democracy for all. But from this it follows that the principles of democratism are violated, not by the draft of the new Constitution of the U.S.S.R., but by the bourgeois constitutions. That is why I think that the Constitution of the U.S.S.R. is the only thoroughly democratic Constitution in the world.

VISUAL SOURCES

Nazi Mythology

Richard Spitz

This is an example of Nazi propaganda art, with its characteristic blend of realistic style and romantic vision. It shows Nazi soldiers and civilian folk marching in brotherly comradeship toward Valhalla, the final resting place of Aryan heroes. Above them, Nazi flags and wounded soldiers are being lifted together toward the same heavens. Stereotypes, rather than distinct individuals, are shown: The soldiers all look almost the same, and on the right there are representatives of civilian youth, middle-aged and elderly people, farmers, and workers. Those being glorified are all males and almost all soldiers. Viewers of this picture are supposed to feel proud, to feel that sacrifices for the state will be rewarded and that the

Photo 13-1

U.S. Army Photo by Garner

greatest glory comes from military service. In subject and style, this picture represents a rejection of the major twentieth-century artistic trends.

Consider: *How this picture fits the image and ideals of nazism as reflected in the documents by Hitler and Goebbels and the statements of the SS officer.*

Socialist Realism

K. I. Finogenov

This example of socialist realism has great similarities to Nazi art: its realistic style, its romantic vision, its propagandistic purpose. In this case, however, the emphasis on economic themes is greater than that on military themes. Painted in 1935 by K. I. Finogenov, it shows Communist party and government leaders, led by Stalin, on a modern Soviet farm. On the right an expert checks the soil. In the background a new tractor is displayed. All the figures are relatively well dressed; no one looks like a peasant farmer.

Consider: *How this picture relates to the role of the government in the Soviet Union and to Stalin's place in it; what insight into the agricultural policy during the 1930s the picture is supposed to convey; how the image presented here fits with Stalin's explanation of collectivization; how this picture compares with that of Joseph II in Chapter 4 (Photo 4-2).*

Photo 13-2

Tass from Sovfoto

Authoritarianism, 1919–1937

This map shows the spread of authoritarian governments in Europe between 1919 and 1937. Although no firm rules apply here, those countries retaining parliamentary democratic forms of government generally had a longer tradition of democratic institutions, were more satisfied winners in World War I, and were located in more advanced industrialized areas in northwestern Europe.

Map 13-1   The Spread of Authoritarian Governments

Parliamentary Democracies

Communist Governments, 1917

Parliamentary Governments that became, at least temporarily, dictatorships or right–wing authoritarian regimes (with dates of change).

Consider: *Taking account of the relevant geography, historical background, and experience of World War I, the commonalities of two or more countries that became dictatorships or changed to right-wing authoritarian regimes.*

SECONDARY SOURCES

Fascism in Western Europe
H. R. Kedward

Both fascism and communism, as they were practiced during the first half of the twentieth century, are traditionally categorized as totalitarian systems. Yet fascism is typically placed on the extreme right of the political spectrum, communism on the extreme left. Indeed, the two usually consider each other archenemies. In the following selection, H. R. Kedward, a British historian at the University of Sussex, takes account of these facts in developing and diagraming a working political definition of fascism.

> **Consider:** *Why the extreme left should be placed next to the extreme right on the political spectrum even though they consider each other enemies; the historical developments that justify using the second diagram for the twentieth century and the first for the nineteenth century; the characteristics of fascism according to Kedward.*

It could be argued that the best way to define fascism is not in a positive but in a negative way, by references to its opposites, but this too presents difficulties. At one time its opposite was naturally assumed to be communism, since fascism was said to be on the extreme Right of politics and communism on the extreme Left. This appeared self-evident when the traditional semicircle of political parties was drawn, i.e.:

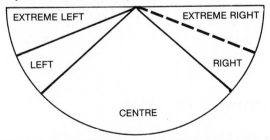

SOURCE: H. R. Kedward, *Fascism in Western Europe: 1900–1945.* Reproduced by kind permission of Blackie and Son Ltd. (Bishopbriggs, Glasgow, 1971), pp. 240–241.

Such a diagram served the political scene of the 19th century when socialism was on the extreme Left and autocratic conservatism on the extreme
Right, but in the 20th century a new diagram is needed in the form of a
circle, i.e.:

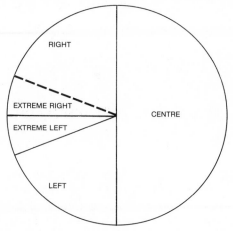

This circular image does greater justice to the realities of 20th-century
politics by recognizing that extreme Left and extreme Right, communism
and fascism, converge at many points and are in some cases indistinguish-
able. Doriot, for example, moved with ease from French communism to his
Fascist P.P.F. without changing his attitudes or methods, and most of the
conclusions on Nazi culture in the last chapter could be applied to Stalinism.
The circle, however, does not minimize the differences which kept the two
systems apart. Travelling the longest route round the circle, it is a very long
way indeed from extreme Left to extreme Right. Thus communism and fascism are as distinct in some respects as they are similar in others.

This was most clearly apparent in the Spanish Civil War. If one looked at
methods, the Communists were as violent, as authoritarian and as tightly
organized as the Fascists; they were both supported by dictators, Stalin on
the one hand and Hitler and Mussolini on the other, and they were both as
intolerant of any deviation from the party line. They were next to each
other on the circle. But if one looked at their history and their ideology the
two had little in common: the Communists stood in the Marxist tradition
and aimed at proletarian revolution, while the Fascists had their national
values and a vision of an organic society. They were quite distinct.

Fascism therefore will only be partly defined by its opposition to communism. It is perhaps more profitable to look for its political opposites
across the circle in the centre, where one finds progressive conservatism,
liberalism and radical individualism. It is at least historically true that in
the countries where these political attitudes were most entrenched — Britain,
France and Belgium — neither fascism nor communism came to power.

Retreat from Totalitarianism

Michael Curtis

In recent years the traditional view of totalitarianism has been called into question. Critics argue that there are such important differences between fascism and communism and between the ideals and policies of various fascist and communist states that it is no longer useful to group all under the single category of "totalitarian." Michael Curtis, professor of political science at Rutgers University, exemplifies this critical approach, emphasizing that while the term totalitarianism may have been useful for some purposes, it now creates more confusion than clarity.

> **Consider:** *How the primary sources support or undermine Curtis' argument; the main distinctions between fascism and communism and whether these distinctions go to the heart of the concept of totalitarianism, making that concept inapplicable to both; whether totalitarianism should be considered only a temporary European development of the 1920s, 1930s, and 1940s.*

Useful as the concept of totalitarianism has been as an explanatory tool for distinguishing political systems, reservations of two kinds are in order. The first is that the concept is only partly applicable to the three countries — Germany, the Soviet Union, and, especially, Italy — out of whose experience the theory was erected, and this has great importance in properly evaluating these countries. The second is that political behavior in the Soviet Union has changed sufficiently to render the concept inadequate. Moreover, the polycentrism of the Communist countries makes a monolithic explanation incorrect. . . .

The totalitarian concept does not sufficiently allow for the enormously different purposes sought by the three ideologies or beliefs, for the different intellectual levels of those beliefs, for the different styles of behavior and symbolic references of the regimes, and for the different groups who supported and benefited by them. Totalitarianism of the left, as Talmon has argued, begins with man, his rationality, and salvation; totalitarianism of the right begins with the collective entity — the state, the nation, or the race.

To offer brief lists of the major characteristics of the belief systems is to illustrate their different purposes. Nazism was characterized by nationalism, racism, emphasis on the *Volk*, anti-Semitism, stress on violence and force, appeal to national unity that would supersede the interests and differences of rank and class. With its rejection of democracy, secularization, rationalism, and positivism, its belief in domestic virtues, its vision of an attractive mythical past and rural harmony, its distaste for industrial civilization and urbanism, nazism was the counterrevolution in action and

SOURCE: Michael Curtis, "Retreat from Totalitarianism," in Carl J. Friedrich, ed., *Totalitarianism in Perspective*. Reprinted by permission of Holt, Rinehart and Wilson (New York, 1969), pp. 63, 109–111, 113. Copyright © 1969 by Holt, Rinehart and Wilson.

ultimately nihilistic in nature. The precapitalist, feudal aspects of nazism are illustrated by the Teutonic imagery, elitist decision-making through the Führer and the Gauleiter appointed by him, the oath of personal loyalty to Hitler, the stress on honor, blood, and soil, the end to the dependence of the German peasant on the market economy. Ernst Nolte has commented that, while Italian fascism recalled a remote but tangible historical era, the Nazis appealed to the prehistoric and the archaic.

The Nazis drew their main strength from the lower-middle class, marginal groups, military desperados, and those who had suffered by greater industrialization. But, uninterested in changing the nature of the social order, the Nazis were prepared to cooperate with those traditional groups such as the military and the bureaucracy that were not regarded as opponents. Though some 40 per cent of the full professors in economics and the social sciences vacated their chairs between 1932 and 1938, many academics, jurists, and even Nobel Prize winners capitulated before the regime. Hitler, in March, 1933, spoke of his regime as "the union between the symbols of the old greatness and the new strength." And the new strength was based on the manipulation of crowds, the display of strength through demonstrations, parades, and mass meetings, the welding of what Hitler, in *Mein Kampf*, called "the enormous human dragon" into a potent political force.

Contrasted with these characteristics are the ends of Marxism: that it seeks a society based on equality and humanitarianism, that it envisages the elimination of political coercion, that it seeks to build a rational social order, an industrialized economy, a higher form of democracy than that existing in the capitalist countries, and that it seeks to create a new type of civilization, internationalist rather than insular and parochial in nature. The traditional social and economic elite groups have no place in such a civilization or new type of society, and a wholly new political instrument is necessary. That the Communist regime distorted these high expectations and ended political liberty is not to deny the loftiness of the ideas.

The differentiation between a counterrevolutionary and a revolutionary purpose is crucial in the evaluation of the Nazi and Communist regimes. The objective of the first remains negative — the downfall of the existing regime — or nebulous, depending on the will of the dictator. The regime is essentially a destructive one in which positive achievement is gratuitous or related only to some destructive function. It is the product of a real dilemma of liberal democracy, a sort of suicidal reaction against a civilization that had failed to provide sufficient emotional satisfaction or material benefits for the mass of the people. In no real way can nazism or fascism be regarded as the continuation or inheritance of the French Revolution. The Nazi movement, as Rauschning wrote, had no fixed aims, either economic or political, either in domestic or foreign affairs. Its strength lay in incessant activity, its Valhalla the lust for power and the quest for adventure.

For Communist countries, the creation of an equalitarian and humane society, while not necessarily observed in practice, is its informing spirit, and action can be related to that fundamental objective. The Russian Revolution began, Deutscher noted, "with the dazzling blaze of a great vision." There is no inherent insistence on violence in the Communist, as in the Nazi or Fascist, system. In the post-Stalin Communist systems, violence is an incidental factor, a means by which to achieve a desired end. But violence was an intrinsic facet of Nazi or Fascist behavior, unrelated to rational purpose. In Italy, the aggressive defenders of "law and order in the streets" and the strikebreakers became the *squadrista*. For Hitler, "force was the first law" and war, the normal condition of mankind. The means as well as the ends of the regimes were different in theory. The Nazi and Fascist regimes saw themselves as perpetual dictatorships from the beginning. The Bolsheviks took power on behalf of the Soviet of Workers' and Soldiers' Deputies, and the dictatorship of the proletariat has always been regarded as a transitional stage toward a free society. . . .

Totalitarianism, after all, has no ontological or essentialist element about it.

Escape from Freedom

Erich Fromm

Many people find that traditional historical categories are inadequate for a deep understanding of nazism. Thus more than most historical developments, nazism has been open to investigation from a psychosocial perspective. One of the earliest to do this was Erich Fromm (1900–1980), a leading German-American psychoanalyst whose classic Escape from Freedom *was first published in 1941. In the following selection from that book, Fromm makes a psychosocial interpretation of nazism, taking care to place this interpretation in a historical context.*

> **Consider:** *How Fromm explains the passive acceptance of the nazi regime by one part of the population and the active support of the Nazis by another part of the population; the main distinctions between the political perspective of fascism, according to Kedward, and the psychosocial perspective, according to Fromm.*

In discussing the psychology of Nazism we have first to consider a preliminary question — the relevance of psychological factors in the understanding of Nazism. In the scientific and still more so in the popular discussion of Nazism, two opposite views are frequently presented: the first, that psychology offers no explanation of an economic and political phenomenon like Fascism, the second, that Fascism is wholly a psychological problem.

SOURCE: Erich Fromm, *Escape from Freedom* (New York: Holt, Rinehart and Winston, 1941), pp. 207–212.

The first view looks upon Nazism either as the outcome of an exclusively economic dynamism — of the expansive tendencies of German imperialism, or as an essentially political phenomenon — the conquest of the state by one political party backed by industrialists and Junkers; in short, the victory of Nazism is looked upon as the result of a minority's trickery and coercion of the majority of the population.

The second view, on the other hand, maintains that Nazism can be explained only in terms of psychology, or rather in those of psychopathology. Hitler is looked upon as a madman or as a "neurotic," and his followers as equally mad and mentally unbalanced. According to this explanation, as expounded by L. Mumford, the true sources of Fascism are to be found "in the human soul, *not in economics*." He goes on: "In overwhelming pride, delight in cruelty, neurotic disintegration — in this and not in the Treaty of Versailles or in the incompetence of the German Republic lies the explanation of Fascism."

In our opinion none of these explanations which emphasize political and economic factors to the exclusion of psychological ones — or vice versa — is correct. Nazism is a psychological problem, but the psychological factors themselves have to be understood as being molded by socioeconomic factors; Nazism is an economic and political problem, but the hold it has over a whole people has to be understood on psychological grounds. What we are concerned with in this chapter is the psychological aspect of Nazism, its human basis. This suggests two problems: the character structure of those people to whom it appealed, and the psychological characteristics of the ideology that made it such an effective instrument with regard to those very people.

In considering the psychological basis for the success of Nazism this differentiation has to be made at the outset: one part of the population bowed to the Nazi regime without any strong resistance, but also without becoming admirers of the Nazi ideology and political practice. Another part was deeply attracted to the new ideology and fanatically attached to those who proclaimed it. The first group consisted mainly of the working class and the liberal and Catholic bourgeoisie. In spite of an excellent organization, especially among the working class, these groups, although continuously hostile to Nazism from its beginning up to 1933, did not show the inner resistance one might have expected as the outcome of their political convictions. Their will to resist collapsed quickly and since then they have caused little difficulty for the regime (excepting, of course, the small minority which has fought heroically against Nazism during all these years). Psychologically, this readiness to submit to the Nazi regime seems to be due mainly to a state of inner tiredness and resignation, which, as will be indicated in the next chapter, is characteristic of the individual in the present era even in democratic countries. In Germany one additional condition was present as far as the working class was concerned: the defeat it suffered after the first victories in the revolution of 1918. The working class had entered the postwar period with strong hopes for the realization of socialism or at least a definite rise in its political, economic, and social position; but, whatever the reasons, it had witnessed an unbroken succession of defeats, which brought about the complete disappointments of all its hopes. By the beginning of 1930 the fruits of its initial victories were almost completely destroyed and the result was a deep feeling of resignation, of disbelief in their leaders, of doubt about the value of any kind of political organization and political activity. They still remained members of their respective parties and, consciously, continued to believe in their political doctrines; but deep within themselves many had given up any hope in the effectiveness of political action.

An additional incentive for the loyalty of the majority of the population to the Nazi government became effective after Hitler came into power. For millions of people Hitler's government then became identical with "Germany." Once he held the power of government, fighting him implied shutting oneself out of the community of Germans; when other political parties were abolished and the Nazi party "was" Germany, opposition to it meant opposition to Germany. It seems that nothing is more difficult for the average man to bear than the feeling of not being identified with a larger group. However much a German citizen may be opposed to the principles of Nazism, if he has to choose between being alone and feeling that he belongs to Germany, most persons will choose the latter. It can be observed in many instances that persons who are not Nazis nevertheless defend Nazism against criticism of foreigners because they feel that an attack on Nazism is an attack on Germany. The fear of isolation and the relative weakness of moral principles help any party to win the loyalty of a large sector of the population once that party has captured the power of the state.

In contrast to the negative or resigned attitude of the working class and of the liberal and Catholic bourgeoisie, the Nazi ideology was ardently greeted by the lower strata of the middle class, composed of small shopkeepers, artisans, and white-collar workers.

Members of the older generation among this class formed the more passive mass basis; their sons and daughters were the more active fighters. For them the Nazi ideology — its spirit of blind obedience to a leader and of hatred against racial and political minorities, its craving for conquest and domination, its exaltation of the German people and the "Nordic Race" — had a tremendous emotional appeal, and it was this appeal which won them over and made them into ardent believers in and fighters for the Nazi cause. The answer to the question why the Nazi ideology was so appealing to the lower middle class has to be sought for in the social character of the lower middle class. Their social character was markedly different from that of the working class, of the higher strata of the middle class, and of the nobility before the war of 1914. As a matter of fact, certain features were characteristic for this part of the middle class throughout its history: their love of the strong, hatred of the weak, their pettiness, hostility, thriftiness with feelings as well as with money, and essentially their asceticism. Their outlook on life was narrow, they suspected and hated the stranger, and they were curious and envious of their acquaintances, rationalizing their envy as moral indignation; their whole life was based on the principle of scarcity — economically as well as psychologically.

Hitler: A Study in Tyranny

Alan Bullock

It is difficult to analyze nazism without focusing on its leader, Adolf Hitler. The close connection between nazism and Hitler raises two questions of particular importance for historians. First, what was the role of the individual in shaping history, here of Hitler in shaping German nazism? Second, to what extent were Hitler and nazism uniquely German developments related to particular characteristics of Germany's past? Alan Bullock, a British historian and author of what has long been considered the most authoritative biography of Hitler, addresses these issues in the following selection from his Hitler: A Study in Tyranny.

> **Consider:** *Whether Hitler should be viewed as an extreme of a broader historical trend affecting not only Germany but Europe as a whole during the 1920s and 1930s; how someone taking a more psychological approach might argue with Bullock's interpretation of Hitler and nazism; how this approach fits with that of Kedward.*

Many attempts have been made to explain away the importance of Hitler, from Chaplin's brilliant caricature in *The Great Dictator* to the much less convincing picture of Hitler the pawn, a front man for German capitalism. Others have argued that Hitler was nothing in himself, only a symbol of the restless ambition of the German nation to dominate Europe; a creature flung to the top by the tides of revolutionary change, or the embodiment of the collective unconscious of a people obsessed with violence and death.

These arguments seem to me to be based upon a confusion of two different questions. Obviously, Nazism was a complex phenomenon to which many factors — social, economic, historical, psychological — contributed. But whatever the explanation of this episode in European history — and it can be no simple one — that does not answer the question with which this book has been concerned, what was the part played by Hitler. It may be true that a mass movement, strongly nationalist, anti-Semitic, and radical, would have sprung up in Germany without Hitler. But so far as what actually happened is concerned — not what might have happened — the evidence seems to me to

SOURCE: Alan Bullock, *Hitler: A Study in Tyranny* (New York: Harper & Row; London: Odhams Press, Ltd.), pp. 805, 807–808. Copyright © 1962 by Alan Bullock.

leave no doubt that no other man played a role in the Nazi revolution or in the history of the Third Reich remotely comparable with that of Adolf Hitler.

The conception of the Nazi Party, the propaganda with which it must appeal to the German people, and the tactics by which it would come to power — these were unquestionably Hitler's. After 1934 there were no rivals left and by 1938 he had removed the last checks on his freedom of action. Thereafter, he exercised an arbitrary rule in Germany to a degree rarely, if ever, equalled in a modern industrialized state.

At the same time, from the re-militarization of the Rhineland to the invasion of Russia, he won a series of successes in diplomacy and war which established an hegemony over the continent of Europe comparable with that of Napoleon at the height of his fame. While these could not have been won without a people and an Army willing to serve him, it was Hitler who provided the indispensable leadership, the flair for grasping opportunities, the boldness in using them. . . .

The view has often been expressed that Hitler could only have come to power in Germany, and it is true — without falling into the same error of racialism as the Nazis — that there were certain features of German historical development, quite apart from the effects of the Defeat and the Depression, which favoured the rise of such a movement.

This is not to accuse the Germans of Original Sin, or to ignore the other sides of German life which were only grossly caricatured by the Nazis. But Nazism was not some terrible accident which fell upon the German people out of a blue sky. It was rooted in their history, and while it is true that a majority of the German people never voted for Hitler, it is also true that thirteen million did. Both facts need to be remembered.

From this point of view Hitler's career may be described as a *reductio ad absurdum* of the most powerful political tradition in Germany since the Unification. This is what nationalism, militarism, authoritarianism, the worship of success and force, the exaltation of the State, and *Realpolitik* lead to, if they are projected to their logical conclusion. . . .

Hitler, indeed, was a European, no less than a German phenomenon. The conditions and the state of mind which he exploited, the *malaise* of which he was the symptom, were not confined to one country, although they were more strongly marked in Germany than anywhere else. Hitler's idiom was German, but the thoughts and emotions to which he gave expression have a more universal currency.

Hitler recognized this relationship with Europe perfectly clearly. He was in revolt against 'the System' not just in Germany but in Europe, against the liberal bourgeois order, symbolized for him in the Vienna which had once rejected him. To destroy this was his mission, the mission in which he never ceased to believe; and in this, the most deeply felt of his purposes, he did not fail.

Revolutionary and Soviet Russia: Stalin's Purges

E. H. Carr

In 1934 a colleague of Stalin was assassinated by a member of the Communist party. Shortly afterward, Stalin initiated mass purges of the Communist party. By 1939, when the purges had ended, vast numbers of people had been executed or imprisoned. Analysts have tried to explain these purges in a variety of ways. In the following selection, E. H. Carr, author of an authoritative, sympathetic multivolume history of Soviet Russia, interprets the causes of the purges, arguing that they were a logical extension of the revolution initiated in 1917.

> **Consider:** *In what ways this interpretation is consistent with the evidence provided in the two documents by Stalin; whether purges, or their like, are an inherent or predictable characteristic of any totalitarian regime; the differences between Stalin's purges and Hitler's efforts to exterminate the Jews.*

First, the purges represented a national backlash against the international aspects of the revolution. Stalin had proclaimed the national goal of "socialism in one country." Alone among the early Bolshevik leaders, he had never lived in western Europe and spoke no Western language. He was notoriously contemptuous of the Communist International and of the prospects of revolution outside the Soviet Union. The victims of the purges included almost everyone associated with the international ideals and aims of the revolution, as well as nearly all the foreign Communists living in Moscow. It is a sobering reflection that, in the party struggles of the 1920's, nearly all the Western observers who understood anything of what was going on favored Stalin as a "safe" man against the hot-headed Trotsky and Zinoviev. Stalin, they felt, would never give the capitalist world any trouble! Trotsky said once that Stalin stood for the primitive, national Russian element in Bolshevism; and if you add that this included a streak of primitive cruelty which Russian backwardness had not yet outgrown, it would, I think, be a fair comment.

Second, the purges represented the conservative reaction which sets in at the second stage of any revolution — the desire to consolidate its achievements, to stabilize and to halt it. The picture here is rather complicated. In everything that pertained to the material power, efficiency, and prosperity of the country, and especially in the intensified drive for industrialization,

SOURCE: Norman F. Cantor, *Perspectives on the European Past*, Vol. I. Reprinted by permission of Macmillan Publishing Co., Inc., pp. 298–299. Copyright © 1971 Macmillan Publishing Co., Inc.

Stalin carried on the revolutionary momentum with enormous vigor. But politically and ideologically, he was a conservative. He wanted no new revolutionary ideas, no innovations, to disturb the solid framework of order and conformity. Emphasis was laid on legality. Old forms and old names — the Council of Ministers, for example — replaced the revolutionary creations. The word *Bolshevik*, suggesting the turbulence of the revolutionary epoch, fell out of favor. The purges exterminated potential troublemakers and disturbers of the peace, old Bolsheviks, people who still dreamed of completing the unfinished work of the revolution. It was the Communists who provided most of the victims. In this aspect the purges resembled a White terror more than a Red terror.

Third — and this is another aspect of the same phenomenon — the purges were the reaction of the hard-headed, practical man of affairs against the utopian intellectual, the man of theory. There may be a personal element here; perhaps Stalin took a malign pleasure in sending to the firing squad the very people who had once despised him for his intellectual deficiencies, his lack of culture, his poor grasp of Marxist principles. Certainly there was no place for independent intellectuals under Stalin, for men who dreamed dreams and nourished revolutionary ideals or split hairs over what Marx or Lenin really intended. Ideological conformity was the counterpart of political and social order, and those who indulged in dangerous thoughts were easy victims of the purges.

The real historical significance of the purges seems to me that they were intended to mark — and did mark — the terminal point of the revolution.

Chapter Questions

1. In light of the evidence and interpretations presented in this chapter about the nature of totalitarianism, how would you explain its appeal or relative success in the twentieth century? In what ways should Italian fascism, German nazism, and Russian communism be distinguished here?

2. Considering some of the theories and practices of totalitarian governments during the 1920s, 1930s, and 1940s, would you conclude that totalitarianism almost inevitably leads to violence and war, or rather that it happens to involve violence and war because of particular historical circumstances of the times? In this respect, should fascism be distinguished from communism? Why or why not?

3. In what ways do Italian fascism and German nazism differ in theory and practice from liberal democracy? In what ways does Russian communism differ from both?

CHAPTER FOURTEEN

World War II and the Postwar World

World War II broke out in 1939 and was even more destructive than World War I. In 1945 Europe emerged from the war facing an overwhelming task of recovery. She had lost her position of dominance in the world, reflected in the successful independence movement among her colonies and the rise of the two new superpowers: the United States and the Soviet Union. Nevertheless, by the early 1960s, Europe had greatly recovered from the war and was enjoying considerable prosperity.

This chapter deals with six developments between 1939 and the early 1960s. First, almost all of Western civilization became embroiled in the war that broke out in 1939 and that did not end until two atomic bombs were dropped on Japan in 1945. What were the origins of World War II? What connections between Hitler, nazism, and appeasement might have led to the outbreak of the war in 1939? How can some of the destruction of the war be explained?

Second, by 1947 the growing hostility between the United States and the Soviet Union became formalized in speeches, policies, and alliances, resulting in a division between Eastern and Western Europe and more broadly between communist and noncommunist countries throughout the world: The Cold War had broken out. The Cold War remains a controversial issue among American historians as well as between Western and Soviet scholars. Why did it occur? What policies characterized the Cold War? How does the Soviet view of the Cold War differ from the American view?

Third, in the 1940s and 1950s there was a growing movement toward regional integration. This was stimulated in part by Cold War alliances and divisions. Specifically, Western European countries made a number of economic steps toward integration, above all through the formation of the Common Market in the 1950s. This trend toward European integration was of great potential significance. But to what extent was it more promise than performance? What concrete developments have occurred that allow us to say that European integration has in fact been taking place?

Fourth, Europe recovered from World War II more rapidly than expected. By the 1950s most countries were back on their feet, thanks in part to aid from the superpowers. By the early 1960s Western Europe was enjoying unprecedented prosperity and relative political and social stability. What

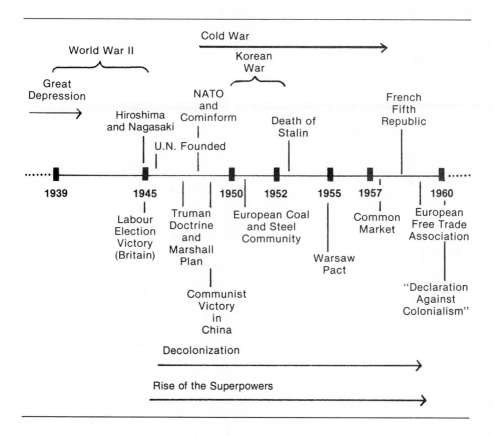

were some of the political and social changes that occurred in this process of recovery? How are they exemplified by the establishment of a Labor government in Britain in 1945?

Fifth, nuclear weapons spread with unexpected rapidity. The potential of nuclear weapons was demonstrated in the final days of the war with Japan. The proliferation of nuclear arms in the 1950s and 1960s seemed to threaten civilization. How have nuclear weapons affected people? What has been the nature of the debate over nuclear weapons? What role could the United Nations play in international disputes that might lead to nuclear war?

Sixth, European powers were unable to hold on to all their colonies in the two decades following the war. What were some of the arguments made and the strategies used in the struggle over decolonization? What role did the United Nations play in this struggle?

While these developments have undergone some modification in the last twenty years, they remain part of the present along with other trends that will be examined in the next chapter.

PRIMARY SOURCES

The Truman Doctrine and the Marshall Plan

During World War II the Soviet Union and the United States were allied against their common enemies, the Axis powers. Shortly after the end of the war, animosity began to reappear between the former allies. By 1947 that animosity had risen to the point where it was formalized in government programs and international policies; the "Cold War" had broken out. In the United States this was most clearly announced in two policy decisions excerpted here. The first is a speech delivered by President Truman on March 12, 1947, to Congress, concerning proposed aid to Greece and Turkey, which appeared in danger of falling under the influence of the Soviet Union. The principles contained in this speech became known as the Truman Doctrine. The second is a statement made by Secretary of State George C. Marshall on November 10, 1947, to Senate and House Committees on Foreign Relations, proposing massive aid to Europe. This proposal became known as the Marshall Plan.

Source: U.S. Congress, *Congressional Record*, 80th Congress, 1st Session (Washington, D.C.: U.S. Government Printing Office, 1947), Vol. 93, p. 1981.

Source: U.S. Congress, Senate Committee on Foreign Relations, *A Decade of American Foreign Policy: Basic Documents, 1941–1949* (Washington, D.C.: U.S. Government Printing Office, 1950), pp. 1270–1271.

Consider: The American perception of the Soviet Union and its allies; the purposes of this foreign policy; how the Soviet Union would probably perceive and react to this foreign policy.

The peoples of a number of countries of the world have recently had totalitarian regimes forced upon them against their will. The Government of the United States has made frequent protests against coercion and intimidation, in violation of the Yalta agreement, in Poland, Rumania, and Bulgaria. I must also state that in a number of other countries there have been similar developments.

At the present moment in world history nearly every nation must choose between alternative ways of life. The choice is too often not a free one.

One way of life is based upon the will of the majority, and is distinguished by free institutions, representative government, free elections, guaranties of individual liberty, freedom of speech and religion, and freedom from political oppression.

The second way of life is based upon the will of a minority forcibly imposed upon the majority. It relies upon terror and oppression, a controlled press and radio, fixed elections, and the suppression of personal freedoms.

I believe that it must be the policy of the United States to support free peoples who are resisting attempted subjugation by armed minorities or by outside pressures.

I believe that we must assist free peoples to work out their own destinies in their own way.

I believe that our help should be primarily through economic and financial aid, which is essential to economic stability and orderly political processes.

As a result of the war, the European community which for centuries had been one of the most productive and indeed creative portions of the inhabited world was left prostrate. This area, despite its diversity of national cultures and its series of internecine conflicts and wars, nonetheless enjoys a common heritage and a common civilization.

The war ended with the armies of the major Allies meeting in the heart of this community. The policies of three of them have been directed to the restoration of that European community. It is now clear that only one power, the Soviet Union, does not for its own reasons share this aim.

We have become involved in two wars which have had their origins in the European continent. The free peoples of Europe have fought two wars to prevent the forcible domination of their community by a single great power. Such domination would have inevitably menaced the stability and security of the world. To deny today our interest in their ability to defend their own heritage would be to disclaim the efforts and sacrifices of two generations of Americans. We wish to see this community restored as one of the pillars of world security; in a position to renew its contribution to the advancement of mankind and to the development of a world order based on law and respect for the individual.

The record of the endeavors of the United States Government to bring about a restoration of the whole of that European community is clear for all who wish to see. We must face the fact, however, that despite our efforts, not all of the European nations have been left free to take their place in the community of which they form a natural part.

Thus the geographic scope of our recovery program is limited to those nations which are free to act in accordance with their national traditions and their own estimates of their national interests. If there is any doubt as to this situation, a glance at the present map of the European continent will provide the answer.

The present line of division in Europe is roughly the line upon which the Anglo-American armies coming from the west met those of the Soviet Union coming from the east. To the west of that line the nations of the continental European community have been grappling with the vast and difficult problem resulting from the war in conformity with their own national traditions without pressure or menace from the United States or Great Britain. Developments in the European countries to the east of that line bear the unmistakable imprint of an alien hand.

British Labor's Rise to Power

Harry Laidler

During World War II, governments became involved in social and economic activities to an unprecedented degree. Although with the end of the war, this changed to some degree, there was still significant acceptance of government involvement in society. In Great Britain this was combined with an increasing acceptance of the Labor party, whose strength had been growing since the end of World War I. In the elections of 1945, this party, made up of a combination of Socialist and trade-union groups, gained a majority and took office, replacing the Conservatives led by Winston Churchill. The new government initiated policies that substantially changed the relationship between the government and the people during the period following World War II. Excerpts from the Labor party platform set forth shortly before the 1945 elections are presented here.

Consider: *The ways in which this platform constituted a major assault on capitalism and "laissez-faire;" how this platform might reflect the experience of*

Source: Harry W. Laidler, "British Labor's Rise to Power," in *League for Industrial Democracy Pamphlet Series* (New York: League for Industrial Democracy, 1945), pp. 24–25. Reprinted by permission of the publisher.

*the Great Depression and the world wars; how a Conservative might argue
against this platform.*

The Labor party is a socialist party, and proud of it. Its ultimate purpose at
home is the establishment of the socialist commonwealth of Great Britain —
free, democratic, efficient, progressive, public-spirited, its material resources
organized in the service of the British people.

But socialism cannot come overnight, as the product of a week-end
revolution. The members of the Labor party, like the British people, are
practical-minded men and women.

There are basic industries ripe and over-ripe for public ownership and
management in the direct service of the nation. There are many smaller
businesses rendering good service which can be left to go on with their
useful work.

There are big industries not yet ripe for public ownership which must
nevertheless be required by constructive supervision to further the nation's
needs and not to prejudice national interests by restrictive anti-social
monopoly or cartel agreements — caring for their own capital structures
and profits at the cost of a lower standard of living for all.

In the light of these considerations, the Labor party submits to the nation
the following industrial program:

1. *Public Ownership of the Fuel and Power Industries* — For a quarter
   of a century the coal industry, producing Britain's most precious national raw material, has been floundering chaotically under the ownership of many hundreds of independent companies. Amalgamation under
   public ownership will bring great economies in operation and make it
   possible to modernize production methods and to raise safety standards
   in every colliery in the country. Public ownership of gas and electricity
   undertakings will lower charges, prevent competitive waste, open the
   way for co-ordinated research and development, and lead to the reforming of uneconomic areas of distribution. Other industries will benefit.
2. *Public Ownership of Inland Transport.* Co-ordination of transport
   services by rail, road, air and canal cannot be achieved without
   unification. And unification without public ownership means a steady
   struggle with sectional interests or the entrenchment of a private
   monopoly, which would be a menace to the rest of industry.
3. *Public Ownership of Iron and Steel.* Private monopoly has maintained high prices and kept inefficient high-cost plants in existence.
   Only if public ownership replaces private monopoly can the industry
   become efficient.

   These socialized industries, taken over on a basis of fair compensation, to be conducted efficiently in the interests of consumers, coupled
   with proper status and conditions for the workers employed in them.

4. *Public Supervision of Monopolies and Cartels* with the aim of advancing industrial efficiency in the service of the nation. Anti-social restrictive practices will be prohibited.

5. *A First and Clear-cut Program for the Export Trade.* We would give State help in any necessary form to get our export trade on its feet and enable it to pay for the food and raw materials without which Britain must decay and die. But State help on conditions — conditions that industry is efficient and go-ahead. Laggards and obstructionists must be led or directed into a better way. Here we dare not fail.

6. *The Shaping of Suitable Economic and Price Controls* to secure that first things shall come first in the transition from war to peace and that every citizen (including the demobilized Service men and women) shall get fair play. There must be priorities in the use of raw materials, food prices must be held, homes for the people must come before mansions, necessities for all before luxuries for the few. We do not want a short boom followed by collapse as after the last war; we do not want a wild rise in prices and inflation, followed by a smash and widespread unemployment. It is either sound economic controls — or smash.

7. *The Better Organization of Government Departments* and the Civil Service for work in relation to these ends. The economic purpose of government must be to spur industry forward and not to choke it with red tape.

The Fearful Choice:
Nuclear Weapons

Philip Toynbee

The intensity of the Cold War and the existence of nuclear weapons on both sides created a tense atmosphere in the West during the 1950s and early 1960s. This atmosphere was reflected in the construction of public and private survival shelters against nuclear attack. It was also reflected in debates over the effectiveness of nuclear weapons to deter the opposing side from attack, the possibility of bilateral disarmament, and the necessity for unilateral destruction of nuclear weapons. In the following selection from a 1956 debate, Philip Toynbee of Great Britain argued for the last position.

> **Consider:** *How Toynbee justifies a policy of unilateral nuclear disarmament; how one might respond to this argument; how the attitude expressed here relates to attitudes expressed by Truman and Marshall.*

SOURCE: Philip Toynbee, *The Fearful Choice* (London: Victor Gollancz, Ltd., 1956), pp. 21–22. Reprinted by permission of the publisher.

It is obvious, surely, that this is an issue which has nothing whatever to do
with party politics and nothing whatever to do with our estimations of
American and Russian society. In the terrible context of nuclear war even
the vital differences between Communism and Western freedom become
almost unimportant. We would infinitely prefer our Western system of
freedom and privacy to prevail in the world; and if we are spared we shall
have an opportunity of trying to ensure that it does so. But even if it didn't
prevail *mankind* would still be given the opportunity of prevailing. Mr.
Kennan has said that anything would be better than a policy which led inevitably to nuclear war. But surely anything is better than a policy which
allows for the *possibility* of nuclear war.

The issue has nothing to do with politics. It has little to do with causes
and highmindedness. Those who have had at least a partial vision of our
destruction are like people who have leant out of the window of an express
train and seen that a bridge is down a little further along the line. They are
urging the driver and their fellow-passengers that the train should be stopped.
But the others reply, many of them from behind their newspapers, that the
train can't possibly be stopped because they have important engagements in
the city. As for the bridge, it may not be down after all, and even if it is the
train will probably manage to jump across it somehow. Besides, it does no
good to the reputation of our railways if express trains are to be halted in
this way. And finally, we ought surely to be aware that there is another express train coming in the opposite direction which will certainly fall down
into the river just as soon as we do.

At the very least, then, let those who wish to continue with the arms-race
be prepared with competent methods of killing off their mutilated families
before killing their mutilated selves. Only when we see that they have made
these preparations shall we be able to believe that they have faced the implications of their policy.

Declaration Against Colonialism

The General Assembly of the United Nations

*Most colonized peoples gained their independence from Western powers during the
twenty years that followed World War II. This reflected both the weakness of
Europe after the war and the strength of anti-imperialist sentiments around the
world. Yet the process of decolonization was difficult in itself and was complicated*

SOURCE: General Assembly of the United Nations, "Declaration Against Colonialism," *Official
Records of the General Assembly*, Fifteenth Session, Resolution 1514, December 14, 1960.

by the ideological differences that divided nations. In 1960, after a bitter debate, the United Nations adopted the following "Declaration Against Colonialism." Although no nation voted against the resolution, Australia, Belgium, the Dominican Republic, France, Great Britain, Portugal, South Africa, Spain, and the United States abstained.

> **Consider:** *Possible reasons why these nations abstained; justifications used by nations for not giving up their colonial possessions; what this declaration reveals about the strengths and weaknesses of the United Nations.*

The General Assembly.

"*Mindful* of the determination proclaimed by the peoples of the world in the Charter of the United Nations to reaffirm faith in fundamental human rights, in the dignity and worth of the human person, in the equal rights of men and women and of nations large and small and to promote social progress and better standards of life in larger freedom,

Conscious of the need for the creation of conditions of stability and well-being and peaceful and friendly relations based on respect for the principles of equal rights and self-determination of all peoples, and of universal respect for, and observance of, human rights and fundamental freedoms for all without distinction as to race, sex, language or religion,

Recognizing the passionate yearning for freedom in all dependent peoples and the decisive role of such peoples in the attainment of their independence,

Aware of the increasing conflicts resulting from the denial of or impediments in the way of the freedom of such peoples, which constitute a serious threat to world peace,

Considering the important role of the United Nations in assisting the movement for independence in Trust and Non-Self-Governing Territories,

Recognizing that the people of the world ardently desire the end of colonialism in all its manifestations,

Convinced that the continued existence of colonialism prevents the development of international economic co-operation, impedes the social, cultural and economic development of dependent peoples and militates against the United Nations ideal of universal peace,

Affirming that peoples may, for their own ends, freely dispose of their natural wealth and resources without prejudice to any obligations arising out of international economic co-operation, based upon the principle of mutual benefit, and the international law,

Believing that the process of liberation is irresistible and irreversible and that, in order to avoid serious crises, an end must be put to colonialism and all practices of segregation and discrimination associated therewith,

Welcoming the emergence in recent years of a large number of dependent territories into freedom and independence, and recognizing the increasingly powerful trends towards freedom in such territories which have not yet attained independence,

Convinced that all peoples have an inalienable right to complete freedom, the exercise of their sovereignty and the integrity of their national territory,

Solemnly proclaims the necessity of bringing to a speedy and unconditional end colonialism in all its forms and manifestations;

And to this end

Declares that:

1. The subjection of peoples to alien subjugation, domination and exploitation constitutes a denial of fundamental human rights, is contrary to the Charter of the United Nations and is an impediment to the promotion of world peace and co-operation.
2. All peoples have the right to self-determination; by virtue of that right they freely determine their political status and freely pursue their economic, social and cultural development.
3. Inadequacy of political, economic, social or educational preparedness should never serve as a pretext for delaying independence.
4. All armed action or repressive measures of all kinds directed against dependent peoples shall cease in order to enable them to exercise peacefully and freely their right to complete independence, and the integrity of their national territory shall be respected.
5. Immediate steps shall be taken, in Trust and Non-Self-Governing Territories or all other territories which have not yet attained independence, to transfer all powers to the peoples of those territories, without any conditions or reservations, in accordance with their freely expressed will and desire, without any distinction as to race, creed or color, in order to enable them to enjoy complete independence and freedom.
6. Any attempt aimed at the partial or total disruption of the national unity and the territorial integrity of a country is incompatible with the purposes and principles of the Charter of the United Nations.
7. All States shall observe faithfully and strictly the provisions of the Charter of the United Nations, the Universal Declaration of Human Rights and the present Declaration on the basis of equality, non-interference in the internal affairs of all States, and respect for the sovereign rights of all peoples and their territorial integrity.

VISUAL SOURCES

The Atomic Bomb

World War II was a turning point in many ways, perhaps most obviously in the nature of weaponry available to human beings engaged in war. In the final stages of World War II efforts to develop atomic weapons came to fruition with the creation of the atomic bomb. This United States Air Force photo shows the atomic bomb exploding over Nagasaki, Japan, on August 9, 1945. This was three days after the first atomic bomb was dropped on Hiroshima. Within a few days Japan surrendered, ending the war. In the decades since 1945 the mushroom-shaped cloud has come to symbolize several things besides the end of World War II: deterrence by nuclear terror; World War III; inhumanity; power out of control; the death of the earth.

> **Consider:** *Your associations to this photo; what other associations people might have; how these associations relate to developments since World War II.*

Photo 14-1

National Archives, U.S. Office of War Information

The Destruction of Europe

This map shows the destruction inflicted on Dresden in the Anglo-American bomb-ing raid of February 13–14, 1945, during the last stages of World War II. As in other "area bombings" made by Allied forces during the war, thousands of civilians were killed in this raid. This shows the blurring of civilian and military targets and the growing use of terror in modern warfare. Military targets such as factories, railway bridges, railway marshaling yards, main railway lines, troop bunkers and barracks, arsenals, and command headquarters were for the most part not signifi-cantly damaged. Instead, the destruction was concentrated on the heavily populated inner city, which was almost completely leveled by fires from incendiary bombing.

Consider: *The possible explanations for this raid and its effects; how warfare conducted in this manner seems to contradict the classic ideals of Western civilization concerning the value of the individual and individual rights.*

Map 14-1   Dresden, 1945

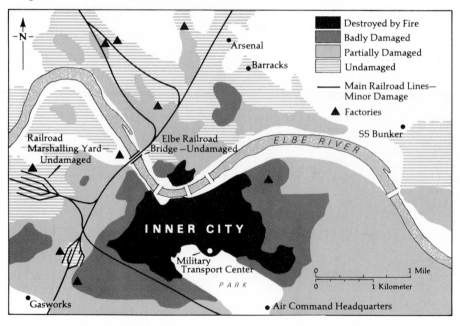

The Cold War and European Integration

This map gives some idea of the movements toward the Cold War and toward European integration in the decades following World War II. Militarily, West and East divided into NATO, led by the United States, and the Warsaw Pact Organization, led by the U.S.S.R. Economically, Western European nations became increasingly tied together through organizations such as the Benelux Customs Union, the European Coal and Steel Community, the European Economic Community (Common Market), and the European Free Trade Association; the East joined in the Council for Mutual Economic Assistance (Conecon). Although military cooperation and economic cooperation were not always linked together, such linkage often did take place.

Consider: *The geographic logic, if any, of the political and economic decisions that were made by the various countries; how maps of the world indicating regional economic cooperation, military alliances, political upheavals, and international "hotspots" might show the extent and intensity of the Cold War and regional cooperation even more fully than this map of Europe.*

Map 14-2   The Economic and Military Division of Europe

SECONDARY SOURCES

Appeasement at Munich Attacked

George F. Kennan

The traditional view in the debate over who was responsible for the outbreak of World War II is that Hitler was emboldened by the unnecessarily weak policy of appeasement pursued by the Western democracies during the 1930s. One element of this appeasement was the Munich Conference of 1938 at which England and France agreed to the dismemberment of Czechoslovakia in return for Hitler's promise to demand no further territories. In the following selection, George F. Kennan, former U.S. ambassador to the Soviet Union and Pulitzer Prize winner for a two-volume work on Soviet-American relations, presents the traditional view of appeasement.

> **Consider:** *From the point of view of the French and British statesmen actually participating in the Munich Conference of 1938, whether Kennan's criticism is justified; the implications of the argument about the causes of or blame for World War II.*

The Munich agreement was a tragically misconceived and desperate act of appeasement at the cost of the Czechoslovak state, performed by Chamberlain and the French premier, Daladier, in the vain hope that it would satisfy Hitler's stormy ambition, and thus secure for Europe a peaceful future. We know today that it was unnecessary — unnecessary because the Czech defenses were very strong, and had the Czechs decided to fight they could have put up considerable resistance; even more unnecessary because the German generals, conscious of Germany's relative weakness at that moment, were actually prepared to attempt the removal of Hitler then and there, had he persisted in driving things to the point of war. It was the fact that the Western powers and the Czechoslovak government did yield at the last moment, and that Hitler once again achieved a bloodless triumph, which deprived the generals of any excuse for such a move. One sees again, as so often in the record of history, that it sometimes pays to stand up manfully to one's problems, even when no certain victory is in sight.

Source: George F. Kennan, *Russia and the West Under Lenin and Stalin* (Boston: Atlantic — Little, Brown, 1961), p. 322. Reprinted by permission of Little, Brown and Company.

The Origins of the Second World War: Appeasement Defended

A. J. P. Taylor

The traditional view attacking appeasement as unjustified and a major cause of World War II has been questioned from different perspectives. Perhaps the most controversial perspective comes from A. J. P. Taylor, a popular outspoken British historian who has written extensively on modern European history. In the following selection from The Origins of the Second World War, *Taylor argues that the appeasers have been unfairly faulted for their policies.*

> **Consider:** *The ways that Taylor and Kennan would disagree about the legitimacy of appeasement rather than the facts of appeasement; the implications of Taylor's argument about the causes of or blame for World War II; the advantages and dangers of looking at appeasement in the 1930s as a historical lesson to be learned for dealing with more recent circumstances.*

He got as far as he did because others did not know what to do with him. Here again I want to understand the "appeasers", not to vindicate or to condemn them. Historians do a bad day's work when they write the appeasers off as stupid or as cowards. They were men confronted with real problems, doing their best in the circumstances of their time. They recognised that an independent and powerful Germany had somehow to be fitted into Europe. Later experience suggests that they were right. At any rate, we are still going round and round the German problem. Can any sane man suppose, for instance, that other countries could have intervened by armed force in 1933 to overthrow Hitler when he had come to power by constitutional means and was apparently supported by a large majority of the German people? Could anything have been designed to make him more popular in Germany, unless perhaps it was intervening to turn him out of the Rhineland in 1936? The Germans put Hitler into power; they were the only ones who could turn him out. Again the "appeasers" feared that the defeat of Germany would be followed by a Russian domination over much of Europe. Later experience suggests that they were right here also. Only those who wanted Soviet Russia to take the place of Germany are entitled to condemn the "appeasers"; and I cannot understand how most of those who condemn them are now equally indignant at the inevitable result of their failure.

Nor is it true that the "appeasers" were a narrow circle, widely opposed at the time. To judge by what is said now, one would suppose that practically all Conservatives were for strenuous resistance to Germany in alliance with

SOURCE: A. J. P. Taylor, *The Origins of the Second World War*, 2nd ed. (New York: Atheneum Publishers, 1965), pp. 291–292. Reprinted by permission of the publisher.

Soviet Russia and that all the Labour party were clamouring for great armaments. On the contrary, few causes have been more popular. Every newspaper in the country applauded the Munich settlement with the exception of *Reynolds' News*. Yet so powerful are the legends that even when I write this sentence down I can hardly believe it. Of course the "appeasers" thought firstly of their own countries as most statesmen do and are usually praised for doing. But they thought of others also. They doubted whether the peoples of eastern Europe would be best served by war. The British stand in September 1939 was no doubt heroic; but it was heroism mainly at the expense of others. The British people suffered comparatively little during six years of war. The Poles suffered catastrophe during the war, and did not regain their independence after it. In 1938 Czechoslovakia was betrayed. In 1939 Poland was saved. Less than one hundred thousand Czechs died during the war. Six and a half million Poles were killed. Which was better — to be a betrayed Czech or a saved Pole? I am glad Germany was defeated and Hitler destroyed. I also appreciate that others paid the price for this, and I recognise the honesty of those who thought the price too high.

The Origins of World War II
Keith Eubank

The issues involved with appeasement, which have so often been a focus for analysis, lead to the broader questions of why war broke out in 1939 and whether it could have been prevented. Keith Eubank, a diplomatic historian from the City University of New York, takes a balanced approach in attempting to answer these questions.

Consider: *Whether anything might have prevented war; how Kennan would react to Eubank's interpretation; the extent to which World War II was a direct consequence of the ideas and doctrines of nazism rather than of political and diplomatic developments of the 1930s.*

The war that came to Europe in 1939 came because the only alternative for Hitler — when faced with a country that would not succumb to threats — was war. Hitler had promised to restore Germany to its rightful place in the world. Poland had received German territory through the Treaty of Versailles. Therefore, Hitler could not back down from Poland; he had to pro-

SOURCE: Keith Eubank, *The Origins of World War II* (New York: Thomas Y. Crowell, 1969), pp. 166–167. Reprinted by permission of Harper & Row, Publishers, Inc. Copyright © 1969 by Keith Eubank.

ceed with his objectives, and the only thing that would be able to alter his course would be war.

Many political commentators since 1939 have claimed that, if nations had acted earlier, there would have been no war. If the League had fought Japan over Manchuria, they claim, or if the League had defended Ethiopia, in 1935, or if France and Britain had invaded the Rhineland in 1936, then Hitler could not have attacked Poland. But it would have been impossible for Britain and France to have entered any kind of war — offensive or defensive, small-scale or large-scale — before 1939, because neither the people nor the governments of the two countries were conditioned to the idea of war. The only way they could accept war after 1918 was for it to be thrust upon them by a series of crises, such as those that finally culminated in the German invasion of Poland. Arguments over when and where Hitler should have been halted, then, are purely academic, because before September 1, 1939 Hitler had done nothing that any major power considered dangerous enough to warrant precipitating a major European war.

Nor was there any existing coalition that could have opposed Hitler's massive forces. For Britain sought to appease Hitler, the French feared a repetition of the bloody sacrifices of 1914–1918, Stalin wanted an agreement with Hitler on partitioning Europe, and the United States rejected all responsibility for Europe. Peace would have been possible in 1939 only if there had existed a great military alliance, including both France and Britain, but headed by the United States and the Soviet Union, that was prepared to defend the governments of eastern Europe. But, until Hitler would force them into an alliance, capitalism and communism were prevented from cooperating to oppose nazism by their ideological differences, jealousies, suspicions, and power politics.

Origins of the Cold War

Arthur Schlesinger, Jr.

The period between the end of World War II and the mid-1960s was marked by the Cold War between the two superpowers emerging from World War II, the United States and the U.S.S.R. Initially American historians analyzed the Cold War with assumptions not too different from policymakers: The United States was only responding defensively to an aggressive Soviet Union intent on spreading its control and communist ideology over the world. But by the 1960s other interpretations were being offered, most notably a revisionist position holding the Cold War to be at least in part a result of an aggressive, provocative American foreign policy. The following is a selection from one of the most influential interpretations of the Cold War, presented in 1967 by Arthur M. Schlesinger, Jr., a modern American

SOURCE: Arthur Schlesinger, Jr., "Origins of the Cold War," *Foreign Affairs*, Vol. 46, No. 1 (October 1967), pp. 45–46. Reprinted by permission of Arthur Schlesinger, Jr.

historian from the City University of New York and former adviser to President Kennedy. Here Schlesinger combines elements of both the orthodox and revisionist interpretations.

Consider: *Whether the Cold War was inevitable or could have been avoided; how the speeches by Truman and Marshall support this position.*

The Cold War had now begun. It was the product not of a decision but of a dilemma. Each side felt compelled to adopt policies which the other could not but regard as a threat to the principles of the peace. Each then felt compelled to undertake defensive measures. Thus the Russians saw no choice but to consolidate their security in Eastern Europe. The Americans, regarding Eastern Europe as the first step toward Western Europe, responded by asserting their interest in the zone the Russians deemed vital to their security. The Russians concluded that the West was resuming its old course of capitalist encirclement; that it was purposefully laying the foundation for anti-Soviet régimes in the area defined by the blood of centuries as crucial to Russian survival. Each side believed with passion that future international stability depended on the success of its own conception of world order. Each side, in pursuing its own clearly indicated and deeply cherished principles, was only confirming the fear of the other that it was bent on aggression.

Very soon the process began to acquire a cumulative momentum. The impending collapse of Germany thus provoked new troubles: the Russians, for example, sincerely feared that the West was planning a separate surrender of the German armies in Italy in a way which would release troops for Hitler's eastern front, as they subsequently feared that the Nazis might succeed in surrendering Berlin to the West. This was the context in which the atomic bomb now appeared. Though the revisionist argument that Truman dropped the bomb less to defeat Japan than to intimidate Russia is not convincing, this thought unquestionably appealed to some in Washington as at least an advantageous side-effect of Hiroshima.

So the machinery of suspicion and counter-suspicion, action and counteraction, was set in motion.

The Cold War:
The Communist Perspective

B. N. Ponomaryov

The Cold War and indeed modern history are interpreted differently in the Soviet Union. While it is sometimes tempting for Americans to pass off such interpreta-

SOURCE: B. N. Ponomaryov et al., *History of the Communist Party of the Soviet Union*, Andrew Rothstein, trans. (Moscow: Foreign Languages Publishing House, 1960), pp. 599, 606–612.

tions as pure propaganda, it must be recognized that perceptions differ greatly in the communist and capitalist worlds; indeed, Communists argue that most American historians are tainted by capitalist ideology and propaganda. The following excerpt is taken from History of the Communist Party of the Soviet Union *(1960), an official publication of the Soviet government. Here the focus is on the end of World War II and the early Cold War period.*

> **Consider:** *The elements of this interpretation most likely to be accepted by Western non-Marxist historians; how this interpretation differs from the perceptions of Truman, Marshall, and Schlesinger, and how these differences help explain the existence of the Cold War.*

The Soviet Union played the decisive role in the victorious conclusion of the second world war, and above all in the annihilation of the most dangerous hotbed of fascism and aggression — Hitler's Germany. The Soviet people bore the brunt of the most terrible war against fascist Germany and her accomplices.

In grim battles against their enemies, the Soviet people victoriously defended their Socialist achievements, the most progressive social and political system, and the freedom and independence of the U.S.S.R., and strengthened the security of their State frontiers.

By their heroic war effort the Soviet people saved the peoples of Europe from the yoke of German imperialism. The Red Army, assisted by the peoples of Europe, expelled the German fascist invaders from Poland, Czechoslovakia, Yugoslavia, Bulgaria, Rumania, Hungary, Austria, Denmark and northern Norway, fulfilling with honour its liberating mission.

The second world war aggravated the general crisis of capitalism. This was most strikingly manifested in the weakening of the world capitalist system, which suffered a serious blow from the break-away of Czechoslovakia, Poland, Bulgaria, Rumania, Albania, Hungary and Yugoslavia.

By smashing German fascism, which represented the interests of the most reactionary and aggressive imperialism, the Red Army helped the German people as well. The foundation was laid for the establishment of a peace-loving German Democratic Republic. The defeat of the Japanese imperialists and the liberation of China from the Japanese invaders paved the way for the victory of the people's revolution and people's democratic system in China, North Korea and Vietnam. . . .

The main foreign policy aim of the Party was to secure a stable and lasting peace, to strengthen Socialism's positions in the world arena, to help the nations that had broken away from capitalism to build a new life. One of the most significant features of the international situation was the radical change that had taken place in the balance of forces in the world arena, in favour of Socialism and to the detriment of capitalism. . . .

As a result of the war the capitalist system sustained enormous losses and became weaker. *The second stage of the general crisis of capitalism set in,* manifesting itself chiefly in a new wave of revolutions. Albania, Bulgaria, Eastern Germany, Hungary, Czechoslovakia, Poland, Rumania and Yugoslavia broke away from the system of capitalism. The revolutions in these countries were governed by the general laws of development, yet they had their specific features, engendered by different social and economic conditions. The people's governments established in these countries carried out a number of important democratic reforms: the people acquired extensive democratic rights and liberties, an agrarian reform was carried out in the countryside, landlord property rights, where they existed, were abolished, and the peasants were given land.

As democratic measures were pushed to their conclusion, the working class in these countries passed to Socialist changes in political and economic life. The new people's governments everywhere confiscated the property of the German and Italian imperialists and of the people who had collaborated with the enemy. The bourgeois elements were smashed in a bitter class struggle. The question of power was thus settled. The dictatorship of the proletariat, in the form of people's democratic republic, triumphed in the countries of Central and South-East Europe. Industry, the banks and transport were nationalised. The economy began to develop along the Socialist path. . . .

In their relations with the People's Democracies the Communist Party and the Soviet Government strictly adhered to the principle of non-interference in their internal affairs. The U.S.S.R. recognised the people's governments in these States and supported them politically. True to its internationalist duty, the U.S.S.R. came to the aid of the People's Democracies with grain, seed and raw materials, although its own stocks had been badly depleted during the war. This helped to provide the population with foodstuffs and also to speed up the recommissioning of many industrial enterprises. The presence of the Soviet armed forces in the People's Democracies prevented domestic counter-revolution from unleashing a civil war and averted intervention. The Soviet Union paralysed the attempts of the foreign imperialists to interfere in the internal affairs of the democratic States.

Major breaches were made in the imperialist chain in Asia too. After years of armed struggle against the landlords, the compradore bourgeoisie and foreign imperialists, the Chinese people, headed by the working class and under the leadership of the Communist Party, overthrew the Kuomintang government and took power into their hands. The People's Republic of China was established in October, 1949, on the basis of the alliance of the workers and peasants with the working class playing the leading role. The bourgeois democratic revolution developed into a Socialist revolution. The establishment of the dictatorship of the proletariat opened the way to the Socialist development of China. . . .

The U.S.A. decided to take advantage of the economic and political difficulties in the other leading capitalist countries and bring them under its sway. Under the pretext of economic aid the U.S.A. began to infiltrate into their economy and interfere in their internal affairs. Such big capitalist countries as Japan, West Germany, Italy, France and Britain all became dependent on the U.S.A. to a greater or lesser degree. The people of Western Europe were confronted with the task of defending their national sovereignty against the encroachments of American imperialism. . . .

The capitalist world headed by the U.S.A. turned with all its strength to the task of reinforcing its weakened links and retaining them in the system of imperialism. To suppress the revolutionary movement it resorted to armed force, economic pressure and direct interference in the internal affairs of other countries. In 1947–1949, the combined forces of international reaction crushed the popular movement in Greece and dealt heavy blows to the liberation struggle waged by the working people of Italy, France and other countries. The monopoly capitalists of the U.S.A., France, Italy and Britain embarked on a large-scale political offensive, with the object of destroying democracy and crushing the working-class movement in their countries. A crusade was organised against the forces of democracy, fascist tendencies in political life became more pronounced and there began the unbridled persecution of Communists. The attacks of the fascist and semi-fascist forces, however, were in the main beaten off and the proletariat retained its most important positions. In some countries the Communists preserved their influence among the masses, in others they even extended it. The strike movement grew in scope and became more militant. The proletariat became better organised and politically more conscious.

The radical changes that took place after the second world war substantially altered the political map of the world. There emerged *two* main *world* social and political camps: the *Socialist* and democratic camp, and the *imperialist* and anti-democratic camp. . . .

The ruling circles of the U.S.A., striving for world supremacy, openly declared that they could achieve their aims only from "positions of strength." The American imperialists unleashed the so-called cold war, and sought to kindle the flames of a third world war. In 1949, the U.S.A. set up an aggressive military bloc known as the North Atlantic Treaty Organisation (NATO). As early as 1946, the Western States began to pursue a policy of splitting Germany, which was essentially completed in 1949 with the creation of a West German State. Subsequently they set out to militarise West Germany. This further deepened the division of Germany and made her reunification exceptionally difficult. A dangerous hotbed of war began to form in Europe. In the Far East the United States strove to create a hotbed of war in Japan, stationing its armed forces and building military bases on her territory.

In 1950, the United States resorted to open aggression in the Far East. It occupied the Chinese island of Taiwan, provoked an armed clash between the Korean People's Democratic Republic and South Korea and began an aggressive war against the Korean people. The war in Korea was a threat to the People's Republic of China, and Chinese people's volunteers came to the assistance of the Korean people.

The military adventure of the U.S.A. in Korea sharply aggravated international tension. The U.S.A. started a frantic arms drive and stepped up the production of atomic, thermonuclear, bacteriological and other types of weapons of mass annihilation. American military bases, spearheaded primarily against the U.S.S.R., China and the other Socialist countries, were hastily built at various points of the capitalist world. Military blocs were rapidly knocked together. The threat of a third world war with the use of mass destruction weapons increased considerably.

Patterns in West European Integration

Donald J. Puchala

Since World War II there have been various moves toward internationalism. One was the formation of the United Nations. A second was the formation of alliances on opposing sides of the Cold War. A third has been regional cooperation and integration in different parts of the world. One of the most striking examples of regional cooperation and integration has been in Western Europe. It was initiated by the formation of the European Steel and Coal Community in 1951 and the European Economic Community (Common Market) in 1958. It has continued to grow. In the following selection Donald J. Puchala, a political scientist from Columbia University, analyzes the extent and significance of Western European integration.

> **Consider:** *Why there was such strong movement toward integration in Western Europe during this period; how this movement toward integration was related to the Cold War; the prospects for further European integration.*

A review of the postwar history of Western Europe makes one immediately aware that a great deal of a political, economic, social and psychological nature has happened in the course of the last two decades' relations among Frenchmen, West Germans, Italians, Belgians, Dutchmen, Luxembourgers and others. Furthermore, almost all of 'what has happened' has had something to do with international integration on the Continent.

First, the great powers of Western Europe, France and West Germany most notably, have ceased preparing for war against one another. We now

SOURCE: Donald J. Puchala, "Patterns in West European Integration," *Journal of Common Market Studies*, Vol. IX, No. 2 (December 1970), pp. 118–119. Reprinted by permission of Basil Blackwell Publisher.

tend to take the new West European security community for granted. But our nonchalance must not blur the fact that the emergence of a 'no war' community on the Continent between 1945 and 1955 was an historically momentous occurrence.

Second, aspects of the national sovereignty and governmental prerogative of several Western European states have been voluntarily transferred to regional policy-making bodies. Over several years these international organizations and supranational institutions have grown in stature in the estimations of European elites. They have found popularity among mass populations. In addition, they have been accorded legitimacy by almost all political strata. Not least important, international and supranational bodies have moved toward expanded functions and jurisdictions.

Third, political transnationality in Western Europe has been increasingly evidenced in the structure and functioning of parties, interest groups and other lobbying organizations. Regional 'umbrella' organizations, established to inject specialized points of view into policy making in the European Economic Community, are the best known transnational groups. But these conspicuous lobbies are really only a small fraction of the total number of newly formed regional associations within which West Europeans of different nationalities share, explore and jointly promote a seemingly unlimited range of political, economic, social and cultural interests.

Fourth, gross transaction flows among Western European countries have both increased greatly in volume and expanded notably in range during the postwar era. West Europeans in the postwar era have been paying a great deal more attention to one another than ever before in history. . . .

Fifth, by almost any attitudinal measure, the twenty-five years since World War II have been a period of fairly dramatic social-psychological change at all levels of Western European societies. National identifications have not altered very much. But, in interesting fashion they have been supplemented by regional identifications. Or, less emphatically phrased, persisting national identifications have not greatly hindered the growth of sympathies for regional integration schemes, nor have they much interfered with federative drives. More than this, and perhaps more significant, West European peoples' feelings about each other have been changing, and most of these shifts in attitude have been in positive directions from enmity to amity and from suspicion to trust.

Sixth, all of the positive features of postwar intra-European relations among governments and peoples must not hide the fact that newspapers published over the years between 1945 and 1970 were cluttered with descriptions of diplomatic crises, debates, confrontations and impasses among West European governments. Several integration schemes failed. Some are failing at present. Conflict has been as conspicuous along the pathway to integration as cooperation has. Whether we choose to use the term 'high politics' or not is a matter of semantic choice. But what we cannot ignore is that certain political issues have continually divided, and continue to divide, West European governments and peoples along strictly national lines. Intermittent crises have been part of European integration.

The Positive Role of the United Nations in a Split World

Dag Hammarskjöld

One of the most idealistic institutions stemming from World War II was the United Nations, formed by agreement of the major powers in 1945 and eventually including most nations of the world. Its primary purpose is to preserve peace, which has become even more pressing with the proliferation of nuclear weapons. But despite some successes, the United Nations has come under attack for favoring policies in opposition to a perceived national interest and for being unable to take effective action when armed conflicts broke out. In the following selection Dag Hammarskjöld, secretary general of the United Nations from 1953 to 1961, analyzes and defends the position and actions of the U.N.

> **Consider:** *Why, according to Hammarskjöld, the U.N. has been unable to resolve many major international problems; how one might respond to this argument; whether policies such as those enunciated by Truman and Marshall support or conflict with the goals and efforts of the U.N.*

With its constitution and structure, it is extremely difficult for the United Nations to exercise an influence on problems which are clearly and definitely within the orbit of present-day conflicts between power blocs. If a specific conflict is within that orbit, it can be assumed that the Security Council is rendered inactive, and it may be feared that even positions taken by the General Assembly would follow lines strongly influenced by considerations only indirectly related to the concrete difficulty under consideration. Whatever the attitude of the General Assembly and the Security Council, it is in such cases also practically impossible for the Secretary-General to operate effectively with the means put at his disposal, short of risking seriously to impair the usefulness of his office for the Organization in all the other cases for which the services of the United Nations Secretariat are needed.

This clearly defines the main field of useful activity of the United Nations in its efforts to prevent conflicts or to solve conflicts. Those efforts must aim at keeping newly arising conflicts outside the sphere of bloc differences. Fur-

SOURCE: Dag Hammarskjöld, "The Positive Role of the United Nations in a Split World," *United Nations Review*, Vol. VII, No. 4 (October 1960), pp. 24–25. Reprinted by permission of the UN Chronicle.

ther, in the case of conflicts on the margin of, or inside, the sphere of bloc differences, the United Nations should seek to bring such conflicts out of this sphere through solutions aiming, in the first instance, at their strict localization. In doing so, the Organization and its agents have to lay down a policy line, but this will then not be for one party against another, but for the general purpose of avoiding an extension or achieving a reduction of the area into which the bloc conflicts penetrate. . . .

Those who look with impatience at present-day efforts by the United Nations to resolve major international problems are inclined to neglect, or to misread, the significance of the efforts which can be made by the United Nations in the field of practical politics in order to guide the international community in a direction of growing stability. They see the incapacity of the United Nations to resolve the major bloc conflicts as an argument against the very form of international cooperation which the Organization represents. In doing so, they forget what the Organization has achieved and can achieve, through its activities regarding conflicts which are initially only on the margin of, or outside, the bloc conflicts, but which, unless solved or localized, might widen the bloc conflicts and seriously aggravate them. Thus the Organization in fact also exercises a most important, though indirect, influence on the conflicts between the power blocs by preventing the widening of the geographical and political area covered by these conflicts and by providing for solutions whenever the interests of all parties in a localization of conflict can be mobilized in favor of its efforts.

Chapter Questions

1. To what extent do the trends described in this chapter give further support to the argument that Western civilization has been on the decline since World War I in comparison to the heights it reached in the nineteenth century? What developments might be cited to refute this argument?

2. How might one make an argument that the fundamental historical shift in the last two hundred years did not come with World War I but rather with World War II, as indicated by the consequences of that war and the developments of the postwar period?

3. Do you think the Cold War was caused primarily by developments related to World War II or by the ideological differences between communist and noncommunist countries? Were there any ways in which the Cold War might have been averted?

CHAPTER FIFTEEN

The Present in Perspective

The most recent decades in Western civilization are particularly difficult to evaluate. They are so much a part of the present that it is almost impossible to gain a perspective on them.

While most of the basic trends of the postwar era examined in the previous chapter continued, some changes have become apparent. The Cold War between the United States and the Soviet Union has diminished in intensity. Europe, and indeed much of the world, has pursued an increasingly independent course from the two superpowers. In the 1960s and early 1970s, radical political and social activism held center stage, but persistent economic problems have dominated people's concerns recently. New technological accomplishments, ranging from space exploration to the production of computers, affect our civilization in many ways. Numerous other familiar trends and events could be added to this necessarily brief list.

This chapter is not organized in the usual way, for the sources are so much a part of the present that the usual distinctions between primary and secondary documents are no longer useful. The selections deal with five recent developments. The first concerns the spread of American institutions in

Europe and the spread of Western institutions in the non-Western world. How do Europeans perceive American influence in Europe? In what ways are Western ideas, values, and products spreading over the non-Western world despite the fall of the colonial empires? What is the significance of the modernization initiated in the West and now spreading to the rest of the world? The second has to do with three social movements: the movement for the liberation of women over the past three decades, the growth of student activism in the late 1960s and early 1970s, and the increase of terrorism during the 1970s and 1980s. How has the position of women been analyzed? What kinds of demands were made by feminists, and how have these demands been justified? What were some of the views of student revolutionaries, and how did these views reflect events of the 1960s? How do terrorist groups justify their views? The third development involves modern communications and their impact. What is the nature of television? In what ways can it affect our lives? The fourth development involves important cultural and intellectual trends. What are some of the characteristics of modern art? What is existentialism? How has the role of ideologies changed in Western civilization since the 1950s? Should the present era be characterized as the "age of the psychological man [woman]" in light of the new stress on the inner life of the individual? The fifth involves connections between the present and the future. What are some of the main problems facing us today? What are the prospects for dealing with those problems?

Here, more than in any other chapter, it will be hard to come to conclusions. There is much ambivalence about recent developments. Our own involvement in these developments makes evaluation of the present even more difficult. At best, the selections in this chapter can throw elements of the present into historical perspective.

The American Challenge
Jean-Jacques Servan-Schreiber

By the mid-1960s there was a growing sense among many Europeans that the United States, although friendly, was becoming overbearing in a variety of ways. Her economic institutions, her capital, and her culture were invading Europe even though Europe had by this time recovered from the devastation of World War II. This sense was particularly strong in France, as evidenced by the following selection from The American Challenge, *a widely popular book first published in 1967. The author, Jean-Jacques Servan-Schreiber, was the publisher of the highly influential magazine* L'Express *and was later elected to France's Chamber of Deputies. Here he suggests that Europe's best hope is to compete and beat Americans at their own game.*

Source: J.-J. Servan-Schreiber, *The American Challenge*, Ronald Steel, trans. (New York: Atheneum House, 1969), pp. 153–154, 156. English translation copyright © 1968 by Atheneum House, Inc. Reprinted by permission of Atheneum Publishers.

> **Consider:** *How Servan-Schreiber's plan relates to the Cold War and other trends toward European integration; alternative strategies that might be useful; what this document indicates about the perception that many throughout the world have of the United States.*

Europeans can regain control over their destiny in this confrontation with the American challenge only by taking stock of themselves and, as we will now try to describe, by hard work and patience. What we must do is not so hard to explain, for the path of our counterattack can be clearly marked out.

1. Creation of large industrial units which are able both in size and management to compete with the American giants.
2. Carrying out "major operations" of advanced technology that will insure an independent future for Europe.
3. At least a minimum of federal power to protect and promote European business.
4. Transforming the relationship between business, the university, and the government.
5. Broader and more intensive education for young people; specialized and continuing education for adults.
6. Finally, as the key to everything else, the liberation of imprisoned energies by a revolution in our methods of organization — a revolution to revitalize the elites and even relations between men. . . .

To build a powerful and independent Europe means strengthening the economic and political bonds of the Common Market. No single nation is strong enough to support efficient production in all areas of advanced technology, for the national framework is too narrow and cannot provide adequate markets for such products. Also, the growing diversification of these products demands a specialization that makes any attempt at national self-sufficiency virtually impossible. . . .

Our back is to the wall. We cannot have both economic self-sufficiency and economic growth. Either we build a common European industrial policy, or American industry will continue taking over the Common Market.

The Dynamics of Modernization

Cyril Black

Although almost all areas of the world that were once colonies of the Western powers gained independence during the quarter century following World War II, the penetration of the rest of the world by Western ideas, values, institutions, and products has been extremely widespread. This is illustrated in this photograph showing a citizen of Kuwait, an oil-rich sheikdom of the Persian Gulf, carrying a Western television set across a road. He is wearing Western-style tennis shoes that were probably manufactured in the Far East. In the background are a bilingual store sign and Western automobiles. Reflected in the glass of the television set is a

Photo 15-1

Bruno Barbey/Magnum

SOURCE: C. E. Black, *The Dynamics of Modernization.* Reprinted by permission of Harper & Row, Publishers, Inc. (New York, 1966), pp. 1–4. Copyright © 1966 by C. E. Black.

modern building probably designed by a Western architect and built under the direction of an international construction firm using both foreign and domestic labor and materials.

This photograph suggests that some of the formerly colonized areas are taking economic, political, and social steps in the same direction as Western industrialized states. Scholars, often strongly influenced by the social sciences, have analyzed these broad, international developments that are sometimes termed "modernization." Cyril Black, professor of history at Princeton, is an outstanding proponent of modernization theory. In the following excerpt from his Dynamics of Modernization, *he analyzes the historical significance of modernization.*

> **Consider:** *The effects of Westernization on non-Western culture as illustrated by this photo; why modernization is such a revolutionary transformation; the ways this analysis reflects a primarily Western point of view; how someone from a non-Western culture might react to this analysis.*

We are experiencing one of the great revolutionary transformations of mankind. Throughout the world in widely differing societies man is seeking to apply the finding of a rapidly developing science and technology to the age-old problems of life. The resulting patterns of change offer unprecedented prospects for the betterment of the human condition, but at the same time threaten mankind with possibilities of destruction never before imagined. The search for an understanding of these forces of change is compelling, for failure may lead to catastrophe. The mastery of this revolutionary process has become the central issue of world politics — the ultimate stake for which peoples struggle in peace and risk annihilation in war. The initiative in guiding this transformation in a manner beneficial to human welfare belongs to those who understand most clearly the ways in which different societies around the world are affected, what must unavoidably be changed, and what must at all costs be preserved.

The change in human affairs now taking place is of a scope and intensity that mankind has experienced on only two previous occasions, and its significance cannot be appreciated except in the context of the entire course of world history. The first revolutionary transformation was the emergence of human beings, about a million years ago, after many thousands of years of evolution from primate life. . . .

The second great revolutionary transformation in human affairs was that from primitive to civilized societies, culminating seven thousand years ago in three locations, the valleys of the Tigris and Euphrates (Mesopotamia), the valley of the Nile, and the valley of the Indus. . . .

The process of change in the modern era is of the same order of magnitude as that from prehuman to human life and from primitive to civilized societies; it is the most dynamic of the great revolutionary transformations in the conduct of human affairs. What is distinctive about the modern era is the phenomenal growth of knowledge since the scientific revolution and the unprecedented effort at adaptation to this knowledge that has come to be demanded of the whole of mankind. Man perceives opportunities and dangers that for the first time in human existence are global in character, and the need to comprehend the opportunities and master the dangers is the greatest challenge that he has faced.

The New Revolutionaries
Tariq Ali

The period between the mid-1960s and early 1970s was marked by considerable political, social, and even revolutionary activism. Perhaps most striking was a series of radical actions by university students throughout Western civilization. Although it is difficult to characterize all these actions, the following excerpt from The New Revolutionaries *indicates some of the more extreme and activist attitudes among those most deeply involved. The author is Tariq Ali, born in Pakistan and a student at Oxford University, where he became a leading revolutionary socialist.*

Consider: *The ways in which Ali's views are revolutionary; the developments of the 1950s and 1960s that are reflected in this analysis; to whom such views might be appealing and why.*

What is absolutely clear is that the revolutionary movement is in a period of upswing throughout the world. The war in Vietnam, the events of May 1968 in France and the invasion of Czechoslovakia symbolize this upswing. Vietnam is at the moment the battle-front against imperialism. France showed the extreme vulnerability of monopoly capitalism and the strength of the working class. Czechoslovakia has initiated the struggle for political revolutions in Eastern Europe and the Soviet Union itself. . . .

Those of us who form the hard core of today's new revolutionaries are still Marxists, but we abhor Stalinism; we believe in Leninism but prefer the emphasis to be upon 'democracy' rather than 'centralism'; we are Guevarist but can appreciate and analyse the mistakes made by Che. We are puzzled by the tendency among many Left factions in the developed countries to devote as much time and energy to attacking each other as to attacking capitalism. The new revolutionaries fight against sectarian tendencies. And what is most important of all, we are not to be bought off by the State. WE mean business.

Source: Tariq Ali, *The New Revolutionaries* (New York: William Morrow and Co., Inc., 1969), pp. 314–315. Reprinted by permission of Peter Owen, London.

The Urban Guerrilla Concept

The Red Army Fraction

While the radical political and social activism that marked the 1960s diminished sharply during the 1970s and 1980s, terrorism practiced by relatively small groups grew to become a major problem in several countries. In Spain, Basque terrorists threatened the authority of the government. In Italy several groups, such as the Red Brigades, created a general sense of insecurity. In Northern Ireland, the Irish Republican Army helped create a civil-war atmosphere. Germany was the site of several terrorist incidents and produced one of the earlier terrorist groups, the Red Army Fraction (sometimes referred to as the Baader-Meinhof Gang). The following is an excerpt from "The Urban Guerrilla Concept."

> **Consider:** *The meaning of being an urban guerrilla; the rationale for the position and activities of the urban guerrilla; who this group perceives as its enemies and its allies and why; similarities and differences between this and the excerpt from* The New Revolutionaries.

If we are correct in saying that American imperialism is a paper tiger, i.e., that it can ultimately be defeated, and if the Chinese Communists are correct in their thesis that victory over American imperialism has become possible because the struggle against it is now being waged in all four corners of the earth, with the result that the forces of imperialism are fragmented, a fragmentation which makes them possible to defeat — if this is correct, then there is no reason to exclude or disqualify any particular country or any particular region from taking part in the anti-imperialist struggle because the forces of revolution are especially weak there and the forces of reaction especially strong. . . .

The concept of the "urban guerrilla" originated in Latin America. Here, the urban guerrilla can only be what he is there: the only revolutionary method of intervention available to what are on the whole weak revolutionary forces.

The urban guerrilla starts by recognizing that there will be no Prussian order of march of the kind in which so many so-called revolutionaries would like to lead the people into battle. He starts by recognizing that by the time the moment for armed struggle arrives, it will already be too late to start preparing for it; that in a country whose potential for violence is as great and whose revolutionary traditions are as broken and feeble as the Federal Republic's, there will not — without revolutionary initiative — even be a revolutionary orientation when conditions for revolutionary struggle are better

SOURCE: Rote Armee Fraktion (Red Army Fraction), *Das Konzept Stadtguerilla* (1971), translated in Walter Laqueur, *The Terrorist Reader* (New York: New American Library, 1978), pp. 176–179.

than they are at present—which will happen as an inevitable consequence of the development of late capitalism itself.

To this extent, the "urban guerrilla" is the logical consequence of the negation of parliamentary democracy long since perpetrated by its very own representatives; the only and inevitable response to emergency laws and the rule of the hand grenade; the readiness to fight with those same means the system has chosen to use in trying to eliminate its opponents. The "urban guerrilla" is based on a recognition of the facts instead of an apologia of the facts. . . .

The urban guerrilla can concretize verbal internationalism as the requisition of guns and money. He can blunt the state's weapon of a ban on communists by organizing an underground beyond the reach of the police. The urban guerrilla is a weapon in the class war.

The "urban guerrilla" signifies armed struggle, necessary to the extent that it is the police which make indiscriminate use of firearms, exonerating class justice from guilt and burying our comrades alive unless we prevent them. To be an "urban guerrilla" means not to let oneself be demoralized by the violence of the system.

The urban guerrilla's aim is to attack the state's apparatus of control at certain points and put them out of action, to destroy the myth of the system's omnipresence and invulnerability.

The "urban guerrilla" presupposes the organization of an illegal apparatus, in other words apartments, weapons, ammunition, cars, and papers. A detailed description of what is involved is to be found in Marighella's *Minimanual for the Urban Guerrilla.* As for what else is involved, we are ready at any time to inform anyone who needs to know because he intends to do it. We do not know a great deal yet, but we do know something.

What is important is that one should have had some political experience in legality before deciding to take up armed struggle. Those who have joined the revolutionary left just to be trendy had better be careful not to involve themselves in something from which there is no going back.

The Red Army Fraction and the "urban guerrilla" are that fraction and praxis which, because they draw a clear dividing line between themselves and the enemy, are combatted most intensively. This presupposes a political identity, presupposes that one or two lessons have already been learned.

In our original concept, we planned to combine urban guerrilla activity with grass-roots work. What we wanted was for each of us to work simultaneously within existing socialist groups at the work place and in local districts, helping to influence the discussion process, learning, gaining experience. It has become clear that this cannot be done. These groups are under such close surveillance by the political police, their meetings, timetables, and the content of their discussions so well monitored, that it is impossible to attend without being put under surveillance oneself. We have learned that individuals cannot combine legal and illegal activity.

Becoming an "urban guerrilla" presupposes that one is clear about one's own motivation, that one is sure of being immune to "Bild-Zeitung" methods, sure that the whole anti-Semite-criminal-subhuman-murderer-arsonist syndrome they use against revolutionaries, all that shit that they alone are able to abstract and articulate and that still influences some comrades' attitude to us, that none of this has any effect on us.

The Second Sex
Simone de Beauvoir

A Feminist Manifesto
Redstockings

It is increasingly recognized that women, both individually and in organizations, have been struggling for changes for a long time. The effort to gain consciousness and understanding of what it means to be a woman — politically, socially, economically, and sexually — has become central to women's struggles for change in the mid-twentieth century. The most important book in Europe and probably all of the West to explore this effort is The Second Sex, *by Simone de Beauvoir, first published in France in 1949. In this book, de Beauvoir, a well-known French novelist, social critic, and existential philosopher, argues that women have been forced into a position subordinate to men in numerous obvious and subtle ways. During the 1960s and 1970s women's struggle for change spread and took on a new militancy. Throughout the West, women were arguing for change in what came to be known, especially in the United States, as the women's liberation movement. Numerous women's organizations formed, and many issued publications stating their views.*

The first of the following two selections on the liberation of women is from The Second Sex. *De Beauvoir stresses the status and role of women as the "Other" in comparison to man. The second selection is an example of one of the more radical statements of feminism. It was issued in July 1969 by Redstockings, an organization of New York feminists.*

> **Consider:** *How de Beauvoir relates women to "Negroes" and proletarians; the handicaps facing women according to de Beauvoir; the primary demands of the Redstockings; how this group justifies its demands; how men might react to this selection; how this relates to student activism and the civil rights movement of the 1960s.*

Source: Simone de Beauvoir, *The Second Sex*, H. M. Parshley, trans. Reprinted by permission of Alfred A. Knopf, Inc., pp. xvii–xxii, xxvii. Copyright © 1952 by Alfred A. Knopf, Inc.
Redstockings, July 7, 1969, mimeograph.

The parallel drawn . . . between women and the proletariat is valid in that neither ever formed a minority or a separate collective unit of mankind. And instead of a single historical event it is in both cases a historical development that explains their status as a class and accounts for the membership of *particular individuals* in that class. But proletarians have not always existed, whereas there have always been women. They are women in virtue of their anatomy and physiology. Throughout history they have always been subordinated to men, and hence their dependency is not the result of a historical event or a social change — it was not something that *occurred*. The reason why otherness in this case seems to be an absolute is in part that it lacks the contingent or incidental nature of historical facts. A condition brought about at a certain time can be abolished at some other time, as the Negroes of Haiti and others have proved; but it might seem that a natural condition is beyond the possibility of change. In truth, however, the nature of things is no more immutably given, once for all, than is historical reality. If woman seems to be the inessential which never becomes the essential, it is because she herself fails to bring about this change. Proletarians say "We"; Negroes also. Regarding themselves as subjects, they transform the bourgeois, the whites, into "others." But women do not say "We," except at some congress of feminists or similar formal demonstration; men say "women," and women use the same word in referring to themselves. They do not authentically assume a subjective attitude. The proletarians have accomplished the revolution in Russia, the Negroes in Haiti, the Indo-Chinese are battling for it in Indo-China; but the women's effort has never been anything more than a symbolic agitation. They have gained only what men have been willing to grant; they have taken nothing, they have only received.

The reason for this is that women lack concrete means for organizing themselves into a unit which can stand face to face with the correlative unit. They have no past, no history, no religion of their own; and they have no such solidarity of work and interest as that of the proletariat. They are not even promiscuously herded together in the way that creates community feeling among the American Negroes, the ghetto Jews, the workers of Saint-Denis, or the factory hands of Renault. They live dispersed among the males, attached through residence, housework, economic condition, and social standing to certain men — fathers or husbands — more firmly than they are to other women. If they belong to the bourgeoisie, they feel solidarity with men of that class, not with proletarian women; if they are white, their allegiance is to white men, not to Negro women. The proletariat can propose to massacre the ruling class, and a sufficiently fanatical Jew or Negro might dream of getting sole possession of the atomic bomb and making humanity wholly Jewish or black; but woman cannot even dream of exterminating the males. The bond that unites her to her oppressors is not comparable to any other. The division of the sexes is a biological fact, not an event in human history. Male and female stand opposed within a primordial *Mitsein*, and woman has not broken it. The couple is a fundamental unity with its two halves riveted together, and the cleavage of society along the line of sex is impossible. Here is to be found the basic trait of woman: she is the Other in a totality of which the two components are necessary to one another. . . .

Now, woman has always been man's dependent, if not his slave; the two sexes have never shared the world in equality. And even today woman is heavily handicapped, though her situation is beginning to change. Almost nowhere is her legal status the same as man's, and frequently it is much to her disadvantage. Even when her rights are legally recognized in the abstract, long-standing custom prevents their full expression in the mores. In the economic sphere men and women can almost be said to make up two castes; other things being equal, the former hold the better jobs, get higher wages, and have more opportunity for success than their new competitors. In industry and politics men have a great many more positions and they monopolize the most important posts. In addition to all this, they enjoy a traditional prestige that the education of children tends in every way to support, for the present enshrines the past — and in the past all history has been made by men. At the present time, when women are beginning to take part in the affairs of the world, it is still a world that belongs to men — they have no doubt of it at all and women have scarcely any. To decline to be the Other, to refuse to be a party to a deal — this would be for women to renounce all the advantages conferred upon them by their alliance with the superior caste. Man-the-sovereign will provide woman-the-liege with material protection and will undertake the moral justification of her existence; thus she can evade at once both economic risk and the metaphysical risk of a liberty in which ends and aims must be contrived without assistance. Indeed, along with the ethical urge of each individual to affirm his subjective existence, there is also the temptation to forgo liberty and become a thing. This is an inauspicious road, for he who takes it — passive, lost, ruined — becomes henceforth the creature of another's will, frustrated in his transcendence and deprived of every value. But it is an easy road; on it one avoids the strain involved in undertaking an authentic existence. When man makes of woman the *Other*, he may, then, expect her to manifest deep-seated tendencies toward complicity. Thus, woman may fail to lay claim to the status of subject because she lacks definite resources, because she feels the necessary bond that ties her to man regardless of reciprocity, and because she is often very well pleased with her role as the *Other*.

Now, what peculiarly signalizes the situation of woman is that she — a free and autonomous being like all human creatures — nevertheless finds herself living in a world where men compel her to assume the status of the Other. They propose to stabilize her as object and to doom her to immanence since her transcendence is to be overshadowed and forever transcended by another ego (*conscience*) which is essential and sovereign. The drama of woman lies in this conflict between the fundamental aspirations of every subject (ego) — who always regards the self as the essential — and the compulsions of a situation in which she is the inessential.

I. After centuries of individual and preliminary political struggle, women are uniting to achieve their final liberation from male supremacy. Redstockings is dedicated to building this unity and winning our freedom.

II. Women are an oppressed class. Our oppression is total, affecting every facet of our lives. We are exploited as sex objects, breeders, domestic servants, and cheap labor. We are considered inferior beings, whose only purpose is to enhance men's lives. Our humanity is denied. Our prescribed behavior is enforced by the threat of physical violence.

Because we have lived so intimately with our oppressors, in isolation from each other, we have been kept from seeing our personal suffering as a political condition. This creates the illusion that a woman's relationship with her man is a matter of interplay between two unique personalities, and can be worked out individually. In reality, every such relationship is a *class* relationship, and the conflicts between individual men and women are *political* conflicts that can only be solved collectively.

III. We identify the agents of our oppression as men. Male supremacy is the oldest, most basic form of domination. All other forms of exploitation and oppression (racism, capitalism, imperialism, and the like) are extensions of male supremacy: men dominate women, a few men dominate the rest. All power structures throughout history have been male-dominated and male-oriented. Men have controlled all political, economic, and cultural institutions and backed up this control with physical force. They have used their power to keep women in an inferior position. *All men* receive economic, sexual, and psychological benefits from male supremacy. *All men* have oppressed women.

IV. Attempts have been made to shift the burden of responsibility from men to institutions or to women themselves. We condemn these arguments as evasions. Institutions alone do not oppress; they are merely tools of the oppressor. To blame institutions implies that men and women are equally victimized, obscures the fact that men benefit from the subordination of women, and gives men the excuse that they are forced to be oppressors. On the contrary, any man is free to renounce his superior position provided that he is willing to be treated like a woman by other men.

We also reject the idea that women consent to or are to blame for their own oppression. Women's submission is not the result of brainwashing, stupidity, or mental illness but of continual, daily pressure from men. We do not need to change ourselves, but to change men.

The most slanderous evasion of all is that women can oppress men. The basis for this illusion is the isolation of individual relationships from their political context and the tendency of men to see any legitimate challenge to their privileges as persecution.

V. We regard our personal experience, and our feelings about that experience, as the basis for an analysis of our common situation. We cannot rely on existing ideologies as they are all products of male supremacist culture. We question every generalization and accept none that are not confirmed by our experience.

Our chief task at present is to develop female class consciousness through sharing experience and publicly exposing the sexist foundation of all our institutions. Consciousness-raising is not "therapy," which implies the existence of individual solutions and falsely assumes that the male-female relationship is purely personal, but the only method by which we can ensure that our program for liberation is based on the concrete realities of our lives.

The first requirement for raising class consciousness is honesty, in private and in public, with ourselves and other women.

VI. We identify with all women. We define our best interest as that of the poorest, most brutally exploited woman.

We repudiate all economic, racial, educational, or status privileges that divide us from other women. We are determined to recognize and eliminate any prejudices we may hold against other women.

We are committed to achieving internal democracy. We will do whatever is necessary to ensure that every woman in our movement has an equal chance to participate, assume responsibility, and develop her political potential.

VII. We call on all our sisters to unite with us in struggle.

We call on all men to give up their male privileges and support women's liberation in the interests of our humanity and their own.

In fighting for our liberation we will always take the side of women against their oppressors. We will not ask what is "revolutionary" or "reformist," only what is good for women.

The time for individual skirmishes has passed. This time we are going all the way.

Televised Violence

Most observers agree that television has had a great impact on the lives of people within Western civilization and throughout the world, but exactly what that impact has been is open to debate. This picture illustrates one of the most controversial issues that have been raised. It shows a television camera crew filming the live action in Vietnam. The images filmed by such crews were displayed on daily newscasts in America and elsewhere, giving civilians a virtual firsthand, up-to-the minute, perhaps overly realistic, impression of what the war was like. However, critics argue that because such images became so common, because they were displayed just before and just after the most mundane of other television shows (typically, situation comedies) and because they were viewed so often from the comfort of a living room, the image of a very real war may have come to seem unreal. Indeed, one must wonder whether this picture itself is not part of a staged scene for a movie (as was the case with a scene the audience sees being filmed in Apocalypse Now, *a major movie of 1979–1980).*

Consider: *Other ways in which the media in the twentieth century have affected people's perception and understanding of war.*

Photo 15-2

Number 1

Jackson Pollock

Twentieth-century artistic styles have tended to become increasingly removed from popular tastes and from what the general public has been used to expecting from art. This was particularly the case with the style of action painting or abstract expressionism, which came to the fore shortly after World War II. The leading painter in this school of art was Jackson Pollock (1912–1956), who executed the work shown here, entitled Number 1, *in 1948. In 1950 Pollock was interviewed by Francis V. O'Connor, a well-known art critic; a selection from that interview follows.*

Consider: *How Pollock's statements and this painting reflect some of the trends of twentieth-century history.*

Mr. Pollock, in your opinion, what is the meaning of modern art?

Modern art to me is nothing more than the expression of contemporary aims of the age that we're living in.

SOURCE: Francis V. O'Connor, *Jackson Pollock*. Reprinted by permission of The Museum of Modern Art (New York, 1967), and Mrs. Lee Krasner Pollock, pp. 79–80. Copyright © 1967 by The Museum of Modern Art.

Photo 15-3

Collection, The Museum of Modern Art, New York. Purchase. Photography by Soichi Sunami.

Did the classical artists have any means of expressing their age?

Yes, they did it very well. All cultures have had means and techniques of expressing their immediate aims — the Chinese, the Renaissance, all cultures. The thing that interests me is that today painters do not have to go to a subject matter outside of themselves. Most modern painters work from a different source. They work from within.

Would you say that the modern artist has more or less isolated the quality which made the classical works of art valuable, that he's isolated it and uses it in a purer form?

Ah — the good ones have, yes.

Mr. Pollock, there's been a good deal of controversy and a great many comments have been made regarding your method of painting. Is there something you'd like to tell us about that?

My opinion is that new needs need new techniques. And the modern artists have found new ways and new means of making their statements. It seems to me that the modern painter cannot express this age, the airplane, the atom bomb, the radio, in the old forms of the Renaissance or of any other past culture. Each age finds its own technique.

Which would also mean that the layman and the critic would have to develop their ability to interpret the new techniques.

Yes — that always somehow follows. I mean, the strangeness will wear off and I think we will discover the deeper meanings in modern art.

I suppose every time you are approached by a layman they ask you how they should look at a Pollock painting, or any other modern painting — what they look for — how do they learn to appreciate modern art?

I think they should not look for, but look passively — and try to receive what the painting has to offer and not bring a subject matter or preconceived idea of what they are to be looking for.

Would it be true to say that the artist is painting from the unconscious, and the — canvas must act as the unconscious of the person who views it?

The unconscious is a very important side of modern art and I think the unconscious drives do mean a lot in looking at paintings.

Then deliberately looking for any known meaning or object in an abstract painting would distract you immediately from ever appreciating it as you should?

I think it should be enjoyed just as music is enjoyed — after a while you may like it or you may not. But — it doesn't seem to be too serious. I like some flowers and others, other flowers I don't like. I think at least it gives — I think at least give it a chance.

Well, I think you have to give anything that sort of chance. A person isn't born to like good music, they have to listen to it and gradually develop an understanding of it or liking for it. If modern painting works the same way — a person would have to subject himself to it over a period of time in order to be able to appreciate it.

I think that might help, certainly.

Mr. Pollock, the classical artists had a world to express and they did so by representing the objects in that world. Why doesn't the modern artist do the same thing?

H'm — the modern artist is living in a mechanical age and we have a mechanical means of representing objects in nature such as the camera and photograph. The modern artist, it seems to me, is working and expressing an inner world — in other words — expressing the energy, the motion, and other inner forces.

Would it be possible to say that the classical artist expressed his world by representing the objects, whereas the modern artist expresses his world by representing the effects the objects have upon him?

Yes, the modern artist is working with space and time, and expressing his feelings rather than illustrating.

The Philosophy of Existentialism

Jean-Paul Sartre

One of the most popular and provocative philosophies to emerge in the mid-twentieth century was existentialism. Although the origins of existentialism can be found in nineteenth-century writers such as Sören Kierkegaard and Friedrich Nietzsche, its most popular exponent was the French novelist, playwright, philosopher, and political activist Jean-Paul Sartre (1905–1980). Sartre's interpretation of existentialism reflects the dilemma of a twentieth-century atheist who can no longer accept traditional ways for determining standards of conduct. The following excerpt is from a lecture given by Sartre in Paris in 1945. In it he is describing the nature of existentialism and responding to critics.

> **Consider:** *What Sartre means when he says that man [or woman] chooses himself [or herself]; the ethical implications of this philosophy.*

Man is nothing else but what he makes of himself. Such is the first principle of existentialism. It is also what is called subjectivity. The name we are labeled with when charges are brought against us. But what do we mean by this, if not that man has a greater dignity than a stone or table? For we mean that man first exists, that is, that man first of all is the being who hurls himself toward a future and who is conscious of imagining himself as being in the future. Man is at the start a plan which is aware of itself, rather than a patch of moss, a piece of garbage, or a cauliflower; nothing exists prior to this plan; there is nothing in heaven; man will be what he will have planned to be. Not what he will want to be. Because by the word "will" we generally mean a conscious decision, which is subsequent to what we have already made of ourselves. I may want to belong to a political party, write a book, get married; but all that is only a manifestation of an earlier, more spontaneous choice that is called "will." But if existence really does precede essence, man is responsible for what he is. Thus, existentialism's first move is to make every man aware of what he is and to make the full responsibility of his existence rest on him. And when we say that man is responsible for himself, we do not only mean that he is responsible for his own individuality, but that he is responsible for all men.

The word subjectivism has two meanings, and our opponents play on the two. Subjectivism means, on the one hand, that an individual chooses and makes himself; and, on the other, that it is impossible for man to transcend human subjectivity. The second of these is the essential meaning of existen-

---

Source: Jean-Paul Sartre, *The Philosophy of Existentialism*, Wade Baskin, ed. Reprinted by permission of Philosophical Library, Inc. (New York, 1965), pp. 35–36.

tialism. When we say that man chooses his own self, we mean that every one of us does likewise; but we also mean by that that in making this choice he also chooses all men. In fact, in creating the man that we want to be, there is not a single one of our acts which does not at the same time create an image of man as we think he ought to be. To choose to be this or that is to affirm at the same time the value of what we choose, because we can never choose evil. We always choose the good, and nothing can be good for us without being good for all.

If, on the other hand, existence precedes essence, and if we grant that we exist and fashion our image at one and the same time, the image is valid for everybody and for our whole age. Thus, our responsibility is much greater than we might have supposed, because it involves all mankind. If I am a workingman and choose to join a Christian trade-union rather than be a communist, and if by being a member I want to show that the best thing for man is resignation, that the kingdom of man is not of this world, I am not only involving my own case—I want to be resigned for everyone. As a result, my action has involved all humanity. To take a more individual matter, if I want to marry, to have children; even if this marriage depends solely on my own circumstances or passion or wish, I am involving all humanity in monogamy and not merely myself. Therefore, I am responsible for myself and for everyone else. I am creating a certain image of man of my own choosing. In choosing myself, I choose man.

The End of Ideology

Daniel Bell

Numerous scholars have argued that the period since World War II constitutes one of fundamental change. In the 1950s many scholars pointed to a declining faith in ideologies and a general convergence of goals and assumptions in Western civilization. An outstanding statement of this view is that of Daniel Bell, a Columbia University and Harvard sociologist with extensive experience in editing magazines such as Fortune, The New Leader, *and* The Public Interest. *The following is an excerpt from Bell's* End of Ideology.

> **Consider:** *What Bell means when he argues that "ideologies are exhausted" and the evidence he uses to support this view; trends of the past few years that confirm or contradict Bell's views.*

The two decades between 1930 and 1950 have an intensity peculiar in written history: world-wide economic depression and sharp class struggles; the

SOURCE: Daniel Bell, *The End of Ideology* (Glencoe, Ill.: The Free Press, 1960), pp. 369–370, 372–373. Reprinted by permission of Macmillan Publishing Co., Inc. Copyright © 1960 by The Free Press, a Corporation.

rise of fascism and racial imperialism in a country that had stood at an advanced stage of human culture; the tragic self-immolation of a revolutionary generation that had proclaimed the finer ideals of man; destructive war of a breadth and scale hitherto unknown; the bureaucratized murder of millions in concentration camps and death chambers.

For the radical intellectual who had articulated the revolutionary impulses of the past century and a half, all this has meant an end to chiliastic hopes, to millenarianism, to apocalyptic thinking—and to ideology. For ideology, which once was a road to action, has come to be a dead end. . . .

The ideologies, therefore, which emerged from the nineteenth century had the force of the intellectuals behind them. They embarked upon what William James called "the faith ladder," which in its vision of the future cannot distinguish possibilities from probabilities, and converts the latter into certainties.

Today, these ideologies are exhausted. The events behind this important sociological change are complex and varied. Such calamities as the Moscow Trials, the Nazi-Soviet pact, the concentration camps, the suppression of the Hungarian workers, form one chain; such social changes as the modification of capitalism, the rise of the Welfare State, another. In philosophy, one can trace the decline of simplistic, rationalistic beliefs and the emergence of new stoic-theological images of man, e.g. Freud, Tillich, Jaspers, etc. This is not to say that such ideologies as communism in France and Italy do not have a political weight, or a driving momentum from other sources. But out of all this history, one simple fact emerges: for the radical intelligentzia, the old ideologies have lost their "truth" and their power to persuade.

Few serious minds believe any longer that one can set down "blueprints" and through "social engineering" bring about a new utopia of social harmony. At the same time, the older "counter-beliefs" have lost their intellectual force as well. Few "classic" liberals insist that the State should play no role in the economy, and few serious conservatives, at least in England and on the Continent, believe that the Welfare State is "the road to serfdom." In the Western world, therefore, there is today a rough consensus among intellectuals on political issues: the acceptance of a Welfare State; the desirability of decentralized power; a system of mixed economy and of political pluralism. In that sense, too, the ideological age has ended.

And yet, the extraordinary fact is that while the old nineteenth-century ideologies and intellectual debates have become exhausted, the rising states of Asia and Africa are fashioning new ideologies with a different appeal for their own people. These are the ideologies of industrialization, modernization, Pan-Arabism, color, and nationalism. In the distinctive difference between the two kinds of ideologies lies the great political and social problems of the second half of the twentieth century. The ideologies of the nineteenth century were universalistic, humanistic, and fashioned by intellectuals. The mass ideologies of Asia and Africa are parochial, instrumental, and created by political leaders. The driving forces of the old ideologies were social equality and, in the largest sense, freedom. The impulsions of the new ideologies are economic development and national power.

Our Psychological Age

Philip Rieff

One of the greatest changes occurring in recent decades may lie not in the external economic, social, or political developments usually pointed to by historians but in the internal life and cultural ideals of Western people. An extremely bold and provocative interpretation along these lines is that of American sociologist Philip Rieff. An admirer of Freud, Rieff has written an extraordinarily perceptive critical analysis of Freud's work in Freud, the Mind of the Moralist. *In the following excerpt from that work, Rieff argues that the present age is one of "psychological man [or woman]," as distinct from the preceding ages of "economic," "religious," and "political man [woman]."*

> **Consider:** *The characteristics of "psychological man [woman]"; how "psychological man [woman]" differs from earlier character types or ideals; how Rieff's interpretation reflects other intellectual developments of the twentieth century.*

In this age, in which technics is invading and conquering the last enemy — man's inner life, the psyche itself — a suitable new character type has arrived on the scene: the psychological man. Three character ideals have successively dominated Western civilization: first, the ideal of the political man, formed and handed down to us from classical antiquity; second, the ideal of the religious man, formed and handed down to us from Judaism through Christianity, and dominant in the civilization of authority that preceded the Enlightenment; third, the ideal of the economic man, the very model of our liberal civilization, formed and handed down to us in the Enlightenment. This last has turned out to be a transitional type, with the shortest life-expectancy of all; out of his tenure has emerged the psychological man of the twentieth century, a child not of nature but of technol-

---

SOURCE: Philip Rieff, *Freud, the Mind of the Moralist.* Reprinted by permission of the University of Chicago Press, and Philip Rieff, pp. 356–357. Copyright © 1979 by The University of Chicago Press.

ogy. He is not the pagan ideal, political man, for he is not committed to the public life. He is most unlike the religious man. We will recognize in the case history of psychological man the nervous habits of his father, economic man: he is anti-heroic, shrewd, carefully counting his satisfactions and dissatisfactions, studying unprofitable commitments as the sins most to be avoided. From this immediate ancestor, psychological man has constituted his own careful economy of the inner life.

The psychological man lives neither by the ideal of might nor by the ideal of right which confused his ancestors, political man and religious man. Psychological man lives by the ideal of insight — practical, experimental insight leading to the mastery of his own personality. The psychological man has withdrawn into a world always at war, where the ego is an armed force capable of achieving armistices but not peace. The prophetic egoist of Western politics and Protestant Christianity who, through the model with which he provided us, also laid down the lines along which the world was to be transformed, has been replaced by the sage, intent upon the conquest of his inner life, and, at most, like Freud, laying down the lines along which those that follow him can salvage something of their own. Turning away from the Occidental ideal of action leading toward the salvation of others besides ourselves, the psychological man has espoused the Oriental ideal of salvation through self-contemplative manipulation. Ironically, this is happening just at the historic moment when the Orient, whose westernmost outpost is Russia, has adopted the Occidental ideal of saving activity in the world. The West has attempted many successive transformations of the enemy, the world. It now chooses to move against its last enemy, the self, in an attempt to conquer it and assimilate it to the world as it is. For it is from the self that the troublesome, world-rejecting ideal of the religious man came forth.

Freudianism closes off the long-established quarrel of Western man with his own spirit. It marks the archaism of the classical legacy of political man, for the new man must live beyond reason — reason having proved no adequate guide to his safe conduct through the meaningless experience of life. It marks the repudiation of the Christian legacy of the religious man, for the new man is taught to live a little beyond conscience — conscience having proved no adequate guide to his safe conduct through life, and furthermore to have added absurd burdens of meaning to the experience of life. Finally, psychoanalysis marks the exhaustion of the liberal legacy represented historically in economic man, for now men must live with the knowledge that their dreams are by function optimistic and cannot be fulfilled. Aware at last that he is chronically ill, psychological man may nevertheless end the ancient quest of his predecessors for a healing doctrine. His experience with the latest one, Freud's, may finally teach him that every cure must expose him to new illness.

An Inquiry into the Human Prospect

Robert Heilbroner

In recent years scholars commenting on our present condition and future prospects have been quite pessimistic. They point to a series of developments in the twentieth century in general and since the 1960s in particular to support their views. One of the most popular of these scholars is Robert Heilbroner, an economist from the New School for Social Research. While personally favoring some form of democratic socialism, Heilbroner questions the ability of either capitalism or socialism to solve problems of the immediate future that are so serious that they threaten our very existence. This is reflected in the following selection from An Inquiry into the Human Prospect *(1980), in which Heilbroner emphasizes the need to end industrial growth while questioning whether we have the ability to do this.*

> **Consider:** *Why Heilbroner is pessimistic about the ability of both capitalism and socialism to end industrial growth; why Heilbroner feels that the problems facing civilization are so difficult to solve.*

What is needed now is a summing up of the human prospect, some last reflections on its implications for the present and future alike.

The external challenges can be succinctly reviewed. We are entering a period in which rapid population growth, the presence of obliterative weapons, and dwindling resources will bring international tensions to dangerous levels for an extended period. Indeed, there seems no reason for these levels of danger to subside unless population equilibrium is achieved and some rough measure of equity reached in the distribution of wealth among nations, either by great increases in the output of the underdeveloped world or by a massive redistribution of wealth from the richer to the poorer lands.

Whether such an equitable arrangement can be reached — at least within the next several generations — is open to serious doubt. Transfers of adequate magnitude imply a willingness to redistribute income internationally on a more generous scale than the advanced nations have evidenced within their own domains. The required increases in output in the backward regions would necessitate gargantuan applications of energy merely to extract the needed resources. It is uncertain whether the requisite energy-producing technology exists, and, more serious, possible that its application would bring us to the threshold of an irreversible change in climate as a consequence of the enormous addition of man-made heat to the atmosphere.

SOURCE: Robert L. Heilbroner, *An Inquiry into the Human Prospect* (New York: Norton, 1980), pp. 149–151.

It is this last problem that poses the most demanding and difficult of the challenges. The existing pace of industrial growth, with no allowance for increased industrialization to repair global poverty, holds out the risk of entering the danger zone of climatic change in as little as three or four generations. If that trajectory is in fact pursued, industrial growth will then have to come to an immediate halt, for another generation or two along that path would literally consume human, perhaps all, life. That terrifying outcome can be postponed only to the extent that the wastage of heat can be reduced, or that technologies that do not add to the atmospheric heat burden — for example, the use of solar energy — can be utilized. The outlook can also be mitigated by redirecting output away from heat-creating material outputs into the production of "services" that add only trivially to heat.

All these considerations make the designation of a timetable for industrial deceleration difficult to construct. Yet, under any and all assumptions, one irrefutable conclusion remains. The industrial growth process, so central to the economic and social life of capitalism and Western socialism alike, will be forced to slow down, in all likelihood within a generation or two, and will probably have to give way to decline thereafter. To repeat the words of the text, "whether we are unable to sustain growth or unable to tolerate it," the long era of industrial expansion is now entering its final stages, and we must anticipate the commencement of a new era of stationary total output and (if population growth continues or an equitable sharing among nations has not yet been attained) declining material output per head in the advanced nations.

The Fate of the Earth

Jonathan Schell

The last few years have been marked by a rekindled arms race between the superpowers, a chilling of relations between the United States and the Soviet Union, and an increasing proliferation of military weapons throughout the world. At the same time there has been some growing awareness of the threat to everyone if a nuclear war breaks out and a new drive among groups within several countries to get governments to limit arms production or proceed toward disarmament. Probably more than any other book, Jonathan Schell's The Fate of the Earth, *which first appeared as a series of articles in* The New Yorker *magazine, served to heighten the consciousness of Americans about the realities of nuclear war and nuclear armaments. The following is an excerpt from that book.*

SOURCE: Jonathan Schell, *The Fate of the Earth* (New York: Alfred A. Knopf, 1982), pp. 3–4, 188, 231.

Consider: *How one might explain the apparent failure of people to do much about the nuclear peril; why national interest may lead to "planetary doom;" what Schell feels must be done; how one might respond to Schell's argument.*

Since July 16, 1945, when the first atomic bomb was detonated, at the Trinity test site, near Alamogordo, New Mexico, mankind has lived with nuclear weapons in its midst. Each year, the number of bombs has grown, until now there are some fifty thousand warheads in the world, possessing the explosive yield of roughly twenty billion tons of TNT, or one million six hundred thousand times the yield of the bomb that was dropped by the United States on the city of Hiroshima, in Japan, less than a month after the Trinity explosion. These bombs were built as "weapons" for "war," but their significance greatly transcends war and all its causes and outcomes. They grew out of history, yet they threaten to end history. They were made by men, yet they threaten to annihilate man. They are a pit into which the whole world can fall — a nemesis of all human intentions, actions, and hopes. Only life itself, which they threaten to swallow up, can give the measure of their significance. Yet in spite of the immeasurable importance of nuclear weapons. the world has declined, on the whole, to think about them very much. We have thus far failed to fashion, or to discover within ourselves, an emotional or intellectual or political response to them. This peculiar failure of response, in which hundreds of millions of people acknowledge the presence of an immediate, unremitting threat to their existence and to the existence of the world they live in but do nothing about it — a failure in which both self-interest and fellow-feeling seem to have died — has itself been such a striking phenomenon that it has to be regarded as an extremely important part of the nuclear predicament as this has existed so far. Only very recently have there been signs, in Europe and in the United States, that public opinion has been stirring awake, and that ordinary people may be beginning to ask themselves how they should respond to the nuclear peril.

We live with one foot in each of two worlds. As scientists and technicians, we live in the nuclear world, in which whether we choose to acknowledge the fact or not, we possess instruments of violence that make it possible for us to extinguish ourselves as a species. But as citizens and statesmen we go on living in the pre-nuclear world, as though extinction were not possible and sovereign nations could still employ the instruments of violence as instruments of policy — as "a continuation of politics by other means," in the famous phrase of Karl von Clausewitz, the great philosopher of war. In effect, we try to make do with a Newtonian politics in an Einsteinian world. The combination is the source of our immediate peril. For governments, still acting within a system of independent nation-states, and formally representing no one but the people of their separate, sovereign nations, are driven to try to defend merely national interests with means of destruction that threaten not only international but intergenerational and planetary doom. In our present-day world, in the councils where the decisions are made there is no one to speak for man and for the earth, although both are threatened with annihilation.

Two paths lie before us. One leads to death, the other to life. If we choose the first path—if we numbly refuse to acknowledge the nearness of extinction, all the while increasing our preparations to bring it about—then we in effect become the allies of death, and in everything we do our attachment to life will weaken: our vision, blinded to the abyss that has opened at our feet, will dim and grow confused; our will, discouraged by the thought of trying to build on such a precarious foundation anything that is meant to last, will slacken; and we will sink into stupefaction, as though we were gradually weaning ourselves from life in preparation for the end. On the other hand, if we reject our doom, and bend our efforts toward survival—if we arouse ourselves to the peril and act to forestall it, making ourselves the allies of life—then the anesthetic fog will lift: our vision, no longer straining not to see the obvious, will sharpen; our will, finding secure ground to build on, will be restored; and we will take full and clear possession of life again. One day—and it is hard to believe that it will not be soon—we will make our choice. Either we will sink into the final coma and end it all or, as I trust and believe, we will awaken to the truth of our peril, a truth as great as life itself, and, like a person who has swallowed a lethal poison but shakes off his stupor at the last moment and vomits the poison up, we will break through the layers of our denials, put aside our fainthearted excuses, and rise up to cleanse the earth of nuclear weapons.

Chapter Questions

1. The closeness of the last twenty years makes it difficult to know what trends and developments will be the most significant historically. Those selected for this chapter are just a few of the possibilities. What others might have been selected? What evidence would demonstrate their importance?

2. It is possible to argue that most of what is claimed to be new about the last twenty years is not really so new, that it is just our impression that it is new because we have been living through it. How might this argument be supported? How might it be refuted?

ABOUT THE AUTHOR

Dennis Sherman is Professor of History at John Jay College of Criminal Justice, the City University of New York, and Adjunct Associate Professor of Humanities at New York University. He received his B.A. (1962) and J.D. (1965) degrees from the University of California at Berkeley and his Ph.D. (1970) from the University of Michigan. He was Visiting Professor at the University of Paris (1978–1979; 1985). He received the Ford Foundation Prize Fellowship (1968–1969, 1969–1970), a fellowship from the Council for Research on Economic History (1971–1972), and fellowships from the National Endowment for the Humanities (1973–1976). His publications include *A Short History of Western Civilization*, Sixth Edition (co-author), *A Study Guide and Readings for the Western Experience* (1983), a series of introductions in the Garland Library of War and Peace, and several articles and reviews on nineteenth-century French economic and social history in American and European journals.

A NOTE ON THE TYPE

This book was set on the Editwriter in California. It belongs to the family of printing types called "modern face" by printers — a term used to mark the change in style of type letters that occurred about 1800. California borders on the general design of Scotch Modern but is more freely drawn than that letter.

Linda Watson 212 337-5020

1-800-722-4726
McGraw-Hill